Entrepreneurship and Business Innovation in the Middle East

Philippe W. Zgheib
Lebanese American University, Lebanon

A volume in the Advances in Business Strategy and Competitive Advantage (ABSCA) Book Series

IGI Global
DISSEMINATOR OF KNOWLEDGE

www.igi-global.com

Published in the United States of America by
IGI Global
Business Science Reference (an imprint of IGI Global)
701 E. Chocolate Avenue
Hershey PA 17033
Tel: 717-533-8845
Fax: 717-533-8661
E-mail: cust@igi-global.com
Web site: http://www.igi-global.com

Library of Congress Cataloging-in-Publication Data

Names: Zgheib, Philippe, 1957- editor.
Title: Entrepreneurship and business innovation in the Middle East / Philippe W. Zgheib, editor.
Description: Hershey, PA : Business Science Reference, 2017.
Identifiers: LCCN 2016053735| ISBN 9781522520665 (hardcover) | ISBN 9781522520672 (ebook)
Subjects: LCSH: Entrepreneurship--Middle East. | Globalization--Economic aspects.
Classification: LCC HB615 .E57787 2017 | DDC 338/.040956--dc23 LC record available at https://lccn.loc.gov/2016053735

This book is published in the IGI Global book series Advances in Business Strategy and Competitive Advantage (ABSCA) (ISSN: 2327-3429; eISSN: 2327-3437)

British Cataloguing in Publication Data
A Cataloguing in Publication record for this book is available from the British Library.

Advances in Business Strategy and Competitive Advantage (ABSCA) Book Series

ISSN:2327-3429
EISSN:2327-3437

Mission

Business entities are constantly seeking new ways through which to gain advantage over their competitors and strengthen their position within the business environment. With competition at an all-time high due to technological advancements allowing for competition on a global scale, firms continue to seek new ways through which to improve and strengthen their business processes, procedures, and profitability.

The **Advances in Business Strategy and Competitive Advantage (ABSCA) Book Series** is a timely series responding to the high demand for state-of-the-art research on how business strategies are created, implemented and re-designed to meet the demands of globalized competitive markets. With a focus on local and global challenges, business opportunities and the needs of society, the **ABSCA** encourages scientific discourse on doing business and managing information technologies for the creation of sustainable competitive advantage.

Coverage

- Ethics and Business Strategy
- Competitive Strategy
- Tacit Knowledge
- Balanced Scorecard
- Joint Ventures
- Cost Leadership Strategy
- Customer-Orientation Strategy
- Adaptive Enterprise
- Differentiation Strategy
- Economies of Scale

IGI Global is currently accepting manuscripts for publication within this series. To submit a proposal for a volume in this series, please contact our Acquisition Editors at Acquisitions@igi-global.com or visit: http://www.igi-global.com/publish/.

The Advances in Business Strategy and Competitive Advantage (ABSCA) Book Series (ISSN 2327-3429) is published by IGI Global, 701 E. Chocolate Avenue, Hershey, PA 17033-1240, USA, www.igi-global.com. This series is composed of titles available for purchase individually; each title is edited to be contextually exclusive from any other title within the series. For pricing and ordering information please visit http://www.igi-global.com/book-series/advances-business-strategy-competitive-advantage/73672. Postmaster: Send all address changes to above address.

Titles in this Series

For a list of additional titles in this series, please visit: www.igi-global.com

CSR 2.0 and the New Era of Corporate Citizenship
Mark Anthony Camilleri (University of Malta, Malta)
Business Science Reference • ©2017 • 398pp • H/C (ISBN: 9781522518426) • US $190.00

Managerial Strategies and Solutions for Business Success in Asia
Patricia Ordóñez de Pablos (University of Oviedo, Spain)
Business Science Reference • ©2017 • 376pp • H/C (ISBN: 9781522518860) • US $195.00

Collective Creativity for Responsible and Sustainable Business Practice
Ziska Fields (University of KwaZulu-Natal, South Africa)
Business Science Reference • ©2017 • 385pp • H/C (ISBN: 9781522518235) • US $200.00

Applying Neuroscience to Business Practice
Manuel Alonso Dos Santos (Universidad Católica de la Santísima Concepción, Chile)
Business Science Reference • ©2017 • 332pp • H/C (ISBN: 9781522510284) • US $200.00

Handbook of Research on Fuzzy and Rough Set Theory in Organizational Decision Making
Arun Kumar Sangaiah (VIT University, India) Xiao-Zhi Gao (Aalto University, Finland) and Ajith Abraham (Machine Intelligence Research Labs, USA)
Business Science Reference • ©2017 • 474pp • H/C (ISBN: 9781522510086) • US $275.00

Strategic Policy-Based Network Management in Contemporary Organizations
Kazuya Odagiri (Sugiyama Jogakuen University, Japan)
Business Science Reference • ©2017 • 186pp • H/C (ISBN: 9781683180036) • US $170.00

Digital Entrepreneurship and Global Innovation
Ioan Hosu (Babeş-Bolyai University, Romania) and Ioana Iancu (Babeş-Bolyai University, Romania)
Business Science Reference • ©2017 • 301pp • H/C (ISBN: 9781522509530) • US $195.00

IGI GLOBAL
DISSEMINATOR OF KNOWLEDGE
www.igi-global.com

701 East Chocolate Avenue, Hershey, PA 17033, USA
Tel: 717-533-8845 x100 • Fax: 717-533-8661
E-Mail: cust@igi-global.com • www.igi-global.com

Editorial Advisory Board

Table of Contents

Detailed Table of Contents

Corporate Intrapreneurship (CIP) is still viewed in many cases in the Arab region as a western concept that does not apply to the Middle East. Whereas Corporate Intrapreneurship (CIP) has been an area of increased interest in the United States and in Europe in the last few decades, stimulated mainly by the hope that it will revitalize and regenerate the manufacturing industry, among others, in these countries, especially in the face of increased competition, in the Middle East CIP is still a somewhat new and sometimes vague concept with little understanding to its benefits and uses. The objective of this chapter is to link intrapreneurship to the well-developed literature on entrepreneurship, to develop a model that will allow us to incorporate those factors that are critical to the intrapreneurial zone of an organization.

The Middle East and North Africa (MENA) region is at a turning point in its development. How MENA region addresses the employment needs of its rapidly increasing population of young people will determine whether the MENA region will become a region characterized by stable, knowledge-based economies that have a dynamic working middle class. Entrepreneurship is considered vital to drive this transition of MENA region. Increased entrepreneurial activities will not only spur job growth but also generate ideas, attract investment and inspire future entrepreneurs to follow footsteps of successful entrepreneurs. This chapter explores the entrepreneurial ecosystem of MENA region. The chapter discusses various challenges and provides specific recommendations to boost entrepreneurial activities in MENA region.

This chapter analyzes the Middle Eastern North African economies' growth prospects and investigates the role of entrepreneurial activities in achieving sustainable economic growth and social development. It explores the existing macroeconomic, political and social characteristics of the region and brings the different literatures together to understand the policy implications of theory and practices. The chapter shows that entrepreneurial activities can cure a lot of problem in the region as long as supported by the central authorities, and the region has a strong potential to be used by the entrepreneurs.

The number of women-owned businesses worldwide has increased significantly, a development that extends to other parts of the world, such as the Middle East and North Africa (MENA). This region's cultural and socioeconomic idiosyncrasies offer unique perspectives on women entrepreneurship. This article provides a critical overview over the situation of female entrepreneurship in the region, which takes into consideration challenges and opportunities on the level of the individual entrepreneurs, as well as on the macro environmental level. We finally discuss constructive solutions in order to increase the number of women business founders.

The aim of this study is to examine how succession planning is carried out in family-owned businesses in Saudi Arabia. The study adopts a qualitative methodology which involves semi-structured, face-to-face interviews. The major findings of the research is that most of the family businesses in Saudi Arabia do not have a proper succession plan due mainly to socio-cultural issues such as mistrust and conflict of interest between the older and the younger members of the family and also subservience of women in the society generally. The implications of the study are discussed including a paradigm shift where women are encouraged and given the opportunity to get involved in the running of their family businesses.

Entrepreneurship has assumed super importance for accelerating economic growth both in developed and developing countries. It promotes capital formation and creates wealth in country. It is hope and dreams of millions of individuals around the world. It reduces unemployment and poverty and it is a pathway to prosper. The word entrepreneur is of French origin and literally means the person that takes between – the middlemen; in a more free translation, the individual who pursues a commercial activity. In spite of various studies, defining entrepreneurship is still a major dispute among researchers and the word entrepreneur still has no common meaning among the academic community. So, espousing a very broad definition for entrepreneurship that incorporates business owners and self-employed individuals and adopting a grounded theory approach with in depth literature review of published documents and data, the core of this chapter is to review critically entrepreneurship in the Middle East with specific focus on Oman.

Corporate Governance systems adequately address problems related to accountability and transparency in developed countries. However, in emerging economies these systems are susceptible to exploitation by self-interest-minded individuals entrusted in managing the organization in some cases, by majority shareholders in other cases and at times by third parties from outside the organization. This exploitation falls under the concept of Agency Theory which emerges as a matter of concern that should be dealt with by Corporate Governance systems. Under the Agency Theory, the author classifies the Agency related problems into three types; "Type One", "Type Two" and "Type Three". All three types emanate from the separation of ownership and decision making complemented by the natural reality of self-interest requiring thus internal mechanisms of control in order to mitigate the Agency problems along with all Agency related costs. The paper then deals with such mechanisms.

Blue ocean strategy includes a consistent pattern of strategic thinking in the creation of new markets in various industries. This chapter examines how to create a blue ocean and its role in improving the construction industry. This is library research alongwith case study. It has been prepared based on information gathered from articles published in international journals and referring to large and reputable builder companies. In the concept of strategy, "Blue Ocean" is referred to two overall scope of blue and red ocean. In this chapter, we used the Kano method for evaluation and selection of the features in the construction industry and then, through a four-step approach, it was decided what features should be removed, innovated, enhanced or improved. Finally, using improved hybrid model of Kano and the pillars of the blue ocean strategy, we concluded that economic factors and psychological factors that impact on the consumers need investment and more attention.

In a world that is swiftly evolving, working life conditions are continuously changing too; this chapter will deal with changing environment and its impact on our lives; it will cover the historical background of healthcare in Lebanon, the entrepreneurial factors affecting the Lebanese hospitals stressing on the working life needs especially the skills needed to learn new things which will provide a better ability to adapt to changing working environments. This chapter also stresses on the role of core competences among entrepreneurs in special fields of social and health care. The healthcare industry has experienced a worldwide growth and proliferation of innovation aimed at improving our lives, its quality and providing better treatment in addition to creating a good working environment enhancing employee performance and self-satisfaction.

Within this diverse and often unstable environment, the social phenomenon of entrepreneurship has emerged. Although this concept is found in many segments of society and individuals, it is often linked to the small business venture, and this environment is where our research will take place. Defining the term presents some challenges because it is more of an activity encompassing a wide range of character traits and skills than just a static concept. Additionally, the Lebanese context may share in the collective nature of a definition, but will also offer unique displays of entrepreneurship that may differ from other societies.

The Lebanese have always been great travelers and emigration played an important role in their history. It became inevitable then that entrepreneurship played a major role in shaping the life of those Lebanese residing outside their motherland, as they had to rely on new and creative ways to sustain their living. Although Lebanese entrepreneurs know how to pinpoint opportunities, they still have limited knowledge of the administrative aspects of managing a business. In other words, Lebanese entrepreneurs have the talent but lack organizational skills. Lebanon is a country where management styles are still traditional. Thus, trying to apply modern management practices can be rather difficult. New technology and product diversification are introduced informally through individual efforts of entrepreneurs.

The Middle East has acknowledged the importance and need of entrepreneurial activities which would flourish the economy and open new opportunities for employment. Providing employment to a young and growing population is the major challenge faced by countries in the MENA (Middle East and North America) region. Everywhere in the world, it is small firms that contribute most to job creation. Their ability to thrive and generate jobs is a function of the environment in which they operate and their capacity to deal with continuous change and build assets for the future. Hence firm competitiveness is high on the development agenda. In today's global environment, firms rather than nations have become the engine of growth, and competitiveness is the key for firms to survive.

Instruments of Islamic finance have recently reemerged as an innovative tool for entrepreneurial transactions. Purpose of this chapter is to: a) define Islamic banking Product; b) compare with nearest western banking equivalent; c) highlight advantages and disadvantages of product; d) state future progression of banking towards convergence or divergence between Islamic and Western banking; and e) finally evaluate the role of client focus and customer driven performance in the future trends of entrepreneurial Islamic funding. This chapter highlights the concept of Islamic Banking. Business is slowly adopting Islamic banking as a rival market to western fractional reserve banking from the perspective of delivering customer value. This synopsis covers 19 instruments of Islamic banking by comparing the advantages and disadvantages of each one to that of conventional banking. Interestingly, the comparative methods result in several findings including the fact that banks must be completely devoted to providing customers with excellent service standards, and must also cater for customers‘ needs and demands. In addition, if Islamic services are desired, then the ones who cater for those needs will survive. Whereas western banks have a higher chance to penetrate the Islamic banking sector, Islamic banks can't provide any conventional banking services due to Sharia'a rules that prohibit fixed or floating payment or acceptance of specific interest or fees for any service. This chapter also concludes with a contrast between Islamic and western banking from a customer perspective.

Foreword

It is a privilege for me to be asked to address a professional expert audience at the vanguard of creation and innovation. I am also thrilled to believe in initiatives and drives. In the sphere of initiatives, I have always wondered: how can we foretell if a new initiative will be successful or if it will result in lethal failure. For each initiative is somewhat a gamble. As if one was left at the mercy of destiny. At the risk of appearing overconfident in the control of one's destiny, I sincerely believe that if one follows a given value system while he is balancing his entrepreneurial drive with a pragmatic thorough understanding of reality, a sort of a conspiracy of events will take place.

It is true that when you add your deep belief, passion, and your positive vision, to the understanding of reality, young talented women and men, can sometimes succeed. This is luck. But the lessons of life taught me that to add magic to this formula, and to put the odds to your advantage, there is a tool box of values, which influence the way "we do" our job and the way "we think" about directing and leading our initiatives and the teams involved. In a true sense, those core values are vital, essential, lasting and intended to direct constructive change. These values are capable to unite and inspire to achieve a healthier, stronger and more productive environment, as well as empower and energize people involved for higher achievements.

The first of those values is definitely the nourishment of the *Entrepreneurial Drive:*It is to celebrate the culture of turning ideas into action and initiatives. to promote the culture of translating dreams into reality and the courage to dare to take initiative. The second is *Hard Work:*Our efforts should transcend the boundaries of duties and responsibilities. We should be committed to go the extra mile to overcome challenges. Hard work blesses the soul. Hard work is fulfilling. Hard work is always a comparative advantage when everything else is at par. Thirdly is *Honesty:* It starts by our deep believe that honesty at the end pays, and there are no shortcuts of dishonesty will be justified enough on the long run. At the end, the ends do not justify the means. What is meant is that acting and interacting with integrity, transparency, and credibility with self and towards others is a sort of a magnetic field generator that disrupt the space around us to our favor. My last value I share with you today is definitely not the least: *Precision.*What I mean, we should train our mind to be precise. Precise in time, in the diagnosis, in the analysis, and in the vision and visualization, in describing and communicating and in the delivery. It is so important to have a high standard of accuracy in everything we do, perceive or think without losing sight of the big picture.

This is a short version of my wisdom, on top of that please move and *be proactive. Be accountable and responsible. Strive to keep up-to-date with advances and changes.* Then the dice will be your ally and you will, more likely, be successful entrepreneurs. In this spirit Dr Zgheib is editing and co-authoring this precious assembly of academic research on innovation and entrepreneurship in the Middle East. I hope this manuscript will contribute significantly in advancing the values of entrepreneurship and innovation.

Neemat Frem
INDEVCO, Lebanon

Preface

OVERVIEW OF THE VALUES OF ENTREPRENEURSHIP AND INNOVATION

In a true sense, core values are vital in innovation. They are essential, lasting and intended to direct constructive change. These values are capable to unite and inspire to achieve a healthier, stronger and more productive environment, as well as empower and energize creative minds that are involved for higher achievements. The first of those values is definitely the nourishment of the *Entrepreneurial Drive.* The second is *Hard Work.* Thirdly is *Honesty.* Last but not least is *Precision.* If we can combine these values against cultural nature in the Middle East where unfortunately, un-precision seems to be in the genes, we can seize opportunities, create tremendous values and help events help society.

ENTREPRENEURSHIP IN THE MIDDLE EAST TODAY

On this special phase of the life cycle of the Middle East region, Business is entering an exciting period with plenty of opportunities for innovation and entrepreneurship. Academic research stands as the witness of time and of change. Yet there is a recipe for success; there is a way to meddle with the law of probability and make the dice roll to our favor. On one hand, there is the passion to create, the desire to progress and the courage to act; On the other hand, there is a thorough assessment of the reality, of one's capabilities and of the challenges we face. A first intuition for a successful recipe is to have a balancing act between the two dimensions; the courage and passion from one side and analytics and synthetics on the other side.

Peoples of the Middle East have so much neglected Mother Nature, heaven's most precious gift. Mankind is now living on borrowed time. It is the duty of today's young generation to live up to this new awareness threshold and to correct what the past generations have done. Eco-Entrepreneurship is focusing on the ecological dimension. The ultimate awareness of societies is when they grasp the environmental friendly dimension. This is certainly a sign of maturity and evolution. It is about understanding that if we do not close the loop of consumption and production, if we do not recognize the subtle balances of the preservation of cycles, life itself can be disrupted and continuous unfolding of evolution will be interrupted.

The Middle East has acknowledged the importance and need of entrepreneurial activities which would flourish the economy and open new opportunities for employment. Providing employment to a young and growing population is the major challenge faced by countries in the MENA (Middle East and North America) region. Everywhere in the world, it is small firms that contribute most to job creation. Their ability to thrive and generate jobs is a function of the environment in which they operate and their capacity to deal with continuous change and build assets for the future. Hence firm competitiveness is high on the development agenda. In today's global environment, firms rather than nations have become the engine of growth, and competitiveness is the key for firms to survive.

TARGET AUDIENCE

This assembly of current research is intended for advancing values of innovation and business entrepreneurship among academics, business executives as well as policy makers of the wider Middle east region. Particular areas that are targeted in this review include 2 main regions: The Near East Levant along the Eastern shores of the Mediterranean, and the Arabian Gulf region. Contributing authors come from a wide variety of business background, as well as regional diversity, including universities from Lebanon, Saudi Arabia, Iran, Turkey, UK, and Africa.

BOOK CONTENT AND CHAPTER DESCRIPTIONS

The early part of the book provides macro-economic overview of business environment in the wider Middle East region. Following part addresses innovation and entrepreneurial drive in a wide variety of business settings, Then, the latter part of the book covers in depth and in extensive variety several country scenarios of a rich entrepreneurial experience in specific sectors, and in diverse business fields. The following section provides a quick coverage of the book by chapter and by author. A quick summary is provided for each section.

Chapter 1: Sustainability of Family Business Entrepreneurship in the Middle East

An entrepreneur that establishes a new venture, in general, works following the logic of 'Going Concern', that is a long-term perspective of survival of the venture, and its future establishment as a market player. For this long-term perspective to survive the initiation, growth and development stages in the market, it needs to satisfy a number of criteria and factors. These criteria and factors include a creative idea, managerial skills, financing and proper financial management, etc. ..., succession planning and sustainable decision-making processes in family businesses

Chapter 2: Cooperative Entrepreneurship in the Middle East

Socio-cultural characteristics as defined by Hofstede lay out the basis for understanding entrepreneurial characteristics within a given society. Masculinity, collectivism, and uncertainty avoidance are related to competitive behavior, then cooperative versus competitive dilemmas are analyzed in the cultural setting of Middle Eastern entrepreneurial activity. The purpose is to prove that a relationship exists between culture, and entrepreneurial attitudes. Among Middle Eastern countries, Lebanon is found to go against generally acceptable relationships between cooperation and entrepreneurial autonomy.

Chapter 3: Corporate Innovation and Intrapreneurship in the Middle East

Corporate Intrapreneurship (CIP) is still viewed in many cases in the Arab region as a western concept that does not apply to the Middle East. Whereas Corporate Intrapreneurship (CIP) has been an area of increased interest in the United States and in Europe in the last few decades, stimulated mainly by the hope that it will revitalize and regenerate the manufacturing industry, among others, in these countries, especially in the face of increased competition, in the Middle East CIP is still a somewhat new and sometimes vague concept with little understanding to its benefits and uses

Chapter 4: Accelerating Entrepreneurship in MENA Region – Opportunities and Challenges

The Middle East and North Africa (MENA) region is at a turning point in its development. How MENA region address the employment needs of its rapidly increasing population of young people will determine whether the MENA region will become a region characterized by stable, knowledge-based economies that have dynamic working middle class. Entrepreneurship is considered vital to drive this transition of MENA region. Increased entrepreneurial activities will not only spur job growth but also generate ideas, attract investment and inspire future entrepreneurs to follow footsteps of successful entrepreneurs. This chapter explores the entrepreneurial ecosystem of MENA region. The chapter discusses various challenges and provides specific recommendations to boost entrepreneurial activities in MENA region.

Chapter 5: Making Innovation Development Policies Work for MENA – The Need for Entrepreneurship

This chapter analyzes the Middle Eastern North African economies growth prospects and investigates the role of entrepreneurial activities in achieving sustainable economic growth and social development. It explores the existing macroeconomic, political and social characteristics of the region and brings the different literatures together to understand the policy implications of theory and practices. The chapter shows that entrepreneurial activities can cure a lot of problem in the region as long as supported by the central authorities, and the region has a strong potential to be used by the entrepreneurs.

Chapter 6: Empowerment Against All Odds – Women Entrepreneurs in the Middle East and North Africa

The number of women-owned businesses worldwide has increased significantly, a development, which extended to other parts of the world, such as the Middle East and North Africa (MENA). This region's cultural and socioeconomic idiosyncrasies offer unique perspectives on women entrepreneurship. We provide a critical overview over the situation of female entrepreneurship in the region, which takes into consideration challenges and opportunities on the level of the individual entrepreneurs, as well as on the macro environmental level. We finally discuss constructive solutions in order to increase the number of women business founders.

Chapter 7: Succession Challenges Facing Family Businesses in Saudi Arabia

The aim of this study is to examine how succession planning is carried out in family-owned businesses in Saudi Arabia. The study adopts a qualitative methodology which involves semi-structured, face-to-face interviews. The major findings of the research is that most of the family businesses in Saudi Arabia do not have a proper succession plan due mainly to socio-cultural issues such as mistrust and conflict of interest between the older and the younger members of the family and also subservience of women in the society generally. The implications of the study are discussed including a paradigm shift where women are encouraged and given the opportunity to get involved in the running of their family businesses.

Chapter 8: Critical Review of Entrepreneurship in Oman

Entrepreneurship has assumed super importance for accelerating economic growth both in developed and developing countries. It promotes capital formation and creates wealth in country. It is hope and dreams of millions of individuals around the world. It reduces unemployment and poverty and it is a pathway to prosper. The word entrepreneur is of French origin and literally means the person that takes between – the middlemen; in a more free translation, the individual who pursues a commercial activity. In spite of various studies, defining entrepreneurship is still a major dispute among researchers and the word entrepreneur still has no common meaning among the academic community. So, espousing a very broad definition for entrepreneurship that incorporates business owners and self-employed individuals and adopting a grounded theory approach with in depth literature review of published documents and data, the core of this chapter is to review critically entrepreneurship in the Middle East with specific focus on Oman.

Chapter 9: Agency Problem Types From a Corporate Governance Perspective

Corporate Governance systems adequately address problems related to accountability and transparency in developed countries. However, in emerging economies these systems are susceptible to exploitation by self-interest-minded individuals entrusted in managing the organization in some cases, by majority shareholders in other cases and at times by third parties from outside the organization. This exploitation falls under the concept of Agency Theory which emerges as a matter of concern that should be dealt with by Corporate Governance systems. Under the Agency Theory, the author classifies the Agency related problems into three types; "Type One", "Type Two" and "Type Three". All three types emanate from the separation of ownership and decision making complemented by the natural reality of self-interest requiring thus internal mechanisms of control in order to mitigate the Agency problems along with all Agency related costs. The paper then deals with such mechanisms.

Chapter 10: Developing Blue Ocean Strategy in Construction Using an Improved Model of Kano

Blue ocean strategy includes a consistent pattern of strategic thinking in the creation of new markets in various industries. This chapter examines how to create a blue ocean and its role in improving the construction industry. This is library research along with case study. It has been prepared based on information gathered from articles published in international journals and referring to large and reputable builder companies. In the concept of strategy, "Blue Ocean" is referred to two overall scope of blue and red ocean. In this chapter, we used the Kano method for evaluation and selection of the features in the construction industry and then, through a four-step approach, it was decided what features should be removed, innovated, enhanced or improved. Finally, using improved hybrid model of Kano and the pillars of the blue ocean strategy, we concluded that economic factors and psychological factors that impact on the consumers need investment and more attention.

Chapter 11: Entrepreneurship and Innovation in the Lebanese Healthcare – Road to Employee Job Satisfaction

In a world that is swiftly evolving, working life conditions are continuously changing too; this chapter will deal with changing environment and its impact on our lives; it will cover the historical background of healthcare in Lebanon, the entrepreneurial factors affecting the Lebanese hospitals stressing on the working life needs especially the skills needed to learn new things which will provide a better ability to adapt to changing working environments. This chapter also stresses on the role of Core competences among entrepreneurs in special fields of social and health care. The healthcare industry has experienced a worldwide growth and proliferation of innovation aimed at improving our lives, its quality and providing better treatment in addition to creating a good working environment enhancing employees performance and self-satisfaction

Chapter 12: The Lebanese Way – A Cultural Propensity Toward Entrepreneurship

Within this diverse and often unstable environment, the social phenomenon of entrepreneurship has emerged. Although this concept is found in many segments of society and individuals, it is often linked to the small business venture, and this environment is where our research will take place. Defining the term presents some challenges because it is more of an activity encompassing a wide range of character traits and skills than just a static concept. Additionally, the Lebanese context may share in the collective nature of a definition, but will also offer unique displays of entrepreneurship that may differ from other societies.

Chapter 13: Lebanese Expatriate Entrepreneurship Worldwide

The Lebanese have always been great travelers and emigration played an important role in their history. It became inevitable then that entrepreneurship played a major role in shaping the life of those Lebanese residing outside their motherland, as they had to rely on new and creative ways to sustain their living. Although Lebanese entrepreneurs know how to pinpoint opportunities, they still have limited knowledge of the administrative aspects of managing a business. In other words, Lebanese entrepreneurs have the talent but lack organizational skills. Lebanon is a country where management styles are still traditional. Thus, trying to apply modern management practices can be rather difficult. New technology and product diversification are introduced informally through individual efforts of entrepreneurs.

Chapter 14: Social and Civic Entrepreneurship in Lebanon and the Middle East

Social and civic entrepreneurship is looking at what is happing around you and coming up with an idea or business plan to take help solve the situation. Social Entrepreneurship makes a person more aware of what is happening around them. It also looks at a problem and finds the best solutions for them. Entrepreneurs around the world are different and their approach to problems are different some work collectively and other induvial. In Lebanon most entrepreneurs are induvial where they work with close families and pass the work down every generation. Also Lebanon encountered many problems from wars to economic problems, that lead to most people working alone and in the private sector. The idea of Social and Civic Entrepreneurship can help the country move forward and get past its current problems. An example of social entrepreneurship is given oh how a simple idea could be used to solve the garbage crises.

Chapter 15: Entrepreneurial Innovation and Islamic Banking

Instruments of Islamic finance have recently reemerged as an innovative tool for entrepreneurial transactions. Purpose of this chapter is to: a) define Islamic banking Product; b) compare with nearest western banking equivalent; c) highlight advantages and disadvantages of product; d) state and defend your opinion about future progression of banking towards convergence or divergence between Islamic and Western banking; and e) finallv evaluate the role of client focus and customer driver performance in the future trends of entrepreneurial funding.

CONCLUSION AND FIELD IMPACT

This book offers a platform of various guidelines for creative minds to venture into entrepreneurship and benefit their surrounding community. In addition, it allows the reader to create a mind map to follow in order to fulfil business dreams, whether it's a private or family business. The most common characteristic among people who aim at becoming an entrepreneur is the fear of risk taking and investment, however, this book aims to stimulate the reader to take risks and transform dreams into reality, by providing concrete examples and case studies around Lebanon, Middle East and the MENA region. By discussing the status of entrepreneurship in various forms in this region, this book puts entrepreneurial innovation in perspective to form an idea of what step to take and how to take it. Naturally, this book is addressed towards entrepreneurs who are already established and would like to expand their knowledge or accelerate their business. It is also beneficial for young adults who aim at launching their own creative businesses and using their skills to benefit the community. Interestingly, it also describes the status of business women in the region, and caters for motivating them into taking action against all obstacles to become entrepreneurs and break the wall of gender in this field. Moreover, by showcasing the different ways a person can be an entrepreneur as well as the issues and obstacles this field is facing, the targeted readers are able to create a holistic idea of what precautions to take, what to focus on and what to avoid in order to reach a successful endeavour. The organization of this book is illustrated in such a way by moving from chapter to chapter that narrows down the ideas of the entrepreneur while reaching one conclusion that is the catalyst for taking action. The book discusses 3 different areas of business practice distributed over 15 chapters, the macro scale discussed is the Middle East and the status of entrepreneurship and business development in the region, the smaller scale is the MENA region where the need for entrepreneurship is discussed for developing countries, and finally the micro scale where business culture is taken into consideration and how It impacts the actions people take towards developing their own businesses. It is important to mention that this book is a very powerful tool for entrepreneurs and non-entrepreneurs alike to benefit from, given the positive impact it creates within the reader by describing the status of the field and the urgent need for it. Finally, by delivering it to the hands of the public, this book will have a great impact on the young generation especially in such a way that allows them to take action and initiate their ideas realistically, while activating their business dreams.

Philippe W. Zgheib
Lebanese American University, Lebanon

Acknowledgment

The book editor wishes to acknowledge the support of all persons involved in the review process of the book. Deep appreciation and gratitude goes to my dean for his feedback and support. Also deep appreciation goes to all authors at various universities of Lebanon, throughout the Middle East, and other parts of the World where scholars carry in their heart and in their mind a genuine concern for business entrepreneurship. My sincere appreciation goes to my colleague Dr. Bassem Maamari for his beautiful spirit of dedication and optimism in the face of adversity.

Sincere thanks go to all those who provided constructive and comprehensive reviews for their unwavering support. Gratitude goes to my colleagues at the Olayan School of Business at the American University of Beirut, also to my inspirational colleagues, at the Adnan El Kassar School of Business in the Lebanese American University, whose enthusiasm motivated me to initially accept the invitation for taking on this project. Special thanks also go to the publishing team at IGI Global, USA, whose support and guidance throughout the process from the initial idea to final issue have been precious.

Special thanks go to my immediate family whose unconditional love, and vibrant energy have kept me going against all odds. My loving gratitude goes to the genius and spirited company of WNYA (Alma, Yara, Naim, and Wadih) who have helped me in various stages of the manuscript. And last but not least, my better half, Nathalie, has kept us all pointed in the right direction aiming for nothing less than the stars through her unfailing support and steady encouragement.

As I hope this book will bring a lasting impact of making our business world, and our daily lives better than we found them, I wish to dedicate the whole effort to Lord Almighty.

Philippe W. Zgheib
December 2016

Chapter 1
Sustainability of Family Business Entrepreneurships in the Middle East

Bassem E. Maamari
Lebanese American University, Lebanon

Ahmad M. Jannoun
Grenoble School of Management, France

ABSTRACT

The sustainability of family businesses with their integral component of entrepreneurial venturing are the result of decades of developmental processes. The role that these family businesses play in any economy can only be described as massive. Therefore, understanding the factors that affect or play a role in the success and continuity of these firms is important, and assessing the level and role of corporate governance in this perspective remains a challenge. The interplay of systems, leadership, accountability, transparency and remuneration, is proving to play a role in family business sustainability.

DOI: 10.4018/978-1-5225-2066-5.ch001

INTRODUCTION

An entrepreneur that establishes a new venture, in general, works following the logic of 'Going Concern', that is a long-term perspective of survival of the venture, and its future establishment as a market player. For this long-term perspective to survive the initiation, growth and development stages in the market, it needs to satisfy a number of criteria and factors. These criteria and factors include a creative idea, managerial skills, financing and proper financial management, etc. ..., succession planning and sustainable decision-making processes in family businesses.

The continuity of the entrepreneurship beyond the first generation of owners is adamant of one of a number of theoretical bases that the scholarly literature on family business describes.

Today, family owned and run businesses (FB) account for almost 95 percent of the firms of the Middle East, providing a major contribution to their respective national economies, and handling 62% of the total commercial exchange within the MENA (Middle East and North Africa) region (Statistics Unkind to Family Business, 2007). These facts are not far from those of many developed economies as reported from Western Europe (IFERA, 2003) and the USA (Beckhard & Dyer, 1983), FB represent similar percentages of their respective economies. Moreover, FB are today the driving economic force within the 'Transition' countries or those that moved from 'controlled economy' to 'open economy' systems such as Azerbaijan, Belarus, Croatia, Estonia, Georgia, Kazakhstan, Kyrgystan, Latvia, Lithuania, Serbia, Ukraine, Uzbekistan, etc.... (Duh, 2012; Rebernik, Tomnic, & Duh, 2007; Pistrui, Welsch, & Roberts, 1997).

Historical observation and previous studies found that one third of family businesses fail within the first four years from establishment (File and Prince, 1996; Bates and Nucci, 1990) and that less than thirty percent of family businesses survive to reach the second generation of managers (Shanker, M.C. & Astrachan, 1996; Kets de Vries, 1994). Moreover, thirty percent of FB cease operating by attrition. Therefore, it is only six to ten percent of FB that remain in the market to their third generation of ownership while almost ninety percent close before reaching that level (Statistics Unkind to Family Business, 2007; IFC, 2008; Berns, Townend, Khayat, Balagopal, Reeves, Hopkins, & Kruschwitz, 2009).

Accordingly, it is very important to see what causes these establishments to wither away with time, and how can business owners change or improve their business situations in order to sustain the operation of their companies.

ISSUES CONFRONTING FAMILY BUSINESSES

Generally speaking, many organic as well as operational problems affect the operation of family owned and family run businesses, from governance to generation gap, from attrition to financial and managerial non-effectiveness.

Governance Problems

Family business is more complex to manage than non-family managed firms. The governance difficulty emanates as the owner is assisted with his/her immediate family in the first generation. These members of the family represent the pool among which the selection of the next CEO will take place. However, these family members are close to each other, they know the strengths and weaknesses of each other so well, that there will always be someone who approves or does not approve any decision taken by the new CEO (who was selected from the group of second generation owners). There is in general a feeling whereby many feel they would have done differently were they to take the same decisions. Moreover, the increase in pressure to audit, or to review and control for past decisions may be taken as a personal attack on the CEO. This may result in family members choosing either to smooth-down the process, or to split the family, where both options damage both the firm's governance as well as the inter-family relationships.

Centralized Decision Making

When a person establishes his/her own firm, success is not necessarily a given. Therefore, when this self-appointed CEO-investor struggles within the market and survives the first few years, his/her self-confidence level increases. The result is more bold decisions. Once the firm becomes a 'going concern', and the results are in the right direction, this owner is afraid to lose this 'personally established firm' that he/she created. As a result, this CEO refuses to share decision-making and the family business is highly centralized for a period of time. The change in management system will occur when the family notices that the business growth process requires a number of 'trusted' managers working together.

CEO at Work and at Home

Being the bread provider for the family, the employer of many of its members, the head of the business' pyramid enjoys full power and authority to run the firm. This, while also being the nuclear family's leader, role-model, and figure-head at home to the family members, and the architect that sets the guidelines and procedures for all the family members who are under that roof. With time, even the more reluctant or rebellious with tend to acknowledge this authority.

Lack of Rules

As a result of the above issues facing the family and the business, the CEO of a family business enjoying full power and authority at work as well as at home, is reluctant to give-up this privilege. The result the CEO is remains in a position not to initiate, support or put the effort into, writing his firm's vision, mission statement, values, rules, and procedures. The lack of such written documents allows the firm more flexibility, but also puts in the hands of the CEO more decision-making power.

Attrition Rate

'Attrition rate' or 'Churn rate' represents the number of the firm members that move out from the firm in a certain period of time. In other terms, it represents an employee's lifetime contribution to a firm. In a family business environment, the occurrence of attrition through different processes results in a major issue for the business' continuity. When the family members leave the firm and the off-springs study something not-related and follow their distinct career paths, the CEO's level of anxiety as to firm continuity increases. On one hand, the owner asks 'Who is going to run the firm when I retire as a CEO?' Is ownership transfer looming around soon? Research proves that this problem faces family-owned businesses across the world and affects their sustainability (Schwartz, 1954; Miller, 1998). On the other hand, the employees of the firm who are afraid to lose their jobs are at risk of leaving the firm to more established career-oriented firms.

These issues not only affect any family business' management and prosperity, but they also affect the economy in which they exist and operate (Duh, 2012). Today, the aging economies are facing a more serious problem in this perspective, because their demographic pyramid is inverted. As a s result, in the EU alone, 34% of all businesses will need to undergo ownership transfers within the coming decade, corresponding to an average of more than six hundred thousand firm every year (Duh, 2012). As a result of the increased awareness of the importance of family business, many studies are initiated on their economic value and contribution, the many challenges facing them (Shanker & Astrachan, 1996), including leadership (Cater, 2006), family harmony (Adendorff, Venter & Boshoff, 2008), succession planning (Tagiuri & Davis, 1996; File & Prince, 1996; Beckhard & Dyer,1983; Barnes & Hershon, 1976), estate planning (File & Prince, 1996), nepotism (Tagiuri & Davis, 1996), institutional weaknesses and poor corporate governance (IFC, 2008). In spite of all the above important factors identified and analyzed, the role of family businesses in developing both the economy and society as well as the corporate governance applied in these organizations and their sustainability are yet to be revisited.

THE BUSINESS ASPECT OF FAMILY BUSINESSES

Definition of Family Business

Beginning with Lansberg, Perrow and Rogolsky (1988)'s question "*What is a Family Business?*", the challenge to uni-dimentionally define FB has taken its toll from researchers (Litz, 2008). They agree to 'what it means' but are short on putting forth a comprehensive and complete definition that they all agree upon (Litz, 2008). The result is more than thirty different postulated definitions in two less than three decades, each focusing on different attributes and factors, from management to stakeholders, and from owners to succession and others (Litz, 2008; Sharma, 2004). The simplest definition is an organization influenced by two or more family member owners, using their ownership rights, family ties and or managerial roles (Tagiuri & Davis, 1996).

Family Business System

Whether FB are different from non-FB in terms of applying managerial theories and related practices, in addition to the need to develop, grow and sustain business through tools and best practices adoption and adaptability to environmental changes is a challenge confronting our better understanding of their operation. Thus researchers have observed, studied and analyzed, and then put forth operational models postulating the attributes of FB.

Bivalent Attributes of the Family Firm

Developed by Davis and Taguiri (1996), this conceptual framework attempts to understand inherent features of the family-owned and family-operated businesses, and attempts to model them into an easy to understand figurative model called "The Three Circle Model", and which is generally taken as a standard tool or model (Gersick, McCollom-Hampton, Davis, & Lansberg, 1997; Admin, 2011). The features in the model are by themselves both advantages and disadvantages to the FB. Derived through research from the overlap of the three components or sub-systems, namely the family, the ownership, and the management of the business. These three factors, represented in three circles, overlap and intersect, creating seven potential areas or positions that the different stakeholder individuals in a FB can take or hold (see Figure 1 below).

The model differentiates between the seven roles of the various stakeholders in the family and the business.

1. External investors, who own part of the business but who do not work in it and are not members of the family.
2. Non-family management and employees
3. Owners who work in the business but who are not family members
4. Family members who own shares in the business but who are not employees
5. Family members who are not actively involved in the business either as employees or owners
6. Family members who work in the business but who do not own shares
7. Inhabiting all three circles are owners who are also family members and who work in the business

The 'Three Circles Model' provides a basic conceptual framework that describes and facilitates the understanding of these intricate organizations where the multi-directional interests of the owners, managers and business intersect, generating a sizeable number of directions, trends, and opinions, all of which leading to tension and conflicts in the family business environment. The "bivalent attributes" concept refers to the dynamics of the FB. The authors suggest that this ensuing overlap is a

Figure 1. The three circle model
Adapted from Taguiri & Davis (1992).

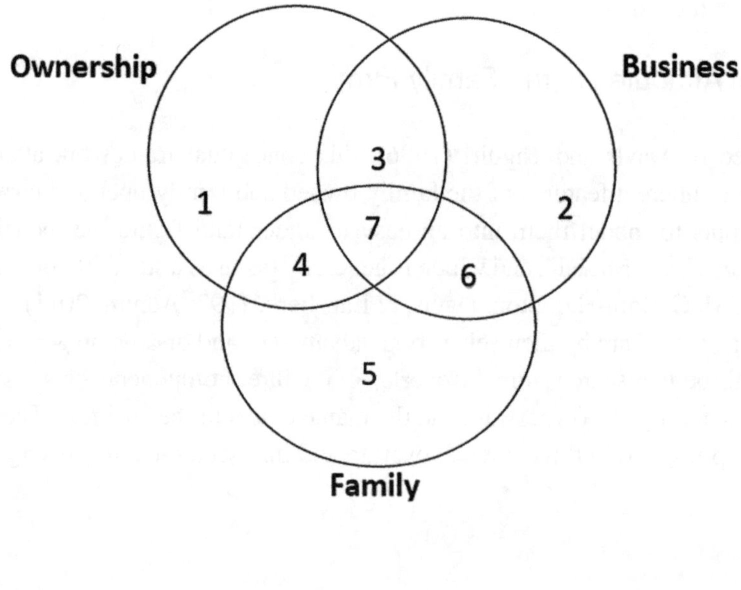

unique feature to the FB, inherent to it, and is at the heart of both advantages and disadvantages for owner family, the business and the related non-family related employees. These bivalent attributes are generated directly by the overlap of the Family, Ownership and Management factors (Tagiuri & Davis, 1996). The acknowledgement and clear definition of these three circles is by itself an achievement for a FB, where the better we define boundaries of interaction, the less overlapping will occur. The resulting outcome is a sustained operation with minimal avoidable conflicts as well as better position to face uncertainty and crises (Admin, 2011). The main 'Bivalent attributes' of the FB are the result of the overlapping between the different components and are namely, 1-Simultaneous Roles; 2-Shared Identity; 3-Common History; 4-Emotional involvement; 5-The private language; 6-Mutual awareness & Privacy; and 7-Meaning of the family Company. These key factors in family set-up issues are defined in their scope as follows:

1. **The Overlap & Intersection of 3 Systems (Family, Ownership & Management):** The Overlap can be a source of tension and conflict as we as a source of Strength and competitiveness. When the interests of the 3 systems are aligned, the overlap is a Source of strength when not aligned viability of the FB is at risk.
2. **Simultaneous Roles:** A member in a family business can belong to up 7 different Sub-groups at the same time, Quick and Efficient decision due to immediate awareness of family/Ownership/Management Interest. Gives the option to retreat into whatever roles give the greatest power in conflict situations.
3. **Emotional Involvement:** Actions and words between relative in Business context are interpreted in term of their meaning in family context. Can Create tension and block communication, or can generate motivation, loyalty and trust.
4. **Mutual Awareness & Privacy:** Temper business decisions with an understanding of their implication on family system.
5. **Meaning of the Family Company:** A Legacy, As Important as a family member, and compete with them for the Founder's time and Resources. Strong Personalized feeling of attachment fad generation to the next.
6. **An Ideological Arena:** That Combines 3 Main Ideologies: Entrepreneurialism, Paternalism and Managerialism.
7. **Family/Business Cross-System Transfer:** The output of the Business system is the output of the family Business and vice-versa

The FB Mobius Strip

Reginald Litz's (2008) study of a different perspective of the family business phenomenon, its sub systems and overlapping effects, results in another conceptualized alternative representation of family business in of metaphor-based diagram. The new perspective suggests the FB interface as a one-sided phenomenon, and names it "The Mobius Strip". The strip is a single band that twists to a full 180 degrees before its two ends reconnect (See Figure 2 below). This provides a continuous connected strip representing a continuum that streams physically unobstructed to all the surfaces, similar to the FB phenomenon, but as two overlapping connected systems. In this continuum, the first system's output becomes the input of the second system and vice-versa (Litz, 2008) as suggested earlier in the scholarly literature on mathematics in 1858 by Ferdinand Mobius and Johann Listing (Litz, 2008).

Litz postulates that the two distinct factors, the family and the business systems, interact together (See Figure 3). Both systems having their respective inputs and

Figure 2. The mobius strip

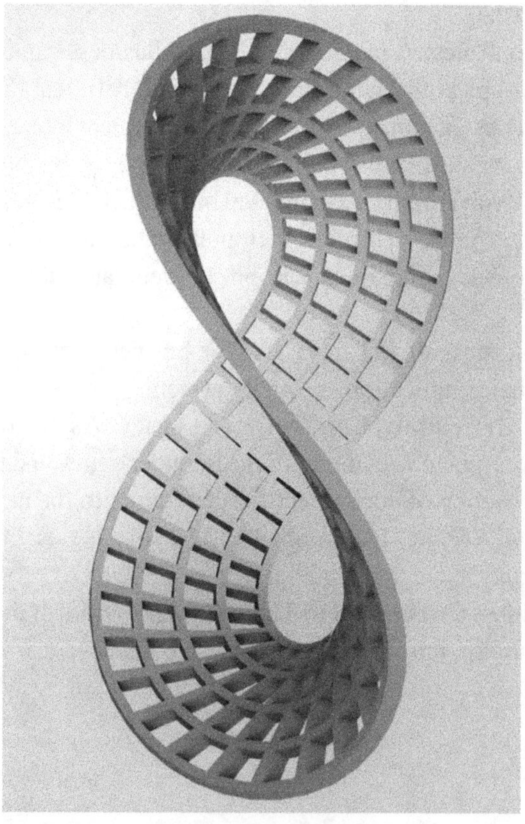

Figure 3. The two distinct systems: Family and Business

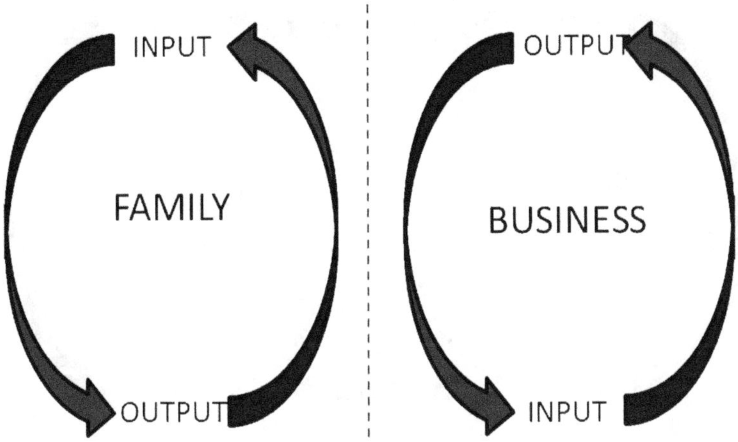

outputs, are perceived as individually effective as long as each one separately meets the requirements put forth by its stakeholders. On the first hand, the inputs of the family system consist of general interpersonal and relational attention focused on the family members and creating an environment encouraging for care and growth. This system is considered effective as long as the inherent relationships among the members of the system are considered functional. Its main outputs are geared toward inter-member relations and customer transactions. On the other hand, the business system‘s effectiveness is measured by its ability to deliver performance, revenues and profitability (Litz, 2008).

Based on that, he postulates that a business turns into a "Family Business" and a family turns into a "Business Family" as cross-system transfers among the two factors occur. As a result, the FB interfaces turn increasingly Mobius-like as a system's outputs are transferred across the interactive system channels to become the input at other system. Such as for example when a new family member join the business, becomes part of the business system input, and contributes to profit generation, where profits are the output of the Business System. These profits are transferred back to the family system in return in the form of family income, that is an input to the Family System itself. Another example is the family business top manager who is not simply top manager or boss, but also in parallel, a father. Similarly, a son or a daughter is not simply an offspring, but also simultaneously, an employee. Thus, in this Mobius-like relationship, one can travel interchangeably all over these 2 systems, as reflective realities, visiting the entire surface without encountering any tangible or system-initiated boundaries (See Figure 4).

Figure 4. Family and Business cross-system

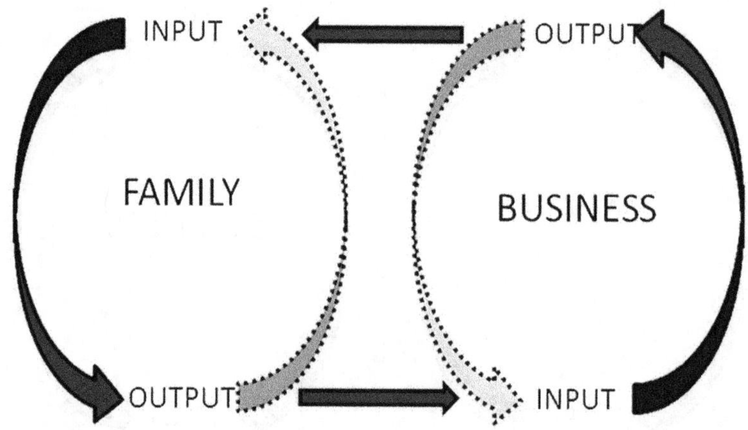

Family Business Sustainability Theories

Research shows that the successful FB entities perform better because they are aware of, and take into consideration, both family and business factors (Sharma, 2004; Olson, Zuiker, Danes, Stafford, Heck, & Duncan, 2003) following targets that are financial and non-financial (Sharma, 2004; Tagiuri & Davis, 1989). Moreover, the alignment of stakeholders' understanding of what constitutes success reduces conflicts leading to synchronized involvement by the family members (Sharma, 2004; Astracham & McMillan, 2003). Thus, the success of the one of the two factors results in internal conflicts and tension that tend to jeopardize the firm's sustainability.

Ernst and Young's "DNA For Sustainable Family Business" Model (2012)

Attempting to identify the key success factors of family business entrepreneurships, Ernst and Young, the Family Business Network International, and Credit Suisse, conducted a joined study to identify the key success factors for family business entrepreneurships. The study was unfolded in 33 countries, the sample included 60% firms in their third generation of family managers, and 43% having more than a thousand employees. The study results are summarized in what is known as the 'Sustainability DNA of Family Business Model' which includes eight critical factors (See Figure 5). These factors are 1-Future management structure; 2-Managing capital; 3-Sustaining growth and profitability; 4-Managing and retaining talent; 5-Culture and responsibility; 6-Balancing risk; 7-Next generation planning; and 8-Effective tax management.

Figure 5. The Sustainability DNA of FB Model
(Young, 2012)

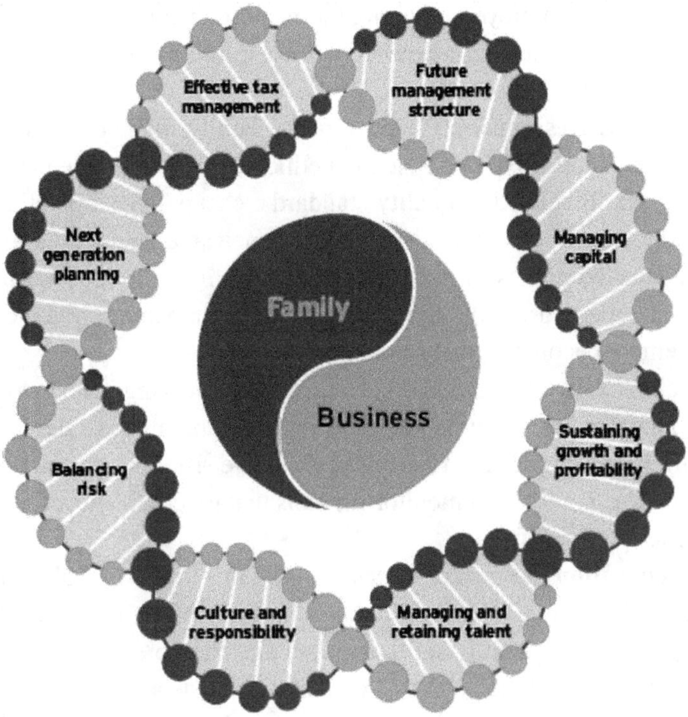

1. **Future Management Structure:** The risk of top position vacancy and lack of successors in FB is a haunting worry to owners whose off-springs may lack skills, qualifications, experience, or interest in the management of the business. Thus, the availability of contingency plans including formulating family charters and appointing non-family executives can contribute to sustainability.
2. **Managing Capital:** The consideration of fresh capital injection to develop the entrepreneurship, restructure it, and sustain its growth plans, need to include new avenues such acquisitions, new subsidiaries, upgrading technology, increasing manpower or machines, or developing new products.
3. **Sustaining Growth and Profitability:** Through exploring new markets and broadening its product-base and business scope a FB may sustain its profitability through optimizing returns and risk mitigation. The firm will have to integrate is activities, innovative in its corporate strategies, and develop synergies for growth while ensuring back-office efficiency that improves bottom and top lines.

4. **Managing and Retaining Talents**: Believing that a company is of the quality of its people puts forth a challenge for family businesses trying to attract and retain qualified employees. Among the major constraints faced are the nepotism applied and the unannounced "Glass Ceiling" strategy against qualified non-family members of staff.
5. **Culture and Responsibility:** Customers, family members, and employees alike are all supportive of a sustained ethical endeavor on the part of the FB, whether that is related to quality standards, cheap labor, operating efficiencies, ethical and legal considerations or renewable energy. As a result, the FB's contested efforts to proactively consider integrating these factors into its modus operands, and relating them to the company's strategic goals and achievement becomes a daily challenge.
6. **Balancing Risk:** Global markets are constantly evolving, with increased volatility. Therefore an increased need to faster adaptability to these changes is pushing FB toward higher flexibility, proactive risk assessment and analysis, better market control and monitoring tools that together, allow for lower risks and better performance.
7. **Next Generation Planning:** Succession planning for FB is a balancing act with high complexity due to the emotional sensitivity of the involved constituents (managing-owner, family, and company) and the objective, financial, legal, technical needs and the diverging personal interests and values. These multi-directional factors and constraints may result in serious internal conflicts of interests affecting the business and its continuity.
8. **Effective Tax Management:** The impact of tax on the FB's potential investment decisions, financing, estate planning, and liquidity on its growth and market competitiveness is vital due to the limitation of sources of resources at hand, and thus management's understanding of these implications becomes detrimental.

Corporate Governance

The Concept of Corporate Governance

As one cannot expect the administrator of other people's funds to be more careful and attentive toward the funds than the money owners themselves (Smith, 2006), and with the publicized financial scandals uncovered implicating reputed global business entities (such as Enron, Xerox, Merrill Lynch, Maxwell, Parmalat, and others), research shows that the most common causes of failure are summarized by managerial incompetence, defective repartition of responsibilities, lack of respect of procedures, ignoring risk management, neglect of the recommendations of internal auditors, inefficiency of external auditors, and managers' greed (see Figure 6 below). These factors, combined with the impact of globalization and pervasive change, are pushing FB to develop and sustain a proper legal framework for monitoring and adapting to change (Cretu, 2012).

As a result, FBs need to revisit their practices of corporate governance including those of integrity, transparency and responsibility (Cretu, 2012). These are defined as follows.

1. **Integrity:** Relates to the truthfulness in approaching one's own, and others' concerns for business and responsibility.
2. **Transparency:** Reflects the organizational thrive for learning, which leads to evolution, improved performance and efficiency and thus to balance and financial stability.
3. **Responsibility:** Corporate Governance responsibility refers to the assumption of clarity of solutions and responsibilities; the present of systems relying on accountability in front of an informed supervisor who has the means to affirm the outcome in an open environment of independence and freedom of examination; where rewards and punishments are continuously functioning without default (Cretu, 2012).

Figure 6. Common causes leading to the financial scandals

Therefore FB are expected to more thoroughly assess and handle risks, improve style and performance of management, find new sources of financing, and reflect operational transparency to stakeholders, which will in return thwart potential business chaos, improve structural organization, allow for higher decision-making degrees of freedom within the boundaries of the applicable best practices, laws and regulations. All of these necessary guidelines for success and sustainability of any business are not evident in the academic research on FB while they are abundantly reported by publicly held firms (Zalivako, 2012), due to their operating sizes and their legal requirements. As a result of the lack of knowledge on FB and the incongruity in the factors considered in assessing FB, a new more generic model is suggested. The new model encompasses five factors labeled as 1) Leadership 2) Transparency 3) Remuneration Measurement 4) Accountability and 5) System, for FB sustainability (see Figure 7 and Table 1).

Corporate Governance in Family Business

As a rule of thumb, the integration of the concept of corporate gorvernance in FB faces more furdles than in other types of firms for many reasons. As FB are managed by their owners who lack discipline and do not necessarily properly thereby articulate their plans, policies, procedures, and practices. These are evident in the

Figure 7. Family business sustainability factors

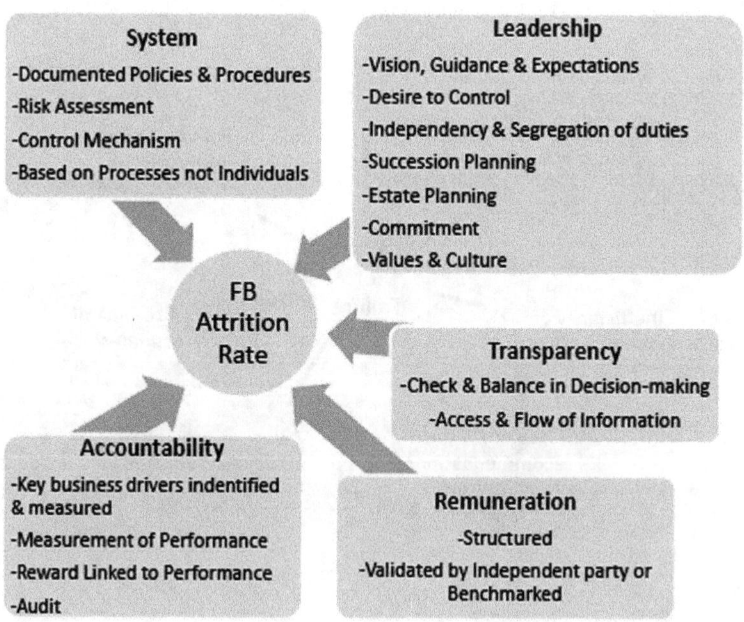

Table 1. List of key corporate governance factors in family business

Factor	Measure
Leadership	Independency and Segregation of duties
	Duality of CEO role / Conflict of interest
	Succession Planning
	Estate Planning
	Vision, Guidance and Expectations
	Desire to control
	Top Management Commitment
	Values and Culture
	Strategic Planning and direction
System	Documented policies and procedures
	Risk Assessment
	Control Mechanisms
	System based of processes not Individuals
Accountability	Structured and Consistent Disciplinary/Corrective actions
	Identification and measurement of key Business Drivers
	Monitoring and measurement of performance
	Internal and external Audit
	Linking Reward to Performance
Transparency	Check and Balances in decision making process
	Access and flow of information
	Structured independently validated remuneration system

performance oversight, ability to attract and retain high skilled talent, and succession planning. Therefore studies show that up to 95% of FB do not reach their third generation of owners (IFC, 2008).

FB often have different and unique characteristics compared to other types of firms. These differences are fue to the nature of management-ownership and to the system-overlap between family and business systems, where family dynamics and generation differences at the managerial level present chanllenges and tension. Therefore, the family dictates the governance system applied in the business (IFC, 2008). Moreover, the continuity, survival and development plans are an integral part of the governance structure (Brenes, Madrigal & Requena, 2011), and are established to support internal relationships and communication between the business executives and the family owners (Berns et al., 2009). As such, corporate governance plays the role of control mechanism, a check and balance tool, providing structure and alignment between the three entities, namely shareholders, the board of directors and company management (Berns et al., 2009). As a solution to the growing concern on the lack of governance in FB comes the Sarbanes-Oxley Act (2002) to reinforce the governance structure, imposing penalties upon non-complying ones (Lander, 2002; Berns et al., 2009). In parallel, the ensuing requirements and standards are used by Fb as a benchmark or reference by those aiming for IPOs or growth, or searching for extenal funding, or looking forward toward sustainable growth and a strategic competitive advantage in their market.

The challenge confronting FB today is that in most of them the family owners control a major stake of the business components, impacting corporate structure and the composition of the board of directors through traditions, culture, netwwork, links and confidence, and the personal power and respect (Berns et al., 2009). It is thus obvious that the thre components of corporate governance structure namely Owners, Board and Top management do in real life overlap, affecting the corporate governance objectivity and the general health state of the business.

Moreover, considering FB through the 3 components (Circles) of family, business and ownership and the integral stages of development and governance structure (Admin, 2011) shows that the family council governing the FB and populated by family members addresses central issues upon their identification (Aronoff & Ward, 2000). Moreover, this council develops protocols and codes of understanding based on the members' shared vision, while educating both managers and family members about ownership responsibilities, management duties, and the boundaries separating family and business. Therefore, this council which sometimes includes non-family business top managers. earns its powerful role as a discussion forum that handles sensitive matters including conflict resolution and succession planning (Admin, 2011). As such, the governance design is set at the board of directors' level by providing advice, monitoring performance, taking or ratifying major decision on executive hiring, new investments and dividends' distribution, appointment of external auditors, and modifying firm charter (Aronoff & Ward, 2000). Thus, the board's absence can cost the FB major strengths and perspective (Admin, 2011).

Although family and non-family businesses have similar operating and functional systems in general, there exist unique attributes for each in terms of priorities, drivers, objectives, strategic plans and decision-making processes. These are mainly generated by the FB's two-systems overlapping process (Family & Business), allowing FB to build on this strength in developing operating synergies explained by the engagement, dedication and commitment of the family executives; while these themselves also presenting a threat, namely that of contradicting priorities, interests and objectives which may negatively impact FB's performance and sustainability (Tagiuri & Davis, 1996; File & Prince, 1996; Koiranen, 2003).

LESSONS LEARNT

The management of a family business which ownership spans across more than one family member, does seem for an external observer from the outside as simple and smoothly running. However, and due to the interrelationship of the three components, namely the family the business and the ownership, the result is seven potential managerial positions of interaction held by the different members of the owner-family (Tagiuri & Davis, 1996). These separately distinctive standing positions increase the complexity of managing FB. Moreover, the absence of, or the mere elasticity of the boundaries of the three components only add to the complexity of the managerial balance, allowing the members of the FB the ability to move across both family and business systems (The Mobious Strip Model) with limited restrictions and boundaries (Litz, 2008), contributing to their flexibility in decision-making.

It is important to mention here that at the start-up of any business, including FB, the interference as well as the pressure from non-managing owners and family members remain limited due to the chance they all give for the venture to grow. During this stage of the life-cycle of the FB, the three components put efforts to align their visions, missions and expectations, work together in synergy, and allowing the FB a unique competitive advantage labeled as 'The Familiness'. The honey moon situation changes to tension as the FB ages and the need to handover to the next generation emerges, or as change and development are needed in management, processes, organization and structure, or as diverging objectives and interests of the family members and owners create conflicts of interest, thereby affecting the FB's sustainability (Ernst & Young, 2012). The result of these tensions and diverging interests is added complexity. This in turn affects the FB's ability to sustain profitability, growth, and development, threatening its viability over time, its capacity to attract and retain talent, intimidating its managerial career plans and future career paths, putting pressure on its organizational structure and culture, and menacing the effective management of its resources and financial capital, thereby putting this viable management FB model at risk. Thus, associating all of the above FB problems to the high attrition rate, resulting in the survival of only 6% of them to their third generation.

To conclude, and as the publically owned corporations have taken a step forward, whether by choice or by compliance, the study recommends that FB move in the same direction, setting forth their corporate governance guidelines, practices and prerogatives within their FB hierarchical structures, in order for them to sustain operation and viability. The first step in the process lies in setting both structured corrective processes and preventive practices within the FB organization with the adequate resilience framework to counter the factors leading to FB failures. These factors include management greed and incompetence, conflicts of interest and duality of roles, lack of respect for procedures, lack of transparency, controls and measures, ignoring risk management, lack of checks and balances (Farazmand, 2014).

REFERENCES

Adendorff, C., Venter, E., & Boshoff, C. (2008). The impact of family harmony on governance practices in South African Greek family businesses. *Management Dynamics: Journal of the Southern African Institute for Management Scientists, 17*(3), 28–44.

Admin. (2011). *The three circle model - Family business framework.* Retrieved Sept.9, 2015 from http:/www.symcoandco.com/resources/article/family-business-framework

Aronoff, C. E., & Ward, J. L. (2000). *La prueba suprema de la grandeza familiar: La elección del nuevo líder.* McGraw-Hill.

Astrachan, J. H., & McMillan, K. S. (2003). *Conflict and communication in the family business (No. 16).* Marietta, GA: Family Enterprise Publisher.

Barnes, L., & Hershon, S. (1976). Transferring power in the family business. *Harvard Business Review*, (July-August), 105–114.

Bates, T., & Nucci, A. R. (1990). *An analysis of small business size and rate of discontinuance.* US Department of Commerce, Bureau of the Census.

Beckhard, R., & Dyer, W. G. (1983). Managing continuity in the family-owned business. *Organizational Dynamics, 12*(1), 5–12. doi:10.1016/0090-2616(83)90022-0

Berns, M., Townend, A., Khayat, Z., Balagopal, B., Reeves, M., Hopkins, M. S., & Kruschwitz, N. (2009). The business of sustainability: What it means to managers now. *MIT Sloan Management Review, 51*(1), 20–26.

Brenes, E. R., Madrigal, K., & Requena, B. (2011). Corporate governance and family business performance. *Journal of Business Research, 64*(3), 280–285. doi:10.1016/j.jbusres.2009.11.013

Cater, J. J., III. (2006). *Stepping out of the shadow: The leadership qualities of successors in family business* (Doctoral dissertation). Wake Forest University.

Creţu, R. F. (2012). Corporate governance and corporate diversification strategies. *Review Of International Comparative Management/Revista De Management Comparat International, 13*(4), 621-633.

de Vries, M. F. K. (1994). The dynamics of family controlled firms: The good and the bad news. *Organizational Dynamics, 21*(3), 59–71. doi:10.1016/0090-2616(93)90071-8

Duh, M. (2012). *Family businesses: the extensiveness of succession problems and possible solutions*. INTECH Open Access Publisher.

Ernst & Young. (2012). *Built to last Family businesses lead the way to sustainable growth*. Available: http://www.ey.com/Publication/vwLUAssets/Built_to_Last/$FILE/ Built_to_Last.pdf

Farazmand, A. (2014). *Crisis and emergency management: Theory and practice*. Boca Raton, FL: CRC Press-Taylor & Francis. doi:10.1201/b16715

File, K. M., & Prince, R. A. (1996). Attributions for family business failure: The heirs perspective. *Family Business Review, 9*(2), 171–184. doi:10.1111/j.1741-6248.1996.00171.x

Gersick, K. E., McCollom-Hampton, M., Davis, J. A., & Lansberg, I. (1997). *Generation to generation: Life cycles in the family business*. Cambridge, MA: Harvard Business School Press.

IFC. (2008). *Guidebook on corporate governance of family-owned enterprises*. Beirut: The Lebanese Transparency Association.

IFERA (The International Family Enterprise Academy). (2003, December). Family businesses dominate. *Family Business Review, 16*(4), 235–250.

Koiranen, M. (2003). Understanding the contesting ideologies of family business: Challenge for leadership and professional services. *Family Business Review, 16*(4), 241–250.

Lander, G. P. (2002). The Sarbanes-Oxley Act of 2002. *Journal of Investment Compliance, 3*(1), 44–53.

Lansberg, I., Perrow, E. L., & Rogolsky, S. (1988). Family business as an emerging field. *Family Business Review, 1*(1), 1–8. doi:10.1111/j.1741-6248.1988.00001.x

Litz, R. A. (2008). Two Sides of a One-Sided Phenomenon: Conceptualizing the Family Business and Business Family as a Möbius Strip. *Family Business Review, 21*(3), 217–236.

Miller, W. D. (1998). Siblings and succession in the family business. *Harvard Business Review, 76*, 22–40.

Olson, P. D., Zuiker, V. S., Danes, S. M., Stafford, K., Heck, R. K., & Duncan, K. A. (2003). The impact of the family and the business on family business sustainability. *Journal of Business Venturing, 18*(5), 639–666. doi:10.1016/S0883-9026(03)00014-4

Pistrui, D., Welsch, H. P., & Roberts, J. S. (1997). The [Re]-Emergence of Family Businesses in the Transforming Soviet Bloc: Family Contributions to Entrepreneurship Development in Romania. *Family Business Review, 10*(3), 221–238. doi:10.1111/j.1741-6248.1997.00221.x

Rebernik, M., Tomnic, P., & Duh, M. (2007). Pitanja sukcesije unutar obiteljskih poduzeća u tranzicijskim privredama. *Društvena istraživanja-Časopis za opća društvena pitanja*, (4-5), 751-779.

Sarbanes, P. (2002, July). Sarbanes-oxley act of 2002. In *The Public Company Accounting Reform and Investor Protection Act*. Washington, DC: US Congress.

Schwartz, E. L. (1954). Will Your Business Die With You? *Harvard Business Review, 32*(5), 110–122.

Shanker, M. C., & Astrachan, J. H. (1996). Myths and realities: Family businesses contribution to the US economy—A framework for assessing family business statistics. *Family Business Review, 9*(2), 107–123. doi:10.1111/j.1741-6248.1996.00107.x

Sharma, P. (2004). An overview of the field of family business studies: Current status and directions for the future. *Family Business Review, 17*(1), 1–36. doi:10.1111/j.1741-6248.2004.00001.x

Smith, W. L. (2006). Goals and characteristics of family-owned small businesses: An international replication and comparison between Middle America and Western Australia Hospitality Providers. *International Journal of Management and Enterprise Development, 3*(3), 212–226. doi:10.1504/IJMED.2006.008821

Statistics unkind to family business. (2007, June 18). *The Star Magazine*.

Tagiuri, R., & Davis, J. (1996). Bivalent attributes of the family firm. *Family Business Review, 9*(2), 199–208. doi:10.1111/j.1741-6248.1996.00199.x

Zalivako, A. (2012). *Die Bauten des russischen Konstruktivismus: Moskau 1919-32; Baumaterial, Baukonstruktion, Erhaltung*. Imhof.

Chapter 2
Cooperative Entrepreneurship in the Middle East

Philippe W. Zgheib
Lebanese American University, Lebanon

ABSTRACT

Socio-cultural characteristics as defined by Hofstede lay out the basis for understanding entrepreneurial characteristics within a given society. Masculinity, collectivism, and uncertainty avoidance are related to competitive behavior, then cooperative versus competitive dilemmas are analyzed in the cultural setting of Middle Eastern entrepreneurial activity. The purpose is to prove that a relationship exists between culture, and entrepreneurial attitudes. Among Middle Eastern countries, Lebanon is found to go against generally acceptable relationships between cooperation and entrepreneurial autonomy. Furthermore, risk avoidance in Lebanon presents a major discrepancy factor with entrepreneurial culture in general.

HISTORICAL OVERVIEW

Collective action on the business level has been rising, initial collaboration started informally between friends and family in societies. It quickly expanded to include networks of interfirm, then formal strategic alliances, consortia to finally reach trade associations (Bird, & Romannelli, 2001, p.219). Historically, all phases of entrepreneurial activities were carried out by a single individual. One man used

DOI: 10.4018/978-1-5225-2066-5.ch002

to manage the perception, the planning and the implementation phase of a new venture. Collective or cooperative behavior evolved with time, allowing a group of individuals under the form of partnerships, networks or corporation to perform as a united body and execute the tasks required more efficiently

The authors of Portraits of successful entrepreneurs and high-flyers (Lam & Kit, 1999) have defined the two critical aspects of this issue: collectivism and individualism.

- **Collectivism:** Collectivism is defined such as the collective welfare is placed above individual welfare. Individual conduct and pursuits are directed at achieving collective harmony, maintained through preserving the social order and following the rules entailed in each relationship.
- **Individualism:** Individualism or the "view of man" as present by Sum Lam (1999), defines the individual in terms of his or her relationship with others which are structured in differential order with different degree of closeness and trust.[…] this relational identity predisposes the individual to consider his or her internal needs in relation to the external environment.(Sum Lam, 1999)

ADDRESSING THE COOPERATIVE/COMPETITIVE DILEMMAS IN ENTREPRENEURSHIP

"The Fundamental issue addressed by this dimension is the degree of interdependence a society maintains among individuals. It relates to people's self concept: 'I ' or 'We' wrote Hofstede in addressing the entrepreneurship dilemmas. (Sum Lam, 1999). Influencing factors in addressing cooperative/competitive dilemmas in entrepreneurship hav ebeen identified. In addressing the cooperative/competitive dilemmas in entrepreneurship, a variety of economical, socio-cultural, historical and other factors are to be studied. (Sweldberg, 2000).

SOCIETIES' PREDISPOSITION

No society is solely competitive or cooperative. All society must possess both traits. For example competitive groups within a society make that society more cooperative by intuition. Mead states that competition does not necessarily reflect conflict and nor does cooperation translates into solidarity. In cooperative societies, she explains, "competition is often introduced and acts as an associative mechanism" (Mead, 1937, p.460). "It is telling that when Gates talks about the competition he lumps them all together. When competitors talk about Gates they single him out." (Dearlove, 1999, p.50) underlining the complexity of cooperation and competitiveness within a market given the relevance of players' size in that particular market. Yet all societies have their particular traits that influence the behavior of members and have a direct effect on the emergence of leaders and entrepreneurs.

THE BENEFITS OF COLLECTIVE OR COOPERATIVE STRATEGIES

Resources: Cooperative strategies, as discussed, by many authors are more rewarding then competitive-individual strategies. Among other benefits, Bird and Romanelli, authors of The Entrepreneurship Dynamic, considered collaboration between founders a tool to ensure a wider acceptance. A second significant advantage to collective strategies is that it provides various member of the team with valued lessons. "Standard designs and processes emerge more easily when collaboration enables founders to find or construct common interests" advance the authors. Finally, not would the team collective strategy serve to pool resources and organize them more effectively and efficiently, but it would as well serve to position the group in a way to be perceived by outsiders as a one united body. (Bird, & Romanelli, 2001)

Stress: Stress is often perceived as work related. Stress that gets translated in physiological symptoms such as coronary heart diseases and disabling ulcers is the individual perception of external demand exceeding one's ability to cater to it with no enough resources to resolve the underlying problem. Several coping methods help relieve stress. Social support is a significant mechanism for entrepreneurial stress.

No one clear cut lesson could be concluded to address the cooperative versus the competitive dilemmas that faces entrepreneurs. It was revealed significant and useful by a large number of research papers, to study the entrepreneur's society in order to understand better his behavior. These studies led their readers, as well to expect the kind of entrepreneurs that will rise from such or such society framework. Yet other studies proved that some societies were strongly cooperative and some others were strongly cooperative, and others provided to clear-cut. (Mead, 1937). Entrepreneurs themselves do not provide a clear cut whether they will prefer cooperation over competition or the opposite. An interesting note is to be drawn; cooperation and competition are two complex systems. Extremely complex systems, in fact, that could only be driven and worked out by a sort of "invisible hand": Collective activity of individual entrepreneurs in a given market place. Vital entrepreneurial networks do not only provide access to resources, but most important it provides the right of entry to various segments to the environment.

In order to study the status of cooperative entrepreneurship in Lebanon it is helpful to start from the past, studying the present and looking into the future. What entrepreneurship in Lebanon is today depends a lot on how it started in small single enterprises and how it grew to what it is today and how it will develop in the future. Lebanon's entrepreneurs emerged mainly right after the long Lebanese wars at the end of the 20th century. Lebanon was struggling to recover from its damaged situation and was seeking every business opportunity to improve. This is explained further by the ESCWA report on Lebanon, with all details on entrepreneurship in Lebanon.

First a clear definition on entrepreneurship is provided, then, further going into the details to explain what cooperative entrepreneurship is, what it entails, and how it is applied globally and in the Middle East in specific considering Lebanon's case, by both highlighting its background and history in relation to cooperative entrepreneurship.

COOPERATIVE ENTREPRENEURSHIP

"A cooperative is an autonomous association of persons united voluntarily to meet their common economic, social and cultural needs and aspirations through a jointly-owned and democratically-controlled enterprise." (MacPherson,1996, p.35). The cooperative form of enterprise is in extensive use throughout the world. It is applied in most market economy countries and to an increasing extent in the newly developing countries. Cooperation is an age-old way of achieving a goal that is beyond the resources of an individual or when working together offers a more practical or favourable solution. The cooperative as a distinct form of company is already over a 150-years old. Its birth occurred at the time when the modern market economy was in its infancy and the need arose for an alternative structure than one based on the ownership of capital or in modern terminology, a company owned by its members and/or customer-owners. Over the years quite substantial commercial and industrial operations have developed on this basis in many countries. The central principles of a cooperative society are that it is open to all, unlimited in membership and, as an alternative to producing a profit on capital invested, produces benefits in the form of services for its members. The most general goal is to create a force on the market consisting of many small companies working together for the same objectives, and in which the aims and methods are decided upon democratically in advance according to the principle that the benefit of the collectively owned and operated business accrues as evenly as possible to all participants.

Basic elements of the cooperative form of enterprise are: Honesty, Openness, Social responsibility and Caring for others. The cooperative firm differs from other types of companies largely because of its ownership model and basic aims. Thus a cooperative enterprise also differs in its structure and operating objectives from other companies in the private sector. What cooperative entrepreneurship seeks to achieve is to bring into the cooperative movement creativity and innovation, market orientation and strategic management. For cooperatives to be entrepreneurial, it is recommended that they be: a) creative, innovative, proactive and calculated risk takers; b) driven by market opportunities and customer preferences; c) business-like in their decision-making processes; d) efficient in the production of goods and services to reduce cost and enhance quality; and e) driven by profits and growth so that members can optimize their benefits and welfare.

The cooperative movement will have to set its course on defining itself as part of the private sector and no longer as part of the public sector. The challenge is therefore how to enter the world of business without sacrificing the social dimension that set the cooperative movement apart from a private business.

PROMOTING ENTREPRENEURS

Taking a gander at the monetary development rates of various economies around the world, we see that one component emerges the most: the economies that support and reinforce business people set themselves up for higher development rates. Financial analysts have perceived the significance of business enterprise since the unbelievable investigation of monetary advancement when the new century rolled over by the colossal Austrian market analyst Joseph Schumpeter. People with vision, willing to go for broke, betting their own particular and financial specialists' assets on new items and techniques shape the motor that consolidates human and physical money to fuel monetary development and advancement.

ENTREPRENEURSHIP

Business is a critical part of a decentralized, market-based way to deal with the effective association of monetary movement. For all intents and purposes all-effective private ventures of all sizes in all parts of an economy, in the created and creating universes, start from the endeavors of individual or little gatherings of business visionaries. The prospect for business enterprise in most creating nations has enhanced astoundingly as bends made in the past are lessening considerably. The disposal of such mutilations will cultivate sound business enterprise for the advantage to social orders. A culmination to this circumstance is that the subsiding way of the State in the economies in creating nations additionally drives more prominent enterprise as State predominance decreases and as new open doors happen with privatization.

The private division's commitments towards monetary development and reasonable advancement are various and multifaceted. A dynamic and developing private segments - whether little, medium-or vast estimated operations - is the important means by which a general public produces livelihood, makes riches and advances material prosperity of its populace. Its commitment towards the lightening of neediness can be considerable.

Moreover, a free and dynamic private segment adds to human advancement by opening up circumstances and alternatives for individuals to pick occupation, utilization and ventures. A just as imperative component is that a thriving private segment will turn into the fundamental generator of assets in the public arena and add to a steady and developing income base from which Governments can attract assets to create and work different instruments, frameworks and exercises supporting monetary development and economical improvement. Accordingly, the part of the business sector has been put to the fore in national and worldwide arrangement exchanges, as it has been progressively perceived that market-based methodologies might frequently show a more powerful method for performing exercises that were initially embraced by the State or in semi open associations. *(The Global Report, 1992).*

COOPERATIVE ENTREPRENEURSHIP

Basic elements of the cooperative form of enterprise are: Honesty, Openness, Social responsibility and Caring for others."

The cooperative firm differs from other types of companies largely because of its ownership model and basic aims. Thus a cooperative enterprise also differs in its structure and operating objectives from other companies in the private sector.

ENTREPRENEURSHIP IN THE MIDDLE EAST

The Middle East has acknowledged the importance and need of entrepreneurial activities which would flourish the economy and open new opportunities for employment. Providing employment to a young and growing population is the major challenge faced by countries in the MENA (Middle East and North America) region. Everywhere in the world, it is small firms that contribute most to job creation. Their ability to thrive and generate jobs is a function of the environment in which they operate and their capacity to deal with continuous change and build assets for the future. Hence firm competitiveness is high on the development agenda. In today's global environment, firms rather than nations have become the engine of growth, and competitiveness is the key for firms to survive. (*Globalization and Firm Competitiveness in the Middle East and North Africa Region, Samiha Fawzy).*

To this end, the Middle East, in different regions, has opened facilities which enhance entrepreneurial skills. Organizations like the "Mediterranean Development Forum (MDF), the "World Bank", and the United Nations Development Programme, have been established to address and answer questions like: It addresses key issues for the future of the region, including: What are the real challenges facing firms' operations and efficiency? Can MENA firms compete in global markets? Which are the key institutional constraints that they face? What are the standards of good corporate behavior that they should follow? How can small- and medium-size enterprises (SMEs) play a more effective role as an engine of growth in the region? What are the reasons behind the observed gap between the actual and potential performance of the tourism sector in MENA? How can MENA's potential in this sector be achieved? Finally, how can governments, firms, business associations, the media, think tanks, and universities participate in building firm competitiveness in the MENA region?

Major actions are being taken to promote statistics databases and "Business Incubators", starting with university campuses and going to privately and publicly owned places.

COOPERATIVE ENTREPRENEURSHIP IN LEBANON

The Lebanese government needs to understand this in its activities. The motor for development is not a greater part for government or open projects. The principle part of the Lebanese government is to support business enterprise. New organizations and advances flourish and offer the economy some assistance with destroying so as to grow to a limited extent the business sectors of set up contenders and supplanting more established innovations. Samples incorporate mobile phone organizations that have taken away part of the business sector for telephones from government worked and possessed wired telephony, huge grocery stores have taken away a major part of the business sector for staple goods from mother and-pop stores in light of more noteworthy effectiveness. Governments that secure the old markets and salaries of existing and less productive organizations keep the inventive annihilation so fundamental to financial advancement.

Since Lebanon's autonomy, at whatever point the financial circumstance crumbled, the private division constantly discovered great motivations to accuse general society part. This slandering has just declined following the end of common strife in 1990 and does almost no to advance the helpful open private exertion that is important to restore the nation. The business group basically can't sit tight for people in general segment to change itself. It must move forward with changes of its own home and add to government push to enhance managerial proficiency. In the event that one backtracks in time, the reputation of the Lebanese monetary "marvel" in the 1950s and 1960s, which kept going until the episode of the common war in 1975, was the doing of the private division while the part of general society area stayed peripheral. The strides taken to modernize state organization, which were started by previous President Fouad Chehab, remain the main genuine changes that Lebanon has known in 59 years of freedom. It is unexpected that the Lebanon of the 1950s and 1960s, which did not have any genuine auxiliary economy, profited from every one of the changes that the district saw after the 1948 disaster or nakba in Palestine, also the ascent to greatness of the oil-rich Arab nations. The stream of capital and business people into Lebanon from those nations and the new open doors that were opened to business visionaries profited Lebanon miraculously and were in charge of what were the nation's brilliant years.

"The Switzerland of the Middle East," the same number of Lebanese jumped at the chance to call their nation, turned into a desert garden amidst extensive provincial turmoil. In any case, it was the true enclosure where a large portion of the Arab world's inside wars were battled through the media. No one acknowledged at the time that these wars were a prelude to the ridiculous strife that the Lebanese needed to persist for over 15 years, and the result of which we are as yet persevering. Amid those days, nobody griped around a wasteful state organization, debasement or expense avoidance, on the grounds that the majority of the nation's intense and smart world class were profiting from the disordered condition of things and were profiting from the economy. Everyone lived as though each was his last day and nobody thought about what's to come. Be that as it may, the success of the free enterprise period bore the seeds of disasters to come.

At the point when one considers the enterprise that prompted a prosperous Lebanon in the 1950s and 1960s and the purpose of the general population of this nation to survive the war years, it appears to be fantastic now to see so little eagerness or private activity to restore the nation's monetary wellbeing. A wide range of reasons are brought out to clarify the absence of legitimate conditions and measures to spare the nation as though they didn't exist before ¬ obviously in various weights and bores. The Syrian vicinity, the Palestinian danger of irritating the sensitive partisan parity, sectarianism, the obstruction of security bodies openly life, the absence of a free legal, Israel and globalization are however a couple of the offenders faulted by various portions of Lebanese society and particularly the business group.

Today things have changed. A large portion of the political and financial tip top, who are persuaded that Lebanon can't get by on the planet's free market economy, are calling for state intercession and a midway arranged economy to rescue benefits that won't be salvageable in the coming decades. For this world class, all methods are adequate to achieve a definitive objective. Unrealistically, they need tailor-made changes to empower the Lebanese to live like the Scandinavians in an expense free shelter as though Lebanon were an oil-rich nation. Without a doubt the state does not have the fundamental elements for genuine change yet the private part experiences a large number of the same weaknesses. It is dampening to realize that the private division does not have a huge number of essentials, for example, dependable information, straightforwardness and a genuine arrangement to change its structure. This absence of vital vision in the business group is most apparent in the consistent quibbling in the middle of brokers and industrialists. Any push to raise traditions obligations gets under the skin of shippers, yet the inability to ensure nearby makers just prompts the industrialists blaming the administration for taking sides. Support for the tourism and managing an account part just estranges those in horticulture and industry. Stuck in the center is the resident, who endures the most. Subsequent to 1990, no private foundation has arranged any genuine arrangement of change for the distinctive areas of the economy. The different councils of business or affiliations could have given the administration a financial vision, however rather have been tormented by consciences and fights. The measurable information once in a while introduced by these establishments is not precise and serves neither a genuine arrangement for the rebuilding the economy nor a push to manufacture a sound database that could be useful to the legislature. As previous Prime Minister Salim Hoss rightly said: "Statistical data in Lebanon is nothing more than a point of view."

COOPERATIVE ENTREPRENEURSHIP IN LEBANON: NEED FOR ACTION

The Lebanese government needs to understand this in its activities. The motor for development is not a greater part for government or open projects. The principle part of the Lebanese government is to energize business. New organizations and innovations thrive and offer the economy some assistance with destroying so as to grow to a limited extent the business sectors of built up contenders and supplanting more seasoned advances. Samples incorporate mobile phone organizations that have taken away part of the business sector for telephones from government worked and possessed wired telephony, expansive grocery stores have taken away a major part of the business sector for perishables from mother and-pop stores as a result of more prominent effectiveness. Governments that secure the old markets and livelihoods of existing and less productive organizations keep the innovative obliteration so fundamental to financial advancement.

GROWTH FACTORS

Financial development happens for the most part due to high rates of capital collection, some as training (human capital) however most in machines, hardware and industrial facilities. In any case, the gathering of capital and instructed work must be upheld by enhancements in innovation. Generally, long haul financial development has been supported by huge increments in profitability because of innovative and authoritative advances. This expansion in efficiency is then deciphered into higher genuine wages, expanding the specialists' ways of life and offering driving force to assist entrepreneurial ventures.

GOVERNMENT REGULATIONS

The significant snags to shaping new organizations or drawing in outside ventures are government regulations, formality and remuneration - all multiplying in the Lebanese economy. Therefore, numerous outside speculators and business people have hauled out of Lebanon, despite the fact that abroad Lebanese people have been effective in business in the Australia, U.S., Saudi Arabia, Canada, Africa, and Brazil, so forth.

Just thoughtful business situations brief gifted business visionaries to put resources into the nearby economy. This lesson can be learned by taking a gander at various countries in Europe, North America or South America. A decent illustration in Europe is Sweden, acclaimed today for the focused proficiency of organizations, for example, ABB (Asea Brown Bovery), Volvo, L.M. Ericsson; with couple of special cases, they all appeared from 1875 to 1915, the prime of Swedish free markets and development. Be that as it may, they are baffled these days; the absolute most fruitful Swedish organizations, for example, ABB, have moved their central station and industrial facilities abroad. Indeed, even in European countries, similar to Italy, with numerous little organizations, administrators gripe about prominent regulations that debilitate and ruin entrepreneurial exercises.

Measurements from the Organization for Economic Cooperation and Development affirm that funding is more bottomless in the U.S. than in Europe, and that America puts a great deal a greater amount of this capital in new businesses. Also, much startup cash is committed to hazardous cutting edge organizations in focuses of entrepreneurial vitality such as Silicon Valley.

The Lebanese government needs to make a Lebanese "Silicon Valley" where entrepreneurial ability and vitality would be sustained and advanced, not just by the standard ace business sector talk administration, yet by abrogating charges on the benefits of recently made firms, annulling formality on speculations, bringing down capital additions and domain assesses, advancing and empowering interests in innovation, and by advancing capital gathering and efficiency. To put it plainly, the administration ought to be master business and work for high rates of financial development. The Lebanese government puts a considerable measure of its assets in infertile political moves. The time has come to move every one of our assets into high return monetary speculations, in this manner advancing and maintaining financial development *(Fadi Asrawi, The Daily Star Online)*.

Most of the information generated about Lebanon indicates that Lebanon is characterized by the presence of SME or in other words "Individual Enterprises", where the father owns, then the son, then the grandson. Moreover, *Banks are too busy lending to the government to worry about the private sector.* Without the right connections, raising finance for small businesses isn't always easy in Lebanon.

An entrepreneur named Badr Hassoun, a soap maker in Tripoli wanted to advertise his football-shaped bars to visiting fans and players during the recent Asian Cup tournament. Because he makes soap in a traditional way with little capital investment and no credit history, he was unable to quickly raise the few thousand dollars he needed to publicize his product and take advantage of the influx of tourists to Tripoli.

Banks and capital markets, the traditional external sources of financing for companies, are largely closed off to entrepreneurs such as Hassoun who want to expand their businesses. Conventional bank loans come with double-digit interest rates and are hard to obtain without a bank account, signatories, and collateral. And even if small businesses are ready to take on this debt, banks are generally unwilling to lend because of the increased likelihood that these borrowers will be unable to make the repayments in the current recession.

This fact of "family owned" businesses, could be considered the main cause of not having adequate cooperative entrepreneurship in Lebanon. Lebanon, in its current position, as the center of the Middle East should be promoting cooperative entrepreneurs, however, this is not yet the case.

Private universities, where cooperative entrepreneurship is enhanced are starting to establish their identities as places of reference in the entrepreneurial world. Yet, a lot more effort should be done on both, the private and the public sector. Special action is being taken for this aspect, and there are individuals as well as organizations who are working for the promotion of cooperative entrepreneurship in Lebanon. An example would be the the Arab Regional Center for Entrepreneurship and Investment Training (ARCEIT), which is attached to the UNIDO Investment and Technology Promotion Office (ITPO) in Bahrain, has just made an agreement with the Beirut Association for Social Development (BASD), to be its focal point in Lebanon. With focal points already in Jordan, Sudan and Syria, BASD is the fourth focal point established by ARCEIT since its inauguration in February this year.

The programme in Lebanon has the full support of the Prime Minister of Lebanon, a protocol formalizing the arrangements is currently being concluded with the

Prime Minister's office. Capacity building activities (training of trainers) will be initiated soon at the BASD. (*Lebanese small businesses are starved for financing, The Daily Star Online).*The ARCEIT is itself a focal point of the Inter-Regional Centre for Entrepreneurship and Investment Training (IRC) of Ahmedabad, India. IRC is the international arm of the Entrepreneurship Development Institute of India and is responsible for building the capacity of institutions in Africa, Asia, Central Asia and Arab countries.

PSYCHOLOGICAL VIEW

A psychological view of the social patterns that influences the creation and development of national entrepreneurs' character in different societies provides a clear description of personality factors empowering competitive or cooperative behavior among entrepreneurs. The following traits were identified by different studies summarized by the researcher Yang (1986), with universal application.

1. Collective orientation,
2. Other-Orientation,
3. Relationship Orientation,
4. Authoritarian Orientation,
5. Submissive disposition,
6. Inhibited disposition, and
7. Effeminate disposition.

These factors raises social-oriented entrepreneurs character as the Yang (1986) study reveals. The collective form of behavior is shaped by the principles of Confucian Ideals. This ideology bases its foundation on the assumption that man only exist in relationship to others. How the new generation will be raised within the family and the society later, plays a critical role in shaping the in favor for "cooperative strategies" individuals. Relational dimensions help explain the personality of entrepreneurs. The relationship between sovereign and subject, father and son, husband and wife, friend and friend structures the personality of the individual and his perception of his role as a relational being. It defines as well, subjects' rights and obligations, which mainly revolve around interpersonal harmony leading to social welfare and stability among social-oriented groups. Other societies cherish a different kind of value such as:

1. High achievement,
2. Competition,

3. Equalitarian values,
4. Enjoyment,
5. Autonomy, and
6. Expression of Oneself.

(Sum Lam, 1999, pp. 138-139).

NORMS AND VALUES

This individualistic relational factor could best be explained by Hofstede's definition of competition driven societies: "individualism stands for a preference for a loosely knit social framework in society wherein individuals are supposed to take care of themselves and their immediate families only." (Sum Lam, 1999, pp. 186). Norms and values that societies adopt greatly influence the individuals' orientation. A matrix table is presented in the Appendix to show how different societies view cooperation and competition.

To summarize the previous findings on influential norms and values of societies, it is significant to point out another research conducted on the correlation between national cultural values and the attitude of entrepreneurs toward cooperative strategies, and which revealed the following: entrepreneurs emerging from masculine and individualistic driven societies were less favorable of cooperative strategies. In all cases, contractual safeguards seemed as a proper tool to protect oneself against other parties' individual goals and aspirations. The authors, Steensman, Marino and Weaver concluded that societies with uncertainty avoidances tendencies had their entrepreneurs appreciate cooperation; both safeguards and partner commonality were considered, in this case. The results of this study as were advanced, stressing the differences among entrepreneurs, bring about some notable implications on the competitive advantage level. Where as feminine and collective societies can see its entrepreneurs rely on cooperative strategies to position their businesses on the global level or to improve innovations developed by other societies. Masculine and individualistic societies would rather focus and be competitive on the technological level. (Steensman, Marino, Weaver, "Attitudes Toward Cooperative Strategies", 2000). This point was advanced and further discussed by Wilken who explained this divergence as "with the transition to collective forms of entrepreneurship expansion and innovation are likely to decrease, either because of the greater caution of collective actors or the unwieldiness of attempting to act in concert" (Wilken, 1979, p. 66).

Also on the socio-cultural norms level, the trust factor seems critical in developing cooperative strategies among market players. As entrepreneurial behavior is often defined as "the pursuit of opportunity without regard to resources currently controlled", a conflict arises naturally as both parties have similar attitudes towards opportunistic behavior.(Burt, 1992). An environment or a society that is supportive of a high level of trust will basically promote: effective communication, lower cost of coordination, high level of exchange, low monitoring efforts and costs and a more performance or goal oriented venture. These factors would eventually lead to lucrative cooperative strategies supporting expansion and efficiency. (Steensman, Marino, Weaver, "Attitudes Toward Cooperative Strategies", 2000).

ECONOMIC PERSPECTIVE

On the economic level, the emergence of cooperative strategies came as the result of the rise in capital requirement of new ventures on one hand, and the limitation that faced individual entrepreneurs on the other. As the result, a group of individuals responded better to the new market conditions and were through the "one for all and all for one" team game, more able to take advantage of the present opportunities.(Wilkin, 1979, p. 66). Individual entrepreneurs contribute to the growth of the economy. Their contribution takes many faces: from the introduction of a high level of competitiveness, to the introduction of all sorts of innovative products and services.... The authors of *The Entrepreneurship Dynamic*, allege that it is time to put the myth of the power of "the Entrepreneur" as a lonely individual to rest and consider more closely the teams of entrepreneurs who work formally or informally together to build new organizations and "create new legitimate market spaces" as specified by the authors.

Competition / Cooperation Prisoners' Dilemmas

In the attempt to grasp the competition / cooperation dilemmas for entrepreneurs a comparison the well known Prisoner's Dilemma can prove helpful: (Axelrod, 1997)

The Prisoners' Dilemma

A and B are two men who rob a bank. The police arrested and placed in two separate jail cells. The prosecutor visits A and B in their cell respectively. He makes clear the options that the two men have: either to confess to the crime or be silent. This model, suggest that no second chance ought to be granted for the other player when defecting the first time. A shortfall of this model is that it fails to acknowledge accidental defections that should not to be responded to in a disciplinary fashion. In real life, accidental defections are looked at closely, and negotiations often help in explaining patterns of behavior. (Swedberg, 2000, p. 220).

REFERENCES

Axelrod, R. (1997). *The complexity of Cooperation*. Princeton, NJ: Princeton University Press.

Bird, C. H., & Romanelli, E. E. (2001). *The entrepreneurship Dynamic: Origins of entrepreneurship and the evolution of industries*. Stanford, CA: Stanford University Press.

Burt, R. O. (1992). *Structural Holes: The social structure of competition*. Cambridge, MA: Harvard University Press.

Chris, I. M. (2000). *Cooperative Entrepreneurship: The Challenge for Unions in the New Millennuim*. International Labor Organization.

Collins, O., & Moore, D. S. (1964). *The enterprisingman*. MSU Business Studies, Michigan State University.

Dearlove, D. S. (1999). *Business the Bill Gates way*. San Francisco, CA: Capstone Publishing Limited.

Gliedt, T. R., & Parker, P. (2007). Green community entrepreneurship: Creative destruction in the social economy. *International Journal of Social Economics*, *34*(8), 538–553. doi:10.1108/03068290710763053

Hakim, Y. H. (2002, March 16). Time for Private Sector to Pull its Weight, Stop "Unending Lament". *The Daily Star*.

Haugh, H. L. (2005). A research agenda for social entrepreneurship. *Social Enterprise Journal*, *1*(1), 1–12. doi:10.1108/17508610580000703

Mead, M. J. (1937). *Cooperation and competition among primitive peoples*. New York: McGraw-Hill Book Company, Inc. doi:10.1037/13891-000

Murphy, P. J., & Coombes, S. M. (2009). A model of social entrepreneurial discovery. *Journal of Business Ethics*, *87*(1), 325–336. doi:10.1007/s10551-008-9921-y

Roper, J. T., & Cheney, G. (2005). The meanings of social entrepreneurship today. *Corporate Governance*, *5*(3), 95–104. doi:10.1108/14720700510604733

Steensma, M. W. (2000). *Attitudes toward cooperative strategies: A cross cultural analysis of entrepreneurs*. Academic Press.

Sud, M., VanSandt, C. V., & Baugous, A. M. (2009). Social entrepreneurship: The role of institutions. *Journal of Business Ethics*, *85*(1), 201–216. doi:10.1007/s10551-008-9939-1

Sum Lam, S. K. (1999). Portraits of successful entrepreneurs and high-flyers: A psychological perspective. Ashgate Publishing Limited.

Swdberg, R. (2000). *Entrepreneurship: The social science view*. Oxford University Press.

Thompson, J. M., Alvy, G., & Lees, A. (2000). Social entrepreneurship- a new look at the people and the potential. *Management Decision*, *38*(5), 328–338. doi:10.1108/00251740010340517

United Nations Department of Economic and Social Affairs (DESA). (1999). *Entrepreneurship and Privatization for Economic Growth and Sustainable Development.* DESA.

Wilken, P. L. (1979). *Entrepreneurship: comparative and historical study*. Norwood, NJ: Ablex Publishing Corporation.

Chapter 3
Corporate Innovation and Intrapreneurship in the Middle East

Philippe W. Zgheib
Lebanese American University, Lebanon

ABSTRACT

Corporate Intrapreneurship (CIP) is still viewed in many cases in the Arab region as a western concept that does not apply to the Middle East. Whereas Corporate Intrapreneurship (CIP) has been an area of increased interest in the United States and in Europe in the last few decades, stimulated mainly by the hope that it will revitalize and regenerate the manufacturing industry, among others, in these countries, especially in the face of increased competition, in the Middle East CIP is still a somewhat new and sometimes vague concept with little understanding to its benefits and uses. The objective of this chapter is to link intrapreneurship to the well-developed literature on entrepreneurship, to develop a model that will allow us to incorporate those factors that are critical to the intrapreneurial zone of an organization.

DOI: 10.4018/978-1-5225-2066-5.ch003

INTRODUCTION

Corporate Intrapreneurship (CIP) is still viewed in many cases in the **Arab** region as a western concept that does not apply to the Middle East. Whereas Corporate Intrapreneurship (CIP) has been an area of increased interest in the United States and in Europe in the last few decades, stimulated mainly by the hope that it will revitalize and regenerate the manufacturing industry, among others, in these countries, especially in the face of increased competition, in the Middle East CIP is still a somewhat new and sometimes vague concept with little understanding to its benefits and uses. This will change because even though the manufacturing industry is still in its infancy compared to the developed countries, yet competition is also strong and if these companies plan to stay in the game and compete, then they need to use whatever tools available and one of them is CIP. In Lebanon in particular where the country prides itself with the human factor, it is greatly advantageous to use this tool especially that it is readily available and can provide strong results.

The objective of this chapter is to link intrapreneurship to the well developed literature on entrepreneurship, to develop a model that will allow us to incorporate those factors that are critical to the intrapreneurial zone of an organization, its size and its dynamics, and to link all of this to the value of the firm. The early part of the chapter discusses entrepreneurship and the profile of an entrepreneur in the hope that an existing large firm can identify entrepreneurs within its structures in order to harness their talents and to add value to the firm. Furthermore, various elements of intrapreneurship are identified, then considers the necessary and sufficient conditions for it to become a value driver within the firm. The various influencing factors are identified and some conclusions are drawn.

DEFINITION OF ENTREPRENEURSHIP

While some may claim that entrepreneurship as a concept started with Adam Smith however the term itself was coined by a French economist Jean Baptiste Say, an admirer of Smith, around 1800. Even though this term has been around since 1800, there is still some confusion concerning the true meaning of the word.

There are many views as to who is an entrepreneur and what an entrepreneurial behavior is. Kuratko et. al (2011) list seven main perspectives on the nature of entrepreneurship. The first is the creation of wealth referring to the undertaking of risks to facilitate production and make a profit. The second perspective is the creation of enterprise which is starting a new business venture that did not exist before. Third is the creation of innovation which is putting together a unique combination that makes existing methods or products obsolete. Next is the creation of change which is to modify or adjust one's ways or skills to better exploit opportunities in the environment. Fifth is the creation of jobs since entrepreneurship involves hiring and developing part of the labor force. Sixth is the creation of value, taken from the perspective of creating value for customers by making use of opportunities previously overlooked. Finally there is the creation of growth because a strong drive towards growth in sales, income, assets and employment are aspects defining entrepreneurship. Perhaps the creation of innovation and change are the perspectives that best describe the role of the entrepreneur in what Schumpeter called creative destruction. Schumpeter described how entrepreneurs through innovation, change and improved work methods often lead to the demise of passive industries or markets that do not manage to evolve.

Nearly 60 years later, Kirzner (1999) stated that the entrepreneur does not create innovation and opportunities but actually is alert to opportunities and therefore is able to exploit them. This concept is close perhaps to the sixth perspective mentioned earlier. Later Kirzner (1999) stated that his view and Schumpeter's view are not necessarily contradicting and can be both accepted. This addition by Kirzner shows that entrepreneurship and entrepreneurial activity as a concept is still developing to this date and although the term has been around for a long time, yet the meaning is still evolving through time.

Most entrepreneurship books, such as the one by Kaplan and Warren (2010) define entrepreneurship today as 'the process of creating something different by devoting the necessary time and effort; assuming the accompanying financial, psychic, and social risks; and receiving the resulting monetary rewards and personal satisfaction'. This definition in particular covers most of what is discussed so far with the exception of the strong drive towards growth. This feature usually accompanies a special type of entrepreneurs, the corporate entrepreneur.

CORPORATE ENTREPRENEURSHIP

Corporate entrepreneurship (CE), also termed intrapreneurship (CIP), also called corporate venturing and intrapreneurship, can be understood as Kuratko et. al (2011) state it, that it is simply entrepreneurial behavior inside mid-sized and large corporations. As in the individual context, entrepreneurship in the corporate context also involves taking risk, innovating new methods or products, creation of change, and the creation of value and growth. Ling et. al (2008) define it as the total of product innovation, business venturing and strategic renewal which encompasses these aspects of entrepreneurial behavior inside the company.

Due to the growing importance of corporate entrepreneurship, several scales were constructed to measure the levels of CIP in the company. One such measure is the Miller and Friesen's index used by Zahra and Covin (1995). The scale items are mostly measured over the past three years span and are as follows: 1) Products or services that the company has launched, 2) Dramatic changes made in the mix of products and services, 3) Major company innovations in its products and services, 4) Strong tendency towards high risk projects, with high rewards, 5) Bold and wide-ranging actions to position itself and its products or services, 6) Strong commitment to R&D, innovation and being the technology leader, 7) Has taken strategies to help it make the best of opportunities in its external environment. Although this index has proved its validity, yet it is difficult to use when evaluating the company environment through the eyes of middle managers and low level (first level) managers.

Therefore a more suitable scale that can measure the company's entrepreneurial environment through the perceptions of the company's managers is the Corporate Entrepreneurship Assessment Instrument (CEAI) developed by Hornsby et. al(2002). This scale made use of 84 Likert-style questions spread over five main areas that the authors determined from previous literature. These five areas are management support, work discretion, organizational boundaries, rewards/reinforcement and time availability. The study performed at the time by the authors confirmed the validity of CEAI as a useful tool for evaluating the entrepreneurial environment. The authors used this instrument in several of their subsequent studies and also Wyk and Adonisi (2011) validated this instrument on a South African sample, giving further confidence that this tool can work in different cultures. The convenience of this tool in assessing the relationship of CE with manager satisfaction is its ability to capture the manager's perception of the environment which is a closer connection to the satisfaction level of that manager, be it a middle manager or first level manager.

The middle manager has been the focus of several researches such as the work of Horsnby et al. (2002) that bases their study on middle managers due to their important role in nurturing communication with diverse range of employees and also encouraging risk in an informal manner. Another research focusing on middle managers is the work of Kuratko and Goldsby (2004) which looks at the middle manager's role in CE from an ethical perspective. While it is acceptable to look at the pivotal role of middle managers in encouraging and implementing entrepreneurial behavior in the organization yet the role of other managerial levels should not be overlooked. Floyd and Lane (2000) present the roles of different levels of management and describe the top manager's role as ratifying, recognizing and directing, the middle manager's role as championing, synthesizing, facilitating and implementing and finally the role of the first level manager as experimenting, adjusting and conforming. From

CORPORATE ENTREPRENEURSHIP AND CORPORATE STRATEGY

The increase in competition and the dynamic aspect of most industries today is compelling companies to adopt an entrepreneurial strategy, often in unique combinations. By doing so they are building their capabilities and shaping their competitive advantage. Once in any of the three models that are different from the opportunist model, discussed above, then a company has decided to include corporate entrepreneurship in its strategy. Barringer and Bluedorn (1999) have identified several dimensions of strategy that are positively related to entrepreneurial intensity in the company. These dimensions are 1) Scanning intensity because it is both necessary to scan the environment to build a good strategy and to capture opportunities, 2) Planning flexibility is necessary for an efficient strategy and necessary to make use of the opportunity in time, 3)Locus of planning, the deeper the locus of planning the more employees are involved and the more intense the entrepreneurial environment and 4) Control systems that are able to monitor the execution of the strategy, can also reward creativity and consequently increase entrepreneurial intensity.

The existence of these positive linkages and the fact that many successful companies such as Google and DuPont are adopting their entrepreneurial vision in their strategies, emphasizes the strong and necessary relation between the two. At this stage, it should also be said that communication plays a very important role and it must be used both ways, regardless of the strategy adopted. Employees must be allowed to express their point of view and their way of seeing things as they are working closely on the process. And continuous feedback from management must be frequent and well measured in order to direct employees' creativity to the right way for better development.

INTRAPRENEURSHIP AND JOB SATISFACTION

Job satisfaction of corporate entrepreneurs and self-paid employees implies higher job satisfaction on entrepreneurs in comparison to corporate employees (Ayranci, 2015; Millan, Hessels, Thurik, & Aguado, 2013). Studies done on entrepreneurship and its nature, purpose, factors, and effects help contribute to the literature. In addition, this study's purpose is to investigate the factors of entrepreneur's job satisfaction on his business in small and medium-sized companies. Results show that there are many factors associated to the entrepreneur's job satisfaction with his enterprise (Ayranci, 2015).Job satisfaction of entrepreneurs and corporate employees distinguishes between two types of job satisfaction- type of work and job security. Comparison with corporate employees, entrepreneurs are more probable to be satisfied with their job in regards to type of work and less probable to be satisfied in regards to job security(Millan et al, 2013).

CORPORATE ENTREPRENEURSHIP IN THE MIDDLE EAST

Research on CE in the Middle East is still in its primitive stages, while recognition for the importance of entrepreneurship is evident, corporate entrepreneurship is still largely unexplored. One reason for this might be the relatively smaller presence of the manufacturing industry in the region when compared to industrial countries such as the United States or Europe. As Zahra et. al (1999) point out that most of the research made on CE (85% at that time) were made on manufacturing firms. Possible reasons according to the authors is the concern for the competitivenes of manufacturing firms in the US and Europe where most of the research has been done and also due to the lack of complete understanding for service firms.

Therefore it can be predicted that with further development of the manufacturing industry, more research and statistics will be made on CE in the region. Meanwhile two good and current examples will be given and the first is the work of Dehghan and Haghighi (2008) which addresses the increasing recognition of Iranian firms for the development of CE in their organizations, focusing on product entrepreneurship and production process entrepreneurship.

Another interesting research is the work of Zimmerman (2010) from Zayed University, UAE; however it studies the case of GE and Intel without really addressing issues in the Middle East region which is necessary to promote the understanding of CE in this region and the extent to which international research applies to it in its own context The issue of company size relation with innovation has received a lot of attention and many researchers have touched on the issue, yet there are many conflicting views and results. Some studies have found a positive relationship between technological change and firm size while others found no relation and even some found a negative relationship (Audretsch and ACS, 1991). Main arguments given in favor of small enterprises are that small firms are more flexible and can employ more motivated engineers or scientists through partial employment programs while large organizations usually suffer from bureaucracy and a heavy inertia to overcome in order to get things done. On the other hand, large companies can benefit from economies of scale and enjoy larger resources necessary for innovation and activities such as R&D.

Drucker (1985) explains these opposing views when he states that it is understandable to build up a conventional wisdom saying that big companies do not innovate. After all, the railroad did not generate the automobile, automobile companies did not succeed in the aircraft business although they tried and none of the giants in the electrical industry managed to dominate the computer industry. Again according to Drucker this is a misunderstanding and bigness is not a hindrance to entrepreneurship rather it is the operation itself. Businesses should not dedicate all its time to running the existing business and taking care of the daily crisis. Businesses should intentionally seek to strengthen the entrepreneurial process in the organization, mainly through policies and procedure Zahra (1996) also entered firm size as a variable into his study, expecting it to be negatively associated with CE but got a result that it had an insignificant effect on CE. The results obtained in the first hypothesis tested in this study are similar to these findings in the sense that the two companies have similar CE perceptions of their managers so size is not an obstacle for Unipak, rather it has its policies and procedures in place to consciously nurture the entrepreneurial spirit needed. Since both companies have entrepreneurial drive set in their corporate values, the two companies have managed to place the right rules and offer the right managerial support to keep the entrepreneurial spirit flourishing. In addition, the result of this hypothesis also supports the idea that in this context age also had no effect.

There is little research on age of companies in years, which makes good sense because what understandably matters in age is where in the life cycle that company lies. No matter what age in years the company is, it could be in any of the stages of venture conceptualization, start-up activities, venture growth, stabilization, diversification, strategic renewal, and/or decline (Kuratko, 2009). This conclusion is obvious in the case of Minnesota Mining and Manufacturing (3M) company that was started in 1902 yet it generates a quarter of its annual sales from products that are less than five years old. The company is famous for its innovation and strategic use of CE with financial gains that speak for itself (Burns, 2008). On the other hand, a company such as Commodore computers was started in 1955 and at the end of 1982 had sales exceeding the best computer companies of the time such as Apple and Texas Instruments, only to fall into decline and announce bankruptcy in 1994, so for those two companies age in years is irrelevant.

The second tested hypothesis is satisfaction levels which resulted in a statistically insignificant difference between UTM and Unipak, however the results arjust on the limit and visually UTM has higher satisfaction levels. Since CE perceptions did not differ, it should be concluded that the reason for the difference in satisfaction is not interpreted by any differences in CE. The reasons for this difference could be any of the factors or a combination of factors of satisfaction that were previously discussed.

The third tested hypothesis is CE levels of perception with seniority that also resulted in similar levels for the two groups. Participants having worked in the company for more than 12 years and participants working for less than 12 years share the same level of perception for CE within the company. This is an area that has not received much attention; however it is reasonable to believe that the managerial level and the entrepreneurial environment have a greater effect on CE perceptions and ability to implement CE than mere years of experience, which can explain the findings in the comparison between the two groups.

As for the results of the fourth hypothesis, it is a clear statistical distinction of the two groups with a clear visual increase in satisfaction with the increase in CE. This is in line with almost all previous results done on American companies. Of special interest is the work of Kuratko et. al (2005) that have tested the effect of CE perception, using also CEAI dimensions and found that perceptions of a CE environment do increase perceptions of satisfaction especially the two dimensions of rewards/reinforcements and work discretion. The authors in this case were studying the effect of satisfaction as a mediator that could enhance the implementation of CE ideas (which they found that it did), however job satisfaction is of importance by itself to the productivity of the company and its managers' loyalty that is worth increasing for many reasons. Again the importance of the finding here is that even in the Lebanese context and in two different companies belonging to the same group, the higher the CE perception, the higher the job satisfaction and all the positive outcomes that come with it, adding to the importance of CE in increasing the company's longevity and performance of the company.

Four types of corporate entrepreneurship exist:

1. **Corporate Venturing:** The process of creating new ventures related to the company's core business,
2. **Organizational Transformation:** Focusing on enhancing operational efficiencies,
3. **Intrapreneuring:** Identification of employees that may have an entrepreneurial aptitude, and
4. **Industry Rule Bending:** Initiating paradigm shifts within an industry through identifying innovative products and processes *(Kenney and Mujtaba, 2007).*

Two dimensions differentiate companies regarding their approaches to corporate entrepreneurship;

1. **Organizational Ownership:** The responsibility for the creation of new business, and
2. **Resource Authority:** The manner in which resources are allocated to corporate entrepreneurship.
3. These two dimensions generate a matrix with four dominant models: the *opportunist*, the *enabler*, the *advocate*, and the *producer (Wolcott & Lippitz, 2007).*

The model of corporate entrepreneurship can be extended to include *intrapreneurship* and *exopreneurship*. Intrapreneurship is the corporate entrepreneurship that focuses on internally generated innovation, while generating innovation outside the organization is defined as exopreneurship. A conceptual model of corporate entrepreneurship is built as a result of these two which shows the *internal, external*, and *strategic variables* that are used to decide on the corporate entrepreneurial posture and activities *(Chang, 2000).*

Recently, several studies were conducted on firms examining the relation between *human resources management* (HRM) and corporate entrepreneurship. It is shown that HRM plays a major role in entrepreneurial firms by affecting its development and growth. In addition, HRM practices are important for creating the appropriate work environment and therefore proved to be the most beneficial to promote corporate entrepreneurship in Small and Medium Sized Enterprises. *(Montoro-Sanchez, Soriano, 2011)*

A study revealed that the cultivation of corporate entrepreneurship is influenced by three main factors:

1. The system of the director board and management,
2. Quality of the entrepreneur, and
3. The corporate strategic entrepreneurial management and the corporate circumstances.

Without these three factors, entrepreneurship is difficult to exist within any corporation *(Jin Chen, Zhaohui Zhu,* and *Wang Anquan, 2005).*

Moreover, corporate entrepreneurship was found dependent on the institutional environment in all its dimensions:

1. **Regulatory:** Laws and governmental policies,
2. **Normative:** Valuation of creativity and innovativeness inside the society, and
3. **Cognitive Dimensions:** Knowledge towards business management.
4. These three dimensions influence both the entrepreneurial orientation and activities of the corporations *(Samuel Gómez-Haro, Juan Alberto Aragón-Correa, Eulogio Cordón-Pozo, 2011).*

Intrapreneurship consists of entrepreneurship within the firm and the environment, structures, processes, channels, management, and systems in which it germinates and grows. Intrapreneurship can be defined as the ability to generate, launch and manage new, innovative opportunities from within existing, larger organizations (Fattal, 2001). Intrapreneurship is the process of uncovering and developing an opportunity to create value through innovation and seizing that opportunity without regard to either resources (human and capital) or the location of the entrepreneur – in a new or existing company (Churchill, 1992). Antoncic and Hisrich (2001) add to the concept of intrapreneurship concept emergent behavioral intentions and behaviors of an organization that are related to departures from the customary. Intrapreneurship is also defined as a process by which individuals inside organizations pursue opportunities independent of the resources they currently control (Steven and Jarillo, 1990); as doing new things and departing from the customary to pursue opportunities (Vesper, 1990); as a spirit of entrepreneurship within the existing organization (Hisrich and Peters, 1998); and as creation of new organizations by an organization, or as an instigation of renewal and innovation within that organization (Sharma and Chrisman, 1999).

- **Identifying Entrepreneurial Talent:** Intrapreneurship has the firm as its boundaries and imagination as its outer limits. It is the entrepreneurial spirit, effort and organization within the firm. It is, therefore, necessary to understand the entrepreneur and the concept of entrepreneurship in order to develop the concept of intrapreneurship that seeks to harness talent and imagination within the firm in order to increase its growth and its value.

Entrepreneurship is synonymous with innovation, creativity and risk-taking. An entrepreneur risks time, effort and money to start, establish, operate, and manage a business for the principal purpose of profit and growth. Entrepreneurs are also seen as people who have the ability to see and evaluate business opportunities, to gather the necessary resources, to take advantage of them, and to initiate appropriate action to ensure success. Their dreams are often viewed as wild (if not crazy) and unrealizable, except for them and their converts.

The entrepreneur is able to recognize potentially profitable opportunities, to conceptualize venture strategies, and to become the key force in successfully moving an idea from the mind to the market place (Johnson, 2001). An entrepreneur has the following qualities: Persistence, Positive thinking, Charisma, Extroversion, High energy, Strong self-image, Strong interpersonal skills, Team spirit, Goal focus, Internal locus of control, Passion, Flexibility, Leadership and visionary tendencies. (Johnson, 2001).

Entrepreneurship is about spotting and exploiting opportunities. Growing firms must be constantly engaged in spotting and exploiting ever newer opportunities or methods of doing business in order to lengthen the life cycle of the firm, and to make its growth path steeper. This requires leadership and the identification of those individuals within the firm who are entrepreneurial, and the creation of a structure and an environment for them that fosters innovation and responsible risk taking.

Entrepreneurs are individuals who want to make a difference. They are effective networking drivers who have know-how as well as know-who. As they create capital by blending creativity with innovation, they manage risk, with self confidence in the face of adversity (Thompson, 1999). Entrepreneurs shift economic resources out of an area of lower and into an area of higher productivity and greater yield (Greig, 2002). They have a good nose to identify business opportunities (Hannu Littunen, 2000). They are independent, spirited, competitive, determined, and achievement oriented (Thompson, 1999). In summary, an entrepreneur takes agency and initiative, assumes responsibility and ownership for making things happen, is open and able to create novelty, manages risks, has the persistence to see things through to some identified end-points, is independent, able to make decisions, and able to make an impact in society (Johnson, 2001). Success factors of entrepreneurship are openness, government relations, finance, experience, managerial skills, capacity to adapt the vision to reality, persistent opportunism, surrendering sovereignty, desire to compete, ability to handle stress, ability to have fun, and commitment..

- **Psychological Profile of the Entrepreneur:** Entrepreneur is typically an optimist, a moderate risk-taker, and a believer in his/her ability to control their own destiny beyond just making money. Taking a more psychological approach, an entrepreneur is a person who is typically driven by certain needs (need to obtain or attain something, need to experiment, need to accomplish or need to escape authority of others). Successful entrepreneurs possess distinctive qualities. Such qualities typically include judgment, perseverance, love of risk, and knowledge of the world and of the business (Praag, 1999), in addition to strong feelings of ownership and control, need for autonomy, assertiveness and dominance, powerful charismatic and ambitious personality (McCarthy, 2003). He or she is the person who perceives the market opportunity and then has the motivation, drive and ability to mobilize resources to meet it. The major characteristics of entrepreneurs include need for achievement, locus of control, propensity to take risk, tolerance of ambiguity, self confidence and innovativeness.

The need for achievement is a strong psychological driving force behind human action has been long proposed as a factor influencing entrepreneurial behavior. It is believed that individuals with a high need for achievement have a strong desire to be successful and are, consequently, more likely to behave entrepreneurially (Thompson, 1999). While individuals with an internal locus of control believe that they are able to control life's events, individuals with an external locus of control believe that life's events are the result of external factors, such as chance, luck or fate. Entrepreneurs are more likely to have an internal locus of control (Littunen, 2000). A person's risk-taking propensity can be defined as his/her orientation towards taking chances in uncertain decision-making contexts. Often the successful entrepreneur exhibits an incremental approach to risk taking, at each stage exposing him/her to only a limited, measured amount of personal risk and moving from one stage to another as each decision is proved (Koh, 1996). Much of the entrepreneurship literature includes risk taking as a major entrepreneurial characteristic (Longenecker, Schoen, 1975).

The manner in which a person perceives an ambiguous situation and organizes the available information to approach it reflects one's tolerance to ambiguity. Entrepreneurs tend to have high tolerance to ambiguity. They strive to overcome unstable and unpredictable situations in order to perform well by managing uncertainty. An entrepreneur is self confident and multi-skilled to make a product, market it and count the money. But above all, entrepreneurs' confidence allows them to move comfortably through uncharted waters in the face of difficulties and discouraging circumstances (Morrison, 2001). Self-confidence is a necessary entrepreneurial characteristic and that it is related to other psychological characteristics, such as internal locus of control, propensity to take risk and tolerance for ambiguity. Finally, and one recurring theme in defining entrepreneurship is innovativeness. It relates to perceiving and acting on business activities in new and unique ways. Entrepreneurs are significantly more innovative than non-entrepreneurs (Greig, 2002). This type person may well be endogenous to the firm (a substantial hidden asset). If so, he/she needs to be identified, evaluated, placed in a nurturing environment, and sufficiently incentivized to achieve his/her potential and a higher firm value (with a stake in that value).

FROM ENTREPRENEURSHIP TO INTRAPRENEURSHIP

Intrapreneurial processes, often haphazardly or due to the initiative and drive of someone or an informal group, go on inside an existing firm, regardless of its size. Intrapreneurship refers not only to the creation of new business ventures, but also to other innovative activities and orientations such as development of new products, services, technologies, administrative techniques, strategies and competitive postures. Its characteristic dimensions are new business venturing, product/service innovation, process innovation, self renewal, risk taking, pro-activeness, and competitive aggressiveness. The concept of intrapreneurship is not about the product/market relatedness to, and the synergy with, the existing business, but rather about emergence, creation and newness (Antoncic and Hisrich, 2003).

The process of intrapreneurship often begins with the recognition of its value within the firm (triggered by internal or external forces). It is followed with the identification of those individuals possessing the above-mentioned entrepreneurial traits, and their organization with the intent to change the profile and the possibilities of the firm. Positive results are more likely to accrue when the employee has a psychological and financial stake in the outcome.

- **Creation of Intrapreneurial Culture:** The shift in values from liking the security of being an employee to starting a business is a factor promoting intrapreneurship (Shapero, 1985). The relationship between certain cultural (religion, politics, education, family, history) and societal factors (economics, policies, institutions, structures) and intrapreneurship is significant (Morrison, A. 2000). Although entrepreneurship activity is present in large companies, the concept of entrepreneurship is commonly linked to small business activity, with the ideal model of business success being the growth of a small business into a corporate giant (Abdel Fadel, 2000). Entrepreneurs within small enterprises have shown dynamism in responding to new opportunities and making speedy adjustment to change faster and better than large corporations (Dejardin, 1998).

Intrapreneurship, as emergent intentions and behaviors, operates, typically, at organizational margins or boundaries not at the organizational core. The challenge to corporate entities, however, is to make intrapreneurship a core business activity- a real value driver.

Intrapreneurship can be viewed as a curious, constantly searching activity at the frontier, not at the core (Sandberg, 1992). This must not be confused with the Research and Development function. R&D departments do generate ideas, products and new services, but are not the center of entrepreneurship. IBM's R&D development was perfectly capable of developing the PC. But the product and the riches and industry transformation it generated was the work of meagerly funded entrepreneurs that ended up competing with IBM and ultimately changing its culture. One should also note that the operating system for the IBM computer was deemed not a big thing for IBM either. This logic created one of the greatest corporations in economic history: Microsoft. At&T's R&D department produced a high quality cellular phone. AT&T, however, did not have sufficient entrepreneurial spirit and talent to see its incredible potential through. The impact of such errors on the growth and the value of AT&T are in the financial record books.

A variety of social and economic factors can stimulate intrapreneurial activity and thus generate more robust economic development. These factors include an increasing focus on capital formation, changing institutional relationships, supportive government programs, reassessment of intellectual property, and new approaches to innovation (Dunphy, Golden, Herbig. 1994). We designate these factors in our model as environmental factors.

Two important factors involved in successful corporate entrepreneurship are organization structure and human resource management practices granting of some degrees of freedom and support to an individual or group of individuals in the organization" (Schuler, 1986). In order to promote intrapreneurial culture, management establishes projects to start an organizational development climate of initiative, to decentralize structure, and to empower employees (Jon Sundbo. 1999). Such empowerment has the purpose of creating innovations, so that the employees function as corporate entrepreneurs or intrapreneur (Pinchot, 1985). In addition to a conducive social environment or culture, the fabric or quality (and suitability) of the human resources in the organization must be carefully selected and nurtured." (Chung, Lai Hong, Gibbons, Patrick T. 1997). An important way of stimulating intrapreneurship is to encourage a personal interest in the business, to promote an informal organization structure with a great deal of individual freedom while ensuring that employees are committed to the company's future growth.

- **Intrapreneurship and Profitability:** Intrapreneurship can create additional shareholder value. Measures can be used to audit the outcome of the process including measurement of the return on investment, return on labor, sales growth, market share, operating and contribution income and productivity. It is proposed that association between intrapreneurship and corporate performance, and hence firm value, will be found to be strong, positive and significant. Intrapreneurship is positively related to growth and profitability of an organization. Intrapreneurship will have practical value resulting in processes that create value for the firm (i.e. in reducing costs and improving performance levels) and products and services that create value in the marketplace (i.e. and for which customers pay). Moreover, firms that fail to engage in intrapreneurial behavior are likely to be slower to react to external threats, and more likely to miss emerging opportunities.

Overview of existing indicators for intrapreneurial effectiveness: Firms need to take stock of their internal entrepreneurial assets, structures, communication systems, efficiency and effectiveness of their intrapreneurial team or unit (new products, processes, services, better delivery or manufacturing systems, response mechanisms to environmental and competitive dynamics, etc.). It is equivalent to counting the strategic and operational assets in a war scenario, and figuring out the most effective way to deploy them.

A nine step model for intrapreneurial applications in hospitals and health related organizations (Cates, 1987) suggests that emphasis to launch a new venture could be placed on cost reduction. The exploring team must be given the necessary time and resources to develop a proposal. The CEO outlines the expected revenue target within five years of operation of the proposed plan. The plan must identify competitive advantages, breakeven analysis, return on investment, and cash flow.

Miller and Frieseen's (1983) of categorized innovative strategy making at an organization. Covin and Slevin (1986, 1992) identified three main related dimensions of intrapreneurship: innovativeness, proactiveness, and risk-taking. The work of Lumkin and Dess (1996) expanded the concept and included two additional dimensions: autonomy and competitive aggressiveness. The continuing work of Guth and Ginsberg (1990) and Zahra (1991, 1993) emphasize innovativeness as a common dimension and adds "the organization tendency to create new businesses or conduct corporate venturing activities" and "strategic renewal in the organizations" taking into account the organization's adaptive capabilities. Antoncic, B. and Hisrich, R.D. (2003) build on the previous research to reach a closer identification of the set of dimensions that explain intrapreneurship as a realistic concept. They came up with an approach that led to an eight dimension model of intrapreneurship: new ventures, new businesses, product/service innovativeness, process innovativeness, self renewal, risk taking, proactiveness, and competitive aggressiveness.

Antoncic, B. and Hisrich, R.D. (2000) generated an external and internal set of intrapreneurship predictors of an organization that if they exist, they will induce or reduce the intrapreneurial activity within an organization. External factors include munificent ones such as dynamism (Zahra, 1991; Khandwalla, 1987), technological opportunities (Guth & Ginsberg, 1990), industry growth (Zahra, 1993), and the demand for new products (Zahra, 1993). They also include hostile factors such as unfavorability of change and competitive rivalry (Zahra, 1993). Internal factors include communication openness (Kanter, 1984), control mechanisms (Kanter, 1989), environmental scanning intensity (Khandwalla, 1977), organizational and management support (Merrifield, 1993; MacMillan, 1986), and organizational values (Guth & Ginthberg, 1990 and Zahra 1991).

REFERENCES

Abdnor, J. (1988). The Spirit of Entrepreneurship. *Journal of Small Business Management, 1*(3), 1–6.

Angeles, M. S., & Soriano, D. R. (2011). Human Resource Management and Corporate Entrepreneurship. *International Journal of Manpower, 32*(1), 6–13. doi:10.1108/01437721111121198

Antoncic, B., & Hisrich, R. D. (2000). Intrapreneurship modeling in transition economies: A comparison of Slovenia and the United States. *Journal of Developmental Entrepreneurship, 5*(1), 21–40.

Antoncic, B., & Hisrich, R. D. (2003). Clarifying the intrapreneurship concept. *Journal of Small Business and Enterprise Development*, *10*(1), 7–25. doi:10.1108/14626000310461187

Arzeni, S. (1992). Encouraging the Entrepreneur. Organization for Economic Co-operation and Development. *The OECD Observer*, (174), 19.

Audretsch, D. Z., & Acs, Z. J. (1991). Innovation and Size at the Firm Level. *Southern Economic Journal*, *57*(3), 739–744. doi:10.2307/1059787

Ayranci, A. E., & Ayranci, E. (2015). A Research on Job Satisfaction Factors of Private Entrepreneurs: The Case of Beylikduzu Organized Industrial Zone. *Procedia: Social and Behavioral Sciences*, *195*(1), 268–277. doi:10.1016/j.sbspro.2015.06.156

Barringer, B. A., & Bluedorn, A. C. (1999). The Relationship Between Corporate Entrepreneurship and Strategic Management. *Strategic Management Journal*, *20*(5), 421–444. doi:10.1002/(SICI)1097-0266(199905)20:5<421::AID-SMJ30>3.0.CO;2-O

Bellone, G., & Goerl, G. F. (1992). Reconciling public entrepreneurship and democracy. *Public Administration Review*, *52*(2), 130. doi:10.2307/976466

Berl, R., Powell, T., & Williamson, N. (1984). Industrial Sales force Satisfaction and Performance with Herzbergs Theory. *Industrial Marketing Management*, *13*(1), 11–19. doi:10.1016/0019-8501(84)90003-8

Bostjan, A. N., & Hisrich, R. D. (2000). Intrapreneurship modeling in transition economies: A comparison of Slovenia and the United State. *Journal of Developmental Entrepreneurship*, *5*(1), 21.

Burns, P. (2008). *Corporate Entrepreneurship*. Palgrave Macmillan.

Cates, N. (1987). S.A.M. *Advanced Management Journal*, *52*(3), 41.

Chang, J. (2000). Model of Corporate Entrepreneurship. *Intrapreneurship and Exopreneurship*, *12*(4), 69–104.

Chen, J., Zhu, Z., & Anquan, W. (2005). A system model for corporate entrepreneurship. *International Journal of Manpower*, *26*(9), 529–543. doi:10.1108/01437720510625449

Chung, L., & Gibbons, P. (1997). Corporate entrepreneurship: The roles of ideology and social capital. *Group & Organization Management*, *22*(1), 10–30. doi:10.1177/1059601197221004

Covin, J. G., & Slevin, D. P. (1986), The development and testing of an organizational-level entrepreneurship scale. Frontiers of Entrepreneurship Research, 1(3), 628-639.

Covin, J. G., & Slevin, D. P. (1991). A conceptual model of entrepreneurship as firm behavior. *Entrepreneurship Theory and Practice*, *16*(1), 7–25.

Dana, L. (1997). A contrast of Argentina and Uruguay: The effects of government policy on entrepreneurship. *Journal of Small Business Management*, *35*(2), 99.

Davies, J., Hides, M., & Powell, J. (2002). Defining the development needs of entrepreneurs in SME's. *Emerald Insight*, *44*(8/9), 24.

De Jordy, H. (1988). Ottawa introduces national policy for entrepreneurs. *Toronto Star*, p. B3.

Ezell, H. (1993). Economic Fears Turn Younger Americans to Entrepreneurship. Journal of Bus[ness. *Record*, *1*(3), 23–32.

Floyd, S. P. (2000). Strategizing throughout the Organization: Managing Role Conflict in Strategic Renewal. *Academy of Management Review*, *25*(1), 154–177.

Greig, C. (2002). So just what is an entrepreneur? And why it actually matters. *Profit Review*, *21*(2), 14.

Guth, W. D., & Ginsberg, A. (1990). Guest editors' introduction: Corporate entrepreneurship. *Strategic Management Journal*, *11*(3), 5–15.

Hornsby, J., Kuratko, D., & Zahra, S. (2002). Middle managers perception of the internal environment for corporate entrepreneurship: Assessing a measurement scale. *Journal of Business Venturing*, *17*(1), 253–273. doi:10.1016/S0883-9026(00)00059-8

Jenssen, H. S. (2002). Public intervention in the entrepreneurial process. *International Journal of Entrepreneurial Behavior and Research*, *8*(3), 173-187.

Johnson, D. (2001). What is innovation and entrepreneurship? Lessons for larger organizations. *Industrial and Commercial Training*, *33*(4), 135–140. doi:10.1108/00197850110395245

Kanter, R. M. (1984). *The Change Masters*. New York: Touchstone, Simon & Schuster.

Kanter, R. M. (1989). *When Giants Learn to Dance*. New York: Touchstone,Simon & Schuster.

Kaplan, J. A. (2010). *Patterns of Entrepreneurship Management* (3rd ed.). John Wiley and Sons, Inc.

Kenney, M., & Mujtaba, B. (2007). A Practitioner View of Organizational Intrapreneurship. *The Journal of Applied Management and Entrepreneurship*, *12*(3), 73–81.

Khandwalla, P. N. (1977). *The Design of Organizations*. New York: Harcourt Brace Jovanovich.

Khandwalla, P. N. (1987). Generators of Pioneering-innovative Management: Some Indian Evidence. *Organization Studies*, *8*(1), 39–59. doi:10.1177/017084068700800104

Kirzner, I. (1999). Creativity and/or Alertness: A Reconsideration of the Schumpeterian Entrepreneur. *The Review of Austrian Economics*, *11*(1), 5–17. doi:10.1023/A:1007719905868

Koh, H. (1996). Testing hypotheses for entrepreneurial characteristics. *Journal of Managerial Psychology*, *11*(3), 12–35. doi:10.1108/02683949610113566

Kuratko, D. (2009). *Entrepreneurship: Theory, Process, & Practice* (8th ed.). Mason, OH: Cengage/South Western Publishing.

Kuratko, D., Morris, M., & Covin, J. (2011). *Corporate Innovation and Entrepreneurship: Entrepreneurial within Organizations* (3rd ed.). South-Western.

Ling, Y., Simsek, Z., Lubatkin, M., & Veiga, J. (2008). Transformational Leaderships Role in Promoting Corporate Entrepreneurship: Examining the CEO –TMT Interface. *Academy of Management Journal*, *51*(3), 557–576. doi:10.5465/AMJ.2008.32626023

Littunen, H. (2000). Entrepreneurship and the characteristics of the entrepreneurial personality. *International Journal of Entrepreneurial Behavior and Research*, *6*(6), 295–310. doi:10.1108/13552550010362741

Longenecker, J., & Schoen, J. (1975). The essence of entrepreneurship. *Journal of Small Business Management*, *13*(3), 26.

Lumpkin, G. T., & Dess, G. G. (1996). Clarifying the entrepreneurial orientation construct and linking it to performance. *Academy of Management Review*, *12*(1), 135–172.

MacMillan, I. C. (1986). Progress in Research on Corporate Venturing. In D. L. Sexton & R.W. Smilor (Eds.), The Art and Science of Entrepreneurship, (pp. 241-263). Cambridge, MA: Ballinger Publishing Company.

Mazzarol, V. G., & Doss, T. N. (1999). Factors influencing small business start-ups. *International Journal of Entrepreneurial Behavior and Research*, *5*(2), 48–63. doi:10.1108/13552559910274499

McCarthy, B. (2003). Strategy is personality-driven, strategy is crisis-driven: Insights for entrepreneurial firms. *Management Decision*, *41*(4), 327–339. doi:10.1108/00251740310468081

Merrifield, D. B. (1993). Intrapreneurial Corporate Renewal. *Journal of Business Venturing*, *8*(5), 383–389. doi:10.1016/0883-9026(93)90020-6

Millan, J. M., Hessels, J., Thurik, R., & Aguado, R. (2013). Determinants of job satisfaction: A European comparison of self-employed and paid employees. *Small Business Economics*, *40*(1), 651–670. doi:10.1007/s11187-011-9380-1

Miller, D., & Friesen, P. H. (1983). Strategy-making and environment. *Strategic Management Journal*, *4*(3), 221–235. doi:10.1002/smj.4250040304

Morrison, A. (2000). Entrepreneurship: What triggers it? *International Journal of Entrepreneurial Behavior and Research*, *6*(2), 59–71. doi:10.1108/13552550010335976

Morrison, A. (2001). Entrepreneurs transcend time: A biographical analysis. *Management Decision*, *39*(9), 784–790. doi:10.1108/EUM0000000006222

Mouritsen, J. N. (2003). Intellectual capital and the capital market: The circulability of intellectual capital. *Accounting, Auditing & Accountability Journal*, *16*(1), 223–234. doi:10.1108/09513570310464246

Praag, M. (1999). Some classic views on entrepreneurship. *The Economist*, *147*(3), 311.

Pryor, A. K., & Shays, E. M. (1993, Spring). Growing the business with intrapreneurs. *Business Quarterly*, *57*(3), 42.

Rein, P. (1988). Understanding and Encouraging Entrepreneurship Internationally. *Journal of Small Business Management*, *3*(1), 111–114.

Robbins, S. M. (2007). *Management* (9th ed.). Pearson Prentice Hall.

Robinson, M. (2001, December). The Ten Commandments of Intrapreneurs. *New Zealand Management. Auckland*, *48*(11), 95.

Schuler, R. (1986). Fostering and facilitating entrepreneurship in organizations: Implications for organization structure and human resources management practices. *Human Resource Management*, *25*(4), 607–629. doi:10.1002/hrm.3930250408

Shapero, A. (1985). Why entrepreneurship? A worldwide perspective. *Journal of Small Business Management*, *23*(4), 25–42.

Sonnenfeld, J. (1985). Shedding Light on the Hawthorne Studies, *Journal of occupational. Behaviour*, *6*(2), 111–130.

Stevenson, H. H., & Jarillo, J. C. (1990). A Paradigm of Entrepreneurship: Entrepreneurial Management. *Strategic Management Journal*, *11*(3), 17–27.

Sundbo, J. (1999). Empowerment of employees in small and medium-sized service firms. *Employee Relations*, *21*(2), 105–127. doi:10.1108/01425459910266385

Thompson, J. (1999). The world of the entrepreneur: A new perspective. *Journal of Workplace Learning*, *11*(6), 209–224. doi:10.1108/13665629910284990

Toulin, A. (1988). Policy aims to inspire entrepreneurs. *The Ottawa Citizen*, p. B8.

Ugonma, O. E. (2003). Psychological Factors Influencing Perceived entrepreneurial Success Among Nigerian Women in Small-Scale Businesses. *Journal of International Women's Studies*, *5*(1), 234–238.

Wolcott, R., & Lippitz, M. (2007). The Four Models of Corporate Entrepreunership. *MIT Sloan Management Review*, *49*(1), 75–80.

Wolcott, R. M. (2007). The Four Models of Corporate Entrepreneurship. *MIT Sloan Management Review*, *49*(1), 75–82.

Wyk, R. M. (2011). An eight-factor solution for the Corporate Entrepreneurship Assessment Instrument. *African Journal of Business Management*, *5*(8), 3047–3055.

Zahra, S. (1996). governance, ownership, and corporate entrepreneurship: The moderating impact of industry technological opportunities. *Academy of Management Journal*, *39*(6), 1713–1735. doi:10.2307/257076

Zahra, S., Jennings, D., & Kuratko, D. (1999). The Antecedents and Consequences of Firm- Level Entrepreneurship: The State of the Field, *Entrepreneurship. Theory into Practice*, *24*(1), 45–65.

Zahra, S. A. (1991). Predictors and financial outcomes of corporate entrepreneurship: An exploratory study. *Journal of Business Venturing*, *6*(4), 259–285. doi:10.1016/0883-9026(91)90019-A

Zahra, S. A. (1993). Environment, corporate entrepreneurship, and financial performance: A taxonomic approach. *Journal of Business Venturing*, *8*(4), 319–340. doi:10.1016/0883-9026(93)90003-N

Zimmerman, J. (2010). Corporate Entrepreneurship at GE and Intel. *Journal of Business Case Studies*, *6*(5), 77–81.

Chapter 4
Accelerating Entrepreneurship in MENA Region:
Opportunities and Challenges

Amir Manzoor
Bahria University, Pakistan

ABSTRACT

The Middle East and North Africa (MENA) region is at a turning point in its development. How MENA region addresses the employment needs of its rapidly increasing population of young people will determine whether the MENA region will become a region characterized by stable, knowledge-based economies that have a dynamic working middle class. Entrepreneurship is considered vital to drive this transition of MENA region. Increased entrepreneurial activities will not only spur job growth but also generate ideas, attract investment and inspire future entrepreneurs to follow footsteps of successful entrepreneurs. This chapter explores the entrepreneurial ecosystem of MENA region. The chapter discusses various challenges and provides specific recommendations to boost entrepreneurial activities in MENA region.

DOI: 10.4018/978-1-5225-2066-5.ch004

1. INTRODUCTION

The increasing size and energy of youth population around the globe pose serious challenges for governments especially in the developing countries. If immediate actions are not taken to utilize the energy of this youth population to create economic activities at home, economies abroad can use this population for their advantage. In order to capitalize on this potential, MENA region needs a sharp increase in rate of job creation. MENA is one of the regions in the world that needs to create millions of jobs in the coming decade. The most important thing to drive this job creation is a business environment, which support entrepreneurs to start new ventures easily and boost economic activity. In order to provide such an environment, governments, NGOs, and business leaders need to first identify the motivations behind entrepreneurs in order to create a healthy and supportive entrepreneurial ecosystem.

The objective of this chapter is to explore these challenges and opportunities and provide recommendations to boost entrepreneurial activities in the MENA region. After introduction, section 2 will explore the current state of entrepreneurship in the MENA region. Section 3 would analyze the entrepreneurial ecosystem in the MENA region to identify various challenges and opportunities for fostering entrepreneurship. Section 4 would offer specific recommendations to improve the entrepreneurial ecosystem and accelerate entrepreneurship. Concluding remarks would be provided in section 5.

2. CURRENT STATE OF ENTREPRENEURSHIP

The MENA region's 60% of the population is under the age of 25. This population is one of the world's youngest workforces. It is expected that more than 100 million young people will be joining this workforce by 2020 (World Economic Forum, 2015). Such a large and motivated young workforce can drive growth and prosperity for entire MENA region. According to a 2015 survey, more than 60% of people wanted to start their own business (Al-Masri, 2016). This situation presents both opportunities and challenges. Unemployment is still an obstacle to the region's development. The Middle East and North Africa regions continue to show by far the highest youth unemployment rates – 28.2 and 30.5 per cent, respectively, in 2014 – and rates have continued to worsen since 2012, particularly for young women (International Labor Organization, 2015). According to an estimate, governments in MENA region had to create 100 million jobs until 2020 in order to meet the alarming unemployment numbers (Albawaba, 2015). The consequences of not doing so could be sever. It would not only result in slowed regional growth but also loss of promising youth to migration. Social unrest is yet another danger.

Accelerating Entrepreneurship in MENA Region

To accelerate job creation in the MENA region, an entrepreneurial environment is necessary. Besides employing their owners, new businesses can provide significant spillover benefits for the economy. Once nurtured into small and medium-sized enterprises (SMEs), these new businesses can significantly contribute to increase the employment and gross domestic product (GDP).

The regional leaders need to address many issues to foster entrepreneurship in MENA region. Some of the pressing issues include identification of promising industries for entrepreneurship, support initiatives for identified industries, role of established entrepreneurs, the education system, the media, the venture capital firms, and the country's culture in encouraging prospective entrepreneurs to start their own ventures. Although the level of early-stage entrepreneurial activity in MENA region is low, the region is rich with innovative ideas and emerging markets and is in a position to produce the next generation of successful leading entrepreneurs (Mervyn, 2015). Most entrepreneurs are involved in necessity business such as shops and farms. These type of businesses employ their owners and lack other opportunities. These businesses usually lack aspiration to grow beyond the needs of their owners. The regional leaders need to focus on innovative entrepreneurs who could use their knowledge and finances to develop new markets. These kinds of entrepreneurial projects can provide the positive spillover effects of increased employment and economic growth. Some governments in MENA region have already started targeted initiatives to boost entrepreneurship. Qatar developed Science and Technology Park to offer support to young innovative minds in developing their ideas. Once young people earned their respective degrees, they can then work in Qatar or advance their skills in other institutions like Qatar Science and Technology Park. The SANAD program in Oman is an initiative to promote entrepreneurship among young people by providing loans and expertise to new graduates. Know about Business (KAB) is another initiative by the Omani government under the auspices of the International Labor Organization (ILO) which focuses on the management training of entrepreneurs to develop their entrepreneurial attitude (Matriano & Suguku, 2015).

The successes of the region's startups should not be underestimated though. According to Wamda, a regional accelerator platform, more than a dozen start-ups – including Bayt, Careem, MarkaVIP, Namshi, News Group, Propertyfinder, and Wadi.com – now have estimated valuations above $100 million. Souq.com, a 3,000-employee company founded in 2005, is poised to be the region's first "unicorn," with a valuation above $1 billion. Yet the regional environment is far from being conducive to entrepreneurship. Wars, terrorism, and political turbulence are plaguing the MENA regions. Besides these factors lack of adequate risk capital, talent, or infrastructure are some other deep-rooted structural problems (Mahroum, 2016). A vast majority of entrepreneurs in the MENA region are small-sized businesses. These types of businesses are very vulnerable to external shocks and need support to survive. Many such businesses do not grow into sustainable small businesses. These small businesses should not be ignored when looking for ways to spur job growth. Around the globe, SMEs employ a large proportion of the workforce and there is scope to do more. The public sector is still the main source of employment in MENA, but this is not sustainable. Family-owned businesses are the backbone of global economy. These businesses contribute around 70-90% of the world's GDP and account for approximately 33% of the Fortune 500 companies. More than 70% of the overall businesses in many countries are family-owned businesses and play a very significant role in driving economic growth and employment opportunities. In the US, approximately 85% of the businesses were family-owned businesses that generated 50% of GDP and 60% of the employment. In France and Germany, family-owned businesses contributed over 50% of GDP. In UK, family-owned businesses contributed over 30% of GDP (Dash, 2016). If these SMEs in MENA are provided adequate support in the form of access to financing, business development services and markets they can grow into large firms and spur job growth across MENA region. There exist few support and development programs for SMEs in MENA region. It is important that governments in MENA region focus on those SMEs that are more labor-intensive businesses to generate more employment opportunities.

3. ENTREPRENEURIAL ECOSYSTEM

Currently MENA region has many entrepreneurial initiatives that encourage entrepreneurial activity. These initiatives include technology incubators, NGOs for developing entrepreneurship, networking associations for wannabe entrepreneurs and university programs to foster entrepreneurship. The entrepreneurial initiatives continue to emerge at a fast pace. MENA governments are increasingly gaining understanding of the value of entrepreneurship and its importance in national economies. Governments in MENA region has low contribution with respect to entrepreneurial initiatives. To date the MENA entrepreneurship ecosystem has grown substantially. The four countries (Egypt, Lebanon, Jordan and the United Arab Emirates) become the leading nations for entrepreneurship development in MENA. These countries are providing finances, incubators and other institutions to support entrepreneurs. Best practices in supporting entrepreneurs are developing gradually in each country (WOMENA, 2015).

The effectiveness and not the number of initiatives is very important. An entrepreneurial ecosystem includes all the elements needed to boost entrepreneurship. This ecosystem has four elements: development of entrepreneurs, financing of entrepreneurs, professional and technical support and operating environment. Various initiatives by government and private sector have contributed to the development of ecosystem in MENA region. Still, iIn MENA region's ecosystem, some elements are undeveloped (such as the regulatory framework) and some are developed (such as advisory). As a result, the entrepreneurial ecosystem in MENA region is currently in an out-of-balance state.

3.1. Development of Entrepreneurs

In order to equip entrepreneurs with required knowledge and expertise to develop and run a venture, individual development is necessary. It helps entrepreneurs build their confidence. There are many enablers of entrepreneur's individual development including mentors, and informal and formal education.

Mentors/advisers are typically successful entrepreneurs who can share their knowledge and experiences with aspiring entrepreneurs. Their success stories can be a source of great motivation and moral support for entrepreneurs in early stages of their entrepreneurial journey. Entrepreneurs can obtain informal education through various sources (such as seminars). Universities also offer many formal entrepreneurship courses and programs. There can be informal education opportunities as well e.g. through advising and mentoring.

The MENA region provides relatively strong informal educational opportunities. Some examples of such programs include Employment For Education in Egypt and Employment For Education in Jordan and the Qualeb Programme in Lebanon. However, the region seriously lacks in formal education opportunities on entrepreneurship. There are insignificant numbers of universities in the MENA region who offer entrepreneurship courses, have established centers for entrepreneurship, and offer a major in entrepreneurship. Few business executives relied on traditional educational institutions (such as universities) for entrepreneurial development (Teh, Al-Dhaafri, & Isakovic, 2015). This situation is alarming because the urge to become an entrepreneur often arises at early stages of education and educational system significantly influences this urge or desire.

Recently, universities in MENA region have started to acknowledge the importance of developing entrepreneurship. These universities have started incorporating entrepreneurship in their education programs. Universities in Saudi Arabia are beginning to strengthen ties with the country's business community through initiatives like the Innovative Industrial Collaboration Program at King Abdullah University of Science & Technology. Oman today has more than 1,200, guarantees free education through high school for boys and girls alike, and boasts a range of public and private universities. At Abu Dhabi University, the Centre of Innovation and Entrepreneurship is bridging the gap between academia and industry by helping students incubate their start-ups. Also, in countries across the region, an organization called

Injaz Al Arab was sending thousands of private-sector volunteers into schools to teach kids financial literacy and the basics of starting a business (Al Ardhi, 2016).

3.2. Financing of Entrepreneurs

The second element of ecosystem involves financing of entrepreneurs. There can be many types of financing support for entrepreneurs. Equity investors can be family and friends, angel investors and venture capital firms. Source of seed capital is often entrepreneur's family and friends. Angel investors provide financing beyond seed capital and venture capitalists get involved when the start-up has proven itself. Conventional debt financing requires collateral and takes long time for approval of credit application. High interest payments of this type of financing could prove a burden on new startups. Microfinance providers offer very small loans to entrepreneurs in poor regions. Government funding programs include funds, short-term loans, guarantees and other financing initiatives for specific industries. These are the industries on the priority list of government.

The financing of entrepreneurs is an underdeveloped element of MENA region's entrepreneurial ecosystem. The network of equity investors is considered a critical source for start-up capital in the developed world. This network is still in its early stages of development nascent in the MENA region and few entrepreneurs are able to tap into the funds provided by family and friends. MENA region also lacks the appropriate regulatory and legal framework needed to develop of a more formal and accessible early-stage financing industry. Very few banks in MENA region have special entrepreneurial programs. A very insignificant number of SMEs in the region have access to debt financing. One reason for this trend could be that SMEs often lack financial transparency and due to region's weak financial infrastructure banks find it difficult to make smart, informed lending decisions. Poor credit information and weak rights of creditors make the situation more complex. The more SME lending by banks with large branch networks implies that SME financing is a relationship business. To ease this tight capital market for entrepreneurs, MENA countries have introduced specific programs encourage SME financing by banks. These special programs include exemptions on bank reserve requirements and credit subsidies. Still, the government support is insufficient to create a healthy financing environment for start-ups. The financial support is very focused on very small businesses and do not cater for medium sized businesses. The financial institutions who do offer financing are not doing enough efforts to promote their programs of entrepreneurial and SME financing.

3.3. Professional and Technical Support

The third element of the ecosystem is professional and technical support for entrepreneurs. There can be many sources of this support. Professional services can be provided by marketing companies, media associations, consulting firms and accounting firms. Depending on the nature of the venture, entrepreneurs may use some or all of this expertise. Incubators can provide office space and support services and charge either a small fee or get share in equity of the start-up. Incubators support the startups until they achieve sufficient scale. These incubators can also provide networking, marketing, advisory, and mentoring. Entrepreneurs can use network associations to connect with experienced entrepreneurs and consultants. These business people and consultants can serve as mentors/advisors to help entrepreneur tackle business challenges. Over last few years, MENA countries launched many initiatives to promote business support by providing support to incubators and network associations. Few examples include information, communication and technology incubators (e.g. Qatar's Science & Technology Park and Egypt's Plug and Play). These incubators provided various support services to aspiring entrepreneurs including mentorship, trainings, and funding. However, improvement is needed in the quantity, and impact of new initiatives. A serious flaw in the ecosystem is that these incubators are focused on technology-oriented businesses. These initiatives also need to provide the basic services to both technology-oriented and non-technology businesses because MENA region needs to spur entrepreneurship in traditional industries (such as manufacturing) as well.

3.4. Operating Environment

The fourth element in the entrepreneurship ecosystem is the operating environment that includes many factors such as the regulatory framework, infrastructure, lobbying organizations, prevailing culture and media.

Governments and chambers of commerce in MENA region can collaborate to simplify rules and provide incentives for entrepreneurs. Reforms are needed in many areas. Current labor laws pose significant workforce bottlenecks and conditions imposed on certain professions and nationalities have made talent acquisition difficult for entrepreneurs. There is a need to develop balanced government policies related to foreign labor that allow gradual induction of foreign labor in local economies to build local skills and capabilities.

The time-consuming and expensive legal process in the MENA region is a big issue. The existing infrastructure needs upgrading to improve the business environment. Road infrastructure is often inadequate and sometimes unsafe. Public transport needs significant improvement. Realizing the pressing need to improve infrastructure, Gulf Cooperation Council (GCC) countries recently announced plans to build a rail network linking Saudi Arabia to the Gulf Cooperation Council (GCC) states. Each of the GCC countries will be responsible for building and costs of establishing the rail link within its borders. The rail network plan was part of a larger drive to increase infrastructure projects across the GCC which were forecasted to exceed $86 billion in 2014, an increase of 77.8 percent over 2013 (MEE, 2015). Besides transportation, the upgrading Internet infrastructure is a necessity for entrepreneurial activity in many parts of MENA region. In Arab states, only 24% of the population used Internet compared with 79% in the US and 67% in Europe. The average Internet speed in the MENA region was 2.73 Mbps, which was a meager fraction of the global average of 8.69 Mbps.

Lobbying is needed by entrepreneurial organizations to force MENA governments to amend certain regulations. These organizations could also create other entrepreneurial support organizations by leveraging their own resources and connections. However, these organizations do not fully developed in the MENA region today. Due to cultural issues, stakeholders still do not feel the urgent need for developing and implementing regulatory reforms and infrastructure upgrades. A large proportion of working population prefers stable government jobs over risky entrepreneurial initiative. Parents generally believe that entrepreneurial activities provide less financial security and prestige. These cultural norms are not easy to change. Part of the challenge is to convince aspiring entrepreneurs that failing in starting their own business is a critical part of the process and failure is often necessary for ultimate success. In the current situation, business failure can bring huge disgrace that hinders subsequent attempts to restart the venture. Given these cultural norms, local media in MENA region does little to promote entrepreneurship. An insignificant number of regional magazines report on entrepreneurship. In this age of social media, there is no social media focus on entrepreneurship. There are very few websites and blogs dedicated for entrepreneurship discussion. These blogs and websites are powerful tools to change attitudes. Media should provide more entrepreneurship-oriented programs. These programs should showcase new ideas and success stories of entrepreneurs.

4. RECOMMENDATIONS

There are some recommendations that regional leaders can use for improving the MENA regions' entrepreneurial ecosystem. The improved ecosystem can boost the entrepreneurship in MENA region. It is important that these recommendations should be implemented in totality, as the isolated implementation of few recommendations is unlikely to improve entrepreneurial ecosystem. Applied in totality, these recommendations can ensure an exponential impact and provide growth in employment and economic activities. These spillover effects would ultimately result in new opportunities for the region's youth.

4.1. Integrate Entrepreneurship in MENA's Culture

Regional leaders need to make efforts so that entrepreneurship become part of the regional culture. This will ensure that entrepreneurship is deeply rooted in the way business is done. This can be done by educating youth, companies and media about the entrepreneurial opportunities.

Successful and established entrepreneurs should encourage the next generation of entrepreneurs. Successful predecessors can provide the most inspiration to the new entrepreneurs. Their involvement can greatly help establish a legitimate and healthy entrepreneurial ecosystem that can generate an exponential growth in entrepreneurship activity. Sharing of ideas and experiences and networking is an important element of entrepreneurial culture. For this purpose, Entrepreneurs can connect with NGOs to build forums that could facilitate sharing of ideas and facilitate networking. One example is mentoring programs. In these programs, aspiring entrepreneurs can benefit from experience and knowledge of their mentors. Another platform could be entrepreneurship service center (Saddi & Soueid, 2011). This center can facilitate meetings between aspiring entrepreneurs and experienced entrepreneurs for idea discussion and feedback to improve business plans. This facilitation and networking is very important because experienced entrepreneurs could counsel new entrepreneurs on various aspects of business such as selection of directors and senior managers and making difficult financing decisions. Entrepreneurs and other entrepreneurial organizations can held entrepreneurship competitions to identify and evaluate high potential business ideas. The selected ideas can be supported by providing necessary support, development, and finances. This way, successful entrepreneurs could themselves become angel investors. When the situation is extremely fragile, as is the case of MENA region, a system to provide support to entrepreneurs in the early stages of their venture development becomes very important. One example of such support is Endeavor, a non-profit organization active in over 10 emerging countries. Endeavor uses a well-defined criteria to select entrepreneurs. Selected entrepreneurs are offered customized services from a volunteer network of business leaders. Successful entrepreneurs can also benefits from the experience and knowledge of other successful entrepreneurs. In order to better assess the venture opportunities, investors, bankers and government officials need training. Government officials need training to formulate effective government policies for entrepreneurship. In this connection, NGOs and successful entrepreneurs can offer an exchange program. In this exchange programs, government officials can be provided temporary work opportunity in the private sector to get practical entrepreneurial experience (Saddi & Soueid, 2011).

Celebrities have prominent positions that can be used to promote entrepreneurship. Celebrities can describe entrepreneurship itself and how entrepreneurs can develop themselves and the country. Highly successful entrepreneurs should receive high visibility. In their policy talks, government officials should highlight success stories of highly successful entrepreneurs. They should promote them as role models and by describing their accomplishments. Such publicity can provide great incentives for aspiring entrepreneurs and help build foundation of a strong economy. Governments should use the public media assets (such as TV) to promote success stories and profile of successful entrepreneurs. Such publicity can help motivate aspiring entrepreneurs and make them feel as part of a large like-minded community of people. This publicity is vital because entrepreneurship in MENA region is not widely practiced or respected (Saddi & Soueid, 2011). NGOs should invite the media to different forums (such as conferences) and individuals should give wide publicity of their views and activities through personal websites, blogs, and social media. Media should regularly cover on regular basis the entrepreneurial issues and success stories.

Schools can educate youngsters about entrepreneurship and help build entrepreneurship culture. Education ministries of MENA region could collaborate with other regional organizations (such as the Arab League) to develop and promote regionally a curricula that include entrepreneurship. In each country, ministries of education can develop policies/guidelines to provide comprehensive entrepreneurship education in universities. In this regards, teachers should be trained first. This training can be made compulsory. Career days can be celebrated in schools and universities where students can be educated about their career prospects in general and specifically about entrepreneurship. Ministries of education may make these initiatives part of accreditation. Teachers can conduct in-class contests where students' business plans are presented and evaluated by experts. University-level students can be provided with the skills and knowledge to start their own venture. More universities should be encouraged to establish major and minor degrees in entrepreneurship. Universities offering degrees in entrepreneurship can also hold specialized seminars. In these seminars, students can work with their professors to create a business plan. This business plan should be presented to angel investors or venture capital firms to attract them finance the business idea. Those students whose major or minor is not in entrepreneurship can also benefit from these opportunities of learning. Universities may also alter the roadmap for existing degrees programs to include a few entrepreneurship-related courses. Universities can encourage faculty to participate in various forums promoting entrepreneurship outside the university. In these forums, university faculty and established entrepreneurs can present their insights and impart training. All these initiatives at various educational levels can help promote a culture of entrepreneurship provided universities and governments collaborate with each other. For example, Start-Up Chile is a program created by the Chilean Government that seeks to attract early-stage, high-potential entrepreneurs to bootstrap their startups using Chile as a platform to go global. The end goal of this program is to position Chile as the innovation and entrepreneurship hub of Latin America. Start-Up Chile has a large portfolio, receiving in between 200 – 250 companies a year (Start-Up Chile, 2016).

Corporate sector can help unlock entrepreneurial potential of their employees to boost corporate entrepreneurship. Corporations can encourage their employees to show their creativity and pursue entrepreneurial activities. Companies can set up internal processes for assessment and funding of entrepreneurial ideas generated by employees. They can provide paid leave of absence to employees for working on their entrepreneurial ideas. When these startups are operational, employers can provide advice and support to these startups. Companies can also build a corporate entrepreneurship forum. This forum could serve as a platform for large companies to discuss their experiences with the entrepreneurship ecosystem. One example of such forum is Aramco Entrepreneurship Center (AEC) setup by Saudi Aramco, Saudi Arabia's state-owned oil company. AEC is an opportunity for Saudi entrepreneurs to access to the resources and expertise they need to allow great ideas to flourish. AEC was established as an incubator to ignite entrepreneurship and help develop local enterprises in the Kingdom of Saudi Arabia. The center provides a variety of exciting programs that offer non-collateralized loans or venture capital partnering, along with the guidance and tools that develop and nurture entrepreneurs and their businesses (Aramco, 2016).

4.2. Expand Scope of Entrepreneurship

There are ways that stakeholders in MENA region can take for an out-of-the-box thinking and solicit new ideas and approaches of entrepreneurship.

In MENA regions, it has been a common practice to promote local entrepreneurial activity by imitating US Silicon Valley (Saddi & Soueid, 2011). UK government started "Silicon Roundabout" program and Germany initiated a "biotechnology hub". Both programs did not live up to the expectations. By attracting larger firms (such as Cisco and Amazon) into the Silicon Roundabout area rents increased and available space decreased. As a result, the smaller UK start-ups that were initially attracted to the area were forced out (Prosser, 2015). There are reasons for that failure. Silicon Valley is home to very large corporations (e.g. Google and Intel). Silicon Valley enjoys presence of a large number of venture capitalists, prestigious educational institutions, reduced costs of failure, strong local industries to help boost R&D, and favorable immigration policies for doctoral level students. (Isenberg, 2010). These factors are not easy for any government to orchestrate. It is therefore important that countries MENA region identify their own competitive advantage and design their entrepreneurship ecosystem to take benefit of those specific advantages. They need to go beyond focus just on technology and look at entrepreneurial opportunities in other areas such as natural resources, environment, and human resources. Governments should identify unmet needs in these areas to boost activity in these areas. One example is Saudi Arabia. For example, Saudi Arabia set up Saudi Industrial Development Fund (SIDF). The SDIF contributes to the realization of the goals, policies and programs of the Kingdom's industrial development, by providing the finance and advisory services needed to support the growth and development of the local industrialization and upgrading the level of the industry performance (SIDF, 2016).

The immigration and naturalization laws are stringent. These laws do not encourage flow of talented and experienced people into the region. This situation put local entrepreneurs at a disadvantaged position because they cannot gain collaboration with foreign entrepreneurs. Governments need to ensure that their labor laws are streamlined to provide a more liberal immigration and visa policy for foreign workers. This can ensure that local entrepreneurs can access the expertise they need.

Governments should also relax the rules of foreign ownership of real estate, business and stock options. The current rules are very stringent and discourage foreign participation in local entrepreneurship. Entrepreneurs should not restrict themselves to their home country and look out for entrepreneurial opportunities in the whole MENA region. To do so, regional leaders need to develop standardized laws and streamlined processes across the whole MENA region. There should also be relaxed policy for foreign labor and imports/exports. There is also a need for active promotion of the value of foreign expertise. This promotion should include active lobbying to the government.

All stakeholders should realize that entrepreneurship is not limited to young people only. Another thing is that not every new startup can be technology-related. There is a need to break this stereotype reinforced by the regional successes in MENA region. Entrepreneurs can be experienced executives from industries and their expertise can be key to the success of any new venture. In a healthy economy, job creation occurs across industries and technology alone may not bring advantage to a country. Therefore, governments, NGOs, and entrepreneurial networks and associations need to encourage entrepreneurial initiatives (such as consumer goods, retail and education) that capitalizes on a country's best available resources. Non-technology incubators should be developed that provide necessary assistance and support to non-technology entrepreneurial initiatives. Another stereotype is that an entrepreneur is necessarily a man. This trend is changing and women entrepreneurs are increasing in MENA region. This is because entrepreneurship provides them more flexible work opportunities. This trend needs support and encouragement from governments, NGOs and entrepreneurial networks and associations because the a major proportion of working-age women population in the MENA region is educated but a majority of it remain outside the labor force. The unemployment rate among working-age women in the MENA is as high as over 40% in some countries. This multifaceted problem needs to be addressed to achieve the desired economic outcomes of having more women in the workplace. There are huge potential economic benefits of increased women's employment. According to recent estimates, by equalizing the man and women participation in labor markets in the MENA region, the regional GDP could increase by 47% over the next decade. The region could realize $600 billion in economic impact annually ($2.7 trillion by 2025) (Ataya, 2016). The "Women Entrepreneurs in Lebanon" project was aimed to give Lebanese entrepreneurial women support, finance, and mentoring. The Prince Sultan bin Abdul Aziz Fund in Saudi Arabia aimed to support Women's Small Enterprises.

Many talented individuals in MENA region have migrated to avail better opportunities abroad where governments are stable and legal and economic systems are more developed. However, even after migration, these individuals often don't break their emotional ties to their home country. These expatriates are a good of source of advice that governments in MENA regions should use to educate future entrepreneurs. These expats can provide advice on several issues such as various reforms to provide enabling environment for entrepreneurship. They can work as mentors of aspiring entrepreneurs and can sponsor local youth to work abroad and gain experience. Upon their return, the youth can use this experience to build their own startup. NGOs and governments can set up business organizations and associations to host networking events. One example of such organization is Lebanese International Business Council (LBC), a non-profit organization that hosts global networking events for Lebanese communities.

4.3. Encourage and Support Entrepreneurships

Regional leaders need to take measure so that prospective entrepreneurs can acquire necessary resources to start their new businesses. There should be a central system set up by governments that promotes entrepreneurship. This system should streamline and shorten the requirements for starting a new venture. Governments can also develop flexible rules for funding these ventures. For example, governments may allow use of crowd funding for new ventures. Governments should reduce the paperwork and approvals required for opening a new venture. Some legal frameworks can be established to encourage investment from venture capital firms and FDI and relaxed capital requirements to start a new venture.

Governments can also support collaboration forums for entrepreneurs and investors. Startup Weekend is a US-based organization that provide networking opportunities organizes for entrepreneurs. For startups looking for growth capital, governments can setup a SME exchange. The structure of this exchange will be similar to the structure of stock exchange but it will target SMEs and will have strict listing requirements (Saddi & Soueid, 2011). Countries in Gulf Cooperation Council (GCC) region pay monthly allowance to while they are employed by the private sector. To promote entrepreneurship, governments can increase this allowance for people who are employed in their own ventures.

The Advanced Management Program and Management Development Scholarships program in Singapore were meant to nurture management of SMEs. These programs coupled with a business-friendly economic policy framework helped boost Singapore's economic growth. Governments in MENA region can follow the footsteps of Singapore and provide subsidized management training programs. Youth microfinance can improve young lives for good and help their businesses grow to become thriving small businesses. It is growing and niche market segment that must be used properly.

Venture capital firms need to broaden their scope of involvement with the entrepreneurial ventures they finance. For the improvement of entrepreneurship ecosystem in the MENA region, venture capital firms should proactively seek entrepreneurs and increase their involvement in the ventures they finance. Venture capital firms can use entrepreneurial networks to find promising startups. They can also look for startups that failed to generate funding from conventional banks. Venture capital firms should have experts to guide and help the entrepreneur in tactical and strategic decision making. At first glance, this deep involvement may seem more than what is norm in USA and Europe but we must understand that entrepreneurs in MENA regions do not have access to the support structure available to entrepreneurs in USA and Europe.

5. CONCLUSION

The MENA regions must provide ample job opportunities to the large population of its unemployed youth. This is not a small task and require creative thinking and decisive actions from the governments. One solution is to encourage entrepreneurship to spur job opportunities and boost economic growth. Time is needed to develop an entrepreneurial culture in MENA region because the concept of entrepreneurship is not neither well understood nor appreciate in MENA region. First step in this regard is to understand what drives entrepreneurship in MENA region and then undertake a comprehensive plan to develop an entrepreneurial ecosystem. It is important that this ecosystem is created quickly to take maximum benefit of one of the world's youngest and fastest-growing workforce.

REFERENCES

Al Ardhi, M. M. (2016, June 4). Arabs Unseen: Golden age of innovation looms for Arab world's entrepreneurs. *The National*. Retrieved July 30, 2016, from http://www.thenational.ae/business/economy/arabs-unseen-golden-age-of-innovation-looms-for-arab-worlds-entrepreneurs

Al-Masri, S. (2016, February 24). *Numbers Don't Lie: Self-Employment Is Thriving In The Middle East*. Retrieved July 28, 2016, from https://www.entrepreneur.com/article/271238

Albawaba. (2015, November 22). *MENA must create 100 million jobs by 2020 to meet unemployment numbers*. Retrieved July 28, 2016, from http://www.albawaba.com/business/mena-must-create-100-million-jobs-2020-meet-unemployment-numbers-771664

Aramco. (2016, May 30). *Aramco Entrepreneurship Center*. Retrieved July 29, 2016, from http://www.saudiaramco.com/en/home/citizenship/economy/aramco-entrepreneurship-center.html

Ataya, L. (2016, May 10). *An Open Call To Innovators: The Middle East Needs More Women Entrepreneurs*. Retrieved July 29, 2016, from https://www.entrepreneur.com/article/275417

Chamlou, N., Klapper, L., & Muzi, S. (2008). *The environment for women's entrepreneurship in the Middle East and North Africa*. World Bank Publications. doi:10.1596/978-0-8213-7495-5

Contessi, S., De Nicola, F., & Li, L. (2012). *International trade, female labor, and entrepreneurship in MENA countries.* FRB of St. Louis Working Paper.

Dash, S. (2016, April 17). *Family First: Securing Continued Growth For Family Businesses In The MENA Region.* Retrieved July 30, 2016, from https://www.entrepreneur.com/article/274231

Djeflat, A. (2002). *National systems of innovation in the MENA region.* World Bank Working paper/Maghtech. http://lnweb18.worldbank.org/mna/mena.nsf/attachments/innovation/$file/rapfin.pdf

Hattab, H. (2012). Towards understanding female entrepreneurship in Middle Eastern and North African countries: A cross-country comparison of female entrepreneurship. *Education. Business and Society: Contemporary Middle Eastern Issues, 5*(3), 171–186. doi:10.1108/17537981211265561

International Labor Organization. (2015, October 8). *MENA region retains highest youth unemployment rate in the world.* Retrieved July 28, 2016, from http://www.ilo.org/beirut/media-centre/news/WCMS_412797/lang--en/index.htm

Isenberg, D. J. (2010). How to start an entrepreneurial revolution. *Harvard Business Review, 88*(6), 40–50.

Kabbani, N., & Kothari, E. (2005). Youth employment in the MENA Region: A situational assessment. *World Bank, Social Protection Discussion Paper, 534.*

Mahroum, S. (2016, May 4). *The Triumphs and Struggles of Arab Startups.* Retrieved July 28, 2016, from https://www.project-syndicate.org/commentary/startups-entrepreneurship-middle-east-by-sami-mahroum-2016-05

Matriano, M. T., & Suguku, D. (2015). Entrepreneurship Growth in Oman: Position, Prospects and Growth of Entrepreneural Education. *IJAEDU-International E-Journal of Advances in Education, 1*(2), 127–131. doi:10.18768/ijaedu.58791

MEE. (2015, February 12). *Rail network project to link GCC states begins.* Retrieved July 30, 2016, from http://www.middleeasteye.net/news/rail-network-project-link-gcc-states-begins-1070205078

Mervyn, D. K. (2015, August 10). *Are Entrepreneurs Born Or Made?* Retrieved July 28, 2016, from https://www.entrepreneur.com/article/249375

O'Sullivan, A., Rey, M.-E., & Mendez, J. G. (2011). Opportunities and Challenges in the MENA Region. *Arab World Competitiveness Report, 2012*, 42–67.

Prosser, D. (2015, November 16). *Silicon Roundabout is getting congested, but it isn't the only hub for tech start-ups.* Retrieved July 29, 2016, from http://www.independent.co.uk/news/business/comment/silicon-roundabout-is-getting-congested-but-it-isnt-the-only-hub-for-tech-start-ups-a6735736.html

Saddi, J., & Soueid, R. (2011). Accelerating entrepreneurship in the Arab world. In *The Forum of Young Global Leaders, World Economic Forum, and Booz & Company.* Retrieved from http://www3. weforum. org/docs/WEF_YGL_AcceleratingEntrepreneurshipArabWorld_Report_

Sadeq, T., & Setti, Z. (2013). Effects of entrepreneurs networking with national values on job growth expectations: A two-level analysis for the MENA region and Denmark. *International Journal of Business and Globalisation, 11*(4), 443–459. doi:10.1504/IJBG.2013.056879

SIDF. (2016). *About Us.* Retrieved July 29, 2016, from http://www.sidf.gov.sa/en/AboutSIDF/Pages/AboutUs.aspx

Start-Up Chile. (2016). *About.* Retrieved from http://startupchile.org/about/

Teh, J., Al-Dhaafri, H., & Isakovic, A. A. (2015). *Entrepreneurial Attitudes and Intentions of Dubai Students.* Academic Press.

Weeks, J. R. (2009). Women business owners in the Middle East and North Africa: A five-country research study. *International Journal of Gender and Entrepreneurship, 1*(1), 77–85. doi:10.1108/17566260910942354

WOMENA. (2015, October 19). *Exploring Trends and Challenges to Scale for Startups in MENA.* Retrieved from http://womena.co/2015/10/19/challenges-to-scale-in-mena/

World Economic Forum. (2015, May 27). *Solving the problem of youth unemployment in the MENA region.* Retrieved July 28, 2016, from https://www.weforum.org/agenda/2015/05/solving-the-problem-of-youth-unemployment-in-the-mena-region/

Zali, M. R., Bastian, B. L., & Qureshi, S. (2013). Promoting innovation in the MENA region: The role of social norms and individual factors in entrepreneurial networks. *International Journal of Business and Globalisation, 11*(4), 413–426. doi:10.1504/IJBG.2013.056877

Chapter 5
Making Innovation Development Policies Work for MENA:
The Need for Entrepreneurship

Mehtap Isik
Bogazici University, Turkey

ABSTRACT

This chapter analyzes the Middle Eastern North African economies' growth prospects and investigates the role of entrepreneurial activities in achieving sustainable economic growth and social development. It explores the existing macroeconomic, political and social characteristics of the region and brings the different literatures together to understand the policy implications of theory and practices. The chapter shows that entrepreneurial activities can cure a lot of problem in the region as long as supported by the central authorities, and the region has a strong potential to be used by the entrepreneurs.

DOI: 10.4018/978-1-5225-2066-5.ch005

INTRODUCTION

This chapter aims to raise practical solutions to the major development and growth problems of the Middle Eastern North African region (MENA), which are theoretically supported. The main answers revealed by the theoretical surroundings are gathered around the entrepreneurial activities. Thus, the chapter proposes that the entrepreneurial activities are not only important for the individuals in the economy, but also for the salvation of the whole economy, in the development perspective. The study is based upon the strong connection between microeconomic and macroeconomic measures and emphasizes the importance of investing on entrepreneurship in MENA. Our analysis calls the policy makers to finance entrepreneurial activities and claims that it worth, because it pays back with economic development and growth at the same time both in the short and long run time.

To this aim, this chapter investigates the forces which drive trade and global integration in fostering economic development for the special case of MENA region. The extent to which we can attribute economic development to economic growth is a question on the one hand; we ask which structural reforms are actually missing in the region to achieve a faster economic growth and whether the pointed structural changes affect the economic measures as would be expected. A detailed investigation on the macroeconomic measures lead us to an answer where microeconomic approaches are required: Entrepreneurship.

Taking the new growth theories into account, the innovation and technological improvements are suggested as the main cure in most of the recipes for triggering development and economic growth at once. Then, the key ingredient in the production process becomes the entrepreneurial ability. In that respect, the institutional design in providing the required support for the innovational activities has to be at the center of the discussions, because the fulfillment of infrastructural necessities are significantly important especially if the macroeconomic environment is not ready for the entrepreneurial activities.

When it comes to Middle Eastern North African (MENA) countries, even in the process of identifying the major problems of the region, entrepreneurship arise as a major answer to many problems of the region. This study questions the existence of appropriate macro environment to support micro decisions of individuals and firms regarding to start-up new businesses and to investments on research and development activities which leads the economic growth and development, eventually.

The first section takes a macroeconomic snapshot of the region to observe its current economic situation in the world. The picture clues in on surprising facts regarding the links between development and growth. Controlling almost 60% of the world's oil, being controlled mostly by very strong autocratic governments, including the world's richest countries and some of the poorest countries together, being in a chronic post-conflict context, having a segmented and highly regulated labor markets, with social relations mainly shaped by Islamic rules, a huge unregistered economic production and almost lack of financial markets, the region differ from other developing regions sharply. Although there are considerable differences among countries in the region, the 90's data on the income inequality, poverty and health care demonstrate relatively low levels of poverty and equitable income distribution in compared to other developing regions. On the other hand, a more recent data shows a relative degradation with an accelerating growth of the other developing regions. In compared to countries in other regions at similar levels of income, the governments in MENA region look like more effective in distributing the social services and aids, but inadequate to support the accumulation of the capital required in manufacturing.

It is widely agreed upon that the economic growth generates suitable but not sufficient conditions for economic development. The poverty and inequality are linked to economic growth in an ambiguous way. Many works following Kuznet (1955) study how the economic growth affects inequality. While many studies shows a negative relation between economic growth and inequality (e.g. Perotti, 1996), some empirical works suggest that economic growth increases the inequality (e.g. Forbes, 2000). Indeed, Panizza (2002) shows that the method of measuring the inequality result in differences in the estimated relationship between inequality and growth. Recent works focus on how inequality affects the growth (Galor, 2011). Doyle and Stiglitz (2014) claim that inequality drags down growth in oppose to Krugman (Budis, 2014).

The way of causality between is not clear. However, empirical evidences show that East Asia has experienced a rapid growth and a relatively low level of income inequality at the same time. In contrast, Latin America and Caribbean region has experienced high levels of income inequality and almost zero economic growth over the same period of time (Birdsall et al., 1995). In the same period, the measures in the MENA region are surprising. Poverty indicators exhibit low levels of poverty and Gini coefficients which are similar to those of Europe with very low rates of GDP growth. (Adams and Page, 2003)

This study takes the tension between income inequality and economic growth into consideration, following Ravillion (2001) who explains how the gains from an economic expansion are utilized by different income groups differ across the countries. In this respect, micro and country-specific approaches can more successfully explain the interaction between economic growth and development in the country at issue. Therefore, economic growth and development policies suggested to a country or a region has to take social and structural elements of the country into account. MENA is a region of its own characteristics in many respects and policies that do not take these specialties into account are off their target. The study claims that policies sourced from new growth theories may be successful, if they are complemented by appropriate structural reforms. Growth strategies should target to balance the speed of growth and well-being of the region. The study analyzes the current financial markets, labor markets and the post-conflict political environment of the region. Also, it is discussed how the oil revenue surplus can be managed so that the infrastructural needs of the region can be fulfilled. In order to compare the macroeconomic conditions of the countries with each other, with European countries and with other developing regions, the data from World's Bank and IMF reports and some cases from countries are used. The effects of Islamic rules on development indices and how these rules would affect the development policies at issue are also discussed, in this chapter.

We organize the rest of the work as follows: In the next section, economic facts about the region are collected. Then, the impacts of political and cultural structure of the region on economic performance are discussed. The next section focuses on why the region needs some policy reforms in its growth and development process, theoretically. The last section, questions the adaptation process and emphasize the need for searching a bunch of compatible policies which respect the distinctive characteristics of the region.

REGIONAL OUTLOOK

Economic Measures

A region is defined by the cultural, social and geographical elements. In that respect different classifications of the countries can be considered. Moreover, different mathematical techniques which handle the time series and cross sectional data of the countries are used to construct the regional data. (Hančlová,et al. 2004, Nielsen, 2011) Due to the reliability and comparability issues, this study mainly focuses on data provided by World Bank to analyze regions' economic activity. The regions are defined geographically as North America, Europe and Central Asia, East Asia and the Pacific, South Asia, Latin America and Caribbean, Middle East and North Africa, Sub-Saharan Africa. As it is defined by World Bank, Middle East North Africa (MENA) region includes high-income countries Bahrain, Israel, Kuwait, Oman, Qatar, Saudi Arabia, and United Arab Emirates together with 13 developing countries Algeria, Jordan, Tunisia, Djibouti, Lebanon, West Bank and Gaza, Egypt, Libya, Yemen, Iran, Morocco, Iraq and Syria.[1]

The countries in MENA region are so diversified that the region can be segmented into subgroups according to various variables such as resource endowments, geographical distances, economic relations and trade unions etc. This study mainly follows the classifications by World Bank and assumes that the region is developing one, but takes the diversification into account and uses the subgroups in analysis.

Figure 1 and Figure 2 shows GDP per capita and GDP per capita growth of the region including all income level countries versus the only developing countries, respectively. The difference between the two groups in GDP per capita income decreases in 1980's and increases from 1990's and on. The GDP growth of developing countries which is significantly higher in early 1980's decrease suddenly and small deviations are seen until recent years. The effect of 2008 crisis is higher on growth of developing countries in the region. The relative position of the region's GDP per capita with respect to the other regions in the world is read from Figure3. Even though the regional data include high income level countries, the regional income gaps between MENA and North America and MENA and Europe and Central Asia are significant. The position of average income of MENA economies change starting in 1990's with the growth of East Asian and Pacific economies. While the East Asian and Pacific region and South Asian region has been decreasing the income gaps with other regions, MENA and Latin America and Caribbean region couldn't achieve such growth trend. Average income of MENA region is behind the World average and the difference has not been decreasing since 1980's.

Figure 4 demonstrates the average GDP per capita growth rates over 10-year periods of the regions between 1980 and 2013. Besides the negative average of 80's

Figure 1. GDP per capita of MENA
Source: http://data.worldbank.org

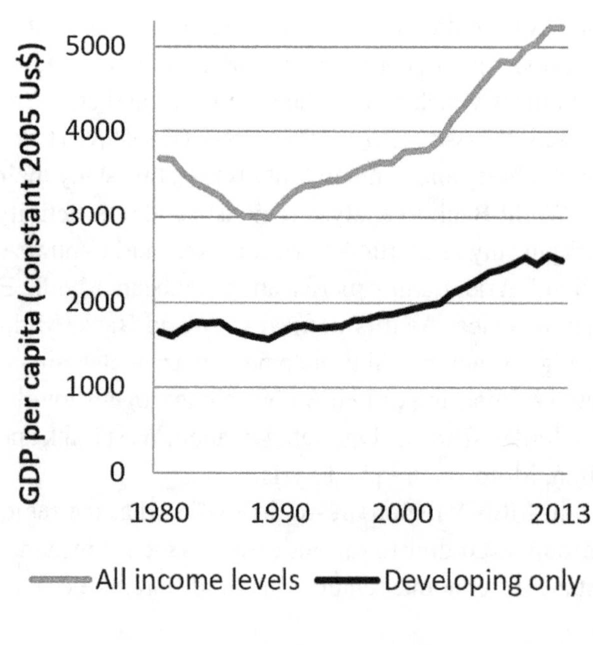

Figure 2. GDP per capita growth of MENA
Source: http://data.worldbank.org

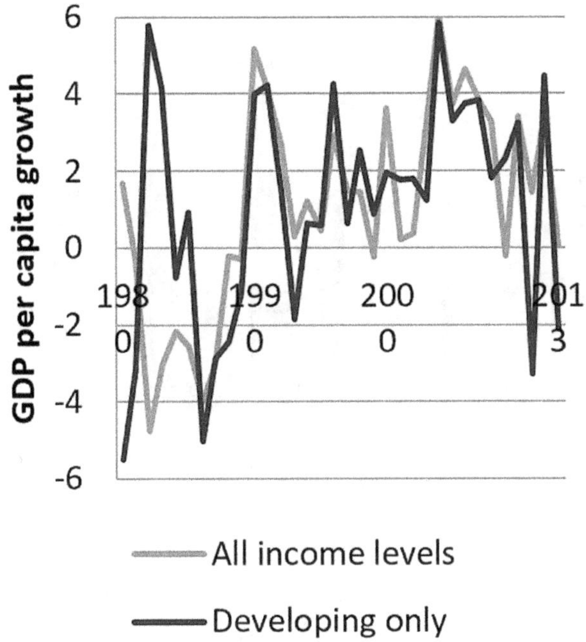

Figure 3. GDP per capita (constant 2005 US$) of Regions (all income levels)
Source: http://data.worldbank.org

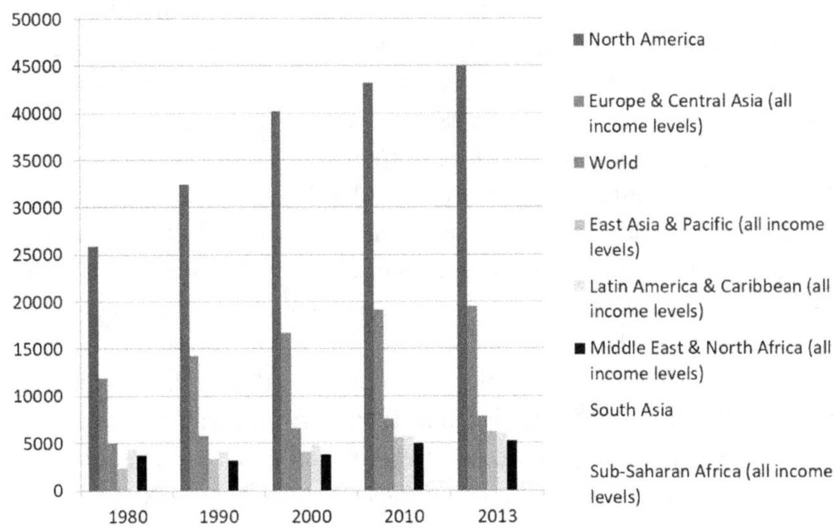

Figure 4. Average GDP per capita growth rates of regions (all income levels)
Source: http://data.worldbank.org

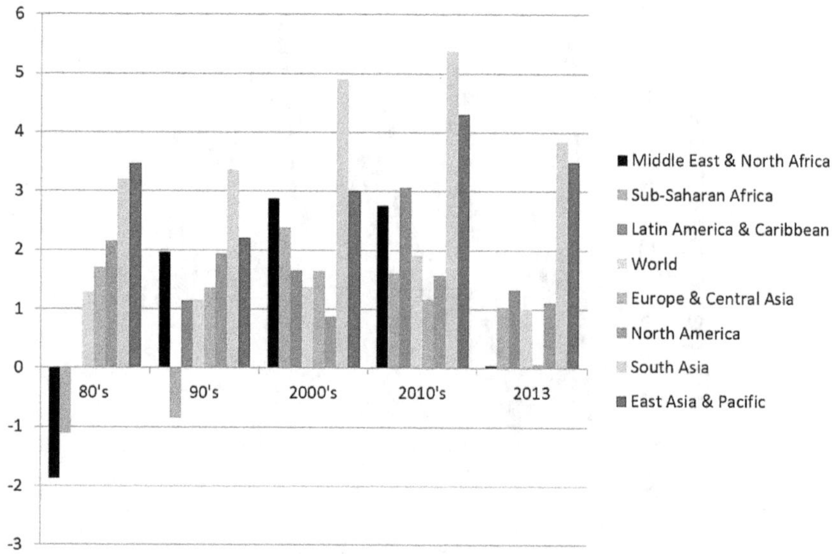

GDP per capita growth, the sharp recovery of 90's is also striking. In Figure 2, we see a continuous decrease in the late 90's, but the growth rate fluctuates around 0.5% and 3.5% until 2000's and stays close to world's average. In the first decade of 2000's, region's growth is slightly higher than the world's average. The V-shape growth rates between 2008 and 2010 point out the 08' crisis. In 2013, GDP per capita growth is negative on the average for developing countries in the region and significantly lower than the rest of the world even though all income levels are included. The recovery period after the 08' crisis looks like not completed yet in any regions. However, MENA and Europe and Central Asia regions are the only ones which experience almost zero growth by the end of 2013. Over the period, MENA's growth rate ranges from -4.8% to 6.7% which is the widest interval that no other region experienced. Although the negative growth rates of 80's are not observed in later years, the sharp decrease at 2012 together with political instability of the region is ringing the alarm bells.

Some major indices regarding the economic growth and development of the countries in MENA as of 2013 are listed in Table 1. A very wide range of countries is observed in which world's richest countries Kuwait, Oman, United Arab Emirates, Saudi Arabia and almost the poorest countries Djibouti, Yemen exist.

Why MENA is a very much diversified region economically and how the policies should be shaped in accordance, cannot be analyzed without understanding the differences in terms of resource endowments, government structures, religious beliefs, cultural values.

Table 1. Indices by countries in MENA

MENA Countries	GDP (millions of US$) (2013)	GDP/per capita ($) (2013)	GDP Growth (%) (2013)	Adult Literacy Rate	Life Expectancy (years) (2012)	HDI (rank)	Gini Index
Algeria	$210,183	$13,304	2,71%	91,8%	71	93	0,35
Bahrain	$32,788	$43,824	5,50%	94,60%	78	44	n.a.
Djibouti	$1,456	$2,998	5,00%	70,00%	61	170	0,39
Egypt	$271,930	$11,085	2,10%	73,90%	71	110	0,30
Iran	$368,904	$15,586	-5,80%	85,00%	74	75	0,38
Iraq	$222,784	$15,188	4,00%	80,20%	69	120	0,3
Israel	$291,357	$32,760	3,00%	97,10%	82	19	0,39
Jordan	$33,678	$11,782	2,80%	93,40%	74	77	0,35
Kuwait	$183,219	$85,660	0,82%	94,00%	79	46	n.a.
Lebanon	$44,352	$17,110	0,90%	89,60%	80	65	n.a.
Libya	$75,456	**	-9,40%	94,20%	75	55	n.a.
Morocco	$104,374	$7,200	4,40%	67,10%	71	129	0,40
Oman	$80,570	$44,052	2,80%	81,40%	72	56	n.a.
Palestine	$4,016	$4,576	*13,8%	95,60%	73	107	n.a.
Qatar	$202,450	$131,758	5,60%	96,30%	82	31	0,41
Saudi Arabia	$745,273	$53,758	4,00%	86,60%	75	34	n.a.
Syria	$73,672	**	**	79,60%	75	166	0,35
Tunisia	$47,129	$11,092	2,80%	88,30%	75	90	0,36
UAE	$383,799	$58,042	4,40%	77,90%	78	40	n.a.
Yemen	$35,955	$3,958	4,40%	63,90%	63	154	0,37

*According to 2012 data
* *Because of domestic problem, there are no correct values.

Resource Endowments

MENA includes the richest countries in oil, gas and mineral reserves. Other than the fact that the countries in the MENA region own 59% of the world proven crude oil reserves, and 45% of the gas proven reserves, minerals such as phosphate (76%), sulfur (18%), bars (15%), strontium (13%), and iron ore (4.3%) in addition to copper, gold and silver constitutes a significant portion of global reserves.[2] In Figure 5, we see that total natural resource rents as percentage of GDP's which are the sum of oil rents, natural gas rents, coal rents (hard and soft), mineral rents, and forest rents is the highest for MENA. Yet, neither the mining activities nor oil and gas productions

Figure 5. Total natural resource rent as percentage of GDP in 2012
Source: http://data.worldbank.org

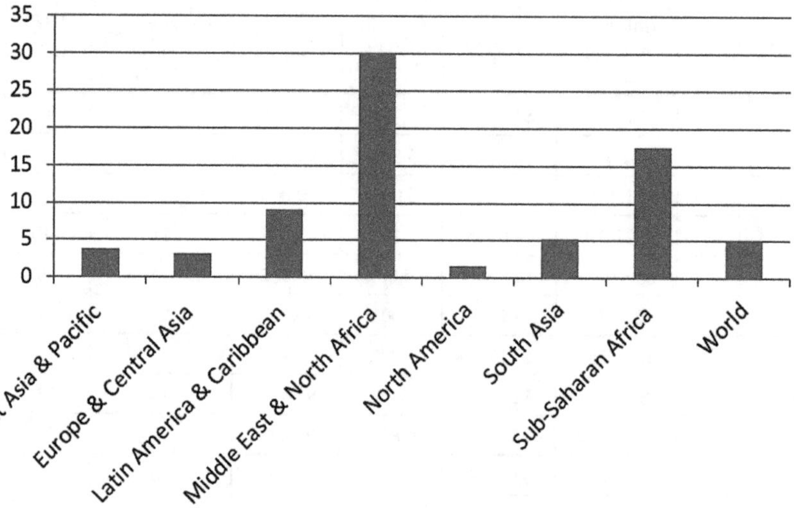

are effective as they are expected with the available capacity. The natural resource endowments of the countries are diversified within the region.

The mismanagement and corruption in revenue management have many consequences on overall economy. Indeed, not only in the MENA region, but many countries all around the world are not able to govern their abundant natural resources, efficiently. In most of the cases, revenues cannot be collected. Even when revenue objectives are achieved, governments take policy actions with respect to the short-term interest. Resource Governance Index (RGI) measures the quality of governance in the oil, gas and mining sector of 58 countries.[3] Norway is the first and Myanmar is the last in the RGI ranking list of the 2013 Resource Governance Index Report. In Table 2, we list the RGI rankings of countries in the MENA region. Those countries appear in *italics* are defined as resource-rich by IMF. Most of the countries in MENA are resource-rich but not able to manage a good governance of resources.

Data given leads to conclude that even though the share of the natural resources on GDP is high, revenues obtained from these resources do not always lead to growth. Indeed, considering that the oil is almost the most crucial factor of production, an obvious question is why all countries endowed with oil are neither the richest nor the most developed ones in the world. Among many other causes that are underlined in the later sections, an economic phenomenon which is named as Dutch Diseases has a crucial role to this end. Corden and Neary (1982) show the effect of revenue surplus obtained from a natural resource on the relative decline

Table 2. Resource governance index ranks

Country	Resource Measured	RGI Rank
Morocco	Minerals	25
Iraq	Hydrocarbons	29
Bahrain	Hydrocarbons	31
Yemen	Hydrocarbons	37
Egypt	Hydrocarbons	38
Kuwait	Hydrocarbons	42
Algeria	Hydrocarbons	45
Saudi Arabia	Hydrocarbons	48
Iran	Hydrocarbons	53
Qatar	Hydrocarbons	54
Libya	Hydrocarbons	55

Source: http://www.resourcegovernance.org/rgi

of internationally tradable manufacture sectors with respect to the non-tradable good's sector. The model explains that as a result of the boom in natural resource sector real income and so the demand for non-tradable service increases. With increasing prices in service sector, real exchange rate appreciates and the tradable manufacture sector lags behind. Indeed, we observe that the developing countries are mainly endowed with a certain natural resource and /or a primary product which constitute a highly significant share of exports. However, variety and maturity of exported products are important variables of income derived from international trade. As the product matures in production process, in other words as the product gets more differentiable, higher profit can be expected. In that respect, considering the role of international trade on economic growth, the natural resources may be considered as a curse rather than a blessing. (Auty R., 1993) Yet, this study suggests that whether the natural resource is a curse or blessing mostly depends on the governments' policies. The analysis shows that the mismanagement of the revenues and the lack of infrastructure required for the development of the lagging tradable sectors are the main cause of the problem.

Although the region has abundant oil, natural gas and mining, the scarcity of water and arable land which are main resources in agricultural production creates a dependency on the imported food and give rise to one of the major policy challenges in the region. Being the most water scarce region in the world, MENA's average water availability per person is approximately 1,200m3/person/year whereas the world's average is approximately 7,000m3/person/year. One half of MENA's population lives under conditions of water stress. Moreover, the population of 300 million today is expected to be around 500 million in 2025 and the per capita availability of water is expected to halve by 2050. The pollution of water resources is another dimension of the problem. Most of the water need is obtained from the Nile, the Jordan and the Tigris-Euphrates river systems. The rest is from winter rain and underground layer of water-bearing porous stone, earth, or gravel. Despite the scarcity, the fact that rivers and lakes in the region are polluted mainly by industrial and domestic wastes is dramatic. (Bakir, 2001) The Nile basin has a large drainage basin and nine countries share it, the Euphrates and Tigris are shared by Turkey, Iraq and Syria and Turkey, Syria, Iraq and Iran, respectively. The Jordan River is one of the small international basins in the world shared by Syria, Jordan, Israel and Lebanon. However, the scarcity of the water supply brings complexities to allocation problem and it adds to Arab –Israeli conflict. (Kliot, 2005)

The use of total water supply in agricultural production, 80%, is significantly higher than the domestic (17%) and industrial use (17%). The mismanagement of agricultural activity plays a crucial role on the water security issue.

The data available in The Statistical Year Book 2012 and 2013 of Food and Agriculture Organization of the United Nations (FAO), shows that in the recent decade the international food and agricultural markets have been experiencing very high price volatilities, directly and adversely affecting the importer countries' food security. Creating a self-sufficient food market is seen as an important task in the region. Governments provide subsidies to the market which amounts to $21.6 billion or 0.7% of the total GDP in 2011 and the irrigation water charges are negligible in most of the countries. The agrarian reform of 50's and 60's which redistributed the land to peasants to smooth out the income inequality and to please an important proportion of the society was mainly targeting to increase the agricultural production. (Warriner, 1962) Although the emancipation of peasantry was resulted to an extent, the targeted level of agricultural production efficiency was not achieved. (Clawson et al., 1971, Springborg, 1977)

Today, governments in the region exerts efforts to improve water supply by investing on large-scaled projects such as desalination, dam construction, inter-basin water transfers, tapping fossil ground water aquifers, and importing virtual water. Sowers et al. (2011) discuss the efficiency of the supply side policies and emphasize the importance of management of water demand. Our investigation on the regional data and theoretical literature points that which of the supply or demand side of water problem should be focused in policies depend on other regional structures. Solving the water and food security problem is one of the most important steps taken in the way of achieving a sustainable growth.

Policies that are provided to cure problems of market economies supported by the growth theories should be carefully updated for the region taking the differences of the region. Indeed, the case of the emancipation of peasantry and the land reform of 50's and 60's can be interpreted as a good step in providing support to entrepreneurial activities. However, missing the creation of individual incentives to achieve profit together with lack of know-how of the new landowners in managing the agricultural activities drew the limits of the production efficiency. Similarly, the privatization of many sectors would share the same destiny with agrarian reform. In that respect, not only the fiscal and monetary policies, but also the supportive/ complementary policies to create the pre-conditions for economic growth play crucial role to foster economic growth and development.

How the policies are practiced by the governments in the region is also of significant importance. The governmental structures in MENA countries are highly dominated by autocracies, religious principles affect economic decisions in the region as well as the cultural life, markets lack basic mechanisms, and most of all, conflicts in the region is the biggest obstacle that prevents any kind of development.

Governance in MENA

Governance is broadly defined as "The traditions and institutions by which authority in a country is exercised" by Kaufmann et al (1999). United Nations Development Programme (UNDP) defines governance as "The exercise of economic, political, and administrative authority to manage a country's affairs at all levels." According to the International Institute of Administrative Sciences, the governance is different than government, and it involves the interaction between the formal institutions and the civil society.

Defining the "good" governance is not a straight forward issue. UNDP (1997) emphasizes the importance of participatory, transparent, accountable, effective and equitable governance. A good governance is supposed to be supported by the rule of law. Representation of each and every different layers of the society in the reallocation process in achieving social and economic development is critical. Public sector management, accountability, legal framework for development, and transparency and information are the key concepts in defining the good governance. Interesting more on the policy management requirements of the governance, World Bank provides a set of governance indicators developed by Kaufmann et al. (2010). Worldwide Governance Indicators (WGI) aim to assess the quality of governance using a research data set provided by a large number of enterprise, citizen and expert survey respondents in industrial and developing countries is used. WGI has six dimensions: Voice and Accountability, Political Stability and Absence of Violence, Government Effectiveness, Regulatory Quality, Rule of Law, Control of Corruption. Estimates are degreed from -2.5 (weakest) to 2.5 (strongest). Table 3 shows the regional averages constructed from the data provided by World Bank. MENA has significantly less scores in all dimensions in compared to other developing regions.

Table 3. World Governance Index (WGI) estimate scores

Averages / Dimensions	MENA	Latin America and Caribbean	South Asia	Sub-Saharan Africa	Europe and Central Asia	North America	East Asia and Pacific
Control of Corruption	-0,2	0,1	-0,6	-0,6	0,4	1,5	0,2
Government Effectiveness	-0,8	0,1	-0,5	-0,7	0,6	1,4	0,1
Political Stability and Absence of Violence/ Terrorism	-0,3	0,2	-1,1	-0,5	0,4	0,9	0,5
Regulatory Quality	-0,2	0,0	-0,7	-0,6	0,6	1,4	0,0
Voice and Accountability	-1,0	0,2	-0,5	-0,7	0,4	1,2	0,2
Rule of Law	-0,1	-0,1	-0,6	-0,6	0,5	1,5	0,3

Source: http://www.resourcegovernance.org/rgi

Whether the democracy is both a necessary and sufficient condition for economic growth is another question, it obviously offers suitable conditions for a market economy to grow. In that respect, questioning the existence of democracy in the region is an important issue, although the answer is obvious. Even in a most broad definition, democracy requires the supreme power to be vested in the people and exercised directly by them or by their elected agents under a free electoral system. However, the practical issues regarding how the power is vested in the people and exercised by them or by representative agents cause a lot of trouble in defining and measuring the democracy in a country. Dahl (1971) points out that the democracy has two dimensions; one is related with public contestation and the other is related with public participation. After Dahl's set of indices, (followed by Gasil 1991, Bollen 1980, 1991, Hadenius 1992) many other measures attempt to scale democracy in countries over years: Economist Intelligence Unit Democracy Index (EIU), Freedom House Index, Neuer Index der Demokratie, Polity index, Polyarchy Dataset, Unified Democracy Scores, Vanhanen's Index of Democracy. Although the list is not full, democracy scores related to MENA are significantly beyond the average. Table 4 shows the three years of EIU Democracy Index which ranges between 0 (most authoritarian) to 10 (most democratic). MENA is the least democratic region in the world. Similarly, Freedom House Index which classifies countries as "free", "partly free" and "not free", measures only Israel as free, Kuwait, Lebanon, Morocco, Tunisia and Egypt as partly free and the rest as not free in 2013.

Once the constitutional democracy is set naturally in a society as it is the case for Western societies, the market economy may be expected to work, properly - Even

Table 4. EIU Democracy Index across regions

Region	2010	2011	2012
North America	8,63	8,59	8,59
Western Europe	8,45	8,4	8,44
Latin America and Carribean	6,37	6,35	6,36
Asia and Austraila	5,53	5,51	5,56
Central and Eastern Europe	5,55	5,5	5,51
Sub-Saharan Africa	4,23	4,32	4,33
MENA	3,52	3,62	3,73
World	5,46	5,49	5,52

Source: Democracy Index 2010, 2011 and 2012 Reports

though the 2008 crisis makes one think about it twice. However, it is not easy to enforce democracy in societies where the preconditions for constitutional democracy are not fulfilled, and it is naïve to wait for a quick positive result. Zakaria (1997) discusses how promotion of democracy in developing countries may cause democracy without constitutional liberalism that produces centralized regimes, ethnic competition, conflict and war.

International democracy aids aim to develop democracy. Huber (2008) defines democracy assistance as "the type of foreign policy that aims explicitly at positively and actively initiating democratization, supporting democratization or strengthening democracy, as well as human rights in foreign countries." He compares the democracy assistance by the US and the EU with respect to the substance, method and recipient of the aids. Both support NGO's related to women, the media and human rights. In general, aids are provided for civil society, political parties and elections and state institutions. Even though it fluctuates over time, the US democracy assistance has been continued since 1990. At the beginning of 2014, in order to support the democracy and governance programming in MENA region, the Obama administration requested $298.3 million from the congress which is almost 2/3 of the one in previous fiscal year. It looks like that the failure of Arab Spring or in most optimistic view the sluggish stage of region's democratization process make international actors to hesitate over democracy assistance.

The Arab Spring which refers a series of revolutionary anti-government non-violent and violent protests and demonstrations, uprisings and armed rebellion that started at the end of 2013 was a breakthrough event and had sharp economic, political and social effects on the region. Protests gave rise to economic, political and in some cases governmental changes in Libya, Egypt, Tunisia, Kuwait, Yemen, Jordan Saudi Arabia, Morocco, Bahrein and Oman. Major conflicts in Sudan and civil war in Iraq and Syria are still going on. The last wave of Israel- Palestine conflict which dates back late 1940's and is very wide-ranging, inflamed the quarrels among the other countries in region. The civil wars and conflicts causing a lot of deaths are turning the hopes on democratization process off.

Along the history of the MENA region, governance of countries changes in a wide range of political regimes which does not include the democracy. After the socialist waves between late 50's and late 90's, which is different from all other forms of socialism in the world and shaped by the Islamic rules, monarchies, dictatorships, autocratic regimes are mostly dominant in the region. After the World War I, the fall of Ottoman Empire and the rise of Republic of Turkey have changed the future of the region forever. The world's superpowers interest on the region with a lot of subsequent political, economic and even cultural interventions that were generally not focused on the region's existing inner dynamics gave rise today's economic and politic conditions with an extraordinary and complex national relations in the region.

Post-Conflict Environment and Government Policies

MENA has always been a scene for, and sometimes subject of, conflicts and wars which give rise today's very complex and confusing economic, political and cultural network under the effect of external forces and internal dynamics. A wide range of religion and ethnic roots have crucial roles in this dynamic. Islam with its different sects is the major religion. Besides the three Abrahamic religions, minorities such as Druze, Yazidi, Baha'i and Zoroastrianism exist. Arabs, Jews, Kurds, Egyptians and Persians live together, not peacefully sometimes. Recent conflicts between two major sects of Islam, Sunni and Shi'a, and between Kurds and Arabs are being most influential than any other time.

Each and every conflict and war have characteristics that are both unique and generic to others in the region. Analysis of these characteristics is beyond the aim of this study. However, the social and economic reasons and results of the conflicts are directly related to policy making process. The policy makers act regarding the short-term conflict resolutions instead of the long-term growth and development. Considering the Iran-Iraq war between 1980-1988, Gulf War between 1990-1991, Iraq war between 2003-2011, Arab-Israeli conflicts beginning with War in 1948, civil wars following Arab spring or the recent ISIS war, it is not wrong to claim that the allocation of natural resources such as oil and especially scarce water sources or fertile arable lands among different religious and ethnic groups has been and is the main cause of conflicts and wars throughout the history. On the other hand, even after the colonial period, first the United Kingdom and then the United States and former USSR (United Soviet Socialist Republics) and now Russia and China are being effective and competing against each other for having potent in the region.

MENA economies are sharply affected by the conflicts in terms of both explicit costs such as loss of labor, physical and human capital, increases in health spending, decreases in productivities, and increases in international debts, and implicit costs such as environmental pollution, high risks of epidemic diseases, decreases in motivation to produce, weakening international trade relations, increase in transaction costs and concessions on policies to resolve conflicts.

The government policies are directed to solve conflicts and post-conflict problems regarding both the domestic politics and international relations. High level of military expenses, the requirement to focus on short-term policies in order to ease the effect of conflicts and wars such as providing huge amount of energy and food subsidies, restrictions in generating government's revenue, pervasive trade policies because of post-conflict political restrictions are only measurable effects on government policies. Conflicts and post-conflict problems challenge the long-term development policies that require increasing investments on specific fields such as education, human rights and necessary institutions for development.

Explicitly, the region has the highest military expenditure per GDP throughout the history since the data is available. The Table 5 shows the years of highest and lowest military expenses of MENA as a percent of GDP, comparing with the other regions. Almost 6% share of military expense in GDP and its growth rate starting from 2008 is certainly remarkable. According to the IHS Jane's Annual Defence Budgets Review in February 2014, defense spending across the MENA region grew by %12.1 which is the highest growth rate of defense spending in the world. The report reveals that Saudi Arabia, Oman, Iraq and Bahrain are featured in the top five growth markets, and defense spending in MENA accounts for %7.8 of worldwide expenditure in 2014.

Being surrounded by a post-conflict environment, the subsidies are widely used by governments to provide short term resolution to social problems. Especially,

Table 5. Military expenses (% GDP)

Country Name	1988	1991	1996	2001	2008	2009	2011	2013
East Asia & Pacific	1,41	1,46	1,44	1,47	1,63	1,74	1,65	1,73
Europe & Central Asia	2,83	2,58	2,17	1,95	1,86	1,98	1,84	1,87
Latin America & Caribbean	1,94	1,58	1,47	1,32	1,31	1,43	1,32	1,32
MENA	7,95	11,6	5,93	6,56	4,11	4,96	4,56	5,93
North America	5,26	4,3	3,21	2,83	3,94	4,35	4,23	3,54
South Asia	3,86	3,31	2,94	3,02	2,60	2,84	2,60	2,51
World	3,43	2,96	2,32	2,26	2,42	2,66	2,46	2,34

Source: http://data.worldbank.org/indicator/MS.MIL.XPND.GD.ZS

subsidies in food and energy sectors have a significant part in governments' budget in the region. In natural resource abundant countries, high level of subsidies is related to the redistribution of surplus created by the abundant resource. Governments aim to reduce shocking impacts of large swings in commodity prices on society. Especially in the post- conflict context, public's expectation to share countries' wealth is generally fulfilled via subsidies. However, subsidy policies are neither oriented for social protection, nor cost-effective. The lack of comprehensive social security system is balanced by supported real wages and incomes and low prices on widely consumed products, so that the governments save the day instead of investing on intensive social security policies that may have permanent resolutions only in the long-term. Similarly, the industrial subsidies such as below-market-price energy inputs are used in order to support certain industries. In some cases, the target is to provide protection to employment in the private sector and in other cases, it is to recover the losses incurred by state-owned enterprises that results from inefficient market structures and subsidized prices. (Sdralevic et al. 2014)

Figure 6 shows that including only petroleum, electricity, natural gas and coal, the pretax subsidies, in the region amounted to 48% of world subsidies. Petroleum products have the highest share, which is about 50%, of the total cost of pretax energy subsidies ($119.3 billion or 4.3% of GDP). Natural gas with 23% ($55.2 billion or 2% of GDP) and electricity with 26% ($62 billion or 2.3% of GDP) follow. On the other hand, food subsidies amounts to $21.6 billion or 0.7% of GDP in 2011. Subsidies on water, financial products, medicines, housing, and other products

Figure 6. Total pretax energy subsidies by region, 2011 ($492 billion; 0.7% of GDP)
Prepared based on data by Sdralevic et al. 2014.

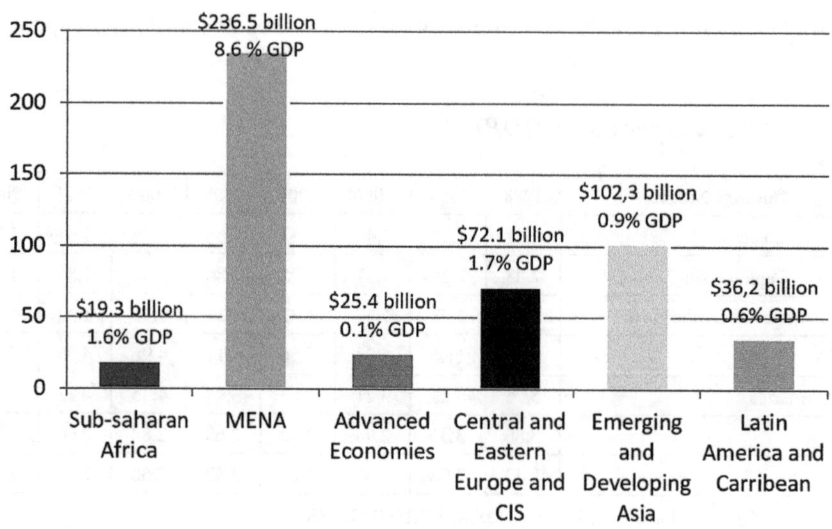

and services that are difficult to measure are maintained in the region, but are not included in the overall estimates of IMF.

Government revenues are generated from mostly oil, natural resources, tax revenues and grants. The distribution of sources varies across countries. Especially in GCC, the share of tax in total revenue is not significant. Figure 7 shows the average value of tax share in government revenue which is the percentage of the total revenue excluding the grants between 2008 and 2012. The oil and other natural resources are the main sources in countries such as Kuwait, Oman, UAE, Iran and Qatar. There are additional fees, fines and rents such as revenue obtained from Suez Canal in Egypt.

Business Environment, Financial Markets, and Islamic Rules' Effects

The role of financial markets in raising the productivity of investments, supporting a strong business environment is crucial for both entrepreneurs and the macroeconomic growth and social development. There exists a two way relation between financial markets and firms: As the firms demand higher investment, financial markets expand, and as the financial markets support higher level of investment, the firm activity accelerates in the economy.

Figure 7. Average tax revenues as a percentage of total government revenue, 2008-2011
Source: http://data.worldbank.org/

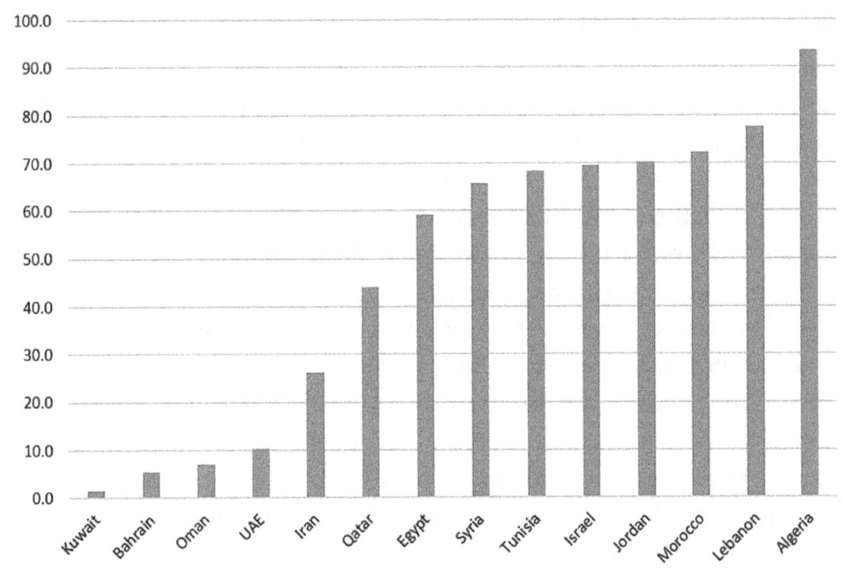

The commercial laws that are defined as a transpose of the European rules by Mallat (2000) and regulations in the region shape the private sector. Governments are dominant and regulatory. State –owned enterprises are significant, and family firms that operate in highly protected markets constitute a large part of the existing private sector. Because of the weak enforcement and laws relating to bankruptcy and liquidation, the exit of firms from business is restricted as well as the entry. Licensing and inspection rules are strict and enforcements of these rules are unpredictable. Allocation of key resources such as credits, physical inputs and infrastructural needs is regulated. Governments apply price controls to subsidize the consumers. In this business environment, it is not easy to find the appropriate conditions to start a business for an entrepreneur. Entrepreneurs are old and had paid jobs before becoming entrepreneurs. Firms are either small with less than 10 workers or very large. Firms report low productivity of labor and capital. (Fawzy, 2002, MacElwee and Al-Riyami, 2003) Especially after the onset of Arab Spring, with undermined business confidence, affected tourist arrivals, and depressed domestic and foreign direct investment, incentives of entrepreneurs to start and run a business is lower. (Yusuf, 2014)

Access to industrial land is a problem in the region. Land markets are segmented with large price differences between privately and publicly owned land and between rural and urban areas. Most of the economic activity is clustered in big cities where the land is restricted. Although the land is limited, there exist idle land because of many reasons such as that the public enterprise that own the land is bankrupt or that the private owner hold the land to increase the price. (Devlin, 2010) Access to credit is another problem. On the average 40% of the firms reveals the credit access as a major constraint. (Beck & Honohan, 2008).

In this type of business environment where a lot of uncertainty exits, the weakness of financial markets is not surprising. Existing studies that are of limited number shows that financial markets are thin and strongly regulated, as the governments impose restrictions and price controls. Creane et al. (2006) develop a comprehensive set of indices to assess the financial market's development in the region. Financial structure is diversified. The GCC countries, especially Bahrain, are in a different position then the rest of the region, in terms of the institutional environment, financial openness and use of the monetary policies which guarantee the long term development of markets. However, government ownership is significant, and market forces cannot properly work in the whole region.

Pearce (2011) investigates the state of financial inclusion in the region, and shows that MENA is behind the regions of similar income on the key indicators of bank deposits and loans accounts per population. World Bank report (2012) shows that credit to private sector ranges from 60% of GDP (Jordan, Kuwait, Lebanon) to 30% of GDP (Algeria, Syria, Yemen). In MENA, the number of firms that use the financial institutions to finance their investment demand is relatively lower than the number of firms in other developing regions. Firms confront much higher collateral requirements to access loans, in compared to their comparators.

Stock markets in the region are small and highly volatile. The share of Foreign Direct Investment (FDI) net inflows in GDP in 2013 is 1,68% in MENA in compared to 3,5% in Latin America and Caribbean and 3,1% in East Asia and Pacific. Iqbal and Nabli (2004) point that non-GCC countries, received net inflows of FDI of about $2.2 billion in 2000 which is nine times less than $19 billion that the group of five Eastern European countries (Czech Republic, Hungary, Poland, Turkey and Russia) together received, three times less than $8 billion what the three East Asian countries (Malaysia, Philippines, and Thailand) received, and twenty two times less than $50 billion what the group of four Latin American countries (Bolivia, Chile, Mexico, and Brazil) received. It shows the potential of the region. However, as Chau et.al (2014) shows that that political uncertainty increased after Arab Spring contributes to the financial volatility. Malik and Awadallah (2013) claim that Arab Spring causes the replacement of old political players with new ones. However, it only led to re-configuration of political power leaving the economic and institutional problems unsolved. With an increasing political uncertainty neither the financial markets completed its global integration nor the business environment improved.

The commercial law that highly influences and shapes the business environment in MENA strongly reflects the effects of Islam which is the widest religion in MENA region. Saudi Arabia, Sudan, Iran, United Arab Emirates and Qatar are governed by Islamic law, sharia. In Algeria, Djibouti, Egypt, Lebanon, Morocco, Tunisia sharia applies in some issues such as marriage, divorce and inheritance. In general, the effect of religious culture on economy is significant all around the region. Qur'an which doesn't include many economic regulations, specifies rules related to the inheritance in detail. Because the extended relatives also reserve a specified amount, the accumulation of capital over generations is prevented. Although a system called waqif which does not exist in Qur'an was created over time to keep family money over generations being tax-free, it never became an efficient way of accumulating the capital. Kuran (2003) discusses the role of Islamic inheritance law on capital accumulation. The lack of corporate structures in Islamic law gave rise of the waqif which are not sufficient to create the conditions for a strong private sector and human and physical capital accumulation. In this regard, the main reason of why MENA economies transferred from reasonable to sluggish levels throughout the 18th century can be identified as the legal infrastructural stagnation. Indeed, Islamic rules of Qur'an do not directly manage the economy either at a macro or a micro level. Two principals regarding the economic decisions were followed in the region: The first one was provisionism that focused on the supplies of essential commodities required for urban life favoring the imports. The second one was fiscalism that mainly focused on raising the revenue in the treasury. Instead of governmental infrastructural investments, the state was directly financing the public goods such as mosques, hospitals and schools. Mainly, waqif founded by rich families were managing the financial flow to support who needed the offered service. They were responsible from the redistribution of income. By the rules, it was possible to protect the family's money from taxes and inheritance rules. Although the system worked partially, it distorted the reallocation of the surplus created by the production. Because the founders of waqif were mainly the close relatives of the rulers and highest officials, they took decisions parallel with ruler's interest. However, they were helping just enough so that an alternative system was not strongly questioned and civil societies couldn't become powerful.

While the market economy was rooting in the Western Europe by naturally finding necessary pre-conditions, the most of the Middle Eastern countries' private sectors, except the oil market, isolated from the international markets. The absence of skills, know-how and accumulated capital and cultural reluctance to be in a network with Western societies worsened the backwards of economies. It should be emphasized that there is no rule against the market economy in Islamic law. Islamic law does not conflict with modern economic developments except issues regarding the interest rates and extreme consumerism. Although creation of the preconditions for market economy such as existence of financial markets, property rights and the entrepreneurial abilities have been prevented in the region, that was most probably not because of the Islamic law itself. The state-centered development policies compatible with Islamic law were not enough to create the required incentives for the development of human capital and financial markets. Moreover, some economic reforms regarding the banking system, stock markets and trade agreements bring the MENA economies closer to the international markets.

Although Islamic banking majorly centers on the GCC countries, Iran and Malesia and constitutes only 1% of the global financial assets, it is a growing sector at an annual rate of approximately 18% between 2009 and 2013, and is projected to grow by an average of almost 20% a year to 2018. Islamic finance assets grew from almost US$200 billion in 2003 to almost US$1.8 trillion in 2013 (International Monetary Fund, 2015). It's not hard to understand why in Cameron's administration finds the future of Islamic finance bright and London volunteers to become a center for it (UK Excellence in Islamic Finance, n.d.).

Labor Market

The region has the highest unemployment rate following Sub-Saharan Africa and it almost doubles the world's average in 2013. World Bank data shows that the unemployment rates are not volatile since 1990 and are between 10% and 11%. As of 2013, the youth unemployment in the region is so severe that it increases up to 51% in Libya. The percentage of unemployed women in the female labor force is more than 20%.

The most significant characteristic of the labor market in the region is that it is dominated by the public sector. In the GCC countries, public employment is an important way of distributing oil revenues to nationals. Having small populations, the GCC countries have been applying open door policies in the labor market for a long time period. IMF data shows that the expatriate labor ranges from 50% of labor in Saudi Arabia to 90% in United Arab Emirates in early 2000's. (Fasano and Goyal, 2004). The labor policies have changed starting from late 1980's. At first, governments and state-owned enterprises took the leading role. Then, in order to nationalize the private sector workforce, mandatory measures such as quantitative regulations have been used. However, enforcing the use of national labor force in private sector had its own drawbacks and created some complexities especially in the long-run. Lower productivities of the nationals together with easy access of private companies to expatriate labor challenge the nationalization policy in labor market. The nationalization policies followed by countries diversify in the region and named after the country such as Emiratization, Omanization etc. The size of labor force and unemployment rates are the effective variables on policies followed. From Bahrein, Oman, Saudi Arabia to Qatar practices different types of mandatory measures. However, neither the job creation process nor the management of existing business environment looks sufficient to realize the nationalization programs. (Al-Waqfi et al., 2014)

The dominance of the government in markets through regulatory actions and state-owned enterprises leads the segmentation of the labor market. Fasano and Goyal (2004) shows that most of the new jobs created by the private sector is in non-oil, services sectors. Paying low wages and requiring low skilled labor, these jobs do not appeal the nationals. Due to high regulation in most of the region, the informality increases. At the same time, the adjustment of the labor market is prevented. Highly protected jobs make the labor almost a fixed input in the production. Thus, firms hesitate to offer new jobs causing higher unemployment rates and segmentation in the market. It also effects the motivation of nationals in taking education. Protected jobs offered by governments have high demand and nationals do not have the incentive to improve their skills over the levels required by these jobs.

The World Bank data shows that the percentage of the population age 15 and above who can, with understanding, read and write a short, simple statement on their everyday life was only about 80% and 5% less than the world's average in 2010. As of 2013, the MENA region has 17 students for every one teacher (a pupil-teacher ratio of 17:1) compared to the world average of 24:1. However, the knowledge level is lower compared to their counterparts in the developed countries as it is justified by international test scores. The quality of teachers is a main explanatory variable. Countries in the region face shortage of teachers. Therefore, those hired to serve as teachers are often not adequately qualified for the position. Most of the countries in the region support the private schools and paid education. The private education sector in MENA is the fastest growing according to report 'Trends in Private Education Investment and Expansion in MENA 2014' by Education Investment.

A QUICK LOOK INTO GROWTH THEORIES

Practices over years have evidently shown that policies which follow Solow's growth model (1956), mainly based upon physical capital accumulation were not sustainable. As the economic structure has changed all around the world, new insights have been required in explaining, analyzing and designing economic theories, policies and practices.

New growth theories following Romer (1989) and Barro (1991) define the growth as a perpetual motion machine. The key concept of the theory is knowledge which is not subject to diminishing returns. Accumulated human capital causes innovations to occur which make capital and labor more productive, and which affect consumption side of the economy as well. The growth is claimed to be self-feeding and sustainable with a strong emphasis on human capital. (Barro et al., 1995; Benhabib & Spiegel,1994; Temple, 1999, 2001a; Easterly & Levine, 2001; Vandenbussche et al., 2006; Cohen & Soto, 2007). Most of the endogenous growth models take for granted the incentives to innovate and to earn higher profits. Indeed, what makes the growth sustainable are mostly the incentives and accumulation of human capital.

More recent criticisms on the growth theories focus on the missing explanation of how the stable equilibrium can be achieved. The strong relation between technologies, institutions and industry are neglected. Institutions related to markets, property rights, monetary exchange and international trade as well as the education and health programs are crucial for creating the proper incentives and fostering the human capital productivity. In that respect, central authorities' direct control over economies can be criticized, and use of policies in action which provide appropriate conditions for individual producers to innovate and to produce effectively can be suggested. The independent and reliable institutions are supposed to govern the required systems such as financial and legal systems. (Nelson, 2005)

There exist substantial theoretical and empirical studies suggesting that financial systems become more developed as countries get richer. At the same time, financial developments accelerate the economic growth. A weakness in the financial system can cause systematic problems for the whole economy. Differences between growth rates of market-oriented economies and of centrally planned economies are put forward by many studies. (Demirgüç-Kunt & Levine, 2004; Stiglitz, 2000; Alfaro et al., 2004; Bruno et al., 2012) In addition to open financial systems, the positive impact of international trade on economic growth through efficient use of resources is theoretically accepted. (Krugman P., & Obsfeld M., 2000) Although the empirical studies in the literature does not fully support the theories (Frankel, J. A. & Romer, D., 1999; Yanıkkaya, 2003; Rodrik, 2005; Herzer D., 2013; Shahbaz,, 2012), existence of the long-run positive effects and that the extend of trade impact on growth is highly related to the policies on education, technology and institutional quality is widely accepted.

Starting from 80's, including MENA economies; many developing countries and centrally-planned economies in Europe shifted their growth strategies towards market-orientation. Complementary policies that support development of financial systems, openness to trade and accumulation of human capital were enacted. (Devlin, 2010) Some of developing countries such as China seem like to achieve growth targets. However, inequality and poverty measures do not mostly follow the fast growth trend. (Kenwood et al., 2013; Kanbur, 2008) Indeed, according to neoclassical growth theories; because accumulation of physical capital is provided by increasing propensity to save, the growth process is stimulated by income inequality. Therefore, a tolerable level of income inequality has a positive impact on physical capital accumulation. However, when human capital is replaced by physical capital, inequality is not anymore a binding constraint for growth. (Galor & Moav, 2004) In this respect, creation of the preconditions for entrepreneurial activities is of crucial importance. As long as the supportive policies for small firms and entrepreneurs are practiced by governments, the economic growth that is achieved by economic activity triggered by human capital, technological advances and profit oriented entrepreneurs can be accompanied by social development and improvements in income equality.

Whether centrally planned or not, the use of government expenditures is always effective in growth and development. Literature shows that the effect of government expenditures on the economic growth is ambiguous. Recent studies shows the importance of type of expenditures in identifying the relationship. Expenditures in the form of investments that provide the required infrastructural structures and accelerate the accumulation of physical capital and labor, increase the quantity and efficiency of factors of production and lead to higher growth. Expenditures on health, education and other services supports the accumulation of human capital, increase the productivity and lead to higher growth. However, beyond an optimal level, the government expenditures may crowd out the private spending and cause inefficiencies in both the factor markets and the final goods markets. According to neoclassical approach increasing tax rates negatively affects the supply side of the economy and it distorts the markets so that economic activity decreases. With respect to the new growth theory, the negative effect of higher tax rates is even higher because the level of technology is negatively affected. However, what Barro (1990) calls as productive government spending may lead to higher level of human capital accumulation and technological improvements offset the negative effects of taxes on the economic activity. (Bergh et al., 2011) Berg and Henrekson (2011) provides a survey on the relation between the government size and the economic growth. They also provides an explanation to the contradictory results in the literature. They suggest that social trust increases the big governments' impact on economic growth. Moreover, market-friendly policies followed by big governments compensate the inefficiencies in the markets created by the high taxes and expenditures.

ENTREPRENEURSHIP AS A GROWTH ENGINE IN MENA

This study brings different literatures together in analyzing the importance of entrepreneurial activities for a sustainable economic growth accompanied by social development. The needs of MENA region in its growth and development process are questioned by taking the existing macroeconomic, political and cultural measures into account. An overall look of the region shows that the countries are from a very wide range of variety and it is almost impossible to adopt a unique formula prepared for economic growth or social development. Especially, the practiced receipts of Western or East Asian world are likely to fall far away from the target. Yet, the measures of region shows us that the entrepreneurial activities may be an answer to many problems at once: Economic growth, income equality and social development. Besides, MENA region has a strong potential to host and enjoy the entrepreneurial activities.

In the region, rich natural resource sectors, oil, gas and minerals, are dominant and creates a pervasive revenue effect in economic activity. The giant governments create an inefficient production process and labor markets are segmented. The unemployment, especially youth unemployment is a major problem not only in economic terms but also accelerating the social unrest and political instability. The scarcity of arable land and water adds a lot of trouble to the existing religious, ethnical and historical conflicts between different groups and countries in the region. Climate change and estimated average temperatures within 30 years which is not suitable to live in makes the problems even worse.

In this respect, the entrepreneurial activities supported by governments in non-oil sectors may solve the problems. Specifically, some sectors have a strong capacity to be expanded by entrepreneurs. Although it is not a complete list, the solar energy, biotechnology, chemical industries, water and air cleaning, agricultural production, Islamic finance, private education are all the sectors on which entrepreneurs can find profit opportunities when the required regulations and policies are supported by the governments. Supporting the infrastructural necessities for human capital and technology required in these sectors and proving the protective and encouraging laws for the entrepreneurs, the central authorities' destructive power is transformed into a creative one. Particularly, the support provided to small and medium enterprises, women and youth plays a crucial role. The successful start-ups would boost the profit incentives of new entrepreneurs and start a perpetual motion in growth accompanied by social development.

The study shows that the use of policies which accelerates the innovation and technology creation in the specified industries enlightens the way to growth and development. However, the microeconomic conditions of each sector and how the firms, new entrepreneurs and governments should proceed in their own decision making process by taking both the individual and social interests into consideration should be analyzed industry by industry and country by country. This type of microeconomic analysis are very much valuable for the macroeconomic policies.

REFERENCES

Adams, R. H. Jr, & Page, J. (2003). Poverty, inequality and growth in selected Middle East and North Africa countries, 1980–2000. *World Development*, *31*(12), 2027–2048. doi:10.1016/j.worlddev.2003.04.004

Alfaro, L., Chanda, A., Kalemli-Ozcan, S., & Sayek, S. (2004). FDI and economic growth: The role of local financial markets. *Journal of International Economics*, *64*(1), 89–112. doi:10.1016/S0022-1996(03)00081-3

Bakir, H. A. (2001). Sustainable wastewater management for small communities in the Middle East and North Africa. *Journal of Environmental Management*, *61*(4), 319–328. doi:10.1006/jema.2000.0414 PMID:11383104

Barro, R. J. (1990). Government spending in a simple model of endogenous growth. *Journal of Political Economy*, *98*(5), 103–125. doi:10.1086/261726

Barro, R. J. (1991). Economic growth in a cross section of countries. *The Quarterly Journal of Economics*, *106*(2), 407–443. doi:10.2307/2937943

Barro, R. J., Mankiw, N. G., & Sala-i-Martin, X. (1995). *Capital mobility in neo-classical models of growth (No. w4206)*.National Bureau of Economic Research.

Beck, T., & Honohan, P. (2008). *Finance for all? Policies and pitfalls in expanding access* (Vol. 41792). World Bank Publications.

Beetham, D. (Ed.). (1994). *Defining and measuring democracy* (Vol. 36). Sage.

Benhabib, J., & Spiegel, M. M. (1994). The role of human capital in economic development evidence from aggregate cross-country data. *Journal of Monetary Economics*, *34*(2), 143–173. doi:10.1016/0304-3932(94)90047-7

Bergh, A., & Magnus, H. (2011). Government size and growth: A survey and interpretation of the evidence. *Journal of Economic Surveys*, *25*(5), 872–897. doi:10.1111/j.1467-6419.2011.00697.x

Birdsall, N., Ross, D., & Sabot, R. (1995). Inequality and growth reconsidered: Lessons from East Asia. *The World Bank Economic Review*, *9*(3), 477–508. doi:10.1093/wber/9.3.477

Bruno, G., De Bonis, R., & Silvestrini, A. (2012). Do financial systems converge? New evidence from financial assets in OECD countries. *Journal of Comparative Economics*, *40*(1), 141–155. doi:10.1016/j.jce.2011.09.003

BudisJ. (2014). Retrieved fromhttp://www.newrepublic.com/article/112278/paul-krugman-vs-joseph-stiglitz-inequality-slowing-recovery

Chau, F., Deesomsak, R., & Wang, J. (2014). Political uncertainty and stock market volatility in the Middle East and North African (MENA) countries. *Journal of International Financial Markets, Institutions and Money*, *28*, 1–19. doi:10.1016/j.intfin.2013.10.008

Clawson, M., Landsberg, H. H., & Alexander, L. T. (1971). *The agricultural potential of the Middle East*. Academic Press.

Cohen, D., & Soto, M. (2007). Growth and human capital: Good data, good results. *Journal of Economic Growth*, *12*(1), 51–76. doi:10.1007/s10887-007-9011-5

Creane, S., Goyal, R., Mobarak, A. M., & Sab, R. (2006). Measuring financial development in the Middle East and North Africa: A new database. *IMF Staff Papers*, 479–511.

Dahl, R. A. (1973). *Polyarchy: participation and opposition*. Yale University Press.

Demirgüç-Kunt, A., & Levine, R. (Eds.). (2004). *Financial structure and economic growth: A cross-country comparison of banks, markets, and development*. MIT Press.

Devlin, J. (2010). *Challenges of Economic Development in the Middle East and North Africa Region* (Vol. 8). World Scientific. doi:10.1142/6762

Easterly, W., & Levine, R. (2001). What have we learned from a decade of empirical research on growth? Its Not Factor Accumulation: Stylized Facts and Growth Models. *The World Bank Economic Review*, *15*(2), 177–219. doi:10.1093/wber/15.2.177

Fasano-Filho, M. U., & Goyal, R. (2004). Emerging strains in GCC labor markets (No. 4-71). International Monetary Fund.

Fawzy, S. (Ed.). (2002). *Globalization and firm competitiveness in the Middle East and North Africa region* (Vol. 3). World Bank Publications. doi:10.1596/0-8213-4989-9

Forbes, K. J. (2000). A Reassessment of the Relationship between Inequality and Growth. *The American Economic Review*, *90*(4), 869–887. doi:10.1257/aer.90.4.869

Frankel, J. A., & Romer, D. (1999). Does Trade Cause Growth? *The American Economic Review*, *89*(3), 379–399. doi:10.1257/aer.89.3.379

Galor, O. (2011). *Inequality, human capital formation and the process of development (No. w17058)*. National Bureau of Economic Research. doi:10.3386/w17058

Galor, O., & Moav, O. (2004). From physical to human capital accumulation: Inequality and the process of development. *The Review of Economic Studies*, *71*(4), 1001–1026. doi:10.1111/0034-6527.00312

Hančlová, J., & Tvrdý, L. (2004). *Classification of the Regions. In Multiregional and Regional Models*. Ostrava: Faculty of Economics, Technical University of Ostrava.

Herzer, D. (2013). Cross-Country Heterogeneity and the Trade-Income Relationship. *World Development*, *44*, 194–211. doi:10.1016/j.worlddev.2012.09.014

International Monetary Fund. (2015). *Islamic finance and the role of the IMF*. Retrieved from: http://www.imf.org/external/themes/islamicfinance/

Kanbur, R., & Michael, S. (2008). *Globalization, Growth, and Distribution: Framing the Questions*. World Bank.

Kaufmann, D., Kraay, A., & Zoido-Lobatón, P. (1999). *Aggregating governance indicators* (Vol. 2195). World Bank Publications.

Kenwood, A. G., Graff, M., & Lougheed, A. L. (2013). *Growth of the International Economy, 1820-2015*. Routledge.

Kliot, N. (2005). *Water resources and conflict in the Middle East*. Routledge.

Krugman & Obstfeld. (2000). *International economics: theory and policy*. Addison-Wesley.

Kuran, T. (1997). Islam and Underdevelopment: An Old Puzzle Revisited. *Journal of Institutional and Theoretical Economics*, *153*(1), 41–71.

Kuran, T. (2004). Why the Middle East is Economically Underdeveloped: Historical Mechanisms of Institutional Stagnation. *The Journal of Economic Perspectives*, *18*(3), 71–90. doi:10.1257/0895330042162421

Kuznets, S. (1955). Economic growth and income inequality. *The American Economic Review*, 1–28.

Leftwich, A. (1993). Governance, democracy and development in the Third World. *Third World Quarterly*, *14*(3), 605–624. doi:10.1080/01436599308420345

Munck, G. L. (2009). *Measuring democracy: A bridge between scholarship and politics*. JHU Press.

Nielsen, L. (2011). *Classifications of countries based on their level of development: how it is done and how it could be done*. International Monetary Fund.

Panizza, U. (2002). Income inequality and economic growth: Evidence from American data. *Journal of Economic Growth*, *7*(1), 25–41. doi:10.1023/A:1013414509803

Pearce, D. (2011). *Financial Inclusion in the Middle East and North Africa: Analysis and Roadmap Recommendations*. World Bank Policy Research Working Paper Series.

Perotti, R. (1996). Growth, income distribution, and democracy: What the data say. *Journal of Economic Growth*, *1*(2), 149–187. doi:10.1007/BF00138861

Ravallion, M. (2001). Growth, inequality and poverty: Looking beyond averages. *World Development*, *29*(11), 1803–1815. doi:10.1016/S0305-750X(01)00072-9

Rodrik, D. (2005). Growth strategies.Handbook of Economic Growth, 1, 967-1014.

Romer, P. M. (1989). *What determines the rate of growth and technological change?* (Vol. 279). World Bank Publications.

Santiso, C. (2001). International Co-operation for Democracy and Good Governance: Moving Towards a Second Generation? *European Journal of Development Research*, *13*(1), 154–180. doi:10.1080/09578810108426785

Sdralevich, M. C. A., Sab, M. R., Zouhar, M. Y., & Albertin, G. (2014). *Subsidy Reform in the Middle East and North Africa: Recent Progress and Challenges Ahead*. International Monetary Fund.

Shahbaz, M. (2012). Does trade openness affect long run growth? Cointegration, causality and forecast error variance decomposition tests for Pakistan. *Economic Modelling*, *29*(6), 2325–2339. doi:10.1016/j.econmod.2012.07.015

Solow, R. M. (1956). A contribution to the theory of economic growth. *The Quarterly Journal of Economics*, *70*(1), 65–94. doi:10.2307/1884513

Sowers, J., Vengosh, A., & Weinthal, E. (2011). Climate change, water resources, and the politics of adaptation in the Middle East and North Africa. *Climatic Change*, *104*(3-4), 599–627. doi:10.1007/s10584-010-9835-4

Springborg, R. (1977). New patterns of agrarian reform in the Middle East and North Africa. *The Middle East Journal*, 127–142.

Stiglitz, J. E. (2000). Capital market liberalization, economic growth, and instability. *World Development*, *28*(6), 1075–1086. doi:10.1016/S0305-750X(00)00006-1

Temple, J. (1999). The new growth evidence. *Journal of Economic Literature*, *37*(1), 112–156. doi:10.1257/jel.37.1.112

UK Excellence in Islamic Finance. (n.d.). Retrieved from: https://www.gov.uk/government/uploads/system/uploads/attachment_data/file/367154/UKTI_UK_Excellence_in_Islamic_Finance_Reprint_2014_Spread.pdf

UNDP. (1997). *Governance and Sustainable Human Development*. United Nations Development Programme.

Vandenbussche, J., Aghion, P., & Meghir, C. (2006). Growth, distance to frontier and composition of human capital. *Journal of Economic Growth*, *11*(2), 97–127. doi:10.1007/s10887-006-9002-y

Warriner, D. (1962). Land reform and development in the Middle East. A study of Egypt, Syria, and Iraq. Land reform and development in the Middle East (2nd ed.). Academic Press.

World Bank Group. (Ed.). (2012). *World Development Indicators 2012*. World Bank Publications.

Yanikkaya, H. (2003). Trade Openness and Economic Growth: A Cross-Country Empirical Investigation. *Journal of Development Economics*, *72*(1), 57–89. doi:10.1016/S0304-3878(03)00068-3

Yusuf, S. (2014). *Middle East Transitions: A Long*. Hard Road.

Zakaria, F. (1997). The rise of illiberal democracy. *Foreign Affairs*, *76*(6), 22–43. doi:10.2307/20048274

ENDNOTES

1 The World Bank categorize countries into 5 groups with respect to their gross national income per capita: Low-income, lower-middle- income, upper-middle-income, high-income and high-income OECD countries. The countries in the low- and middle- income groups are labeled as developing.

2 *Source: OPEC Annual Statistical Bulletin 2014*

3 RGI evaluates four key components: Institutional and Legal Setting to assess whether the laws, regulations and institutional practices enable comprehensive disclosures, open and fair competition, and accountability; Reporting Practices to evaluate the actual disclosure of information and reporting practices by government agencies; Safeguards and Quality Controls to measure the checks and oversight mechanisms that guard against conflicts of interest and undue discretion, such as audits; Enabling Environment to understand the broader governance environment generated using over 30 external measures of accountability, government effectiveness, rule of law, corruption and democracy.

Chapter 6

Empowerment Against All Odds:
Women Entrepreneurs in the Middle East and North Africa

Bettina Lynda Bastian
American University of Beirut, Lebanon

ABSTRACT

The number of women-owned businesses worldwide has increased significantly, a development that extends to other parts of the world, such as the Middle East and North Africa (MENA). This region's cultural and socioeconomic idiosyncrasies offer unique perspectives on women entrepreneurship. This article provides a critical overview over the situation of female entrepreneurship in the region, which takes into consideration challenges and opportunities on the level of the individual entrepreneurs, as well as on the macro environmental level. We finally discuss constructive solutions in order to increase the number of women business founders.

INTRODUCTION

Middle Eastern and North African countries (MENA) have made some progress in reducing inequalities between men and women during the past decades, especially since many countries are signatory to the Millennium Development Goals (MDGs) that include the promotion of gender equality and empowerment of women. Entrepreneurship of women has moved into the center of attention. For example, experiences

DOI: 10.4018/978-1-5225-2066-5.ch006

with female entrepreneurship abroad reveal that its acceleration may have similar positive economic effects on countries like the large-scale entry of women into the labor market (Kauffman Foundation, 2014). The potential of female entrepreneurs in the MENA to contribute to growth, development and job creation has therefore received increasing attention by researchers, policy makers and the larger public. The percentage of women entrepreneurs has increased significantly in many countries over the past years, for example in Egypt their share grew from 20% in 2008 up to 35% in 2010 (OECD, 2014). Despite these promising developments, the rates of women that start their own ventures are amongst the lowest rates of general entrepreneurial activities worldwide. Entrepreneurial activities of women aggregate to a strikingly low rate of only 4% (Global Entrepreneurship Monitor (GEM), 2013), with men in most MENA countries establishing more than two thirds of businesses. Women-led businesses in the region are 60% more likely to remain a single person firm without any employees. Moreover, only 1/10 of women in the region expect their business to grow and to hire additional personnel in the coming years (GEM, 2013). Women also tend to perceive less market opportunities than their male counterparts and this gap in the Mena region, again, is the greatest across all global regions (GEM, 2013).

This chapter aims to give an overview over the topic of female venturing in the region and identifies factors that affect women entrepreneurs in their activities. In this context, the chapter will address challenges and opportunities on the level of individual entrepreneurs to show what motivates women in the region to start their own freelance activities. Moreover, we will draw on pivotal macro-environmental factors that were shown in previous research to affect female entrepreneurial behavior.

THE LEVEL OF THE INDIVIDUAL WOMAN: MOTIVATORS AND DE-MOTIVATORS

Push and Pull Factors

On the level of individual entrepreneurs research has been interested to understand motivations and entrepreneurial opinions that underlie actions and behaviors. In this context, scholars often draw on the pull-push model (Uhlaner & Thurik, 2007) and contextualize it within the realm of Middle Eastern societies. Push factors are the result of the dissatisfaction of individuals with their current situation, which could be rooted in organizational issues (e.g. restructuration, lack of flexibility, organizational changes). Moreover, push factors such as the economic situation, unemployment, gender inequality, and others could be found in the macro environment (Verheul et al., 2006). The dissatisfaction of concerned individuals with their labor conditions might make them inclined to select self-employment (Verheul et al., 2006). In numerous studies, women in the region reported problems they faced when trying to integrate into the labor market (Naguib & Jamali, 2014). Already the participation rate of women in the labor market is very low, and averages 23% compared to a world average of 50% (ILO, 2013). Furthermore, there are about twice as many young women unemployed in the region (43.9%) compared to male peers (22.9%) (ILO, 2013). Moreover, women who had employment positions often experienced gender discrimination in the workplace such as pay dispersions and 'glass ceilings' (Jamali, 2009). Other important push factors of women in the region included financial security, lack of job opportunities, and low income, especially for migrant workers and expatriates in the Gulf region (Naguib & Jamali, 2014).

Pull factors, on the other hand, suggest that individuals are attracted to entrepreneurship by a prospect of greater material or non-material benefits, often as a result of favorable conditions and structures, such as technological progress, changes in consumer behavior, policy initiatives in favor of entrepreneurs, and increases in the standard of living (Verheul et al., 2006). Many women in the region seem to be motivated by a combination of both factors. Much research on the topic has been done in the UAE, where pull factors often dominated decisions of women to start their own business. Next to the possibility of a double income for the family, women were especially drawn into entrepreneurship by the prospect of independence and professional accomplishment (Tlaiss, 2013), the possibilities to more flexibly combine family and professional life, as well as by the professional challenge that required a lot of creativity from them (Naguib & Jamali, 2014)

Self-Efficacy

Women were shown to have humble levels of self-confidence regarding their entrepreneurial potential, and that independent from their actual educational and experience level (Boyd and Vozikis, 1994). This phenomenon is referred to as low self-efficacy (Boyd and Vozikis, 1994), which indicates that women have a weak belief in performing well in entrepreneurship, and they tend to value and perceive their skills, experiences and competencies significantly lower than those of men with comparable levels (Chen et al., 1998). This phenomenon was observed with women in different societies across the globe, and it starts at an early age, as research on teenage girls and boys showed, where self-perceptions significantly impacts entrepreneurial options in the future for girls compared to boys (Wilson et al., 2004) and remain a constraint for most women (not for men) even after launching their ventures, with significant effects on venture growth (Kirkwood, 2009). Women seem to be more affected in their career choices by lack of confidence and their own perceptions of self-efficacy than men (Wilson et al., 2007). A lack of self-confidence and self-efficacy starts at an early age, as research on teenage girls and boys showed, where self-perceptions significantly impacts entrepreneurial options in the future for girls compared to boys (Wilson et al., 2004). Such perceptions have been shaped by described gender stereotypes in society that impose certain expectations regarding female behavior long before professional and educational measures can affect female confidence. We will come at a later stage to cultural macro environment in the MENA region that are patriarchal, male-dominated, and characterized by traditional ideas regarding the roles of the different genders in society (Hofstede, 1994; Omair, 2008).

A lot of research in the MENA region shows that women entrepreneurs, against the odds of gendered and traditional societies, display high levels of self-confidence and conviction in their abilities to start and run a business (Zamberi Ahmad, 2011). Especially in very traditional societies in the Gulf or Iran, those women that actually started their own business compensated for the hardships and difficulties imposed on them by norms and traditions with high self-confidence, enthusiasm, and determination (Javadian & Singh 2012; Zamberi Ahmad, 2011). In the Kingdom of Saudi Arabia (KSA) surveys showed that self-confidence is the third biggest motivator for Saudi women entrepreneurs after the need for achievement and independence (Sadi & Al Ghazali, 2010). On the other hand the region has great female potential that remains mainly untapped for entrepreneurship and seems to support the thesis of low self-efficacy of women. For example, the MENA region is the only region in the world with a reverse gender gap in math and sciences on elementary and secondary school levels. In the region girls outperform boys across the region and in mixed as well as in sex segregated classrooms (Thacker 2011). Moreover, according to the UNESCO (Yahia, 2014), the region possesses the highest number of female researchers in the world, with an average of 38% compared to other regions such as North America and Western Europe (32%). The percentage of women in research worldwide is 30% (Yahia, 2014). Yet, women participation in entrepreneurship does not reflect this potential. This may also be due to a lack of female role models.

Lack of Female Role Models

A positive mindset, added to the will and confidence to succeed, is as important for entrepreneurial success as ideas and skills. However, it is hard for women in general to imagine themselves as successful business founders if most of the role models, if not all, are males. Entrepreneurship is associated with personalities such as Steve Jobs, Jeff Bezos, Bill Gates, or Fadi Ghandour from Aramex. Entrepreneurship is essentially masculinized; entrepreneurial behavior is being understood as masculine behavior. Women entrepreneurs are less visible in mass media and that although significant numbers of very successful female entrepreneurs exist worldwide and in the MENA region. This invisibility of female entrepreneurs also reflects in higher education. Entrepreneurial education worldwide is based nearly exclusively on the experiences of men and on studies related to traditionally male owned businesses, which then represent the basis that shape students' expectations (Jones, 2013). Male experiences and expectations also reflect in the way curricula are conceived and in the gendered language that is used to describe course content, and many women do not actually apply for entrepreneurship courses because they feel the courses don't fit well with their personalities (Jones, 2013). In consequence, this leads to very low enrollment of women in entrepreneurship courses, although women represent the majority of students at business schools worldwide (AACSB, 2013).

Role models motivate women when they perceive similarity to them in terms of attitudes, behavior and achievements. Moreover, they also play an important role in the MENA context to create legitimacy for female entrepreneurial activities. In surveys and interviews many women repeatedly referred to Khadija, Prophet Muhammad's first wife who was a successful businesswoman, as an inspiration and role model. An Arabic saying points to her pivotal role in history: "Islam did not rise except through Ali's sword and Khadijah's wealth". Muslim women across social and cultural borders draw on Kahdija's example and also generate legitimacy for their own activities, since Khadija's story is an example of how Islam allows women to establish and run their own business and to manage financial assets, without the interference of male family members and husbands (Al Dajani & Marlow 2010; Naguib & Jamali 2015).

Social Networks

Entrepreneurship takes place within a social space and every person is embedded in a social network that is composed of personal and professional, informal and formal relations (Birley, 1985). Such networks play an important role for business activities because they entrepreneurs them to gain access to knowledge, information, physical assets, skills and other resources (Kogut and Zander, 1992). Men and women use their social networks differently: the former tend to rely on social relations that could be relevant for their business, for example, other entrepreneurs, industry participants, competitors, etc. (Burt, 2000). These people give access to new perspectives and information regarding business opportunities, markets, customers, strategies, and others. On the other hand, women business starters tend to use social networks in an ineffective manner, since they rely more on private and family contacts that typically share similar ideas and understandings regarding entrepreneurial topics (Burt, 2000). This limited social network creates a great disadvantage for women right from the start: they miss out on professional connections that could share their experiences and support them through mentorship.

Research on the MENA region confirms that women entrepreneurs across the region rely predominantly on a network of family and very close friends (Erogul & Mc Crohan, 2008; Weeks 2009). This has to do in part with cultural restrictions regarding women's mobility and societal in-acceptance when it comes to their interaction with males outside their families, as is the case of many women in the Gulf countries (Zamberi Ahmad, 2011). In such patriarchal setting private family networks are often the only sources for women that can offer financial support, professional assistance and facility provision besides emotional encouragement. These social networking limitations of women lead to a situation where they are disadvantaged from the start since they miss out on important professional experiences of network partners, and support through potential mentorship. The above mentioned low participation rates of women in the region in the labor market imply that women have very little professional exposure and few opportunities to develop necessary managerial skills and business acumen in order to develop and grow their ventures. Lack of professional experience prohibits women to be prepared for the basics like finance and accounting, compliance with laws and regulations, as well as marketing. Many female business owners lack strategy and planning – all important topics that need to be communicated to lenders and possibly investors – thus, for them relevant social contacts that could help to prepare them, would be of pivotal importance.

MACRO ENVIRONMENTAL FACTORS

Quite a few discrepancies regarding the level of female entrepreneurship have been attributed to different cultures, notably, different values, beliefs and behaviors that prevail within countries. Culture reflects in a country's social, political and legal institutions (e.g., families, governments, laws and regulations), and it also influences people's behavior (Zahra & Wright, 2011). Mena countries are predominantly male oriented societies, which ascribe to men the role of bread earners and heads of family. On the other hand, the role of women is predominantly seen as caregivers, wives and mothers (Hofstede, 2001). Moreover, Arab societies are collectivistic, and as such emphasize conformity with family and tribes (Hofstede, 2001). Family members, for example, are expected to submit their individual needs and aspirations under the goals of the group (e.g. the family). However, entrepreneurial endeavors require the opposite; notably, entrepreneurship necessitates independence, autonomy and pro-activeness on behalf of women (and men), all traits that clash with existing traditional cultures. The professional choices of women are clearly influenced by their 'readings' of what is socially acceptable and desirable for different genders (Jamali, 2008). In the prevailing patriarchic, male dominated culture men are endowed with large authority over women in terms of financial responsibility, inheritance, marriage and divorce (Kazemi, 2000), which makes it very difficult for women to challenge these assigned roles. The culture reflects in gendered assumptions regarding the behavior of men and women, and women are expected to be more intuitive and relationship focused, whereas men are supposed to be decisive and dominant (Hofstede, 1994; Omair, 2008). Entrepreneurship by definition of being proactive, risk-taking, innovative, autonomous and competitively aggressive (Dess & Lumpkin, 1996) contradicts the traditional ideas regarding gender, and women entrepreneurs are therefore obliged to continuously navigate and negotiate their entrepreneurial engagements with families and friends.

Albeit, more liberal views and values have been introduced to MENA countries over time – especially in the professional arenas - modern values seem to affect men and women very differently. My own research on the topic shows that men benefit much more from such an environment, and feel incited to search for greater professional liberties, such as freelance activities. On the other hand, female motivation to seek individual professional fulfillment and to start a business has not been affected by the introduction of more modern values (Bastian & Zali, 2016). Basically, women remain constrained in their entrepreneurial efforts by patriarchal traditions. Local laws often also reflect and enforce certain cultural values, thus constitutional and statutory provisions often hamper female entrepreneurial aspiration. Some examples are Jordan, Kuwait, in the UAE and even in Palestine, where husbands can prevent their wives from working; or Jordan, Kuwait, Egypt; Oman, Saudi Arabia, the UAE, Yemen women cannot apply for their own passports; or, as in Lebanon, Palestine and many other confer citizenship to their children. In most Mena countries men are legally the 'head of the household' and they have the entire decision power about the family residence. Moreover, as head of the family they are responsible for obtaining all official documents regarding family members.

Women also experience open disapproval for their entrepreneurial activities. In her research on female entrepreneurs in Lebanon, Jamali (2009) reports that women faced difficulties in striking a balance between family and work responsibilities, because families refused support, and exercised societal pressure on women who leave behind their households and kids in the pursuit of a professional venture. Research in other MENA context, like Palestinian embroiders in Jordan reveals how women are forced to constantly negotiate their entrepreneurial roles with their husbands and extended families, in the form of insurances they have to give that all family obligations would still be met. This creates additional barriers for female entrepreneurs regardless of their social status (Al Dajani & Marlow 2010). In some countries, such as the KSA, restrictions on female mobility outside their homes, makes business venturing very challenging, since for example direct commercial transactions with strangers and men outside their family are prohibited (Zamberi Ahmad, 2011).

Religion

The region is the cradle for the three book religions, Judaism, Christianity and Islam. Yet, the majority of people in the region adhere to Islam. The exception is Lebanon where there exists a strong Christian population too, as well as Israel, which defines itself as Jewish state, but which is not part of this overview. In all societies Islam has a strong and defining impact on women's role and status in society (Erogul & McCrohan, 2008; Zamberi Ahmad, 2011). In media and also research, Islam is often portrayed as a religion adverse to women's rights and a source of their subordination, since it (like all other book religions) endows men with important authority over their daughters, sisters and wives in all areas of their lives, such as financial decisions, inheritance, marriage and divorce (Kazemi, 2000). However, Islam remains a pivotal spiritual and social force in daily life (Sidani, 2005) and several studies view Islam as an enabler for women empowerment rather than an obstacle. Such studies point to the positive perception of Islam amongst female entrepreneurs who rather feel inspired by its teachings (Madichie & Gallant, 2012; Tlaiss, 2015).

A recent study by Tlaiss (2015) focuses on how Islamic teachings and values have contributed to the success of Muslim women entrepreneurs in establishing and growing their businesses. The study shows that Islam is not an obstacle to female development, and in the contrary has helped women to construct their entrepreneurial career in the context of a patriarchal and traditional society. Women were shown to internalize the regulations of Islam regarding business ethics, notably ethics related to hard work (amal salih) and ethics linked to the strive for excellence and perfection in work (itqan). These work related values allowed women to develop competitive work practices and to create legitimacy for their activities in a social environment dominated by Islam. Many female entrepreneurs were particularly proud of their role and drew on Mohamad and his first wife Khadija who both were traders and businesspeople as example. Again the attempt to live up to the achievements of their role models encouraged and motivated women to become better and more ethical entrepreneurs (Tlaiss, 2015)

Governmental Support

Governments can support entrepreneurs through policies, regulations, programs and financial backing (Naguib & Jamali, 2015; Zamberi Ahmad, 2011). As previously mention, many states in the region have announced their commitment to maintaining international standards to achieve more development for women. For example, many countries are signatory to the Millennium Development Goals (MDGs) that include the promotion of gender equality and empowerment of women. In this context, governments play a pivotal role at the macro level, as they have the capacity to improve or impede women's empowerment and entrepreneurship in the MENA. However, the governmental efforts and impact on female entrepreneurship vary from country to country. In some case, as in the UAE, governments have played an important role in encouraging women to enter freelance activities and to catalyze startups (Tlaiss, 2013). During the past years, the UAE government has promoted entrepreneurship and small and medium sized enterprises in general through numerous programs and forums. Although there is no specific organization that is dedicated to support women entrepreneurs, various initiatives foster female entrepreneurs. They include business incubators, science parks, and specialized training programs. Moreover, numerous associations have been established by the government that intent to empower women through education and support. Amongst others, the Emirates Businesswomen Councils (EBWC) has been very active in their support for female entrepreneurs. EBWC was established as an initiative of the Federation of the UAE Chambers of Commerce and Industry. This association provides support in form of mentoring, training, and others to female business starters. It also lobbies on behalf of women entrepreneurs, facilitates research about issues and problems related to women entrepreneurs, and functions as hub to connect Emirati women with international and national organizations. Other associations, such as the UAE Women's Organizations/Associations also provide social and health services, especially for women in more traditional sectors. Women are motivated to invest in more traditional areas that also preserve Emirati heritage and are provided with a secure income. The Department of Economic Development (DED) in Dubai started the Intilaq programed in 1999 that supports home based enterprises and micro enterprises of women, by providing them special trade licenses for women who would otherwise be unable to fulfill the necessary legal requirements in order to trade to get business assistance and bank loans. Moreover, the Intilaq program provides entrepreneurship and management training. Such governmental initiatives have proved to have encouraging results for female entrepreneurial intentions (van Horne et al., 2011).

In other cases in the region, the role of the government was shown to be more of an obstacle that creates and maintains a work and career environment based on gendered rules and regulations, and government show a deficit in understanding the particular challenges and difficulties faced by women entrepreneurs (Welsh et al., 2014; Zamberi Ahmad, 2011). Most countries in the region still have sparse governmental support, and often lack important legal reforms, which involve women in decision making, in order to improve this situation (Al Ghazali, 2010; Welsh et al., 2014).

Little Access to Finance

Access to credit is one the greatest concern for all new ventures, but especially for women owned businesses. A recent study by the IFC (2014b) estimates that about 70% of female ventures in developing and emerging countries receive no or too little funding by financial institutions in order to support and grow their ventures. The credit gap, which is the difference between the required and the actual levels of debt of a new venture, is estimated at about $280 billion. According to the IFC, the credit gap for women in the MENA region is the largest one worldwide. The lack in funding is approximately $271,000 per women-owned SME (compared to approximately $18,700 per women-owned SME in East Asia) (IFC 2014b). On average, women owned enterprises in the region have a 10% larger credit gap than men owned ones. Banks and other credit givers tend to perceive women as riskier customers, mainly because credit officers typically interact much less with women as clients and have very little information about this customer group. Moreover, women in the region tend to have smaller businesses for which financial institutions tend to expect lower returns due to their size. Nevertheless, a recent study by Goldman Sachs (2014) demonstrates that access to capital is vital for the entire economy as it has a direct impact on per capita incomes of people. If the credit gap can be closed by 2020, average per capita income could increase by 12%.

In most other countries, governments still fail to compensate for this gap in funding and this lack of support was frequently cited by female entrepreneurs as one of the biggest obstacles for women to start their own businesses (Welsh et al., 2014; Zamberi Ahmad, 2011). Positive attitudes towards female entrepreneurs on all levels – state administration, banks and lending organizations – are fundamental to nurture female business starters and their communities.

SOME SOLUTIONS TO INCREASE FEMALE ENTREPRENEURSHIP IN THE REGION

There exists no silver bullet solution to foster female entrepreneurship and to tap into the great potential of women in the MENA region. Impediments for women are complex. The above article has identified the following:

- Dissatisfactory conditions for women in the labor market and work place and gendered economies that push them into entrepreneurship because of lack of professional development opportunities.
- Low levels of self-confidence and efficacy on behalf of women regarding their abilities as entrepreneurs.

- Entrepreneurship as discipline is gendered
- Lack of female role models in entrepreneurship
- Lack of sufficient government support to promote empowerment of women
- In many countries in the region we find still high regulatory and legal impediments for women's development and self-determination
- prevailing patriarchic and male dominated culture is not conducive for female entrepreneurship

Many MENA societies are gendered and social norms and traditions often discourage women, and place little importance on female agency such as entrepreneurship outside their house. In fact in many contexts, c cultural norms and traditions even restrict female physical mobility and limit a woman's possibility to participate in the labor market and to gain important managerial experience that could prove useful for future entrepreneurial ventures. Moreover, entrepreneurship is still perceived as a male "trade" and not very suitable for women. Such situations place a lot of responsibility on entrepreneurship training in the region. In the current context, entrepreneurial education seems to be more important for women compared to men in order to increase confidence and belief in their own abilities. There still exists a lack of proper advice and support networks that could provide coaching and training in this sense. Especially within environments that provide little support for entrepreneurs, public advice facilitates entrepreneurial processes. Moreover, the number of mentoring networks is on the rise in different entrepreneurial ecosystems in the region. Yet, mentoring still requires to be tailored to the needs of female entrepreneurs, who often have to fulfill typical female functions like family and household and combine them with their roles as business starters, and often are overwhelmed with it.

It is also important to raise women's awareness for these topics and help them understand how such conditions have influenced their individual choices and often constrained their professional potential. Role models are of great importance in helping to increase female self-efficacy and to set an example of what is possible. Role models motivate us because we perceive similarity to them in terms of attitudes, behavior and achievements. Many successful women entrepreneurs and business leaders in the region exist, and examples are: Hafia Al Kaylani (founder of the Arab International Women's Forum), Rana Shmaitelly (founder of the Little Engineer); the young Hind Hobeika (Instabeat), the successful Lebanese designer Nada Debbs, and many others. The stories of these women can motivate other women to emulate them and go beyond their limits. To date, women entrepreneurs and innovators tend to receive far less attention in media than male counterparts, and therefore are less visible. We need to bring these stories more to the attention of the larger public. We also need to integrate these biographies and their business experiences into our teachings in higher education; and in our teachings at school before girls develop a negative expectation regarding their professional potentials.

In all MENA countries, certain socio-cultural obstacles limit women's entrepreneurial endeavors. These obstacles are deeply rooted in traditions and old customs, which cannot be changed overnight. But many of these barriers for women are non-financial in nature, and raising awareness will contribute to create an environment that is more conducive of female venturing. Moreover, national governments need to support female entrepreneurs with campaigns that aim at changing public opinion regarding working women. There has to also be increased awareness on behalf of policy makers regarding biases against women in legal rights and regulations, and these need to be addressed. This involves the promotion and introduction of laws that fight gender discrimination in the public and private sectors, granting women equal rights, for example, to enter into contracts or to property, as well as to education. Media, especially those that are government controlled or supported, need to pay more attention to coverage of female entrepreneurship in terms of content and quantity.

The state also has an interest in closing the financing gap for female entrepreneurs, which requires thoroughly assessing all challenges facing female entrepreneurs and allocating the necessary resources in order to reduce financial gaps. Governmental actions need to be accompanied by private funding alternatives, which increasingly involve female investors. A recent longitudinal study on the crowdfunding platform 'Kickstarter' that involved 22.000 entrepreneurs found that crowdfunding proved a very adapted solution for female entrepreneurs. As crowdfunding is possible with very small investment amounts, many crowdfunding investors are women that are also more likely to invest into female projects. Moreover, fundraising campaigns by women had higher success rates than those by men (Marom, 2014). Equally, we should increase the number of women who invest into women, for example female angel investors, who are affluent individuals that invest in new ventures, need to play a greater role in order to close the capital gap. Women currently represent about 23% of all business angel investors (an increase of 14% since 2005) (Klein, 2014) and women owned ventures that received angel capital represent 20% (Klein, 2014). Recent analysis of the global venture capital (VC) and micro-venture firms industry revealed that only 7% of investing partners in such firms are women. Globally, 12% of venture rounds and just about 10% of all venture dollars invested went to startups founded by women. However, the research showed that VC firms that were founded by women or have a relatively high percentage of women partners tend to invest significantly more into female ventures, and these investments represent a high share of their profits (Tech Crunch, 2016). Creating more stewardship also on behalf of governments, private sector and women themselves for women founded businesses is also essential to create better success perspectives for female entrepreneurs and incite more women to launch a career as entrepreneur.

Moreover, a recent study on entrepreneurs in Latin America finds that female and male entrepreneurs seek mentor support to help in their growth. However, men were more likely to seek for mentors outside their family and friends' connections (Inter-American Development Bank, 2014). It is necessary to change female habits by offering them platforms, such as increased representation of women on trade fairs and trade missions in order to give them more opportunities for networking. It will allow learning from female role models, which also might incite increasing numbers of women to consider entrepreneurship as a serious and viable professional path. Research on entrepreneurial advice seeking found that public advice sponsored by local governments proved very valuable for entrepreneurs in the MENA region (Bastian & Tucci, forthcoming). The data indicates that entrepreneurial performance increased with more support entrepreneurs received from public advising institutions as strategically important advice source. Public advice can supply firms with information, coaching and consulting on numerous innovation relevant matters, (e.g. recent technology trends, market development, sector analysis, market opportunities, and guidance through entrepreneurial and innovation processes).

"Soft" issues, notably lack of self-confidence appear to be a major cause for the low rates in female entrepreneurship within the MENA region. We need to find a portfolio of options that can help reducing the gender gap in entrepreneurship in our region and promote momentum for job creation. Supporting women entrepreneurs is not only a question of social fairness and ethics, but also essential for economic growth and prosperity of Mena societies. It is essential for a sustainable future.

REFERENCES

AACSB. (2014). *Business School Data Guide.* Retrieved January 03, 2015 from: http://www.aacsb.edu/~/media/AACSB/Publications/data-trends-booklet/2014-business-school-data-guide.ashx

Al-Dajani, H., & Marlow, S. (2010). Impact of women's home-based enterprise on family dynamics: Evidence from Jordan. *International Small Business Journal,28*(5), 470-486.

Al-Ghazali, B. M., Yusoff, R. M., & Sadi, M. A. (2013). Women Entrepreneurs in Bahrain: Motivations and Barriers. *Jurnal Teknologi, 64*(2), 139–143. doi:10.11113/jt.v64.2251

Bastian, B., & Zali, S. (in press). Entrepreneurial motives and their antecedents of men and women in North Africa and the Middle East. *Gender in Management, 31*(7).

Birley, S. (1985). The role of networks in the entrepreneurial process. *Journal of Business Venturing, 1*(1), 107–117. doi:10.1016/0883-9026(85)90010-2

Boyd, N. G., & Vozikis, G. S. (1994). The influence of self-efficacy on the development of entrepreneurial intentions and actions. *Entrepreneurship Theory and Practice, 18*, 63–63.

Burt, R. S. (2000). The network structure of social capital. *Research in Organizational Behavior, 22*, 345–423. doi:10.1016/S0191-3085(00)22009-1

Chen, C., Green, R., & Crick, A. (1998). The self-efficacy expectations and occupational preferences of females and males. *Journal of Business Venturing, 13*(4), 295–316. doi:10.1016/S0883-9026(97)00029-3

Erogul, M. S., & McCrohan, D. (2008). Preliminary investigation of Emirati women entrepreneurs in the UAE. *African Journal of Business Management, 2*(10), 177–185.

GEM (Global Entrepreneurship Monitor). (2012). *Global Entrepreneurship Monitor 2012 Women's Report*. Retrieved March 20, 2016, from: http://www.babson.edu/Academics/centers/blank-center/global-research/gem/Documents/GEM 2012 Women's Report.pdf

Hofstede, G. (1992). *Cultural Dimensions in People Management-The Socialization Perspective. In Globalizing Management–Creating and Leading the Competitive Organization*. New York, NY: Wiley & Sons.

Hofstede, G. H. (2001). Culture's consequences: Comparing values, behaviors, institutions and organizations across nations. *Sage (Atlanta, Ga.)*.

IFC. (2014). *Women, Business and the Law 2014*. Retrieved January 16, 2015 from: http://wbl.worldbank.org/~/media/FPDKM/WBL/Documents/Reports/2014/Women-Business-and-the-Law-2014-Key-Findings.pdf

ILO. (2013). *Global Employment Trends for Youth 2013: A generation at risk*. Retrieved 27.4.2015 from: http://www.ilo.org/global/research/global-reports/global-employment-trends/youth/2013/lang--en/index.htm

Inter American Development Bank. (2014a). *WEGrow: Unlocking the Growth Potential of Women Entrepreneurs in Latin America and the Caribbean*. Retrieved on January 16, 2015, from: http://services.iadb.org/mifdoc/website/publications/98704705-c7cc-416c-b103-7797dac0844a.pdf

International Finance Corporation (IFC). (2014b). *Women owned SMEs: A business opportunity for financial institutions. A market and credit gap assessment and IFC's portfolio gender baseline*. Retrieved 3 Jan. 2015 from: http://www.ifc.org/wps/wcm/connect/b229bb004322efde9814fc384c61d9f7/WomenOwnedSMes+Report-Final.pdf?MOD=AJPERES

Jamali, D. (2008). A stakeholder approach to corporate social responsibility: A fresh perspective into theory and practice. *Journal of Business Ethics*, *82*(1), 213–231. doi:10.1007/s10551-007-9572-4

Jamali, D. (2009). Constraints and opportunities facing women entrepreneurs in developing countries: A relational perspective. *Gender in Management: An International Journal*, *24*(4), 232–251. doi:10.1108/17542410910961532

Javadian, G., & Singh, R. P. (2012). Examining successful Iranian women entrepreneurs: An exploratory study. *Gender in Management: An International Journal*, *27*(3), 148–164. doi:10.1108/17542411211221259

Jones, S. (2013). *Gendered Discourses of Entrepreneurship in HE: The Fictive Entrepreneur and the Fictive Student*. Retrieved January 03, 2015 from: http://www.google.com/url?sa=t&rct=j&q=&esrc=s&frm=1&source=web&cd=6&ved=0CD0QFjAF&url=http%3A%2F%2Fwww.isbe.org.uk%2Fcontent%2Fassets%2FBest_Conference_Paper-_Sally_Jones.pdf&ei=0QmvVIjEA4rtatPVgLAE&usg=AFQjCNE45n0jg8ECHs8RlGaaxg2v3hs2ig&bvm=bv.83339334,d.d2s

Kauffman Foundation. (2014). *Sources of economic hope: Women's entrepreneurship*. Retrieved 3 Jan. 2014 from: http://www.kauffman.org/~/media/kauffman_org/research%20reports%20and%20covers/2014/11/sources_of_economic_hope_womens_entrepreneurship.pdf

Kazemi, F. (2000). Gender, Islam and politics. *Social Research*, *67*(2), 453–474.

Kirkwood, J. (2009). Is a lack of self-confidence hindering women entrepreneurs? *International Journal of Gender and Entrepreneurship*, *1*(2), 118–133. doi:10.1108/17566260910969670

Klein, K. (2014). Rise of female Angel investors fuels women-run companies. *Business Week*. Retrieved on January 03, 2015 from: http://www.businessweek.com/articles/2014-09-10/angel-investing-rise-of-women-investors-fuels-women-run-companies

Kogut, B., & Zander, U. (1992). Knowledge of the Firm, Combinative Capabilities, and the Replication of Technology. *Organization Science*, *3*(3), 383–397. doi:10.1287/orsc.3.3.383

Lumpkin, G. T., & Dess, G. G. (1996). Clarifying the entrepreneurial orientation construct and linking it to performance. *Academy of Management Review, 21*(1), 135–172.

Madichie, N. O., & Gallant, M. (2012). Broken silence: A commentary on womens entrepreneurship in the United Arab Emirates. *The International Journal of Entrepreneurship and Innovation, 13*(2), 81–92. doi:10.5367/ijei.2012.0071

Marom, D., Robb, A., & Sade, O. (2015). Gender Dynamics in Crowdfunding (Kickstarter): Evidence on Entrepreneurs, Investors, Deals and Taste-Based Discrimination. *Investors, Deals and Taste-Based Discrimination.* Retrieved 26.10.2016, from: file:///C:/Users/bb21/Downloads/sade_presentation.pdf

Naguib, R., & Jamali, D. (2015). Female entrepreneurship in the UAE: A multi-level integrative lens. *Gender in Management: An International Journal, 30*(2), 135–161. doi:10.1108/GM-12-2013-0142

OECD. (2014). *Women in Business 2014. Accelerating Entrepreneurship in the Middle East and North Africa Region.* Retrieved January 15, 2014 from: http://www.keepeek.com/Digital-Asset-Management/oecd/development/women-in-business-2014_9789264213944-en#page1

Omair, K. (2008). Women in Management in the Arab Context. Education, Business and Society. *Contemporary Middle Eastern Issues, 1*(2), 107–123. doi:10.1108/17537980810890293

Sachs, G. (2014). *Giving credit where it is due. How closing the credit gap for women owned SMEs can drive global growth.* Retrieved January 03, 2015 from: http://www.goldmansachs.com/our-thinking/investing-in-women/gmi-report-pdf.pdf

Sadi, M. A., & Al-Ghazali, B. M. (2010). Doing business with impudence: A focus on women entrepreneurship in Saudi Arabia. *African Journal of Business Management, 4*(1), 1–11.

TechCrunch. (2016). *The first comprehensive study on women in venture capital and their impact on female founders.* Retrieved on October 17, 2016, from https://techcrunch.com/2016/04/19/the-first-comprehensive-study-on-women-in-venture-capital/

Thacker, S. (2011). *An exception to the gender gap in education: The Middle East and North Africa.* Retrieved on 30.11.2016, from: http://blogs.worldbank.org/arabvoices/exception-gender-gap-education-middle-east-north-africa

Tlaiss, H. (2013). Entrepreneurial motivations of women: Evidence from the United Arab Emirates. *International Small Business Journal.*

Tlaiss, H. A. (2015). How Islamic Business Ethics Impact Women Entrepreneurs: Insights from Four Arab Middle Eastern Countries. *Journal of Business Ethics, 129*(4), 859–877. doi:10.1007/s10551-014-2138-3

Uhlaner, L., & Thurik, A. R. (2007). Postmaterialism influencing total entrepreneurial activity across nations. *Journal of Evolutionary Economics, 17*(2), 161–185. doi:10.1007/s00191-006-0046-0

Verheul, I., Stel, A. V., &Thurik, R. (2006). Explaining female and male entrepreneurship at the country level. *Entrepreneurship and Regional Development, 18*(2), 151-183.

Weeks, J. R. (2009). Women business owners in the Middle East and North Africa: A five-country research study. *International Journal of Gender and Entrepreneurship, 1*(1), 77–85. doi:10.1108/17566260910942354

Welsh, D. H., Memili, E., Kaciak, E., & Al Sadoon, A. (2014). Saudi women entrepreneurs: A growing economic segment. *Journal of Business Research, 67*(5), 758–762. doi:10.1016/j.jbusres.2013.11.040

Wilson, F., Marlino, D., & Kickul, J. (2004). Our entrepreneurial future: Examining the diverse attitudes and motives of teens across gender and ethnic identity. *Journal of Developmental Entrepreneurship, 9*(3), 177–197.

Yahia, M. (2014). *Women's gap from education to research.* Retrieved 30.11.2016, from: http://blogs.nature.com/houseofwisdom/2014/03/womens-gap-from-education-to-research.html

Zahra, S. A., & Wright, M. (2011). Entrepreneurships next act. *The Academy of Management Perspectives, 25*(4), 67–83. doi:10.5465/amp.2010.0149

Zamberi Ahmad, S. (2011). Evidence of the characteristics of women entrepreneurs in the Kingdom of Saudi Arabia: An empirical investigation. *International Journal of Gender and Entrepreneurship, 3*(2), 123–143. doi:10.1108/17566261111140206

Chapter 7
Succession Challenges Facing Family Businesses in Saudi Arabia

Ignatius Ekanem
Middlesex University, UK

Latifah Abdulmohsen Alrossais
Middlesex University, UK

ABSTRACT

The aim of this study is to examine how succession planning is carried out in family-owned businesses in Saudi Arabia. The study adopts a qualitative methodology which involves semi-structured, face-to-face interviews. The major findings of the research is that most of the family businesses in Saudi Arabia do not have a proper succession plan due mainly to socio-cultural issues such as mistrust and conflict of interest between the older and the younger members of the family and also subservience of women in the society generally. The implications of the study are discussed including a paradigm shift where women are encouraged and given the opportunity to get involved in the running of their family businesses.

DOI: 10.4018/978-1-5225-2066-5.ch007

INTRODUCTION

Saudi Arabia is a very rich and big country in the Middle East, and currently the country is striving towards stability and growth which largely depends on public and private sectors. In the recent years the statistics for family business were high where in among the top 100 companies 45 companies were family owned businesses. Generally, 90 per cent of the businesses in Saudi are family-owned while only 5 percent were surviving the third generation and most of the companies which were successful were less than 65 years old. The total number of businesses operating in Saudi Arabia was 763,589 in 2009 (Ministry of Economy and Planning, 2009). The Saudi government is aware of the impact of such businesses to the economy of the country and hence has presented several methods of addressing this challenge that might affect both family and afterwards the economy of the nation. There are important issues that need to be differentiated in order to separate the businesses and the family loyalties, employing only the most competent family members as managers and the need to come up with resource to match with the best managerial practices.

The past decade has been characterized by the adoption of 'Saudization' and economic policy of localization that encourages local nationals to take up jobs and embark on running businesses that were owned by foreign nationals (AsadSadi & Henderson, 2007). This has to some extent led to benefits in developing opportunities for Saudi nationals, but also led to problems in having family members to run their family entities, especially those who have secured better jobs elsewhere. On a micro level, however, family businesses are a family property and are expected to benefit the family, thus control rests on family members, most notably the eldest male member, who makes all major decisions, often with little voices on the contrary (Nakauchi & Wiersema, 2014).

The history of family businesses in Saudi Arabia can be viewed from the traditional and cultural orientation of the country, where family bond and unity is highly regarded. The need to retain wealth in the family counts towards ensuring that the profile of the family is raised and this can be of importance even at the time of marriages. This implies that family property is to be entrusted to the most senior members of the family who, may be viewed with awe and assumed to have the experience for the same. This poses two challenges, first, succession issues, which must be shared among old members of the family and secondly, the challenge of having to pass the business to someone who may not be able to run the same (Nakauchi & Wiersema, 2014). Family enterprises are mainly concentrated in the fields of hospitality, services and retail, which tend to have high level of customer contact, thus increasing the importance of the owner (or patriarch), and indirectly poses new potential challenges when the owner is no longer able to remain active in the management of the business.

It has been found that the rate of failure of family business in Saudi Arabia is staggering and the problem is that with such failure, business stability in the country is volatile as is the problem of sustaining employment (Wagner-Tsukamoto, 2008). The failure of family businesses in an economy that is largely run by family businesses is a worrying trend, but this speaks more about the internal management aspects of such entities. When businesses fail, joblessness increases, the family source of income is also affected and social vices may increase. This means that business failure is not just a simple issue as it impacts on the general economy of the whole country. There are many perspectives from which the situation of family business can be viewed; the cultural issues including gender situation in Saudi Arabia, the personal views of the owner of the business, extended family circumstances and influence, and the specific industry situations (i.e. competition). All these are a multitude of variables that denote that family businesses (especially small and medium) entities are in a delicate situation and their survival is harder than large entities.

Recently the government has shown willingness to allow women to take active role in certain aspects of the society. For instance, the country has had the first elected woman minister, Norah Al Faiz (Time, 2009), but this is a far cry from the realities in lower levels of the society, where there are cultural challenges that exist. However, it is clear that there are progresses taking place, and this might imply that there may also be positive impacts on family businesses, for instance it was reported in a local magazine that women are becoming proactive in running their businesses and they can also be entrusted with family businesses (Carayannis & Papadopoulos 2011). While the circumstances are changing and may require changes to be initiated even in family businesses, the challenges facing family businesses in a country that has a lot of diversity and influences are many. This is an issue that should be looked into and possible solutions proposed. It is vital for the family businesses to be made stable, and this can be done by ensuring that their internal operations are carefully managed. This study seeks to explore the challenges facing family entities in the Kingdom with the view of proposing solutions that can sustain succession and prosperity of these businesses.

This study will be important in showcasing the need for ensuring that management practices are improved to support development of businesses in Saudi Arabia. The research can provide valuable advice for business owners, government entities and prospective business managers on how to ensure that sufficient measures are taken to sustain the future of businesses in Saudi Arabia.

The aim of this study is, therefore, to examine how succession can be made successful in businesses that are family-owned in Saudi Arabia, especially when the patriarch is not able to run the business any more. Specifically, the study investigates:

- Whether formal management and planning styles are used in family business entities in Saudi Arabia.
- How business succession is carried out in family businesses in Saudi Arabia
- The extent of influence of socio-cultural issues in managing succession of family run businesses in Saudi Arabia

This study is aimed at filling a gap in the literature by shedding light on managerial issues and the features of family businesses in Saudi Arabia. As family businesses in Saudi Arabia tend to fail as soon as the owner stops active management, the question is, is this a leadership crisis or are there other issues that might be contributory to this problem. A number of views have been expressed and various theories have been given, most of which highlight that the challenges of continuity of family businesses are many.

LITERATURE REVIEW

Family Businesses: The General View

The significant impact of family business on domestic economies is a concept that has been highlighted by many writers, through job creation, innovation and accumulation of capital. Although they agree on the impact of family business, there is no agreed definition of the term family business. There are scholars who define family business as the participation of more than one family member in the operation and ownership of a private capital company. The family members have control over the company which makes it operate actively and the business is closely managed by the family members over generations (Kanoo, 1995; Carayannis & Papadopoulos, 2011). According to Nakauchi and Wiersema (2014) family business is described as any organization where the decisions and management is affected by the succession leadership of the family member.

There are three approaches that the scholars have used to define the term family business. The first approach presents it as ownership of a project; a business is classified as family if a family has more than 50 percent of its shares (Binder, 1994). The second refers to the emotional perception of the family members towards a business (Daily & Dollinger, 1993). The third approach looks at the management of the business by the members of the family (Tagiuri & Davis, 1992).

According to Lyman (1991) the family-business managers display less reliance on the written policies and have more personal approach and trust their employees to a greater extent. Similarly, McGivem (1989) indicates that the advantages of working in a family business are; good relationships and greater chance of decision making once accepted by the family members. The challenges of working with a family business include lesser professionalism, no clear lines of authority and no availability of options to non-family members (McGivem, 1989). In relation to conflicts, Kootstra, (2009) established that there are different methods of solving such cases like use of litigation, arbitration and mediation but the most effective one for family businesses is mediation.

In regard to the studies that focus on the Arab family business environment, there are only few available. The study by Afifi (2002) is about the compatibility between the characteristics of family businesses and the requirements of successful management change. The study concluded that the family business is better able to manage change in the instances of equality of conditions than companies without it. The study also states that a family business has a tendency of resisting change.

There are a number of questions that have been discussed in forums, conferences and general debates about Saudi Arabia. The key question is about succession and especially after the break up prominent family businesses in Saudi. There are writers that have pointed out the critical issues that family businesses face and have suggested the need to have reforms through the joint stock ventures to enable them go through the impacts of globalization (Ramady, 2010). It is a fact that most of the family businesses in Saudi started as trading houses and have grown into conglomerates (Sfakianakis, 2009).

There is significant impact of the culture in Saudi Arabia that shapes the managerial practices of the family business. The families in Saudi Arabia live together and conduct businesses together. The bigger families have the ability to own and dominate the private sector within the Kingdom. This means that there is a need to consider the concept of family and its importance in the study about family business in Saudi Arabia. There is need for awareness of the importance of families in daily life. The tradition detects that older and senior people are well respected and hence this should not be counter argued.

According to Tagiuri and Davis (1992), majority of the family business owners desired to see their business transferred to the next generation but it is estimated that only 70% will survive into the 2nd generation while 90% will not make it to the 3rd generation. Succession is a very essential aspect of family business that many families face than other issues. Ward (2011) argues that succession is essential to the existence of the firm with the potential for the success or failure of the business. Succession is defined as the family business that will be passed on for the next generation of the family to manage and control. Theorists also agree that family businesses highly depend on the succession plan (Nakauchi & Wiersema, 2014). However, researchers have pointed out that family businesses do not implement the succession plans and in some instances such firms do not have the succession plan (Ward 2011; Blodgett, Dumas, & Zanzi, 2011).

Management and Planning in Family Businesses

Business sustainability is a major objective that is of as much importance as is the profit making objective. Businesses are created by entrepreneurial qualities that are in an individual(s) and the success of the business depends on how these individuals manage to organize all operations that pertain to the business (Kets de Vries, 2013). According to Dawson (2005) businesses tend to grow when there are adequate measures that guarantee relevance to the market, but also effective management of internal capabilities. Kets de Vries (2013) focuses on the qualities of the owners in determining success of privately owned businesses and indicates that such entities tend to fair very well when the owners are all entrepreneurial. This is a subjective view that places the chances of success purely on individual capability, but ignores the role that business environment plays in the management of family entities.

Morelli and Sangiorgi (2006) studied how family run entities are developed by exploring the approaches used by the managers of these entities. It was found that there is a difference in the way family entities are managed between countries. However, there was general consensus in that the managers who are mainly owners of family run entities tend to engage in different management approaches when running their entities. Drawing from Fayol's principles of management and Drucker's views on scientific management Kootstra (2009) notes that the established views of management are never considered necessary in running family run entities. Planning in a family run business is considered to be a short term task that should not be worrying the owners because they can change their plans depending on evolving situations (Kootstra, 2009).

By the same token, Nakauchi and Wireman (2014) argue that the length of planning and importance that is attached to the same by business managers is linked to the level of power that is being wielded. For instance, owners of businesses can change their plans at whim as a sign of power and authority, and they need not be accountable to anyone. This view is however different from the findings by Kemp (2013) and Nakauchi and Wiersema (2014) who indicate that business owners of family run entities tend to have long term plans that have been developed over the years. The approaches to managing businesses by such owners is therefore often less formal, but very strict on what the owners view to be crucial to their entities.

Wagner-Tsukamoto (2008) posits that the challenge facing owners of family run entities, which informs their choice of management styles, is often linked to their desire to win over their customers, and at the same time have loyal employees. To this extent, business owners may engage in less autocratic approaches when dealing with some of their trusted workforce, but remain more autocratic when dealing with others. This may imply that management and planning of family run entities, is clearly linked to the level of control that is desired. Kootstra (2009) explores the ways managers change their tact when engaging their workforce. To a large extent, this denotes the desire of these managers to adapt to situations as they develop.

Another view that is linked to family run entities is that in understanding how management and planning of family entities take place, it is necessary to first understand that these entities tend to be sole proprietorships with some degree of partnership (Nakauchi, & Wiersema, 2014). Wagner-Tsukamoto (2008) provides a more elaborate view by stating that family run entities often have one main voice that might overrule all the others and this tends to make such businesses more autocratic in management and planning because eventually there is no voice of reason, but voice of command. This is not to say that it is a disadvantage to have one main voice. If anything, Kemp (2013) indicates that family run entities are quick in decision making, which is a competitive advantage issue. The challenge, however, is in readiness to include the views of other members of the family in running such entities, a challenge that is difficult to overcome (Nakauchi & Wiersema, 2014).

Succession as a Process

According to the studies of executive succession, succession is treated as a process not as an event (Nakauchi & Wiersema, 2014; Chung & Luo, 2013; Sullivan & Perrenoud, 2012; Frynas & Mellahi 2011). There are particular steps and procession before and after the succession takes place. The problems that may occur at every phase of the process can be identified prior to the beginning of the succession process (Brockhaus, 2004). Davis and Harveston, 1998) point out that personal skills, family and development of the organization are very important aspects in the progress of the family business in initial stages and final stages. The life cycle model developed by Churchill and Hatten (1997) explores the succession process from a father to the son in the family business. The model defined four states: the first stage is about the *owner-management* in which the owner is the first and the only member of the family directly involved in the business. The second stage is the *training and development stage* in which the family members especially the children learn the business. The third stage is the *partnership stage* which is between the father and the son and the last stage of succession process is the *power transfer* in which the successor is given responsibility.

Another framework about the succession model is provided by Nordqvist, Wennberg, and Hellerstedt, (2013). In this model, the succession process is broken down in seven stages. This process takes place in the 24 years tenure of the business founder or owner (Handler, 1994). The first stage is *pre-business stage* in which the successor is partially aware of the concepts of the organization. The second stage is the *introductory stage* where the successor is exposed to the family members dynamics and the firm. The *introductory-functional stage* is the third stage where the successor moves to part time job at the organization. The fourth stage is the *functional stage* where the successor becomes a full time member of the company. The fifth stage is referred to as the *advanced functional stage* during which the successor assumes managerial responsibilities. The sixth stage is called the *early succession stage* where the successor takes up the presidency of the company and the last stage is the *mature succession* stage where the successor becomes the 'de facto leader' of the firm.

The succession process can also be understood by the theory of George Kelly on the concept of transition theory. The Transition Theory states that a psychological process which is founded on the role of the players' construction systems that there are others who try to join in a social enterprise (Chesson, 2012). This means that each phase is conceptualized and it is associated with the specific role behavior on the side of the founder and the next generation members and the transition from one stage to the other depends on the role behavior transition (Kootstra, 2009; Becker, 2013).

The Role of the Founder

The founder is very important in family business. There are several studies which have focused more on the role of the founder in the success of the family owned business (Block, 2012; Ward, 2011; Bocatto, Gispert, & Rialp, 2010; Zellweger & Sieger, 2012). The main aspect of the founder is the leadership style and how they initiate the successors into the business. The characteristics of the founders normally manifest themselves as a requirement for the achievement and power (Zellweger & Sieger, 2012), together with the internal locus of control and there is reflection of a deep-seated desire for immortality (Bocatto et al., 2010). There are various theorists who have investigated the root of these psychological characteristics of the founders of the business. The family business can be a way in which the founders realize a way of handing conflicts that have developed in them during childhood. The founders find an opportunity to realize power and self-esteem that they were denied while they were still young. There are three significant senses that the founders gain from their business: first, they start business to escape the authority of powerful figures since they have unresolved conflicts with their parents (Lin, 2014). The second sense is since the firm is viewed by the founder as the 'baby' and the 'mistress', the employees are seen as tools for shaping the company. The workers are denied the chance to have the power in the organization. This means that those who are not pleased can leave (Becker, 2013). The last sense is the business represents an extension of himself, the process of succession become mixed up when the founder has personal concerns that he will leave behind (Nakauchi & Wiersema, 2014).

There are other researchers such as Kets de Vries (2012) which provides a clearer picture of the characteristics of the founders and the drive in the entrepreneur. The study found that people that desire to run their own businesses because of need for control are known to have serious difficulties when it comes to dominance and submission. Such entrepreneurs have a strong distrust of the world around them which is reflected in the way the firm is operated. They work hard in protecting their little world from dominance of the 'evil' forces.

Litz (2012) suggests that the difficulty of letting go of power has been created by the attitude of the founders. They kill the business they have devoted their life to build up by failing to offer a lifeline to the viability and continuity of organization. The owners of the business fail to appreciate the fact that at some point of their life there will be a replacement of their position in the company. If a successful owner of a business who has clear vision and have achieved a lot in the business does not have the courage and the ability to appoint the successor, this will be done by the legal representative (Sharma, & Hoy, 2013).

Berrone, Cruz, and Gomez-Mejia, (2012) argue that most of the founders have the characteristics of appointing successors that are bound to fail. The inadequate successors are selected by the founder who is described as the *false prophet's watchful waiter* and *loyal servant* (Berrone et al., 2012). The false prophets are those people whose competence is not a factor in their selection hence their choice is unrealistic (Litz, Pearson, & Litchfield, 2012). The problem with the founder and the succession process has been a key research concept and many solutions have been offered. The challenge of overcoming the resistance of the founders to hand over to successors can be addressed in different approaches. Litz (2012) suggests that helping the founders to be self-aware is an approach that will encourage them to think about replacement and appointing successors. Another approach is by encouraging the business founders to establish several ventures. The founder can continue to be a founder of a new frontier and give chance to others to control and manage other businesses (Litz, 2012).

Perspective of the Next Generation

The perspective of the next generation family members is also an important aspect of the research in looking at the factors that lead to the success or failure of businesses. The early writing on family business succession placed much emphasis on the concept of the founder and the entrepreneur as the central figures in the business system of the family. The individual family members of the business founder were grouped together into "the family". However, researchers such as Danco (1981) focuses on the spouse while others focus on the relationship between the father and the son. The study by Davis and Harveston (1998) looks at the conflict between individuals in the family which needs to be given more focus today. The study of offspring's by Sharma and Hoy (2013) examines the concept of reluctant heir and the entry mode of the business family successors.

Davis and Harveston (1998) also look at individual perceptions of satisfaction their working relationships with the fathers. The findings suggested that working with the father as a boss can be satisfying in much family business. Ward (2011) points out that there is high level of resistance from the second generation managers of being in the company. Davis and Harveston (1998) suggest that the involvement of family members in the business does not mean that it should be the first born of the family; other members can also join family business and manage them.

The theory by Rogal (1989) examines the need to have the family members to plan and make a quality decision about the type of career they would like to pursue. The process of accessing the ability, interests and the successor of the family business is a very crucial role. This cannot be replaced with any other process if the succession has to succeed (Dyer, 2003). The importance of communication and discussion by the family members is very critical regarding the career choice. Pradhan and Ranajee (2012) present a case study about the five family firms to describe three dimensions of sibling association and its importance in the transition process. The three dimensions are; bonding against rivalry, autonomy against dependency and leadership versus paralysis. Appreciating the unique characters, ability and talents of each family member minimizes the level of rivalry among them (Pradhan & Ranajee, 2012). This will create a process of individualism that will enable the members not to be stereotyped but encouraged to work together.

SOCIO-CULTURAL ISSUES IN SUCCESSION

In the previous sections, issues of planning, management, innovation, and family have been examined. These issues inform the broader business environment that an organisation has to run within. The environment of a business can be defined within the political, economic, social, technological and legal framework (Becker 2013). In a society that is influenced greatly by the cultural aspects, the social environment plays a key role in determining how decisions are made and the management issues that are involved. Family run entities have strong influence of the family and thus the social cultural processes.

Kemp (2013) notes that family run entities have a key person who makes key decisions, which are often based on broader social issues such as:

- The role of religion: from a religious point of view, the place of women is clearly stated and they must remain subservient to their male counterparts. Thus, if a family does not have male children, the children of the next immediate family who are male (i.e. nephews) must run the entity (Pradhan & Ranajee, 2012).

- The kind of perception that is to be relayed to the clients: The main issue here relates to the image that the owner of business has created among clients. Family run businesses are identifiable by the patriarch who has personal touch and contact with clients and thus his active participation in business is an assurance to clients (Erdem, 2010). The owner or eldest family male member is therefore the nerve centre of the business, should this person leave by any reason, this might also mean that clients will lose faith in the ability of the business to serve their interests, because, their assurance and contact is gone (Kemp, 2013). Wagner-Tsukamoto (2008) implies that in such a case the issue of developing future leadership arises and the owner of business has to be questioned on their ability to develop leadership. In recent studies, Becker (2013) and Chesson (2012) indicate that business development that is based mainly on social structures is difficult to run and external help needs to be sought by existing leadership.
- The role played by women or men in the business: As discussed in previous sections of this research, in societies that are male dominated, the role of women is never clear because, there is no open acceptance that they are subservient, and yet there are no active steps taken to support the view to the contrary. In Saudi Arabia, the role of women is to be mothers and stay at home. Their involvement in running commercial entities is not considered, thus they remain less influential and never even considered in issues of succession (Wagner-Tsukamoto, 2008). Becker (2013) argues that this is biased leadership that does not benefit from the wealth of a certain section of the society.

Pradhan and Ranajee (2012) suggest that Hofstede's views on cultural dimensions cannot be ignored especially when examining the societies and business entities in the Middle Eastern world. Becker, (2013) and Nakauchi, and Wiersema (2014) indicate that in Saudi Arabia, male dominance is evident in all aspects of life and thus, business decisions and succession are more likely to be made by or benefited from by male members of the family. This situation means that women are not to be considered for any significant position and their risk averse nature is also not to be benefited from (Kootstra, 2009). The fact that women are left out of succession does not have any bearing with their ability but is purely a social dictate issue.

RESEARCH METHODOLOGY

The study adopts a qualitative approach which involves semi-structured, face to face interviews. The sample in this research includes a total of 6 respondents who are managers or executives of various family firms in Saudi Arabia. The qualitative approach is the only way this sample can assist the researchers to achieve the objectives of the study. The researchers strongly believe that reality is made up of events and objects as they are understood and perceived in the consciousness of human beings (Descombe, 1998). This is why the research makes use of family members who are managers or executives of various family firms in Saudi Arabia to gather information and make generalizations.

Respondents were given a copy of the questions to be asked in the interview in order to give them time to prepare and allow for any possible objections or clarifications to be raised and addressed before the interview commenced. This approach helped in putting the mind of the respondents at ease by reassuring them that they were better placed to answer the questions being asked as well as affording them plenty of time to come up with their answers.

Although the interviews followed a pre-determined topic guide, respondents were encouraged to go into as much depth as possible. This led to other questions naturally being raised as more information was provided. As a result of this, each interview lasted for at least an hour and a half, while the longest interview took two and a half hours to complete and some participants were interviewed up to three times.

The data in this study were collected and analysed using an inductive process of recording, tabulation, coding, and constantly comparing emerging codes and categories with data until meaningful ideas emerged (Yin, 2009; Ekanem, 2007). Categories were allowed to emerge according to the topics emphasised by each participant related to succession planning in their organisations. The process of analysing the data began as soon as the researcher started collecting data. It was ongoing and inductive as the researcher was trying to make sense of the data collected (Shaw, 1999).

The data analysis utilised a set of techniques such as content analysis, pattern-matching, and explanation-building technique (Yin, 2009; Ekanem, 2007). Content analysis involved listening to and transcribing the tapes, reading the transcripts to list the features associated with issues of succession planning and establishing categories which were then developed into systemic typology. These features included management and planning styles used in family business in Saudi Arabia, training and qualifications required when choosing managers and successors.

Pattern-matching technique involved examining whether there were any interesting patterns and how the data related to what was expected on the basis of common sense or previous theory (Yin, 2009). It also involved examining whether there were inconsistencies or contradictions in the narratives between the executives and managers. Explanation-building technique allowed series of linkages to be made and interpreted in the light of the explanations provided by each respondent (Yin 2009; Ekanem 2007. The aim was to build a general explanation based on cross-case analysis.

ANALYSIS OF FINDINGS AND DISCUSSION

The business industries that were interviewed include construction (brick lying), hospitality (restaurant, hotel), oil equipment, and academic institution (computer college). The need to gather data from respondents representing various industries was crucial, because the research examines the situation of family businesses in Saudi Arabia and thus it would be representative to collect data from various respondents instead of one line of business. The profile of the case study firms is as shown in Table 1.

The respondents were highly educated with diplomas, bachelor and masters' degrees, although the qualifications were not all related to what they were doing. The respondents had sufficient managerial experience. Based on the information given above, only one respondent had experience of less than 10 year. The others had more than ten years' experience and this is a good thing for their businesses. However, considering that some had qualifications that were not in line with their work, experience seem to count more in making them either effective or otherwise in their management and leadership roles.

Table 1. Summary profile of companies

Respondent	Industry	Who was Interviewed	Number of Interviews	Qualifications	Years of Managerial Experience
A	Hospitality	Owner- manager	2	Diploma	< 10
B	Construction	Manager	1	Diploma	10-15
C	Academic institution	Owner-manager	2	Bachelor degree	10-15
D	Hospitality	Manager	3	Bachelor degree	15-20
E	Restaurant	Owner-manager	3	Bachelor degree	>20
F	Oil equipment	Owner-manager	1	Masters' degree	>20

The Generation of Business

The first open ended question wanted to know the generation in which the current managers belong in order to understand the success or the period that the company has been in operation. Respondent A and D were from different business sectors and the organisations that they work for have been in place for many years and are family owned business. Respondent E stated that he was the fifth generation in the business and the family. This means that there have been five family generations which have been able to guide through the family. Respondent B was the second generation but the company has been in place for a long time because there were many successors within a single generation. Respondents C and F were from the third generation of their companies.

Training and Academic Qualifications Required When Choosing Managers and Successors

The questions in this section were aimed at looking at the management styles used in family businesses in Saudi Arabia. Most of the managers trained in areas that are not related to the business. There is no evidence of management training. This was captured from respondent C who stated that:

Most of the family members do not go for any formal training or management training. They just learn from others at place of work. There is no academic qualification in the management of family business

This is the perspective that was agreed by all the respondents as emphasised by respondent E:

Being a family member, especially male first born, is enough qualification (laughing). I know some people may not agree with me, but I took this from my father and I have worked here successfully for a long time. So I think it is important that the business is given to the children who show interest in running it

Similarly, respondent D remarked: “qualification and training of the family member is not key aspect in succession process.” However, there were those who felt that there is a need to have training in the area of management and the speciality area of family business because it will help in proper management. This was a comment after a follow-up question on the perspective of the respondents on academic qualification.

Performance of the Family Members in the Company

It was noted that it was not easy to monitor the performance of family members because they are perceived to be "above the law" as explained by respondent A:

Family members do not operate within the policies and the regulations of the company in many occasions. This is because they are guaranteed their job in the company or other family business.

Another respondent (Respondent C) commented that "performance is not equal to promotion or salary compensation for family members." These respondents saw performance as something that is not considered for family members either in managerial positions or just as employees.

The Succession Plans Put in Place

This was the second objective of the study which sought to establish the succession processes put in place by the family business in Saudi Arabia. The respondents stated that the key strategy they use in the business to ensure that it is sustainable in the next generation is to ensure that the culture that was established by the founders and the forerunners of the business is maintained. The respondents further pointed out that having trust and cohesion in the family ensures that the members are ready and willing to work together. This means that they are working hard to ensure that there is peace and cooperation among the family members. There were other aspects that were outlined to ensure that the company lives beyond its generation such as training and mentoring of the possible successors of the business.

Respondent A clearly pointed out that the main reason why businesses fail is because of lack of or poor succession plan. The respondent asserted that most of the family business in Saudi Arabia did not have a succession plan while others have already a designated person to take up the business such as the male member and the first born of the family. The respondent stated that having a clear succession plan that gives every member of the family an opportunity to become the CEO of the company ensures that the designated person work hard and show the interest to take up the business.

Selection Procedures for Family Members in the Organization

There was a general agreement by respondents that there is a need to have proper plans for succession of the business. This view was captured from the interview with Respondent B who stated:

In my view, planning should be done before hand. You cannot just pick someone because he is a member of family and put them to business, they can fail you.

Similarly, Respondent C stressed that 'without planning, failure is possible any time. For instance, I have heard of companies where there was no planning and for this reason the persons who were picked for the job did not know what to do'

However, respondent A stated that there was no proper plan for succession of his business but only the culture where the first male child of the current CEO takes up the family business. He emphasised:

We know the male child will run the business. So, any other plan may not succeed. But I am saying that the male persons who are chosen should be trained in business from an early stage so that they can be in a position to do well.

This means that there are no processes of carrying out succession processes in his organisation. Other respondents, E and F were of the same opinion, but they stated that it would be good to get consultants to run the business. Their view thus advocates planning for external help where necessary. Respondent D indicated that the business should decide what to do when the time comes and should not rush to any unrealistic conclusions about giving the children the work or leadership if they are not ready. He commented:

I cannot put someone in business just for the sake of making them leaders because they are my family. This is a no-no for me. I must always ensure that the person who is chosen is one that can actually do the right thing and can be fully accountable to me.

Similarly, Respondent E stated: 'I consider that any business that is successful has good planning in place to guide all that is taking place. If you are a business person and you do not have plan, then what kind of business are you running? I have been planning everything that we do, this is my policy'

Influence of Socio-Cultural Issues

One of the research objectives was to establish the influence of socio-cultural issues in managing succession of family run businesses in Saudi Arabia. The concept of cultural patterns and influence of the performance of the company was also a key objective of the study. Respondent A pointed out that the cultural aspect in which women are seen as those who can only take care of the family and children impacts on the success of the business. Women such as spouses of the founder or the leaders of the business do not offer any contribution to the business. They are not given leadership or even roles as employees in the business. The female members of the family are not considered in the business succession processes in Saudi Arabia. The respondent also stated that female are seen as objects and they are not respected at work place. This hinders the success of the business. If the family business owners do not have a male child, he will go to the level of marrying another wife so as to get one. The respondent further stated that even the female members of the family who have been to school are taking up training in field considered suitable for female such as religious studies, nursing, and so on. Hence, they are not trained to take up managerial roles in family businesses.

Respondent A pointed out that most businesses are cultured in a manner that the first born male child of the family is the rightful successor of the business. He stressed:

As you know in Saudi Arabia, it is the male children that inherit. They are thus the ones to run the business. However, things are changing, but for now, that is the situation.

This means that other family members already know their fate because they do not have chances of becoming the leaders of the company. The family business is likely to fail if the designated successor does not have the competency and the interest to run the business.

The Sources and Impact of Family Conflict on Succession Planning

This question wanted to establish the impact and the source of conflict in family business. Most of the respondents stated that extended family where the owner has more than one wife brings conflict. Respondent A, stated that:

Extended family always struggle on who to inherit the company and how they should be treated but this should actually not be an issue that divides families, but what can you do. In my understanding and in our culture and religion, the family must be looked after, so if my father had two or three women, all children are his and sharing should be done in a good way especially if a business is at stake

The respondents also observed that being at the top of the company is the ultimate goal of any family member hence every person strives to be at the top of the company. There is conflict in the family if the current CEO favours particular individuals in the family. Family conflict can result from outsiders such as the advisors and the board members. The board members may make a decision in the best interest of the company which may affect the family fabric. For example, as indicated by Respondent B:

If a particular person who is a designated successor of the company is left out of key managerial appointment may bring power struggle in the family.

There are other sources of conflict that were mentioned in the interview such as talents and shortcomings or weaknesses of the individuals being emphasized over the help they can bring to the family. The current people in position who do not want to let go of the company leadership even if their retirement age has come are also a source of conflict in the company. They may be grooming their own children to take up the business operations that are still young and not able to take over the business. The brothers and other family stakeholders such as cousins may want to take over the company. This brings issues which may result into family business failure as pointed out by Respondent C:

I think it is vital that an organisation knows who is to succeed the owner when the time comes. This should be within the articles of running the organisation. Failure to do this might result in the failure of the organisation.

The impact of family conflict was well presented during the interviews. The respondents stated that there is bound to be “failure and poor performance” when there is family conflict. These were the terms used by all the respondents.

CONCLUSION

The main issue being discussed in this research has been the question of dealing with business failure in Saudi Arabia, when the owner has left or is not able to continue running the entity. It is a major problem that has hailed the country for a long time, and the researchers were motivated to examine what can be done to deal with it. Business management and sustenance of the business are important issues that any economy needs. In Saudi Arabia, the patriarchs tend to consolidate power and know all secrets about the business, yet are unwilling to pass these to the generations that follow. In such instance, when the patriarchs are not able to manage their entities, business failure is imminent and this leads to poverty in the family and in the whole society, this is an issue that needs to be addressed.

There were three fundamental research questions that the study sought to address. The question about managers of family business following formal management style was answered in which most of the managers are not trained as managers.

They are simply selected to lead in which they learn while working. There were few managers who go to school and take up management and leadership training. The succession plan of the family business was also a major research question that has been addressed in the study. The study has established that most of the family businesses do not have a proper plan.

In this study, it was found that there are many factors that contribute to such challenges, and these have to do with trust, the subservience of women in the society and also challenges of conflict of interest between children and the older family members. These are issues that cannot be ignored, and solutions should be identified. It was thus necessary to gather data from family owned businesses, by interviewing owners and managers of businesses that are family owned and drawn from various industries.

Implications of the Study

This study has established that there are a number of challenges facing family owned organisations in Saudi Arabia. It is clear that most of the family owned businesses share one common problem and that is of perpetuity, but this problem is a culmination of a number of challenges, i.e. trust, lack of commitment by children, and the male society challenge.

One of the main challenges facing family businesses in Saudi Arabia has been found to be the problem of trust, where the business owners who are generally older members of the family are not keen to entrust the entity to the younger members of their families. In other words there is generational mistrust between the old and the young, with the old feeling that the young or their children are not up to the task. This makes them (the owners) to consolidate power and knowledge about the business to themselves and no one else.

With such a situation, it becomes difficult to provide any leadership or guidance that sustains the business because skills are not passed on. For instance, the owner knows everything about the business but the younger ones have no clue about anything. This jeopardises the future of the business if all of a sudden, it has to fall in the hands of the children. There is need to ensure that trust is built. This is no easy task, and it calls for change in perception among the owners about what their children can do.

Saudi Arabia is male dominated and this has been for a long time. Women tend to be subservient to their male counterparts and are not allowed to do much. This situation has caught the attention of the international community and there have been effort to deal with it. Recently, the King named first woman cabinet minister, and this is a step in the right direction. Much have to be done to provide women with the kind of support that they need to do their businesses. There is need to ensure that a space is opened for women to run businesses. In some families where women are the only children or are old members of the family, the business can easily pass to uncles and nephews who may not have any desire to run such businesses. There is need to have a paradigm change in the society to include women in running businesses. There are success stories about few women in Saudi Arabia and this implies that given the chance, they can really embark on beneficial business activities for their families. It is also evident that women are keen in doing something that is of economic benefit and are also risk averse, a quality that can make them to be good at running their family entities to greater benefits.

It is also important that in some circumstances, businesses can be placed under the leadership of a professional management organisation. It is evident that succession is a major challenge because children may also not wish to run the businesses or know how to do the same. In such a case, the businesses may fail. It would be good if a consultancy organisation is entrusted with the business in a clearly given agreement so that the continuity of the business can be guaranteed. This again calls for the owners of the businesses to adapt and accept that the business can be entrusted to others.

In families where there are young children, this can be a very good option, and the agreement can state that the children can be trained and be allowed to take over the management and leadership after a certain age, which will be beneficial to them and to the business as well. There are a number of professional consultancy bodies in Saudi Arabia that can be contracted for this purpose. The government can also seek to support this initiative by creating business support departments in every city that can help support the growth of businesses.

One of the challenges that were identified in this study is the fact that the owners tend to consolidate power and knowledge and are reluctant to pass these on to their children. This poses imminent threats to the entity because the children cannot then run the entity. It would be important to groom the children in the line of business, i.e. even occasionally allowing them to come to the shop-floor at an early age. This will instil in them the business acumen that they will require when the responsibility is left to them.

While it is not good to patronise the children, the owners can discuss the interests of the children and those who wish to learn business management can be trained, so that they can come out of university and schools with the knowledge and skills that are in line with their business areas, and be able to take over the entity.

Family businesses are prevalent in Saudi Arabia and there is need to ensure that in the curriculum at schools, there is an inclusion of business management modules. In so doing, it would be possible for the children to learn how to run a business or some may develop interest in the same and will focus on running their businesses. This should be encouraged and it calls for the government through relevant ministries to roll out plans to include modules of business and entrepreneurship.

Limitation of the Study

The study has several limitations which suggest the implication for further research. The major limitation of the study is the extent to which the study can be generalised to wider population of family businesses in Saudi Arabia. Due to the relatively small sample of respondents who took part in the study, it would not be wise to assume that their views represent that of the general population at large. It would require a larger sample for the views collected to represent the views of family businesses in Saudi Arabia.

REFERENCES

Afifi, M. (2002). Compatibility between the characteristics of family businesses and the requirements of successful change management. Family Business Forum in the Arab World, Jeddah, Saudi Arabia.

Asad Sadi, M., & Henderson, J. C. (2007). In search of greener pastures: Al-Marai and dairy food business in Saudi Arabia. *British Food Journal, 109*(8), 637–647. doi:10.1108/00070700710772426

Becker, T. E. (2013). Nepotism and the Commitment of Relevant Parties. *Nepotism in Organizations*, 129.

Berrone, P., Cruz, C., & Gomez-Mejia, L. R. (2012). Socio-emotional wealth in family firms theoretical dimensions, assessment approaches, and agenda for future research. *Family Business Review, 25*(3), 258–279. doi:10.1177/0894486511435355

Binder. (1994). *The quest for growth: A survey of UK private companies.* London: Author.

Block, J. H. (2012). R&D investments in family and founder firms: An agency perspective. *Journal of Business Venturing*, *27*(2), 248–265. doi:10.1016/j.jbusvent.2010.09.003

Blodgett, M. S., Dumas, C., & Zanzi, A. (2011). Emerging trends in global ethics: A comparative study of US and international family business values. *Journal of Business Ethics*, *99*(1), 29–38. doi:10.1007/s10551-011-1164-7

Bocatto, E., Gispert, C., & Rialp, J. (2010). Family-Owned Business Succession: The Influence of Pre-performance in the Nomination of Family and Nonfamily Members: Evidence from Spanish Firms. *Journal of Small Business Management*, *48*(4), 497–523. doi:10.1111/j.1540-627X.2010.00306.x

Carayannis, E. G., & Papadopoulos, C. B. (2011). The innovation diplomacy concept and the Hellenic-American innovation bridge as a special case-in-point. *J Knowl Econ*, *2*(3), 257–326. doi:10.1007/s13132-011-0056-5

Chesson, P. (2012). Scale transition theory: Its aims, motivations and predictions. *Ecological Complexity*, *10*, 52–68. doi:10.1016/j.ecocom.2011.11.002

Chung, C. N., & Luo, X. R. (2013). Leadership succession and firm performance in an emerging economy: Successor origin, relational embeddedness, and legitimacy. *Strategic Management Journal*, *34*(3), 338–357. doi:10.1002/smj.2011

Churchill, N. C., & Hatten, K. J. (1997). Non-market-based transfers of wealth and power: A research framework for family business. *Family Business Review*, *10*(1), 53–67. doi:10.1111/j.1741-6248.1997.00053.x

Daily, C. M., & Dollinger, M. J. (1993). An empirical examination of ownership structure and family and professionally managed firms. *Family Business Review*, (5): 117–136.

Danco, K. (1981). *From the other side of the bed: A woman looks at life in the family business*. Cleveland, OH: University Press.

Davis, P. S., & Harveston, P. D. (1998). The influence of family on the family business succession process: A multi-generational perspective. *Entrepreneurship Theory and Practice, 22*, 31-54.

Dawson, M. (2005). *The Consumer Trap: Big Business Marketing in American Life*. Urbana, IL: University of Illinois Press.

Denscombe, M. (1998). *The Good Research Guide*. Buckingham, UK: Open University Press.

Dyer, W. G. (2003). The Family: The Missing Variable in Organizational Research. *Entrepreneurship Theory and Practice, 27*(4), 401-416.

Ekanem, I. (2007). Insider Accounts: A qualitative research method for small firms. *Journal of Small Business and Enterprise Development, 14*(1), 105–117. doi:10.1108/14626000710727926

Erdem, F. (2010). *Family Business Reputation: A Literature Review and Some Research Questions. Electronic Journal of Family Business Studies*, 4(2).

Frynas, G., & Mellahi, K. (2011). *Global Strategic Management*. New York: Oxford University Press.

Handler, W. C. (1994). Succession in family business: A review of the research. *Family Business Review*, *7*(2), 133–157. doi:10.1111/j.1741-6248.1994.00133.x

Kanoo, K. H. (1995). Family Businesses and the Road to Survival. *Eastern Region Chamber of Commerce Economic Symposium*. Kingdom of Saudi Arabia.

Kemp, L. J. (2013). Modern to postmodern management: Developments in scientific management. *Journal of Management History*, *19*(3), 345–361. doi:10.1108/JMH-02-2011-0005

Kets de Vries, M. F. (2012). Star Performers: Paradoxes wrapped up in enigmas. *Organizational Dynamics*, *41*(3), 173–182. doi:10.1016/j.orgdyn.2012.03.010

Kets de Vries, M. F. R. (2013). *Organizational paradoxes: Clinical approaches to management*. New York: Routledge.

Kootstra, G. L. (2009). *The incorporation of design management in today's business practises: An analysis of design management practises in Europe*. Design Management Europe: ADMIRE programme.

Lin, W. T. (2014). Founder-key leaders, group-level decision teams, and the international expansion of business groups: Evidence from Taiwan. *International Marketing Review*, *31*(2), 129–154. doi:10.1108/IMR-07-2012-0120

Litz, R. (2012). Double roles, double binds? Double bind theory and family business research. In Understanding Family Business: Unique Perspectives. Springer New York.

Litz, R. A., Pearson, A. W., & Litchfield, S. (2012). Charting the future of family business research perspectives from the field. *Family Business Review*, *25*(1), 16–32. doi:10.1177/0894486511418489

Lyman, A. R. (1991). Customer service: Does p make a difference. *Family Business Review*, *4*(3), 303–324. doi:10.1111/j.1741-6248.1991.00303.x

McGivem, C. (1989). The dynamics of management succession: A model of chief executive succession in the small family firm. *Family Business Review*, *2*(4), 401–411. doi:10.1111/j.1741-6248.1989.tb00007.x

Ministry of Economy and Planning. (2009). *Statistical Yearbook*. Riyadh: Author.

Morelli, N., & Sangiorgi, D. (2006). Managing globalization and local issues in service design: on the convergence between opposing demands of industrialisation and personalisation of service performance. *Proceedings: D2B – The first international design management symposium*.

Nakauchi, M., & Wiersema, M. F. (2014). Executive succession and strategic change in Japan. *Strategic Management Journal*.

Nordqvist, M., Wennberg, K., & Hellerstedt, K. (2013). An entrepreneurial process perspective on succession in family firms. *Small Business Economics*, *40*(4), 1087–1122. doi:10.1007/s11187-012-9466-4

Pradhan, S., & Ranajee, J. (2012, December). Value Creation by Family-Owned Businesses: A Literature Review. *The IUP Journal of Business Strategy*, *IX*(4), 35–45.

Ramady, M. A. (2010). *The Saudi Arabian economy: policies, achievements and challenges*. Spingler.

Rogal, K. H. (1989). Obligation or Opportunity: How Can Could-Be Heirs Assess Their Position? *Family Business Review*, *2*(3), 237–255. doi:10.1111/j.1741-6248.1989.00237.x

Sfakianakis, J. (2009). *Challenges facing family businesses in Saudi Arabia*. Accessible at: www.Arabnews.com

Sharma, P., & Hoy, F. (2013). Family business roles. *The Landscape of Family Business*, 113.

Shaw, E. (1999). A guide to the qualitative research process: Evidence from a small firm study. *Qualitative Market Research: An International Journal*, *2*(2), 59–70. doi:10.1108/13522759910269973

Sullivan, K. T., & Perrenoud, A. (2012). *Executive Succession Planning*. ELECTRI International and Arizona State University.

Tagiuri, R., & Davis, J. A. (1992). On the goals of successful family companies. *Family Business Review*, *5*(1), 43–62. doi:10.1111/j.1741-6248.1992.00043.x

Time. (2009). *Leaders and Revolutionaries* [Online]. Available from http://content.time.com/time/specials/packages/article/0,28804,1894410_1893847_1893841,00.html

Wagner-Tsukamoto, S. (2008). Scientific Management revisited: Did Taylorism fail because of a too positive image of human nature? *Journal of Management History*, *14*(4), 348–372. doi:10.1108/17511340810893108

Ward, J. L. (2011). *Keeping the family business healthy: How to plan for continuing growth, profitability, and family leadership*. Macmillan. doi:10.1057/9780230116122

Weathington, B. L., Cunningham, C. J. L., & Pittenger, D. P. (2010). *Research Methods for the Behavioral and Social Sciences*. Hoboken, NJ: John Wiley & Sons, Inc.

Yin, R. (2009). *Case Study Research: Design and Methods*. London: Sage.

Zellweger, T., & Sieger, P. (2012). Entrepreneurial orientation in long-lived family firms. *Small Business Economics*, *38*(1), 67–84. doi:10.1007/s11187-010-9267-6

Chapter 8
Critical Review of Entrepreneurship in Oman

Neeta Baporikar
Namibia University of Science and Technology, Namibia

ABSTRACT

Entrepreneurship has assumed super importance for accelerating economic growth both in developed and developing countries. It promotes capital formation and creates wealth in country. It is hope and dreams of millions of individuals around the world. It reduces unemployment and poverty and it is a pathway to prosper. The word entrepreneur is of French origin and literally means the person that takes between – the middlemen; in a more free translation, the individual who pursues a commercial activity. In spite of various studies, defining entrepreneurship is still a major dispute among researchers and the word entrepreneur still has no common meaning among the academic community. So, espousing a very broad definition for entrepreneurship that incorporates business owners and self-employed individuals and adopting a grounded theory approach with in depth literature review of published documents and data, the core of this chapter is to review critically entrepreneurship in the Middle East with specific focus on Oman.

DOI: 10.4018/978-1-5225-2066-5.ch008

INTRODUCTION

In recent years, the promotion of entrepreneurship as a possible source of job creation, empowerment and economic dynamism in a rapidly globalizing world has attracted increasing policy and scholarly attention (Baporikar, 2014). Entrepreneurship has assumed super importance for accelerating economic growth both in developed and developing countries. It promotes capital formation and creates wealth in country. It is hope and dreams of millions of individuals around the world. It reduces unemployment and poverty and it is a pathway to prosper. Entrepreneurship is the process of exploring the opportunities in the market place and arranging resources required to exploit these opportunities for long term gain (Baporikar, 2002, 2007). Economists have been trying to relate economic development to entrepreneurial activity. However, apart from several theories, empirical findings do not allow us to draw any definite conclusions on the connection between overall economic development and any aspect of entrepreneurship. It is important though to identify the different ways in which economic development is facilitated. These generally are:

- **Growth of Capital Stock:** Capital is one of the key elements of entrepreneurship, and when more capital is available it is assumed that entrepreneurial activity will be facilitated.
- **Technological Progress:** Technological progress is imported as well as endogenous to the entrepreneurial activity. New technology is sometimes adopted by the entrepreneur, while in other instances developed through the knowledge base that is established by past entrepreneurial activity.
- **Endogenous Increase of Personal Wealth:** In the case that the entrepreneur or the worker will accumulate wealth from own work, it is expected that this wealth will be directed to new or further entrepreneurial activity.

Thus, entrepreneurship and entrepreneurial activities play an important role in the daily business environment. Entrepreneurship has also crucial role in the world economy. Entrepreneurship is an interesting topic as it deals with the behaviour of the firm entrepreneur and the entrepreneur's main competencies. However, the field of entrepreneurship world over is evolving (Baporikar, 2011, 2013). Further the networked economies are playing a greater role in creating level playing field and facilitating rise of entrepreneurship world over (Baporikar, 2015b). The concept of an entrepreneur is refined when principles and terms from a business, managerial, and personal perspective are considered. In almost all of the definitions of entrepreneurship, there is agreement that we are talking about a kind of behaviour that includes: initiative taking, the organizing and reorganizing of social and economic mechanisms to turn resources and situations to practical account and acceptance of risk or failure. To an economist, an entrepreneur is one who brings resources, labour, materials, and other assets into combinations that make their value greater than before, and also one who introduces changes, innovations, and a new order. To a psychologist, such a person is typically driven by certain forces; the need to obtain or attain something, to experiment, to accomplish, or perhaps to escape the authority of others. To one businessman, an entrepreneur appears as a threat, an aggressive competitor, whereas to another businessman the same entrepreneur may be an ally, a source of supply, a customer, or someone who creates wealth for others, as well as finds better ways to utilize resources, reduce waste, and produce jobs others are glad to get.

Thus, entrepreneurship refers to a process that is dynamic and creates incremental wealth. The wealth is created by individuals who assume the major risks in terms of equity, time and/or career commitment or provide value for some product or service. The product or service may or may not be new or unique, but value must somehow be infused by the entrepreneur by receiving and locating the necessary skills and resources efficiently and effectively. Entrepreneurship is thus considered as the process of creating something new with value by devoting the necessary time and effort, assuming the accompanying financial, psychic, and social risks, and receiving the resulting rewards of monetary and personal satisfaction and independence that comes with it. This definition stresses four basic aspects of being an entrepreneur regardless of the field. First, entrepreneurship involves the creation process, creating something new of value. The creation has to have value to the entrepreneur and value to the audience for which it is developed. Entrepreneurship has assumed super importance for accelerating economic growth both in developed and developing countries. It promotes capital formation and creates wealth in country. It is hope and dreams of millions of individuals around the world. It reduces unemployment and poverty and it is a pathway to prosper. Entrepreneurship is the process of exploring the opportunities in the market place and arranging resources required to exploit these opportunities for long term gain (Baporikar, 2002). It is the process of planning, organizing, opportunities and assuming. Thus it is a risk of business enterprise. It may be distinguished as an ability to take risk independently to make utmost earnings in the market. It is a creative and innovative skill and adapting response to environment.

Given entrepreneurship's potential to support economic growth, it is the policy goal of many governments to develop a culture of entrepreneurial thinking. This can be done in a number of ways: by integrating entrepreneurship into education systems, legislating to encourage risk-taking, and national campaigns. An example of the latter is the United Kingdom's Enterprise Week. Outside of the political world, research has been conducted on the presence of entrepreneurial theories in doctoral economics programs. Many of these initiatives have been brought together under the umbrella of Global Entrepreneurship Week, a worldwide celebration and promotion of youth entrepreneurship, which started in 2008. Some of the countries have even established separate institutions to develop entrepreneurship. Debate on the value and importance of entrepreneurship at the national level has almost reached consensus in developed societies. Unfortunately, this is not the case in many developing countries. Developed economies produce 10 times more new ventures per adult per year compared to countries in the Middle East (World Bank, 2010). In most of these countries, the problem is not lack of entrepreneurship, but rather a negative macro environment and infrastructure, which channels entrepreneurial activity into unproductive and destructive economic directions. This is especially visible in three core issues: opportunity to enter, access to capital, and access to skill and knowledge (UNDP, 2004). Furthermore, most of the entrepreneurship activity in these countries is 'necessity entrepreneurship' and not opportunity driven (Reynolds et al., 2004). A prevailing high unemployment situation, when combined with low social welfare infrastructure, pushes people in these countries to start a business in order to survive. In addition, many of these businesses are in the informal sector because of the rigid and expensive new business start-up process, thus limiting their ability to expand through formal channels of resources (Reynolds et al., 2004). Based on the recent 'Doing Business 2010' report, the last 40 positions in ease of doing business are all occupied by developing countries. The overall lack of entrepreneurship development in many of these countries can be attributed to hostile entrepreneurial environments. On the positive side, there have been some new entrepreneurship development initiatives, especially in the Gulf region. For example, the Qatar Science and Technology Park, Knowledge Economic City in Saudi Arabia, Knowledge Oasis, Oman and Dubai's Mohamed bin Rashid Al-Maktoum Foundation are all promising initiatives that are much needed. India is also a promising role model for other developing countries, and is one of the oldest countries that have developed successful entrepreneurship development initiatives (Gupta, 1989). But, with approximately 50% living below the poverty line with high population growth rates in the world, these government efforts need to be accelerated and organized. The only way forward in these countries is through emphasizing endogenous development rather than depending on external aid or foreign investments alone. Encouraging entrepreneurship will do developing countries more good, in terms of long-term growth and gains in productivity, leading to better entrepreneurship and economic development. The word entrepreneur is of French origin and literally means the person that takes between – the middlemen; in a more free translation, the individual who pursues a commercial activity. As Bruyat and Julien (2001) point out, defining entrepreneurship is still a major dispute among researchers and the word entrepreneur still has no common meaning among the academic community. There are several approaches to this issue, which come from different viewpoints and have their roots within the theory that each scholar adopts as the basis for his or her research. The explanation and presentation of the various streams that dominate the definition debate is not within the spectrum of this work. Anyone interested in studying the lively dialogue on this issue can refer to some of the many papers that deal with it. So, adopting a very broad definition for entrepreneurship that incorporates business owners and self-employed individuals, the core of this chapter is to review critically entrepreneurship in the Middle East with specific focus on Oman. The chapter is organized as follows: Section 1 provides the background, followed by literature review. Section 3, 4 and 5 examine country profile of Oman, issues pertaining to entrepreneurship development and barriers to entrepreneurship development in Oman. Section 6 concludes the discussion.

BACKGROUND

An entrepreneur is one who creates a new business in the face of risk and uncertainty for the purpose of achieving profit and growth by identifying significant opportunities and assembling the necessary resources to capitalize on them (Zimmerer & Scarborough, 2008). The French economist Richard Cantillon is generally recognized with being the first to think up the phrase in the context of what we view today as entrepreneurship in about 1730. He defined entrepreneurs as risk takers, in the sense that they purchased goods at certain prices in the present to sell at uncertain prices in the future. Entrepreneurs attempt to forecast and act upon change within markets. The entrepreneur is a bearer of uncertainty (Cantillon, 1755). The entrepreneur bears the uncertainty of market dynamics (Knight, 1921, 1942). Thus entrepreneur can be defined as "an individual who is enterprising, disposed to risk-taking and willing to stake his future for larger good of resources and society". Entrepreneurs are major contributors to economic growth, development, and prosperity; see Schramm (2006a) and Baumol, Litan, Schramm (2007). Entrepreneurs are responsible for a large share of technological innovation in products and production processes, driving economic transformation and international trade. Entrepreneurs establish new forms of organizations and employ new types of business methods. Economic theory must keep up with these critical developments by understanding the fundamental contributions of entrepreneurs. Such an understanding is essential for formulating economic policies that do not restrict productive entrepreneurs. Yet, despite the essential nature of their economic contribution, the importance of entrepreneurs has not been recognized fully in neoclassical economics. Thus, it is important to understand, the economic framework to recognise the economic contribution of the entrepreneur. Entrepreneurs play a central role in the modern economy because they are the prime movers – the makers of firms. Entrepreneurs are fundamental to economic equilibrium because they set the economy in motion. Firms are responsible for practically all economic activity outside of government: innovating, pricing, contracting, employing resources, labor, and capital goods, raising financial capital, organizing production, and marketing goods and services. In equilibrium, firms create markets as well as organizations, making both types of institutions endogenous. Economic equilibrium, including prices, allocation of goods, and the structure of transactions, thus depends on the actions of entrepreneurs. The discussion draws upon the microeconomic analysis in Spulber (2008) in which not only entrepreneurs, but also firms, markets, and organizations are endogenous.

Yet, as individuals, entrepreneurs are distinct from firms. An individual engages in entrepreneurial activities before the firm is established and then becomes an owner after the firm is established. Richard Cantillon introduced the entrepreneur in 1732 in his path-breaking economic treatise. The theory of the entrepreneur has undergone cycles of revival and neglect throughout the history of economic thought. Jean-Baptiste Say (1841, 1852) provides the first comprehensive discussion of the entrepreneur in economic analysis, emphasizing the effects of the entrepreneur's reputation, judgment, and risk bearing on profit. Entrepreneurs are central to Frank Knight's (1971) discussion of risk, uncertainty, and profit. Knight emphasizes both the supply of and demand for entrepreneurship. Joseph Schumpeter (1934, p. 75) identifies entrepreneurship as "the fundamental phenomenon of economic development. The carrying out of new combinations we call 'enterprise'; the individuals whose function it is to carry them out we call 'entrepreneurs.'" Schumpeter (1934, p. 66) further observes that "new combinations are, as a rule, embodied, as it were, in new firms which generally do not arise out of the old ones but start producing beside them." These classical themes are developed further in the modern literature on the entrepreneur. Mark Casson's (1982, p. 23) discussion emphasizes intermediation by entrepreneurs: "an entrepreneur is someone who specializes in taking judgmental decisions about the coordination of scarce resources," see also Casson (2003). Casson (1982, 2003) describes the entrepreneur as a coordinator and middleman. Casson (1982, p. 84) argues that the firm provides market-making activities to address each of these: contact making via search or advertising, specification and communication of the trade to each party, negotiation, transport and administration, monitoring of quality, and enforcement. Casson (1982, chapter 9) concludes that the entrepreneur "specializes in providing market-making services." The entrepreneur builds the firm as a "market making organization" to reduce the transaction costs of intermediation. Casson (1982, p. 84) identifies various obstacles to trade including no contact between buyer and seller, no knowledge of reciprocal wants, no agreement over price, need to exchange goods and pay taxes, no confidence in product descriptions, and no confidence that restitution will be made for default. Casson (1982, p. 97) points out that "For information flows as complex as those required for the operation of a market, social convention is usually unable to provide the degree of structure required. Greater sophistication is called for and this necessitates the use of purpose-built organizations. Among these purpose-built organizations are market-making firms."

Hellmann (2007) models the entrepreneur as an intermediary in the market for inputs needed to establish a firm and shows how the entrepreneur convinces suppliers of complementary resources to commit to the new venture. Baumol (1968) emphasizes the function of the entrepreneur as locating new ideas, putting them into effect, and exercising leadership. Baumol (2006) argues that the innovative entrepreneur relies on price discrimination to raise funds for innovation. Baumol (1993) presents theoretical models that examine the innovative activities of the entrepreneur, see also Baumol (2002, 2006). Baumol (1993) contrasts innovations that are substitutes from those that are complements, and shows how incentives can differ for firms engaged in complementary innovation.

COUNTRY PROFILE OF OMAN

Oman is an interesting case since, unlike many neighbouring nations that rely almost entirely on oil revenues, in Oman several non-energy business sectors, such as tourism and light manufacturing are expanding rapidly (Baporikar, (2015c). According to some, the Omani economy is one of the freest economies in its region. The Oman government has worked hard to create infrastructure to fuel and support a rising generation of entrepreneurs (Baporikar, 2015a). The Sultanate of Oman is an Arab country located on the eastern side of the Middle East, bordering the United Arab Emirates, the Kingdom of Saudi Arabia, and Yemen. It has a population of approximately 2.8 million, and covers 309,500 square kilometers. When the current Sultan, Qaboos bin Said, assumed power in 1970, a new era began in the modern history of the country. Pre-1970 Oman was characterized by political turmoil in the South and the interior, national illiteracy, poverty, and widespread diseases. Since then, a renaissance period of infrastructure developments in all sectors, fueled by oil capital, positioned Oman as one of the most progressive countries in the Middle East. The discovery of oil during the last century was a cornerstone in the development of the infrastructure and economy in the region. For the past 41 years, Oman's main export has been oil, which is still the backbone of the economy and constitutes around 80% of total government revenue. Although oil has been the source of much of the economic and social prosperity in the past, it has become, to some degree, blight in relation to developing a strong, diversified, innovative economy.

Besides, as the population grew faster than the economy could sustain, serious economic challenges have arisen. The growth in population has outstripped the capacity of higher education institutes and the job market. This has created two main challenges for the government - unemployment and provision of opportunities for higher education. These economic and social dilemmas have been key factors in pressurizing the government to look at entrepreneurship and self-employment, especially among the young. However, fostering indigenous entrepreneurship is not going to be easy for a country that has a small private sector and low national entrepreneurial activity, *'Oman's economy is suffering from an underlying entrepreneurial malaise, which without action, will hinder economic growth'* (Porter, 2003, p. 51). For instance, in 2003, fewer than 2 in 100 were starting a new business, compared to 1 in 10 in the US (MOM, 2005). In the last ten years there has not been a single IPO issued for a new high-growth venture in the Muscat Securities Market (MSM). However, entrepreneurship has been a buzzword, especially among young people between the ages of 18-34 (Chen & Lai, 2010). They have recognized the various benefits of starting-up new businesses. According to Badulescu & Dodescu (2010), the motivations for business start-ups among potential women entrepreneurs are driven mostly by the 'self-achievement desire', 'need for more money' and 'desire for a higher social and professional status'. Entrepreneurs demonstrate a need to achieve, a willingness to exploit a challenge, to persevere, to work hard and driven by self-belief, but tempered with the ability to be flexible and to delegate to others when necessary as well as willingness to listen to advice and to recognize that they are not experts in every aspect of their business (Goodbody Economic Consultants, 2002).

Allen (2006) stressed that entrepreneurs do not wait for someone else to make the decision, or solve the problem, or even ask for the problem to be solved; they recognize problems as opportunities and takes it upon themselves to solve them. Management specialists, policy makers, researchers, and practitioners view entrepreneurship in various perspectives. Goel, Vohra, Zhang, & Arora (2007) briefly define it as the activity of establishing and managing a business for profit and growth. This notion resembles closely what McMullan, Long and Graham (in Lena & Wong, 2004) said that entrepreneurship is an instrumental factor driving the emergence and growth of new businesses. In a parallel note, Smallbone and Welter (2001) said that entrepreneurship includes self-employment and part-time businesses, while Bhide (2000) relates it to venture creation and ownership of small and medium enterprises. In the present day, however, Oman is an interesting case. Unlike many neighboring nations that rely almost entirely on oil revenues, in Oman several non-energy business sectors, such as tourism and light manufacturing are expanding rapidly. According to some, the Omani economy is one of the freest economies in its region. The Oman government has worked hard to create infrastructure to fuel and support a rising generation of entrepreneurs. In 2009, the Ministry of Education launched the "I'm an Entrepreneur" campaign to create more awareness about entrepreneurship amongst students and recent unrest has doubled Oman efforts. For example, other governments might make note that His Majesty Sultan Qaboos already established a Fund for the Development of Youth Projects (known today under the name 'Sharakah') in collaboration with the private sector to provide capital and assistance for business projects set up by young Omanis. A royal Decree exempts the Fund from company income tax for 10 years and from corporate tax and tax on profits for five years. Also, non-governmental organizations are now active, such as Injaz – Junior Achievement in the Middle East. Hence, when one visits Oman today, one can see that it is a contemporary country with highways, sleek new airports, satellite TV dishes and a range of public and private universities.

Entrepreneurship Development

Entrepreneurship development is concerned with the study of entrepreneurial behaviour, the dynamics of business set-up, development and expansion of the enterprise. Entrepreneurship development (ED) refers to the process of enhancing entrepreneurial skills and knowledge through structured training and institution-building programmes. It basically aims to enlarge the base of entrepreneurs in order to hasten the pace at which new ventures are created. This accelerates employment generation and economic development. Entrepreneurship development focuses on the individual who wishes to start or expand a business. Small and medium enterprise (SME) development, on the other hand, it also focuses on developing the enterprise, whether or not it employs or is led by individuals who can be considered entrepreneurial. Furthermore, entrepreneurship development concentrates more on growth potential and innovation than SME development does. However, many of the lessons learned from experiences in both types of development are similar. Entrepreneurship is promoted to help alleviate the unemployment problem, to overcome the problem of stagnation and to increase the competitiveness and growth of business and industries. Various attempts have been made to promote and develop entrepreneurship in all economies. Oman is also gearing up for entrepreneurship development as it is also shifting from being merely an oil-based economy.

Before discussing further issues in entrepreneurship development, it is essential to understand that entrepreneurial activities do not take place in a vacuum. Hence, it becomes important and is imperative to consider the specific institutional context in which they operate. Within the wider social, cultural, and political contexts, based on GEM's entrepreneurship model, Figure 1, highlights the fact that there are basic requirements (e.g., institutions, infrastructure, macroeconomic stability and education), efficiency enhancers (e.g., higher education, technological readiness and market size), and a number of innovation and entrepreneurship conditions that all contribute to firm expansion, entrepreneurship development and, eventually,

Figure 1. Institutional context and its relationship to entrepreneurship
Source: Modified from GEM, 2010.

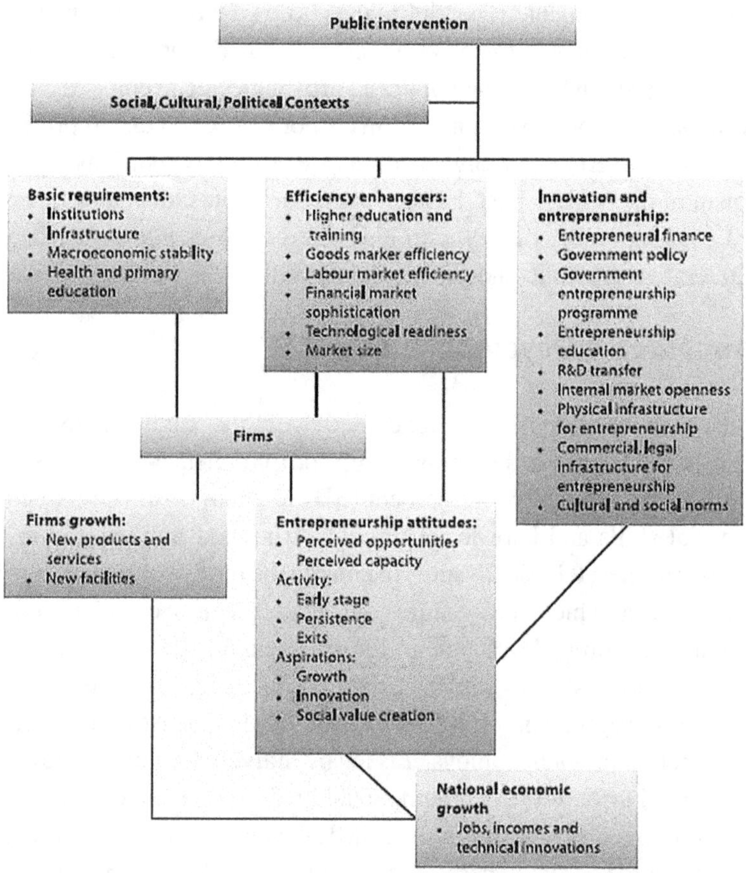

national economic growth. While these factors also have an impact on established firms, new entrepreneurs are particularly sensitive and the presence of these conditions can have a significant positive impact on their development. Given this framework, policymakers have to choose suitable policy instruments in order to stimulate positive entrepreneurial attitudes within a society, and encourage entrepreneurs to recognize valuable business opportunities and pursue skills to capitalize on them. Most importantly, governments need to encourage entrepreneurs' aspirations to grow, innovate and help entrench these social values in order to promote sustainable competitiveness. Through the provision of supportive resources and policies, policymakers can help increase entrepreneurship activities for greater national competitiveness and sustained economic growth.

Entrepreneurship Role and Phases of Economic Development

The World Economic Forum (2011) classifies entrepreneurial activities according to three stages of economic development: factor-driven, efficiency-driven and innovation-driven. Factor-driven economies are largely extractive, whereas efficiency-driven economies and innovation-driven economies add increasing amounts of value in their production of goods and services. The hallmark of efficiency driven economies is scale, whereas that of innovation-driven economies is creativity GEM (2012). It is further notable that the entrepreneurship percentage is generally higher in the factor driven economies than in efficiency and innovation economies, not only in the region but on average overall. Some of the realities of entrepreneurship are given based on Shane (2008). They are:

- People are more likely to start companies in places that are poorer, with high rates of unemployment than richer places with low rates of unemployment.
- The typical startup is an ordinary, barely innovative, homebased business that starts and stays tiny.
- Entrepreneurs do not select industries because they are good for startups but rather because they know these industries.
- The typical entrepreneur, who is a middle-aged person, starts a business because they do not like working for someone else and because they are just trying to make a living.
- People are more likely to go into business for themselves if they are unemployed, work part-time, have changed jobs often and make less money.
- Obtaining higher levels of education makes people more likely to start businesses. Studying fields or subjects that correspond to occupations in which many people run their own businesses is likely to increase a person's chances of starting a business.
- Most entrepreneurs do not systematically search for, or evaluate, their new business ideas
- More people even start companies before they have identified a business idea than the other way around.
- The typical business is started by a single person alone or with their spouses working together.
- It does not take a large amount of money to start a business and the most common source of capital for a new business is personal savings.

ISSUES IN ENTREPRENEURSHIP DEVELOPMENT

Entrepreneurship has received much attention from both scholars and policy makers during the past decades because there is a growing need in many countries for entrepreneurs to enhance economic growth and development. Entrepreneurial activities provide employment opportunities and increase competitiveness. Policy makers and scholars around the world are trying to learn how they can stimulate entrepreneurial activities as well as understand why some people choose entrepreneurial careers and others do not. Entrepreneurial behavior can be looked at from either internal or external viewpoints of an individual. The internal viewpoint looks at the personality traits of an individual such as, locus of control, risk taking, need for achievement, problem solving, innovation, creativity perception and work values in relation to entrepreneurial activity. Many social scientists have different views about entrepreneurial intentions of people and diverse studies focus on the effect of personality characteristics on attitudes towards entrepreneurial activities (Bonnett & Furnham, 1991). Although the results vary across the studies, these studies do indicate a link between entrepreneurial intention and some personality factors. These include self- confidence; risk taking ability; the need to achieve and locus of control. Other researchers have sought the entrepreneurial personality in risk-taking propensity; internal locus of control; tolerance for ambiguity; over-optimism, and need for autonomy (Delmar, 2000). Rotter (1989) developed the concept of locus of control as a force responsible for an individual's decision to become an entrepreneur. In addition, he says that individuals with a high internal locus of control are more likely to become entrepreneurs, than those of high external locus of control. Miao & Ying (2008) have studied the effects of entrepreneurial traits on entrepreneurial orientation. He identified entrepreneurial traits as need for achievement, risk propensity and locus of control. The dimensions of entrepreneurial orientation include innovativeness, risk taking and pro- activeness. Their finding indicates that entrepreneurial traits positively affect entrepreneurial orientation.

Yonca and Atsan, (2006) in their research work on "The entrepreneurial characteristics of Turkish university students" explored the entrepreneurship orientation by comparing entrepreneurially inclined students with non-entrepreneurially inclined students. Their study indicated that except for tolerance for ambiguity and self-confidence, all entrepreneurial traits are found to be higher in entrepreneurially inclined students, as compared with not so inclined students. That is, entrepreneurial students found to have higher risk taking propensity, higher internal locus of control, a higher need for achievement and higher innovativeness. Wang and Wong, (2000) have done a study on the entrepreneurial spirits of university students in Hong Kong and Singapore. The study concentrated specifically on the role of some personality characteristics including risk taking propensity; tolerance of ambiguity; internal locus of control; innovativeness; independences, and motivational factors (love for money, desire for security, and desire for status) rather than the differences in the contextual factors. The study of Henderson and Roberson (2000) also provides a useful insight into perception of young adults towards entrepreneurship. The study shows that the respondents perceived entrepreneurship mostly from the view of innate characteristics. Still most of them thought that entrepreneurial traits should be also nurtured by external factors.

The external viewpoint examines things like, culture, role models, work experiences, education and environment. McClelland, D, Pilon, D (1983) argued that some societies have cultural attitudes which translate into primary socialization practices that foster entrepreneurial individuals. Some studies take into account the relation between entrepreneurial attitudes and cultural, social, economic, political, demographical, contextual and situational factors. Timmons (1990) refers entrepreneurial behavior as a way of thinking, reasoning, and acting that is opportunity-directed, and leadership-balanced. He acknowledged that the entrepreneurship personality can be either acquired or inborn. Further the factors which can affect attitudes towards entrepreneurial activities can be classified into regulatory factors (e.g. institutions and policies); cognitive factors (e.g. knowledge of how to start ventures and obtain financial support); and normative factors (e.g. the perception of entrepreneurship as a career); which were used to explain both types and levels of entrepreneurship in different countries. Begley et al. (1997) compared the role of social- cultural factors on attitudes towards entrepreneurial activities in a four dimensional model. The study indicated that only social status of entrepreneurs might be predicted as factor to start a business.

Barnett (1993) after studying more than 70 viewpoints of scholars on entrepreneurs and entrepreneurship concluded that it is not easy to come up with a consensus definition from the literature. It is people's experience, knowledge and commitment that influence their decisions to become entrepreneurs and these factors have roots in their behaviors and attitudes. Luthje and Franke (2003) produced a model with contextual factors affecting attitudes towards entrepreneurial activities. The study reveals that the attitude toward self-employment might be linked to two contextual factors (perceived barriers and perceived support). Moreover, many previous studies indicate a link between entrepreneurship and education (Galloway & Brown, 2002; Henderson and Robertson, 2000. Furthermore, a study by Global Entrepreneurship Monitor (GEM, 2001) indicated that people with limited education are less likely to participate in entrepreneurial initiatives. Since the education offered by a university generally influences the career selection of students, universities can be seen as potential sources of future entrepreneurs. Hill (1988) argues that he scope and structure of entrepreneurial education is different in different context. From these review, we realize entrepreneurial intention is a function of entrepreneurial attitudes. Entrepreneurial attitudes are in turn affected by many variables which include the business environment; opportunities to start a business; personal characteristics necessary to start a business; risk taking and use of social networks. In a comprehensive review of the literature, Pedersen and McCormick (1999) reported on deficiencies related to lack of supportive institutions (financial, state and social/labour); low trust and accountability; limited access to capital and sub-contracting; and rent-seeking and corrupt practices, ensuing low entrepreneurship development. This is to a certain extent true in Oman also. The governance mechanism, inefficient parastatal industry, strong foreign presence, concentrated production, informal dominance, limited capital and lending, etc. in combination with inefficient management practices were further highlighted as detrimental to enterprise development. More recently, several studies have pointed toward improvements in the Middle East business environment in general and Oman in particular. Last but not the least is the cultural aspects. Culture is another important factor that explains cross country differences in SME development as entrepreneurs' decision-making is influenced by their cultural backgrounds. The term "culture", as discussed here, is defined as "the collective programming of the mind that distinguishes the members of one group or category of people from another" (Hofstede, 1991). On the basis of this definition, Hofstede (1980 and 2001) proposed a five-dimensional model for analysing national cultures as given in Figure 2.

Abundant empirical literature has demonstrated the relationship between entrepreneurial activities and cultural dimensions, and has found similar results. In general, low power distance, individualism, low uncertainty avoidance, and long-term orientation are associated with entrepreneurial activities and innovation (Shane, 1993, 1995; Thomas and Mueller, 2000; and Jones and Davis, 2000). Collectivism can be a good support to subsequent implementation after invention (Nakata and Sivakumar, 1996). Masculine cultures emphasize the value of performance, competition and success, while feminine countries may be more successful in the service sector due to the strong focus on relationships (Luczak and Mohan-Neill, 2009). Thus, Oman needs to understand and integrate the various dimensions of entrepreneurship development, entrepreneurial attitudes and behavior of its nationals, youth and women into all its entrepreneurial planning activities mainly when it targets development of the small and medium sized (SMEs). Women and young people's entrepreneurial attitude has generally been ignored in SMEs' development and plans in Oman. We believe a joint effort from educational institutions, entrepreneurial development offices in governmental side and private sector will promote more entrepreneurial attitudes via intentions and Oman will have more enterprises.

Figure 2. Five dimensional model for analysis of national culture
Source: Hofstede, 1980 and 2001.

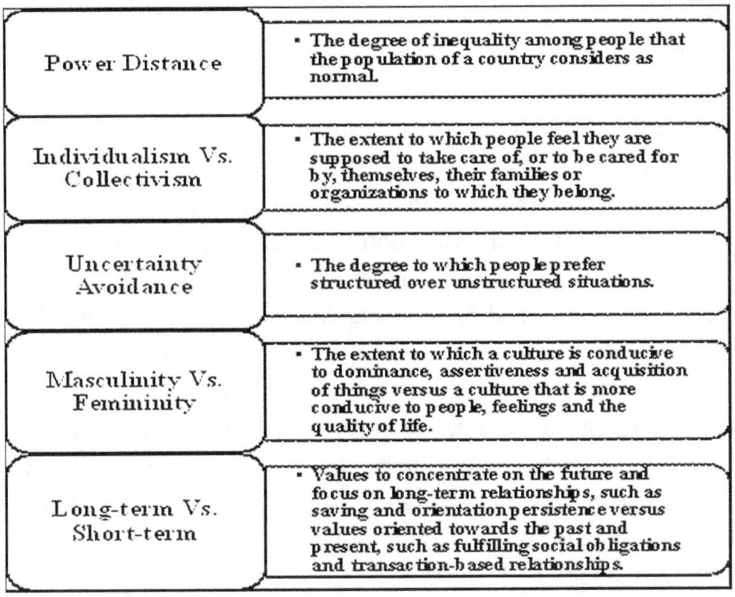

Barriers in Oman Entrepreneurship Development

As with all the GCC countries, the barriers for entrepreneurship development in Oman relate to:

- Limited access to capital.
- Lack of developed financial institutions.
- Averse or minimal risk taking behaviour.
- Lack of clarity about demand-supply market dynamics.
- Lack of clever marketing techniques.
- Lack of competitive spirits.
- Lack of access to high quality support services.
- Lack of work culture.
- Lack of broad set of skills – languages, numeric, logic, interpersonal skills and business understanding due to poor educational background.
- Lower levels of creativity and innovation.
- Absence of homegrown angel investors and seed accelerators.
- Assured life style.

ACHIEVING SUSTAINABLE ENTREPRENEURSHIP DEVELOPMENT

There is a pervasive tendency to equate entrepreneurship development (ED) with self-employment. Many self-employed individuals are indeed entrepreneurs, but the majority are not. Their businesses are simply microenterprises in the informal sector, with little growth potential. The promotion of self-employment is a worthwhile objective, but it should not be confused with ED. Entrepreneurship development programmes that in reality focus only on self-employment are less likely to succeed in creating economic growth. Entrepreneurship development should be about helping people start and grow dynamic businesses that provide high value added. In determining the difference, it is useful to look at potential growth sectors or geographic areas and to explore criteria for selecting beneficiaries who are entrepreneurial. A needs assessment before programme formulation is useful. An analysis of high-growth economic sectors enables more focused support to entrepreneurs in the most promising sectors of the economy. Entrepreneurship development programmes should be formulated to identify risks and determine the likelihood of success, identify the factors that affect the levels of entrepreneurship in a country. These factors include the perception of opportunity, degree of respect accorded to entrepreneurs, acceptance of wide disparities in income and a family environment which is oriented towards business. Entrepreneurship development programmes require a selection process that attempts to identify those target groups that have some of the key prerequisites for entrepreneurial success. While it can be argued that public funds should be spent on those who most need help, a selection process deploys limited resources where they are most effective, to the overall benefit of the community. Beneficiaries may be individuals and/or groups. An entrepreneurship development programme should help aspiring entrepreneurs to recognize and design unique, innovative business opportunities, based on an analysis of local conditions and their own special skills. The programme can help the entrepreneur to diversify based on his/her basic knowledge of a product or skill in a certain sector without distorting the local markets. In a truly entrepreneurial approach, innovative capacity matters more than the size of the market. Diversification can be accomplished by introducing a novelty or new product feature, stressing quality or value added, anticipating a new market or even creating a market.

Thus, entrepreneurial development programmes may have to include support for:

- *Entrepreneurship orientation and awareness.*
- *Development of the competencies (skills, experience and attitudes) necessary to recognize a market opportunity and organize the resources to meet it.*
- *Improvement of business performance for growth and competitiveness.*

ED training is usually more effective when linked to finance and other services such as marketing, quality assurance and productivity improvement. For example, involving the development banks at an early stage of the support process helps to prepare the entrepreneur for the credit process and facilitates the bank's appraisal of the business plan. Successful entrepreneurship also depends on supportive and coordinated government policies. Entrepreneurship is conducive to economic growth and the creation of employment. Government programmes and policies have a significant impact on the level of entrepreneurship within a country. While many governments profess support for entrepreneurial businesses, they often lack specific policies and coordinated programmes designed to support entrepreneurial activity.

In Oman, the major factors impeding the development of entrepreneurship is the lack of adequate skills in terms of exposure, creativity and business ideas to start and establish businesses. However, there are other obstacles to successful entrepreneurial development initiatives like protective environment, funded education, lack of competition and inadequate schooling in terms of curriculum and overall development. Further, liberalizing imports, ending monopolies and opening public services to private-sector provision of goods and services enhance the conditions for entrepreneurship growth. GEW in Oman is underway. Entrepreneurship workshops are taking place at various higher education institutes. Startup Weekend Oman is scheduled and form 2013, the Cisco Entrepreneur Institute and Amideast are giving away two scholarships to attend a Starting a Business Course in Arabic for two of the winners. So also, the Sharakah Youth Fund is offering a workshop on "Budgeting for Start-up Businesses" in the morning, and Cisco/Amideast again will be involved covering two sessions on "Growth & Expansion" and "Leadership for Growth." These forays indicate that entrepreneurship development in Oman is heading in a right direction and much needs to be seen in the days to come. At a glance once can see today, there are emerging trends of entrepreneurship be it, youth, rural, women or tourism etc., Baporikar, (2011).

However, fostering entrepreneurship is a long term process. It also involves ensuring that markets for capital, labour, goods and services are working well. It also requires that impediments to entrepreneurship be removed and that conditions be established in which innovation and risk-taking can flourish. Government policy-makers also seek to foster entrepreneurship through programmes which, for example, augment the supply of information and enable reliable transportation of goods and services, encourage networking, facilitate the provision of finance, and seek to create positive attitudes towards entrepreneurial activity. Focused policies that facilitate access to finance, professional services and training for start-up companies, that simplify business registration, reporting and taxation, etc. are essential to entrepreneurial venture creation. Seminars and the study of entrepreneurial development abroad can be included in programmes addressing entrepreneurship policy. Several economies globally and especially in the Asia-Pacific region have designed and put into operation entrepreneurship development programmes. The main players are government, academia, the private sector and the media. Most of the policy programmes for SME development conducted by governments feature entrepreneurship development as an important component. Various agencies have placed SME and entrepreneurship development at the centre of their agendas and oversee these programmes at the national level.

Areas of opportunities and innovative practices seem to be related to ICT and mobile phones, including mobile banking (Etzo & Collender, 2010, Baporikar, 2014b). Other innovative businesses seem to be emerging in creative industries (Lobato, 2010). It is noted that most Oman entrepreneurs are involved in often in trade and service activities. Nevertheless, while these business owners might not be introducing radical innovations to the market, they are, like other entrepreneurs, taking risks and demonstrating persistence and creativity while trying to make a living (Baporikar, 2015d). Several institutions, universities and R&D centres across Asia and the Pacific are designating entrepreneurship development as their core function. Over the years, many of these agencies have emerged as centres of excellence for example: Entrepreneurship Development Institute, India. Similarly, institutions and universities in Oman should take the lead. The private sector as well as NGOs plays a vital role in promoting entrepreneurship in various countries. In this context, the role of the media assumes great importance. The media provides a powerful means of creating an entrepreneurial culture in society, particularly through its influence on collective and individual perceptions and attitudes. The media educates and enhances entrepreneurship by conveying positive messages and knowledge that are crucial in building supportive social attitudes (and even systems) towards generating entrepreneurial activity (Hang & van Weezel, 2007). This understanding of media's role and impact is still in infancy in many pf the Arab countries due to them being governed in monarch systems.

SOLUTIONS AND RECOMMENDATIONS

While business incubators and accelerators, co-working spaces, entrepreneur networks, technology demo days, favourable government regulations and programs, and mentoring are all wonderful tools for use in the effort to create entrepreneurial cities, ultimately, they are just that – tools. As such, they run the risk of becoming a disconnected set of tactics without a guiding strategy or clear purpose. Can they sustain entrepreneurial activity in the long run? Are they actually transforming their cities in deep and lasting ways, or will this be yet another passing fad in the field of economic development? To answer these questions, we must first understand what it is we are actually trying to accomplish by implementing these tools. Of course, all economies today want more jobs, more wealth and more tax revenue. Oman is no exception. But, these are outcomes that represent the longer-term effects of entrepreneurial activity.

I would submit that the shorter-term, intermediate objective is to *develop* entrepreneurs so that, in turn, they can successfully engage in the kinds of restructuring necessary to develop their businesses. These successful businesses will create the economic development that is sought. 'Developing' entrepreneurs is not accomplished merely by bringing them together, giving them less paperwork to complete, providing them with laboratory or office space, or pumping up their businesses with venture capital. It is achieved by evolving their entrepreneurship *skills*. To date, there has been surprisingly little thought given to the skills required for successful entrepreneurship, especially in Arab world. These skills seem to be taken for granted, a situation arguably fuelled by scholarly squabbles over the attribution for entrepreneurship success to innate traits, behaviours, attitudes and mental cognition as well as the confusion created by the misapplication of terms such 'capabilities' capacity building' or competencies'. At the end of the day, none of these factors captures the root cause of entrepreneurship success, which is the mastery of a skill set, and skill is the only factor that can truly be learned and developed. Skill is essentially applied knowledge. Through strategic, focused and intensive practice, with regular feedback on progress (via a coach), entrepreneurs can develop their skills (Lichtenstein & Lyons, 2010). This, leads to the question, "What are the skills of entrepreneurship?" Based on Lyons (2009), tool for assessing entrepreneurship skills called the Readiness Inventory for Successful Entrepreneurship (RISE), which is web-based and consists of 30 skills organized according to four broad categories of skill: Transformation Management, Relationship Management, Business Management, and Organizational Process Management, Oman should undertake to assess and then develop those skills especially in the youth who are the potential entrepreneurs. The RISE can then be used to track the entrepreneur's skill development. The more developed an entrepreneur's skills, the better ability to grow and sustain business. When taken together for the entire city or country, this successful business development activity yields economic transformation, and it enables the community to assume the mantle of a 'true entrepreneurial nation.'

It all starts with *entrepreneurship skills and* not a collection of tools. So some of the suggested strategies to fuel these skills and promote entrepreneurship include:

- Improve access to capital and develop financial institutions.
- Focus on improving competitive spirits in schooling.
- Promote risk taking behaviour through sports and personality development activities.
- Provide access to high quality support services.
- Organize training programmes to develop clarity about demand-supply market dynamics, clever marketing techniques.
- Professionalize work culture.
- Rework on curriculum in schools and teaching methodology to ensure acquisition of broad set of skills – languages, numeric, logic, interpersonal skills and business understanding due to poor educational background.
- Promote creativity and innovation.

FUTURE RESEARCH DIRECTIONS

Going forward, SMEs and entrepreneurs will play an increasingly important role in buoying Oman's future. To promote long term success and economic sustainability, further research to understand how the government of Oman should prepared to don the roles traditionally carried out by accelerators, needs to be undertaken. Oman's entrepreneur ecosystem needs strong government push and adequate support to create entrepreneurs both men and women (Gerard & Al-Riyami, 2003). Studies on models of entrepreneurship development contextualized to Oman's culture and economy needs to be developed so that there is value addition to the government's job creation efforts and will also lead to entrepreneurship and economic development. Gromb and Scharfstein (2005) partial equilibrium model in which an investor owns two potential projects that depend on managerial ability is also interesting and more suitable for developing countries like Oman where the governance is of a different kind. Studies regarding approaches and methods to adopt this model would be interesting. In this model, the projects must be completed one after the other. The manager must devote effort to improve the chances the first project will be successful. The outcome of the projects provides information about the manager's ability. They interpret the first project as that of an established firm, and they interpret outsourcing of the second project as an entrepreneurial firm. The distinction between existing and new firms has to do with different labor-market incentives for managers, with higher-ability managers preferring to become entrepreneurs. The incentives of entrepreneurs and managers differ because their tasks differ. The entrepreneur is concerned with defining the new firm, which is by definition a market entrant. The manager, who works for an established firm, takes into account the potential continuation of existing business. The entrepreneur is building an organization and works independently. In contrast, the manager of an established firm is part of an existing hierarchy, often with bureaucratic inertia, risk aversion and inefficiencies that are observed in many large business organizations see Carl Schramm (2006b). Another interesting area is to study the relationship between entrepreneurial activities and cultural dimensions, specially based on the low power distance, individualism, low uncertainty avoidance, and long-term orientation associated with entrepreneurial activities

CONCLUSION

Small businesses are the lifeblood of any economy. But this sentiment resounds even more deeply with the Gulf, as the region looks to utilize human capital and diversify its economy. The small Gulf State of Oman has been tackling the issue of unemployment among its citizens by adopting stringent policies on localization. But the Sultanate is yet to make headway in creating a suitable ecosystem for entrepreneurs. Right now there are only two options for employment - Omanis can either enter the private sector or the public sector and there is a need for third option – self-employment or 'entrepreneurship', which in turn will fuels job creation Baporikar, (2014). Entrepreneurs say that Oman's current economic infrastructure is unfavorable for start-ups and the list of hurdles remains daunting for would-be business owners. The process for starting a company tends to be slow, right from opening of the company, to acquiring all the correct licenses, and then to actually begin operations. Many businessmen feel that such kind of delays eventually end up costing more than an entrepreneur could afford at that stage.

Hence, an ideal market for a budding entrepreneur is one in which there is support from their government (in the form of access to funding and support services) and where there is a clear demand for their products and services. The government has to continue to put in place the enabling environment, which includes supportive regulations, access to funding and provision of support services like marketing and other business planning services. "[The government must] identify the focus areas and priorities for Oman's economic growth, then make these opportunities visible and available to the private sector, including large companies, SMEs and entrepreneurs. Big changes in government rule in these nations will be slow to take hold. However, as the case of Oman shows, faced with an opportunity to tackle high youth unemployment and channel youth dissent, fueling an organic entrepreneurial revolution at the grassroots level is increasingly looking like the smartest strategy for today's leaders in the Arab world. Put simply, entrepreneurship in this part of the world is the best remedy for one of the root causes of discontent among youth - unemployment.

REFERENCES

Allen, S. (2006). *Entrepreneurship is an attitude*. Retrieved from http://entrepreneurs.about.com/b/2006/10/07/

Badulescu, A., & Dodescu, A. (2010). Entrepreneurial training and attitude toward entrepreneurship: Assessing the impact of Antr ES programme. *Proceedings of the 5th WSEAS International Conference on Economy and Management Transformation, 2*.

Baporikar, N. (2002). *Entrepreneurship and Small Industry (Theory and Practice)*. Mumbai, India: Himalaya Publishing House.

Baporikar, N. (2007). *Entrepreneurship Development and Project Management*. Mumbai, India: Himalaya Publishing House.

Baporikar, N. (2011). *Entrepreneurship Development and Project Management*. Mumbai, India: Himalaya Publishing House.

Baporikar, N. (2011). *Entrepreneurship. In Emergent Trends* (1st ed., p. 14). VDM Verlag.

Baporikar, N. (2013). *Entrepreneurship and Small Industry (Theory and Practice)*. Mumbai, India: Himalaya Publishing House.

Baporikar, N. (2014). Strategic Management Overview and SME in Globalized World. In K. Todorov & D. Smallbone (Eds.), *Handbook of Research on Strategic Management in Small and Medium Enterprises* (pp. 22–39). Hershey, PA: Business Science Reference. doi:10.4018/978-1-4666-5962-9.ch002

Baporikar, N. (2014). Youth Entrepreneurship in Indian Scenario. *International Journal of Asian Business and Information Management, 5*(2), 74–84. doi:10.4018/ijabim.2014040106

Baporikar, N. (2014b). Information Strategy as Enabler of Competitive Advantage. *International Journal of Strategic Information Technology and Applications, 5*(1), 30–41. doi:10.4018/ijsita.2014010103

Baporikar, N. (2015a). Entrepreneurship in Sultanate of Oman: A Case Approach. *International Journal of Asian Business and Information Management, 6*(4), 14–26. doi:10.4018/IJABIM.2015100102

Baporikar, N. (2015b). Role of Entrepreneurship in Networked Indian Economy. In P. Ordóñez de Pablos (Ed.), *Technological Solutions for Sustainable Business Practice in Asia* (pp. 36–59). Hershey, PA: Business Science Reference. doi:10.4018/978-1-4666-8462-1.ch003

Baporikar, N. (2015c). Effect of National Culture on Development of International Business in the Sultanate of Oman. In B. Christiansen (Ed.), *Handbook of Research on Global Business Opportunities* (pp. 268–288). Hershey, PA: Business Science Reference. doi:10.4018/978-1-4666-6551-4.ch013

Baporikar, N. (2015d). Societal Influence on the Cognitive Aspects of Entrepreneurship.[IJCESC]. *International Journal of Civic Engagement and Social Change*, *2*(4), 1–15. doi:10.4018/ijcesc.2015100101

Barnett, C. G. (1993). *Defining Entrepreneurship*. Paper delivered at the 7th annual conference of small business, Southern Africa.

Baumol, W. J. (1968). Entrepreneurship in Economic Theory. *The American Economic Review*, *58*, 64–71.

Baumol, W. J. (1993). *Entrepreneurship, Management, and the Structure of Payoffs*. Cambridge, MA: MIT Press.

Baumol, W. J. (2002). *The Free-Market Innovation Machine: Analyzing the Growth Miracle of Capitalism*. Princeton, NJ: Princeton University Press. doi:10.1515/9781400851638

Baumol, W. J. (2006). *Entrepreneurship and Invention: Toward Their Microeconomic Value Theory*. Special Session on Entrepreneurship, Innovation and Growth I: Theoretical Approach, American Economic Association Meetings.

Baumol, W. J., Litan, R. E., & Schramm, C. J. (2007). *Good Capitalism, Bad Capitalism, and the Economics of Growth and Prosperity*. New Haven, CT: Yale University Press.

Begley, T. M., Wee-Liang, T., Larasati, A. B., Rab, A., & Zamora, E. (1997). *The Relationship Between Social-Cultural Dimensions and Interest in Starting A Business- A Multi-Country Study, Frontiers of Entrepreneurship Research*. Wellesley, MA: Babson College.

Bhide, A. (2000). *The origin and evolution of new businesses*. New York: Oxford University Press.

Bonnett, C., & Furnham, A. (1991). Who Wants to be An Entrepreneur? A Study of Adolescents Interested in a Young Enterprise Scheme. *Journal of Economic Psychology*, *12*(3), 465–478. doi:10.1016/0167-4870(91)90027-Q

Bruyat, C. A., & Julien, P. A. (2001). Defining the field of research in entrepreneurship. *Journal of Business Venturing*, *16*(2), 165–180. doi:10.1016/S0883-9026(99)00043-9

Cantillon, R. (1755). *Essay On The Nature Du Commerce in General*. London: Fletcher.

Casson, M. (1982). *The Entrepreneur: An Economic Theory*. Totowa, NJ: Barnes & Noble Books.

Casson, M. (2003). *The Entrepreneur: An Economic Theory* (2nd ed.). Cheltenham, UK: Edward Elgar. doi:10.4337/9781843765639

Chen, Y. F., & Lai, M. C. (2010). Factors influencing the entrepreneurial attitude of Taiwanese tertiary-level business students. *Journal of Social Behavior and Personality*, *38*(1), 1–12. doi:10.2224/sbp.2010.38.1.1

Delmar, F., & Davidsson, P. (2000). Where do they come from? Prevalence and characteristics of nascent entrepreneurs. *Entrepreneurship & Regional Development*, *12*(1), 1–23. doi:10.1080/089856200283063

Etzo, S., & Collender, G. (2010). Briefing: The mobile phone revolution in Africa: rhetoric or reality? *African Affairs*, *109/437*(437), 659–668. doi:10.1093/afraf/adq045

Galloway, L., & Brown, W. (2002). Entrepreneurship Education at University, A Driver in the Creation of High Growth Firms? *Education + Training*, *44*(8/9), 398–405. doi:10.1108/00400910210449231

Gerard, M., & Al-Riyami, R. (2003). Women entrepreneurs in Oman: Some barriers to success. *Career Development International*, *8*(7), 339–346. doi:10.1108/13620430310505296

Global entrepreneurship Monitor. (2000). London: GEM Research Association, London Business School.

Goel, A., Vohra, N., Zhang, L., & Arola, B. (2007). Entrepreneurs and entrepreneurship: A cross cultural comparison of India and China. Indian Institute of Management Ahmedabad Journal, 1-33.

Goodbody Economic Consultants. (2002). *Entrepreneurship in Ireland*. Dublin, Ireland: Goodbody.

Gromb, D., & Scharfstein, D. (2005). *Entrepreneurship in Equilibrium*. Working Paper. London Business School.

Gupta, S. K. (1989). Entrepreneurship development: The Indian case. *Journal of Small Business Management*, *27*(1), 67.

Hellmann, T. (2007). Entrepreneurs and the Process of Obtaining Resources. *Journal of Economics & Management Strategy*, 16.

Henderson, R., & Robertson, M. (2000). Who Wants to be An Entrepreneur? Young Adult Attitudes to Entrepreneurship as a Career. *Career Development International*, *5*(6), 279–287.

Hills, G. (1988). Variations in university entrepreneurship education, An empirical study of an evolving field. *Journal of Business Venturing*, *3*(2), 109–122. doi:10.1016/0883-9026(88)90021-3

Knight, F. H. (1921). *Risk, Uncertanity and Profit*. Chicago: University of Chicago Press.

Knight, F. H. (1971). *Risk, Uncertainty and Profit*. Chicago: University of Chicago Press.

Lichtenstein, G. A., & Lyons, T. S. (2010). *Investing in Entrepreneurs: An Approach for Strengthening your Regional and Community Economy*. Santa Barbara, CA: Praeger/ABC-CLIO.

Lobato, R. (2010). Creative industries and informal economies: Lessons from Nollywood. *International Journal of Cultural Studies*, *13*(4), 337–354. doi:10.1177/1367877910369971

Lüthje, C., & Franke, N. (2003). The Making of an Entrepreneur: Testing A Model of Entrepreneurial Intent among Engineering Students at MIT. *R & D Management*, *33*(2), 135–147. doi:10.1111/1467-9310.00288

Lyons, J. S. (2009). *Communimetrics*. New York: Springer. doi:10.1007/978-0-387-92822-7

McClelland, D., & Pilon, D. (1983). Sources of adult motives in patterns of parent behavior in early childhood. *Journal of Personality and Social Psychology*, *44*(3), 564–574. doi:10.1037/0022-3514.44.3.564

MOM. (2005). *Third symposium on employing national manpower*. Shinas, Oman: Ministry of Manpower.

Pedersen, P. O., & McCormick, D. (1999). African Business Systems in a Globalising World. *The Journal of Modern African Studies*, *37*(1), 109–135. doi:10.1017/S0022278X99002955

Porter, H. (2003). A Culture of Enterprise. *Business Today,* 51-52.

Reynolds, P. D., Bygrave, W. D., Autio, E., & Arenius, P. (2004). *GEM 2003 global report*. Babson College.

Rotter, J. B. (1966). Generalized expectancies for internal versus external control of reinforcement. *Psychological Monographs*, *80*(1), 609. doi:10.1037/h0092976 PMID:5340840

Schramm, C. J. (2006a). *The Entrepreneurial Imperative: How American's Economic Miracle Will Reshape the World (and change your life)*. New York: Harper Collins.

Schramm, C. J. (2006b). *Entrepreneurial Capitalism and the End of Bureaucracy: Reforming the Mutual Dialog of Risk Aversion*. Presented at the American Economic Association meetings, Boston, MA.

Smallbone, D., & Welter, F. (2001). The distinctiveness of entrepreneurship in transition economies. *Journal of Small Business Economics*, *16*(4), 249–262. doi:10.1023/A:1011159216578

Spulber, D. F. (2008). *The Theory of the Firm: Microeconomics with Endogenous Entrepreneurs, Firms, Markets, and Organizations*. Cambridge, UK: Cambridge University Press.

Timmons, J. A. (1978). Characteristics and role demands of entrepreneurship. *American Journal of Small Business*, *3*, 5–17.

UNDP. (2004). *Unleashing entrepreneurship: Making business work for the poor: Report to the Secretary-General of the United Nations by the Commission on the Private Sector & Development*. New York: UNDP.

Wang, C., & Wong, P. (2004). Entrepreneurial interest of university students in Singapore. *Technovation*, *24*(2), 161–172. doi:10.1016/S0166-4972(02)00016-0

World Bank. (2010). *Doing Business 2010*. Washington, DC: The World Bank Group, IFC and Palgrave MacMillan.

Yonca, G., & Atsan, N. (2006). Entrepreneurial characteristics amongst university students: Some insights for entrepreneurship education and training in Turkey. *Education + Training*, *48*(1), 25 – 38.

Zimmerer, T. W., & Scarborough, N. M. (2008). *Essentials of entrepreneurship and small business management: the foundations of entrepreneurship*. Pearson Education.

KEY TERMS AND DEFINITIONS

Barriers: Anything serving to obstruct, or preventing, access, or progress. Anything or something that limits a quality or achievement or the act of limiting or the condition of being limited or cause delay. Barriers come in many forms and from many sources. They can be temporary or permanent. When evaluating a barrier, it is necessary that one looks at all the activities that precede the delay as well as the activities that follow the delay.

Business: Pertains broadly to commercial, financial, and industrial activities.

Challenges: Something that by its nature or character serves as a call to make special effort, a demand to explain, justify, or difficulty in a undertaking that is stimulating to one engaged in it.

Competence: Refers to the capacity of individuals/ employees to act in a wide variety of situations. It's their education, skills, experience, energy and their attitudes that will make or break the relationships with the customers and the products or services that are provided.

Creativity: Creativity is defined as the tendency to generate or recognize ideas, alternatives, or possibilities that may be useful in solving problems, communicating with others, and entertaining ourselves and others.

Develop: To progress from earlier to later or from simpler to more complex stages of evolution; to aid in the growth of; strengthen or to grow by degrees into a more advanced or mature state.

Entrepreneur: An individual engaged in the process of starting and growing one's own business or idea. One undertakes risk to start an enterprise not only for profits.

Entrepreneurship: The capacity and willingness to develop organize and manage a business venture along with any of its risks in order to make a profit. The most obvious example of entrepreneurship is the starting of new businesses.

Entrepreneurial Process: Creativity and its links to enterprise, the three stage process of entrepreneurship; opportunity screening; innovation and competitive advantage; acquiring resources.

Environment: Important or essential in relation to a plan of action; highly important to an intended objective.

Impact: To have effect on, effect of coming into contact with a thing or person; the force exerted by a new idea, concept, technology, or ideology, the impression made by an idea, cultural movement, social group, it is to drive or press (an object) firmly into (another object, thing, etc.) so as to have an impact or strong effect (on).

Initiative: Readiness to engage in daring or difficult activity, the condition of being initiated into some experience or sphere of activity: knowledgeableness.

Management: The act or manner of managing; handling, direction, or control. Skill in managing; executive ability: the technique, practice, or science of managing and dealing.

Resource: Capability, ingenuity, initiative, quick-wittedness; also refers to source of economic wealth, esp. of a country (mineral, land, labour, etc.) or business enterprise (capital, equipment, personnel, etc.), means of doing something.

Sustain: To support, hold, or bear up; endure without giving way or yielding and to keep up or keep going, as an action or process.

Chapter 9
Agency Problem Types From a Corporate Governance Perspective

Nazih Khalil El-Jor
Lebanese American University, Lebanon

ABSTRACT

Corporate Governance systems adequately address problems related to accountability and transparency in developed countries. However, in emerging economies these systems are susceptible to exploitation by self-interest-minded individuals entrusted in managing the organization in some cases, by majority shareholders in other cases and at times by third parties from outside the organization. This exploitation falls under the concept of Agency Theory which emerges as a matter of concern that should be dealt with by Corporate Governance systems. Under the Agency Theory, the author classifies the Agency related problems into three types; "Type One", "Type Two" and "Type Three". All three types emanate from the separation of ownership and decision making complemented by the natural reality of self-interest requiring thus internal mechanisms of control in order to mitigate the Agency problems along with all Agency related costs. The paper then deals with such mechanisms.

DOI: 10.4018/978-1-5225-2066-5.ch009

AN OVERVIEW OF AGENCY THEORY

One of the simplest and most straight forward concepts of Corporate Governance implies the process by which companies are managed and controlled. A main issue in such a process is the delegation of authority within the governance chain[1]. As far back as the sixteenth century, Adam Smith brought up the issue of such delegation resulting in the separation of ownership and decision making and the ineffectiveness of such arrangement mainly due to the fact that managers would never handle the interests of shareholders with the same vigilance as they would their own interests leading to waste in resources. The work of Berle and Means (1932) on the same subject serves as the basis for the various debates that place managers in a position to work for their best interests rather than the interests of the organization. These debates have sprung numerous concepts upon which was built the principles for corporate governance. In our chapter, we have limited the framework of corporate governance principles in businesses mainly to the issues pertaining to the "Agency Theory" and its effects of the business' management thus highlighting the consequences of the separation of ownership (shareholders) and control (management) in modern corporations with private ownerships and the need to implement internal mechanisms of control in order to mitigate the agency conflict(s) along with their related costs and subsequently increase the firm performance.

Jensen and Meckling (1976) define the agency relationship as a contract under which one party (the principal) engages another party (the agent) to perform some service on their behalf. As part of this, the principal will delegate some decision-making authority to the agent. In terms of financial results, the agency problem refers to the conflict of interest arising between creditors, shareholders and management because of differing goals (Investopedia, 2008). The agency problem emanates from the arrangement. Jensen and Meckling criticize theories of the firm as being actually theories of markets in which firms operate, and they advance a theory of firm behavior that focuses on the firm itself. On the other hand, Fama and Jensen (1983) note the narrow set of circumstances under which it is efficient for the functions of decision management, decision control, and residual risk bearing to be combined to the same agents; namely, for small, noncomplex organizations where residual claims are restricted to decision agents, or residual claims are held by other agents with special relationships to decision agents (e.g., family members). Business associates whose goodwill and advice are important to the organization are also potential candidates for holding minority residual claims of organizations that do not separate the management and control of decisions.

Inherent in any principal-agent relationship is the understanding that the agent will act for and on behalf of the principal. The agent assumes an obligation of loyalty to the principal that he will follow the latter's instructions and will neither intentionally nor negligently act improperly in the performance of the obligation. An agent cannot take personal advantage of the business opportunities the agency position uncovers. A principal, in turn, places trust and confidence in the agent. These obligations bring forth a relationship of trust and confidence between principal and agent.

Theoreticians of the Agency Theory delve on the conflict of interest between the agents (executives) and the principles (shareholders) in which the latter aims at maximizing the profits of their firm while the agents aim at maximizing their personal gain, often at the detriment of the firm. Thus the Agency Theory is based on the shift of interests between those of the executives and those of the shareholders and the study of Agency relationship in private businesses leads to a "Type One" Agency problem between the managers and the owners.

The development of broad types of business endeavors has given rise to numerous forms of associations that brought about, among others, different forms of Agency problems and different systems of governance. A general point of interest to us is the family businesses that are characterized by a concentration of ownership and that have a grave Agency problem often referred to as "Type Two" Agency problem emanating from the conflict of interest between majority and minority shareholders[2]. Corporate governance mechanisms provide some form of protection for the interests of these shareholders who otherwise are left at the mercy of the decision makers acting to enhance their own benefits.

In most relatively small family businesses, the governance chain is modest and is constituted of three simple layers. These are made up of family member shareholders, the board of directors made of yet family members and the company managers who, in most cases are family members too. In typical larger publicly quoted companies the size of these organizations necessitates additional layers of managers and in many cases additional layers of investors. This labyrinth of layers creates the situation of "Type Three" Agency problem resulting from the multitude of layers between the ultimate principle (the investor), the final agent (the manager) and the conflicting interests of each player within the governance chain.

A corporation, on the other hand, is a legal entity liable for income tax paid on an annual basis. This has to be done before the corporation can determine how much money it has left to distribute as profits. This profit or after-tax net income is segregated in a retained earnings account on the corporation's books out of which eligible shareholders receive their profits. However, profit distribution is not mandatory by law and the decision to distribute or not distribute lies in the hand of the corporation's board of directors which may decide to keep these profits in the corporation to use in funding new endeavors or as working capital. This creates "Type Four" Agency problems where, the board, whether influenced by the CEO or not and acting in all good intentions may decide, contrary to the desires, interests and expectations of the shareholders, not to give out dividends but to reinvest it in the company.

Type One Agency Problems

Agency problems take root when the investor opts for becoming a shareholder without being involved in company affaires often giving the company's managers a free hand in deciding on matters such as objectives and strategies to meet the latter. As a result, managers' actions determine profitability and returns, thus directly affecting the investor's interests in one way or another.

Looking at the relationships established within organizations between those who own the business and those who run it, these constitute Agency relationships analogous to a contract whereby the agent is delegated, by the principle, the responsibility of making decision to maximize the returns of the latter. Thus the ideal agent is the person who makes decisions aimed at maximizing the equity value of the principle rather than his own. Agency conflicts arise when the opposite happens and when it does so at the detriment of the principle's property. In such situation "Type One" Agency relationship occurs between the owner and the manager. These situations resulting in Agency problems cannot be avoided mainly due to the fact that there is no perfect contractual agreement that can be drawn in these state of affairs and furthermore there is no perfect agent who would put the company's interests before his own.

Since agency relationships are usually more complex and unclear (in terms of what specifically the agent is required to do for the principal) than contractual relationships, agency carries with it special ethical issues and problems, concerning both agents and principals. Ethicists point out that the classical version of agency theory assumes that agents i.e., managers should always act in principals' (owners') interests. However, if taken literally, this entails a further assumption that either (a) the principals' interests are always morally acceptable ones or (b) managers should act unethically in order to fulfill their "contract" in the agency relationship. Clearly, these stances do not conform to any practicable model of business ethics.

We should, at this point, bring up the basic assumption made in relation to Agency Theory that self-interest motivates both the principle and the agent. Accordingly, agents are most likely to pursue objectives driven by self-interest which could digress and possibly clash with those of the principals. Agency Loss has been applied to establish the extent of the gap between the consequences of the agent's actions and the best expected outcome for the principle. That gap increases as the self-interests diverge thus increasing the Agency Loss and decreasing them as the self-interests converge. In many situations, the principle, well aware of the state of affairs could simply look the other way given the acceptable size of the gap and admit a fact of life that can be maintained under control. In other situations when matters go out of hand and the gap size becomes intolerable, Agency problems could set the course for undesirable outcomes both for the principle and the agent translated into organizational misfortune.

All in all, contractual imperfection and improper behavior lead to incongruence between the interests of the owners and those of their managers leading to Agency costs. These costs can be identified as *coagulation costs,*[3]*nurturing costs*[4] and *inconsistency costs*[5]. The magnitude of such costs relates to the firm structural characteristics and the agent's risk appetite. The larger the organization, the more formal processes become while bureaucracy sets in bringing with it organizational politics and its burden on costs. On the other hand risk taking by the agent is directly proportional to his flair for politicizing. Human nature and contractual statutes provide the perfect concoction for Agency problems.

In the case of Type One Agency problems however, two main situations emerge that need consideration; the first situation relates to what could be referred to as "ethical peril" resulting from the ambiguity of the agent's behavior and his attitude towards risk, especially when such risk results in his best interest and will increase his welfare at the detriment of the principles' interests. In such situation the principle ends up holding the short end of the stick, should matters go the wrong way while the agent, in a worst case scenario, ends up achieving no personal gain.

The second situation results from the information asymmetry that develops between the agent and the principle mainly due to information withheld from the latter. The agent, by virtue of position and privileges, can juggle information back and forth and feed the principle parts of it in doses as the situation requires while keeping things under tight control. This information asymmetry constitutes the crucial element for appropriate action in appropriate instances of the company affairs for the intended purposes of the agent. The information in question here relates to matters of opportunities whose benefits could swing one way or another depending on how these are handled, when and by whom.

Type Two Agency Problems

In Family businesses, Agency costs are of a different type since family members are directly associated in the running of the business. Family ties create an atmosphere of commitment, loyalty and altruism. These result in a long term orientation and reduce incentives for managers' individual opportunism while increasing the focus on the business' long term interests for the benefit of its owners. In family businesses, Type One Agency costs, due to managerial opportunism, do not arise as managers are long term oriented and would unlikely be given the opportunity to make short term strategic decisions for their own benefits. It should be noted at this point that often individuals placed in managerial positions are chosen on the basis of who they are rather than what their qualifications are. In many cases these would be family members chosen because what is important to the principle is loyalty and trust instead of skills and aptitude.

In situations where equity ownership is concentrated, controlling shareholders can and often do expropriate private benefits such as non-proportional profits distribution at the expense of the minority shareholders thus creating conflicts of interest between them and the minority shareholders resulting in the second Type of Agency problem. This tendency of power abuse results in various outcomes at the detriment of the minority shareholders such as the use of company assets as collateral for personal loans, the placement of family members or friends in sensitive positions or the buyout of company assets at discounted prices. This type of Agency problem annuls the benefits attained from the reduction of Type One Agency problems burdening the company with additional Agency Costs.

Various governance mechanisms exist to reduce the expropriation risk of minority equity and further decrease the decline of a firm's profits. These could vary from the elimination of duality[6], since the combination of chair of the board and CEO has been shown in a multitude of studies to increase agency costs where the interests of majority shareholders dominate that of non-controlling minority shareholders (Braun and Sharma, 2007), to the board independence[7] where outsider directors within that board are totally independent from the CEO to whom they would otherwise be expected to hold allegiance. Board independence signifies a relatively meaningful size of the board being made up of outsiders with no allegiance to neither the CEO in whatever possible way.

Type Three Agency Problems

In large public organizations we would find within the governance chain extra layers of management ranging from functional to executive to corporate and further, extra layers of investors such as beneficiaries and trustees. The ultimate beneficiary, the investor, uses collective funds such as pension or trust funds typically controlled by trustees who invest in public companies. These in turn, through investment managers, would invest in a multitude of companies on behalf of the investor. As it turns out, the ultimate beneficiaries have no idea of the companies they have a financial stake in and would therefore have no say or power to directly influence the latters' boards. Internally, the company's board can be viewed as the principle having the company's senior executives as their agents managing the company through yet another layer of functional managers. Between the board and the ultimate managers at the bottom of the governance chain there are many layers of agents requiring reporting mechanisms subject to malfunction at one point or another.

Perils emanate from the distance within the governance chain between the ultimate beneficiary and the functional manager. Thus the expectations of one may not be the same as that of the other, nor would be those of the parties in between them, creating Type Three Agency problems. Investment managers could be after increasing their bonuses, executives could be striving for increased earnings while functional managers could be bucking for promotions. On the other hand, the ultimate beneficiary could be concerned with long-term security from an investment while the investment manager would be seeking short-term growth from the same investment. All the above would eventually lead to results that are probably not in the best interest of the ultimate beneficiary.

Type Four Agency Problems

In the majority of corporations the most immediate use of profits is for expansion of corporate properties for the purpose of generating additional profits or for competitive necessity. Type Four Agency problems emanate from retention conflicts that occur as a result of managerial decisions which, in most case, could be to the best interest of the organization and indirectly could render managers' lives easier. Whenever possible, given the organizational structure and the type of board governing, managers may influence the decision to increase retained earnings in order to finance some projects which would not necessarily enhance shareholder wealth, but could be in the best interest of the company at that specific instance in time. Such high-flying managerial investment policies may not produce results that are clearly apparent to the shareholders as it may be to management. Many shareholders do not have the knack to analyze or understand complex financial planning nor perceive projected project results on which management could have invested great effort and time in preparing.

Whether good intentions are present or the best interest of the company is considered, the fact that it is not what the shareholders wish, it is a problem to them. Although this type of Agency problem does not harm or is in nature not to the disadvantage of the shareholders, when it is not congruent with their desires it is considered as a problem to them and thus has been classified as another Agency problem. It should be further noted that the resultant corporate growth grants to management a larger power base, job security, greater prestige/status, and an ability to dominate the board and award themselves higher levels of compensation. On the other hand, shareholders would prefer higher levels of cash distributions, especially where the company has few internal positive Net Present Value investment opportunities, hence producing a clash of interests between principal and agent.

Type Five Agency Problems

There are instances where conflicts of interest may also arise between shareholders and managers with respect to the timing of cash flows. Shareholders will be concerned with all future cash flows of the company into the indefinite future. However, management may only be concerned with company cash flows for their term of employment, leading to a bias in favor of short term high accounting returns projects at the expense of long-term positive NPV projects. For example, research and development (R&D) expenditures would tend to decline as top executives approach retirement (Dechow and Sloan, 1991). This is because R&D expenditures reduce executive compensation in the short-term, yet the retiring executives won't be around to reap the benefits of such investments. Healy (1985) also posits that time horizon agency conflict may also lead to management using subjective accounting practices to manipulate earnings prior to leaving their office in an attempt to maximize performance-based bonuses.

AN UNDERSTANDING OF CORPORATE GOVERNANCE

Corporate Governance matters as we label them today have long been an integral part of business conduct and have slowly but surely evolved over time in financial institutions, private family businesses and conglomerates. They have taken shape in mergers, acquisitions, expropriations, confiscations, privatizations and hostile takeovers, to name but a few throughout the political, financial and corporate world.

It is not until recently, following a wide wake of major corporate failures, damage and disenfranchisement, mostly in the Western world, that corporate governance became a subject of interest to policy makers, regulators, economists, investors, corporate executives and scholars. Many have attempted to delineate the topic in various approaches and ended up describing the "same elephant" but from different angles. The debate over the topic of corporate governance has taken a wide spread view as seen in the compiled definitions below:

Corporate governance is the system by which companies are directed and controlled. Cadbury Code (1992)[8]
The whole set of legal, cultural, and institutional arrangement that determine what public corporations can do, who control them, how control is exercised, and how the risks and returns from the activities they undertake are allocated Blair (1995)
Corporate governance is most often viewed as both the structure and the relationships which determine corporate direction and performance. The board of directors

is typically central to corporate governance. Its relationship to the other primary participants, typically shareholders and management, is critical. Mc Ritchie (1999)
Corporate governance is the process carried out by the board of directors, and its committees, on behalf of and for the benefit of the company's stakeholders, to provide direction, author it, and oversight to management. Sobel (2005)
The system by which business corporations are directed and controlled. The corporate governance structure specifies the distribution of rights and responsibilities among different participants in the corporation, such as the boards, managers, shareholders and other stakeholders, and spells out the rules and procedures for making decisions on corporate affairs. It provides the structure through which the company objectives are set, and the means of attaining those objectives and monitoring performance. Hawkama (2008)[9]

In most definitions of corporate governance structures and systems of control constantly stick out and most appropriately constitute a main pillar of the subject matter. One key component of these systems related issues are the controls by which managers are held accountable to those who have a legitimate claim on the business. Another key component is the structure of the board and its role in the strategic guidance of the organization, its accountability to the shareholders and its ability to effectively oversee and monitor management. Standards have been proposed which, in some countries, are set by law stipulating that managers and board members are required to be informed, act in the best interest of the shareholders[10] and other stakeholders[11], act in good faith, with due diligence and care while ensuring compliance with applicable laws. What has also emerged as another requirement lately is the increased accountability not only to shareholders but to a wider social interest.

The basic concepts of Corporate Governance within the corporate law have only lately been addressed and only recently have regulators and academics given due importance to the adequate practice of governance in the corporate world. Yet the subject remains very much disputed both at the corporate and the regulatory levels. This divergence in standards is due to various factors that could be explained by a country's stage of economic development, the patterns of wealth accumulation in particular societies and in many cases cultural, social and political attributes. The legal framework of governance also varies depending on the traditional civil, common or theocratic law practices. In civil law countries corporate governance practice follows strict rules that have been codified and legislated. In theocracies these same rules are extracted from religious scriptures and interpreted as principles of conduct that are officially established as rules governing the faith and practice of that particular religion while in common law countries it's the principles of appropriate conduct that form the basis of corporate governance.

It is not until the release in the early 1990s of the Cadbury Code on corporate governance practice in the United Kingdom that a genuine development in corporate governance modern literature was established. This code became the standard reference for what followed on the subject of corporate governance. The Organization of Economic Cooperation and Development (OECD) corporate governance guidelines in the late 1990s, complemented by the International Corporate Governance Network's (ICGN) governance practices and policies for global or multinational applications, the Sarbanes-Oxley legislation in the United States and the European Union's Code of Corporate Governance, all have laid the groundwork for best practices. Other governance codes took shape in several other countries, these include the French governance code review by Daniel Bouton, the corporate governance code in Italy, the development of the Spanish code of corporate governance by the Aldama commission and the German governance code by Gerhard Cromme. Elsewhere around the globe, in Latin America, Asia and developing Europe individual guidelines and governance codes are continuously being introduced.

In the Arab world numerous efforts were undertaken on the topic of corporate governance. Substantial work was done by "Hawkamah", the Institute of Corporate Governance in Dubai which released in 2008 the results of its Corporate Governance Survey of Banks and companies in the Middle East and North Africa. The study was conducted in collaboration with the Washington-based International Finance Corporation (IFC), an affiliate of the World Bank. Other work also took place in various GCC states where corporate governance principles and guidelines were established such as the 2002 Oman Codes of Corporate Governance, Saudi Arabia's Corporate Governance Regulations in 2006, Qatar's Corporate Governance Codes in 2009, the UAE's Governance Rules and Corporate Discipline Standards in 2009, Bahrain's Corporate Governance Codes in 2011 and Kuwait's Corporate Governance Principles in 2012, to name a few.

In the absence of Lebanese corporate governance legislation, the Lebanese Transparency Association (LTA) and the Lebanese Corporate Governance Task Force (LCGTF) launched in 2006 the Lebanese Code of Corporate Governance (the Code), a voluntary code of corporate governance aimed for the Lebanese joint-stock companies, mainly Small and Medium Enterprises (SMEs) along with Family Owned Enterprises (FOEs). The Code established principles for board governance and company performance. It was inspired mainly by the OECD corporate governance principles along with other international good governance best practices.

Lately, corporate governance has established a standalone identity as a specialized field of study.

However, as a result of corporate debacles around the globe, regulators throughout are moving towards the establishments of standards and principles of corporate conduct in an attempt to monitor, control and regulate the latter. Nevertheless, the extents to which investors' rights are protected are fundamental indicators of corporate governance and corporate finance evolution in particular countries. In the case of developed countries Corporate Governance systems adequately address the problems of corruption related to accountability and transparency among all concerned. By contrast, in emerging economies, less developed Corporate Governance systems are susceptible to exploitation by self-interest-minded individuals from within the organization, mainly those entrusted in managing it, bringing up the question of Agency Theory.

Governance Mechanisms

Corporate Governance practices, in line with Agency Theory, provide the mechanisms to insure that self-seeking agents act in the best interests of principles rather than their own. In order to keep the actions of these agents within the organization under control, Corporate Governance mechanisms provide the necessary framework to do so. This framework is built around regulative and legal procedures that are based on codes and best practices. They establish the rules and regulations required to monitor, regulate and restrict the behavior of all players against the identified ethical peril brought about by their behavior.

Information asymmetry problems which are a major component of Agency problems transpire from the fact that while principles need quality information to monitor and control their organization, agents determine the caliber of that information since they have it and they control its flow. Since the basis for proper corporate governance lays in the integrity of information and in the prevention of its misuse, a crucial governance mechanism entails the establishment of an adequate information system providing accurate and timely information for all corporate stakeholders of the organization. This is required since those opportunists who control information have the comparative advantage to impose their influence of many aspects running the business both from and administrative and a logistics perspective.

Safeguarding the ultimate beneficiaries is built into the governance chain reporting mechanism. Information required by the various parties within the chain to control and monitor the performance of other parties range from quantitative to qualitative, from analyst reports to performance reports and from detailed operating reports to limited reports, all depending on who generates the information and who receives it. When it comes to the Board of Directors, information disclosure is imposed by statutory requirements. However, managers on the other hand have great leeway when it comes to what information they need to present and to whom depending on their view of the company's strategic purpose and strategic direction. Internal reporting mechanisms, external monitoring requirements and investor intended appeals do not always necessarily match in many instances as each is meant for a purpose, not necessarily congruent. Each fits requirements of the parties concerned and meets their best self-interest no matter how far spread out from the others'.

Corporate Governance is continually changing and undergoing reforms around the world. The governance chain is not the perfect mechanism to control and monitor business conduct within the corporate world. Each of the chain's parties is after their own self-interest and they do so by setting their own measures and targets incompatible with those of the ultimate beneficiary. There big gaps as to the division of power among the chain players gives each a certain level of "information ownership" not available to the other payers.

CONCLUSION

Since agency relationships are usually more complex and unclear (in terms of what specifically the agent is required to do for the principal) than contractual relationships, agency carries with it special ethical issues and problems, concerning both agents and principals. Ethicists point out that the classical version of agency theory assumes that agents should always act in principals' interests. However, if taken literally, this entails a further assumption that either (a) the principals' interests are always morally acceptable ones or (b) managers should act unethically in order to fulfill their "contract" in the agency relationship. Clearly, these stances do not conform to any practicable model of business ethics.

A familiar real-life example is large corporations' lay off dilemma. Conventional wisdom holds that investors are rewarded when companies thin their employment rosters because operating costs are lowered, in theory leading to greater profits. This expectation is often made explicit in news reporting surrounding a downsizing episode; the reports highlight whether investors seem pleased or displeased with an announcement of a mass layoff, and the often-stated assumption is that corporate management has undertaken the layoffs in part, if not in whole, to please shareholders and enhance their wealth. In this instance it is obvious that shareholders' interests are advanced to the detriment of at least one other constituency, namely the employees. In such cases, observers question whether it is ethical to serve the principals' interests when those actions harm a large number of people, and whether the benefits shareholders receive are commensurate with the harm inflicted on the laid-off employees.

Along the same lines, others have noted that traditional agency theory makes little mention of what obligations, moral or otherwise, principals have to their agents. The emphasis lies almost exclusively on what agents should or must do for the principals, relying, in turn, on a vague assumption that principals will compensate agents adequately for their services. Some ethics scholars argue that principals have obligations as well. In the example above, some would argue that not only is it unethical to harm employees to obtain improvements (often marginal) in shareowners' wealth, but also that the shareholders have moral obligations directly to the employees as an extension of the ethical employer/employee relationship (i.e., not to harm them arbitrarily, among other obligations). This ethical problem is only complicated by the reality that, as noted above, principals are often institutions rather than individuals.

Meanwhile, consistent with the conventional formulation of the theory, agents are seen as having ethical duties to the principals. If managers act in self-interest—a rather negative assumption—and it fails to serve the best interests of the shareholders, they may, according to some views, have fallen short on their ethical responsibilities. In a larger sense, some see the traditional agency model as a simplistic, even deceptive, justification for traditional economic power relationships, specifically that large wealth holders can extract concessions from weaker economic beings. Certain scholars have argued that from a broader social perspective, there are many kinds of principal-agent relations, and included among these is the fact that shareholders may be seen as agents to managers, employees, and the broader society.

REFERENCES

Abbasi, M. Z. (2009). Legal analysis of agency theory: An inquiry into the nature of corporation. *International Journal of Law and Management*, *51*(6), 401–420. doi:10.1108/17542430911005936

Agrawal, A., & Mandelker, G. (1987). Managerial Incentives and Corporate Investment and Financing Decisions. *The Journal of Finance*, *42*(4), 823–837. doi:10.1111/j.1540-6261.1987.tb03914.x

Baysinger, B., & Butler, H. (1985). Corporate governance and the board of directors: Performance effects of changes in board composition. *Journal of Law Economics and Organization*, *1*(1), 101–124.

Berle, A., & Means, G. (1932). *The Modern Corporation and Private Property*. New York: Macmillan Co.

Blair, M. (1995). *Ownership and Control*. Rethinking Corporate Governance for the Twentieth Century.

Bonazzi, L., & Islam, S.M.N. (2007). Agency theory and corporate governance: A study of the effectiveness of board in their monitoring of the CEO. *Journal of Modelling in Management, 2*(1).

Braun, M., & Sharma, A. (2007). Should the CEO also be the Chair of the Board? An Empirical Examination of Family-Controlled Public Firms. *Family Business Review, 20*(2), 111–126. doi:10.1111/j.1741-6248.2007.00090.x

Brennan, M. J. (1994). Incentives, Rationality, and Society. *Journal of Applied Corporate Finance, 7*(2), 31–39. doi:10.1111/j.1745-6622.1994.tb00403.x

Core, J., Holthausen, R., & Larcker, D. (1999). Corporate governance, chief executive officer compensation, and firm performance. *Journal of Applied Corporate Finance*.

Dechow, P. M., & Sloan, R. G. (1991). Executive Incentives and the Horizon Problem: An Empirical Investigation. *Journal of Accounting and Economics, 14*(1), 51–89. doi:10.1016/0167-7187(91)90058-S

Denis, D. J., & Denis, D. K. (1995). Performance Changes Following Top Management Dismissals. *The Journal of Finance, 50*(4), 1029–1057. doi:10.1111/j.1540-6261.1995.tb04049.x

Denis, D. J., Denis, D. K., & Sarin, A. (1997). Agency Problems, Equity Ownership, and Corporate Diversification. *The Journal of Finance, 52*(1), 135–160. doi:10.1111/j.1540-6261.1997.tb03811.x

Easterbrook, F. H. (1984). Two Agency Cost Explanations of Dividends. *The American Economic Review, 74*(4), 650–659.

Eisenhardt, M. K. (1989)... *Agency Theory: An Assessment and Review, The Academy of Management Review, Vol, 14*(1), 57–74.

Fama, E. F. (1980). Agency Problems and the Theory of the Firm. *The Journal of Political Economy, Vol, 88*(2), 288–307. doi:10.1086/260866

Fama, E. F., & Jensen, M. C. (1983). Separation of Ownership and Control. *The Journal of Law & Economics, 88*(2), 301–325. doi:10.1086/467037

Haugen, R. A., & Senbet, L. W. (1981). Resolving the Agency Problems of External Capital through Options. *The Journal of Finance, Vol, 36*(3), 629–647. doi:10.1111/j.1540-6261.1981.tb00649.x

Healy, P. (1985). The Effect of Bonus Schemes on Accounting Decisions. *Journal of Accounting and Economics, 7*(1-3), 85–108. doi:10.1016/0165-4101(85)90029-1

Investopedia. (2008). Retrieved from: www.investopedia.com

Jassim, A., & Dexter, C. R. (1988). Agency theory: Implications for financial management. *Managerial Finance Year Journal, 14*(4).

Jensen, M. C. (1986). Agency Costs of Free Cash Flow, Corporate Finance and Takeovers. *The American Economic Review*, *76*(2), 323–329.

Jensen, M. C. (1993). The Modern Industrial Revolution, Exit and the Failure of Internal Control Systems. *The Journal of Finance*, *48*(3), 831–880. doi:10.1111/j.1540-6261.1993.tb04022.x

Jensen, M. C., & Meckling, W. H. (1976). Theory of the Firm: Managerial Behavior, Agency Costs and Ownership Structure. *Journal of Financial Economics*, *3*(4), 305–360. doi:10.1016/0304-405X(76)90026-X

Jensen, M. C., & Murphy, K. J. (1990). Performance Pay and Top-Management Incentives. *Journal of Political Economy*, *98*(2), 225–264. doi:10.1086/261677

Jensen, M. C., & Ruback, R. S. (1983). The Market for Corporate Control: The Scientific Evidence. *Journal of Financial Economics*, *11*(1-4), 5–50. doi:10.1016/0304-405X(83)90004-1

Kaplan, S. N. (1989). The Effects of Management Buyouts on Operating Performance and Value. *Journal of Financial Economics*, *24*(2), 217–254. doi:10.1016/0304-405X(89)90047-0

Kaplan & Reishus. (1990). Outside Directors and Corporate Performance. *Journal of Financial Economics*, *27*(2), 389-410.

Morck, R., Strangeland, D., & Yeung, B. (2000). *Inherited wealth, corporate control and economic growth: the Canadian disease*. Working Paper. National Bureau of Economic Research: 6814.

Prendergast, C. (2001). *Consumers and Agency Problems*. NBER Working Paper No. 8445. National Bureau of Economic Research.

Shivdasani, A., & Yermack, D. (1999). CEO involvement in the selection of new board members: An empirical analysis. *The Journal of Finance*, *54*(5), 1829–1853. doi:10.1111/0022-1082.00168

Sobel, P. (2005). *Auditor's Risk Management Guide: Integrating Auditing and ERM*. CCH Inc.

ENDNOTES

1 The governance chain establishes the relationships among the various groups involved in the governance of the organization.

2 Shareholders are also known as residual claimers since they basically control whatever remains after the concerned stakeholders such as preferred shareholders, bondholders and convertible bondholders get their share of equity.

3 Costs incurred by agent in an attempt to justify actions aimed at aligning own interests with those of the principle thus further solidifying the credibility of his decisions.

4 Costs incurred from the monitoring requirements entailing performance audits, budget restrictions and compensation policies in line with the agent's opportunistic behavior.

5 Costs that constitute the income difference due to decisions made by the agent and those that would have otherwise maximized the interests of the principle. These costs can never be nullified in situations where control is delegated.

6 CEO duality refers to the situation when the CEO also holds the position of the chairman of the board. Such situation is seen by some as a benefit and by others as a detriment to the situation.

7 An independent board is a corporate board that has a majority of outsider directors who are not company employees, are not affiliated with the top executives of the firm and have minimal or no business dealings with the company to avoid potential conflicts of interests.

8 A committee that was established in 1991 by the British Financial Reporting Council, the London Stock Exchange and the accountancy profession to look into the financial aspects of Corporate Governance following the sudden collapse in the UK of companies that were publishing healthy financial accounts resulting in an increasing lack of investor confidence in the honesty and accountability of listed companies. The committee's was forever after known as the Cadbury Committee named after its chairman Sir Adrian Cadbury.

9 The Institute for Corporate Governance is being set up by a group of international institutions, including the Dubai International Financial Centre (DIFC), Organization for Economic Cooperation and Development (OECD), UAE Ministry of Finance and Industry, Centre for International Private Enterprise (CIPE), International Finance Corporation (IFC), the Union of Arab Banks (UAB), Dubai School of Government (DSG), Young Arab Leaders (YAL), and

the Institute of Management Development (IMD). Hawkama aims to promote corporate sector reform and good governance, assist the countries of the region in developing and implementing sustainable Corporate Governance strategies, with the aim of facilitating the economic and financial integration of the region with the rest of the world. Corporate Governance codes and standards will be adapted to national requirements and objectives, and will foster regional co-operation which in turn will facilitate exchange of knowledge and allow countries to learn from successful experiences.

10 Shareholders are also known as residual claimers since they basically control whatever remains after the concerned stakeholders such as preferred shareholders, bondholders and convertible bondholders get their share of equity.

11 These are categorized into three general tiers; the first tier being investors, the second tier being creditors and the third tier being employees, suppliers, customers, government, community and society.

Chapter 10
Developing Blue Ocean Strategy in Construction Industries Using an Improved Model of Kano

Mohammad Abdolshah
Islamic Azad University – Semnan, Iran

Fariborz Ahmadzadeh
Islamic Azad University – Semnan, Iran

Afshin Abbaspour
Islamic Azad University – Semnan, Iran

ABSTRACT

Blue ocean strategy includes a consistent pattern of strategic thinking in the creation of new markets in various industries. This chapter examines how to create a blue ocean and its role in improving the construction industry. This is library research alongwith case study. It has been prepared based on information gathered from articles published in international journals and referring to large and reputable builder companies. In the concept of strategy, "Blue Ocean" is referred to two overall scope of blue and red ocean. In this chapter, we used the Kano method for evaluation and selection of the features in the construction industry and then, through a four-step approach, it was decided what features should be removed, innovated, enhanced or improved. Finally, using improved hybrid model of Kano and the pillars of the blue ocean strategy, we concluded that economic factors and psychological factors that impact on the consumers need investment and more attention.

DOI: 10.4018/978-1-5225-2066-5.ch010

1. INTRODUCTION

In many countries, the construction industry is an indicator of economic activity which affects a wide range of communities as well as end consumers, experts in home sales, construction companies, project planners, government and government agencies and also manufacturers of raw materials for construction (P. Ballesteros Pe'rez, MCG l.-C., JP Pastor-Ferrando, 2010). Today, mass production is not profitable regardless of the actual needs of the end consumer, and competition for a larger share of existing industries, it is not profitable as in the past, and in some cases, even causes the loss of capital, and loss of position in market, and as a result we see, in the form of phenomena such as "empty house", or "excess supply". The industry, in the field of manufacturing technology, to some extent, goes along with the world, but in the field of marketing and sales, to a large extent, this has been left behind. Mass production and lack of attention to customer needs, has led to this point that, instead of adjusting production with customer needs, customers have to acceptance what has come to fruition.

Producers only focused on the competition for production, and to reduce costs in some cases they turn toward the improper use of them, which over time, it imposes many expenses for buyers. For example, according to the situation of stagflation in Iran, the majority of buyers purchases according to their budget, and often are seeking for lower housing area, but today most housing are big area, in addition to the increased cost to the manufacturer, it causes to reduce selling and supplement. Today, the definition of a successful company is not only the satisfaction of our customers, but the company is successful which create value for its customers, which in return, the companies that creats value for their customers, finally, create a win-win economic relationship (Ching-Chow Yang, K.-J. Y., 2011). Thus the concept of value creation and the blue ocean in the construction industry became important and it will make the industry porpuseful and modernised.

The goal of Blue Ocean Strategy is to make meaningless competition through the creation of a new space for mutual profit. A space in which, due to the lack of exploration and evaluation, is empty of competitors and a lot of profit. In this strategy via the systematic and continuous steps, it is provided a new field of activity for the company, innovation and avoiding competition is a priority (Amburn, C. k. R., 2008).

2. RESEARCH BACKGROUND

Blue Ocean Strategy which was published in 2005 by Professor Chan Kim and Renée Mauborgne, drew a lot of attention among academics and experts. This process, in its agenda has the retention of existing customers and attracts new customers (Ching-Chow Yang, K.-JY, 2011). Blue Ocean Strategy is the result of two decades of research and study on more than 150 strategic movements of the world, in more than a number of different industries during the last 100 years. This approach is formed from two strategies at the same time, the strategy of differentiation and cost reduction strategies. At the same time, the organization offers a series of methodologies and management tools to create an unrivaled, new market space. The authors of Blue Ocean Strategy believe that the only way to win the competition, is stop trying to win the competition and instead of entering the red ocean of bloody competition, to enter the infinite market space of ocean water, and to create demand. A market in which, the rules are not specified in, and there are opportunities for profitable growth. In short, instead of getting a larger share of the cake, we should seek to enlarge the cake. Chan Kim and Renée Mauborgne, the authors of the book, with a revolutionary in the field of management and strategy, innovative approach in terms of the proposed business altogether. They offer new and innovative philosophy through criticizing the dominant paradigm in the field of strategic thinking, which is based on participation in the competition, straight face and blood flow, and ultimately the formation of red ocean (ocean of blood), in whci business takes place upon it in a peaceful environment, away from the bloody conflict, and in the blue ocean zone (R.Toulayi, 2008).

Blue Oceans, both in the past and the present, are the characteristics of all businesses. For example, if we go back a hundred years ago, many of the basic and main industries such as automobile, petrochemical, health and management consulting, at the time, or completely were unknown, or were just emerging. Also, if we go back 30 years ago, then we will see that many of the multi-billion dollar industries were not existed significantly in the past three decades, such as mobile phone industry, biotechnology, and home videos. But in spite of this, so far, the nature and the concept of the ocean water are largely unknown. In the last 25 years, the main focus of strategic thinking has been on competitive strategies, and competition is rooted in the center of the strategy pattern. With this attitude, it is not surprising that today's organizations, in the form of a skillful, learned how to compete with each other, and by analyzing the basic elements of the economic structure in the industry, they have been able to take a strategic position such as differentiation, cost reduction, or focus. Thus far, there are little practical guidelines and practical instructions on how to create a blue ocean in the world. In most of performed researches, the main focus of the authors is to explain what they did not consider the ocean water. Few have focused on the use of this method in order to improve the status quo, and innovations in the market. Amir Abbas Kaviani in his article explains how this method in the field of banking, the wipe out the theory and converted it to action. Author of the article explained the methods of banking services and attract new customers by banks (Kavyani, AA, 2013). But in general, researchers have emphasized the benefits of using this method. Roohollah Tavalaee describes in blue ocean chapter, as a revolution in strategic management, how this method, the ability to enter into organizations, and established how it is described, based on basic steps Strategy (Toulayi, 2008). Amir Navidi in his essay evaluated this strategy in the field of entrepreneurship, and the merits of the matter, and that is to explain the entrepreneur and the special place that is considered for the people, and the ways that they put forward (A. Navidi). Thus, considering the above, most studies have been done so far, to describe above mentioned strategy. Frank Papa and Philip C. Slocum, in their article, in the field of orthopedics, have used the Blue Ocean Strategy in the development and improvement of education and required care, as well as cost reduction in this branch of medicine (Philip C. Slocum a, Frank Papa b 2014). Jaka Lindica, Mushca Bavda and Helena Kovacicb, in the article further growth through the blue ocean, concepts for economic policy, on research they did on Amazon and Solvenian companies, the survey results showed that the gap between macro-level policy economic, to achieve a higher level of economic growth, as well as macroeconomic and business. The result was that, the strategy is different for each company, depending on the size, type of industry, and whether they cooperate or not, and that, the same organization can make use of a strategy to advance the goals. (Jaka Lindica, MB z., *, Helena Kovacicb., 2012). Jen T. Young, in the article, the impact of change management chain hotels, the hotel chain in Taiwan, showed how, Blue Ocean Strategy can affect change in public image. And also showed how Blue Ocean Strategy can change policies during the transition period, due to the change in hotel management assistance (Yang, J.-t., 2012). Burke et al., (Andrew Burke, A. v. S., and Roy Thurik., 2009), in a study entitled, "Blue Ocean compared to competitive strategy: Theory and Evidence," examined the Dutch retail industry during the years 1982 to 2000. The study had two important differences compared to other researches. First, test priorities of blue ocean, compared to competitive strategy, are presented in the form of short and long term, and the other is that the results of this analysis provides the first statistical results, which proves blue ocean strategy at the corporate level, has successful application. Burke et al., (Andrew Burke, A. v. S., and Roy Thurik., 2009), in their study, they used a model that was introduced in 1921 by Harol Hotelling. It states that, until the presence in a specific market profitable, more and more suppliers enter the market, it has reached saturation point, in this case, are all in the head to head. Parvynn and colleagues, in a study entitled, "Understanding the function and structural features Blue Ocean practices in sales management" presented. In this study, the role of value creation mechanisms will be discussed during the company's sales strategy. Using the process of value creation and strategic marketing as theoretical methods, principles of Blue Ocean Strategy, in this study, and practices in sales management activities, is classified (Pita Pitta, D., 2012), the research entitled, "Issues related to the weak economy: blue ocean and new product development." In this chapter, we have investigated the use of Blue Ocean Strategy with the aim of producing new products. The results show that, using this method, companies can organize product offers and services, to provide services to new customers and to lest its industrial competitors. Their results provide concepts for manufacturing new products, and the management team and senior management.

3. KANO EVALUATION MODEL

Kano and Tisuji believed that two features should be adhered reviewed to assess the quality of anything: Intuitive features and mental characteristics. According to this model, the qualitative characteristics fit into five groups and based on these characteristics, the questionnaire is set, and each of these features are divided into two groups. (Ching-Chow Yang, K.-J. 2011)

- **Highly Attractive Attributes:** Firms should raise these factors, and even create new highly attractive attributes to acquire non-customers; (Ching-Chow Yang, K.-J. 2011)
- **Attractive Charm Features With a Very High Quality:** In the absence, the features of the results should be established.
- **Quality Features with Very Low Attraction:** If any, it should be kept at the same level or decline.
- **One-Dimensional Quality Features:** Feature shows the relationship between customer perception and satisfaction. (Ching-Chow Yang, K.-J. 2011)
- **Quality Features with High Value-Added:** In the absence, it must be developed.
- qualitative characteristics with lower value, if any, it should be dropped, but come down to a level that does not cause discontent.
- **The Essential Quality Features:** The lack of feature causes discontent, but it also does not necessarily lead to happiness (Ching-Chow Yang, K.-J. 2011).
- **Critical Quality Characteristics:** It is very important for the client, and in the absence, it must be developed.
- **Essential Qualitative Characteristics:** It is important for the client, but does not have a significant impact on satisfaction levels, and it should be kept at the same level.
- **Ineffective Qualitative Characteristics:** A feature in which lack or existance of it does not create any kind of satisfaction or dissatisfaction. (Ching-Chow Yang, K.-J. 2011)

- **Potential Quality Features:** If you look at the results, it should be improved, as has the required potential for satisfaction.
- **Unimportant Quality Characteristics:** It should be removed.
- **Reverse Quality Features:** Features that its presents causes dissatisfaction, and its absence will be satisfied, if any, should be removed. (Ching-Chow Yang, K.-J. 2011)

Figure 1 shows the process of creating value for customers, the improved hybrid model of Cano and Blue Ocean Strategy, which was developed on the basis of the above mentioned strategies.

Figure 1. Model of 'value of customer' based on integration of refined Kano's model and 'blue ocean' framework (Ching-Chow Yang, K.-J. Y, 2011)

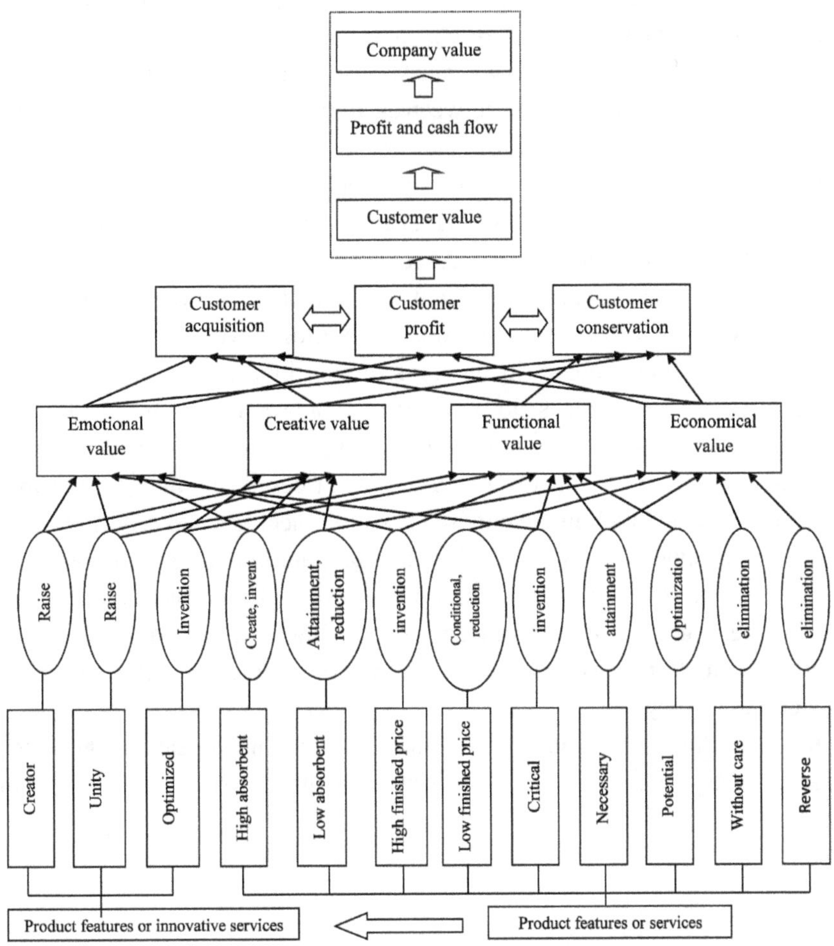

4. BLUE OCEAN, REQUIREMENTS AND APPROACHES

Blue Ocean Strategy is a pattern of strategic thinking to create new markets and businesses in various industries. In this type of environment, rather than the use of traditional instruments in the competitive environment, including market analysis, review of the existing competitors in the market, and the methodology of these, such as by exploring and creating new demand, it is trying to maintain existing customers and attract new customers. Table 1 shows the tools available in the Blue Ocean Strategy, to create a new market, and then, Table 2, deals with the questions raised at the beginning of the formation of a blue ocean.

According to what was said so far from the Blue Ocean Strategy, and describing the current situation in the construction industry in the country, it caused author to explain the review of this strategy in the industry. As noted, the ocean water is based on innovation, so the question is that the construction industry is now, to what extent is consistent with the desires of customers? To what extent product manufacturers have innovation and try to meet their customers' needs?

In response to the above question it must be said that, unfortunately, in this industry, there was little communication between customers and suppliers, and production strictly is according to their condition, such as taste and facilities available to production. Because of large amounts of housing, which in terms of quality and features are at a classified level, we are faced with the phenomenon of mass production, of course, provide the competition for market share among producers, thus, considering conditions, it appeares to need more water in the ocean, the industry is feeling.

One of those in the construction industry, by those involved and is considered less mass is branding problem in the construction industry. When it created the brand in the industry, as well as clothing, the kind of product we provide, for classes or provide a wide range of community. This requires careful analysis of consumer needs in terms of design, quality of materials, the prices, the applicant's age, marital status, and the area, which in the end, the desired objectives and criteria for selecting the right product, on the table. For example, automobile companies in most regions of the world, there are shopping facilities specific to the client. The same applies to the construction industry can also be implemented to grant long-term loans, limited auction sales, branding developed by people who are engaged in the construction industry.

Here, according to the context of formation of the blue ocean, or the four-step approach, we try to explain the blue ocean strategy, in the case of construction companies.

Table 1. The tools in the Blue Ocean Strategy

Row	Description	Actions
1	Analysis of the competition scene	1. Drawing situation: each company based on the critical success factors of the industry, and value creation key factors for the industry. 2. Map the current state of strategy formulation of the organization: To determine the factors that the industry invests now, in terms of products, services and delivery on the competition and investment.
2	Rivals Mapping	Competitors are divided into three categories: 1. pioneers: those who innovete value or to create innovative values. 2. Followers: those who reform current values or are to improve the values that have already been realized. 3 Survival or permanent resident: those that mimic the way forward and, without innovation or improvement, process simulation.
3	Framework of different pathways of innovation in value	1. Evaluation of alternative industries in the implementation of ocean water, due to this, the new arena created by substitute products, not affected in the short term, it is necessary, because otherwise, all investments made fruitless and the product will be marginalized. 2. Evaluation of strategic groups within the industry: As an alternative to searching across industries, creating blue oceans is possible by examining the strategic groups can be in unknown areas, open areas of work and services, blue ocean. 3. Study customer chain: The aim of any industrial customers, it will be seen that the industry and products, taking their normal target. Based on the principle of innovation in ocean water can be focused on non-target customers, created a new market. 4. Study of products and services supporting the often complementary products and services, exist untapped value. Important defining the overall solution, which followed their customers when selecting a product or service. 5. Evaluation of functional and emotional attributes: some industries compete largely based on profit calculations. The main character and systematic structure of these industries is a logic-oriented tradition. Other industries compete largely on emotional characteristics, the basic characteristics and systematic structure of these industries is their emotional and exciting. 6. Evaluation of the time managers with the shed in the area could actively shape their future, and are demanding a new ocean. This time, it may be more difficult than other routes were introduced in the past, but with a similar systematic approach can be achieved.
4	Four step approach	1. Create: factors that can completely new value for customers to create new demand. (Ching-Chow Yang, K.-JY, 2011) 2. Eliminate: to reduce costs, eliminate any factor or element that does not create value for the customer, or the customer is reducing. (Ching-Chow Yang, K.-JY, 2011) 3. Raise: factors or attributes that can cause the creation of absolute value for customers. (Ching-Chow Yang, K.-JY, 2011) 4. Reduce: Anything that has repeatedly been designed, which may increase their costs without having to make gains, are adjusted.

Table 2. The questions raised in the founding of the Blue Ocean Strategy in the construction industry

Row ردیف	Description	Questions Raised
1	Application	Is there a reason that customers buy new goods or services? That is if new products meet the needs of the **consumer?**
2	Price	Whether large customers are able to purchase a new product or service?
3	Expense	Is the cost of goods or services, in such a way that it can be presented with profitability to the market?
4	Ability	Is the company able to address its capability gap as soon as possible?
5	Implementation	Is it possible to transfer the ideas or imitate it? Have measures been taken to lack of transport or imitation?

First Step: Create

The recommended way to do that is to create an office supply order, or working closely with the client, as mentioned above, the construction industry is the least relevance in the fields in the views of customer's relationship for the production. The actions that can be performed in the office are noted as follows:

- To attract customers with marketing techniques, and offering face to face.
- Collecting requests and opinions.
- Economic and technical computing.
- Provide advice and recommendations to the customer.
- Conclusion of the contract.

During the above steps, producers can collect the views of customer, technical changes have shared with him, then economic calculations done, and then do the necessary agreements, to produce. This process leads, sales guarantee and buyer's quite good, which is a deal win - win for both parties (Amburn, C. k. R., 2008)

Step Two: Eliminate

In this step, one of the most important steps that should be done contract work is the elimination of bureaucracy to the customer, and provides all administrative services and banking. Due to the high volume of bureaucracy in the country, as well as large volumes of bureaucracy in this industry, one of the factors that buyers face is very welcome.

Step Three: Invention

In this step, the measures that lead to innovation and the creation of new service areas will include:

- Provide after-sales services to customers.
- Provision for future customer needs.
- Product updates, and provides advice to the update.

Including those in the construction industry has remained completely foreign and unknown, after-sales service. Creating infrastructure to deliver these services can be a very lucrative new market ahead of its producers, the big automotive companies today benefit from the service and parts business sales are more than selling product. (Amburn, C. k. R., 2008)

Fourth Step: Reduce

This is step one of the key competitive advantages, because the entire infrastructure created for the creation of a new arena, regardless of the stage, you may be faced with defeat. Among the measures that could be cited in this step include:

- Reduce the cost when delivered, by increasing the possibilities.
- A decrease in property prices set by contracts, property restitution, since the agreement.

5. BLUE OCEAN STRATEGY DEVELOPMENT IN THE CONSTRUCTION INDUSTRY, USING KANO

In 2001, the theory of the life cycle raised quality features, and suggested that the qualitative characteristics can be changed, for example, there are attractive features with no importance and may be in a range to feature leveling are important. In order to confirm the idea of the life cycle, quality characteristics that had been raised by Cano, Lofegern, Whittle and Gustafsson (2011), performed a studyin the field of quality appeal theory in two stages (in 2003 and 2009). Although there are several studies related to the Kano theory, but in view of the importance of quality features that have been ignored by previous researchers, in the answer to this problem in 2005, Yang (see Part Three of this article), reviewed the Kano model, and the quality of the main characteristics of the units, divided into two sub-groups, and totally eight groups were emerged (Ching-Chow Yang, K.-J. Y, 2011).

Figure 2. The formation of a blue ocean in a four-step approach

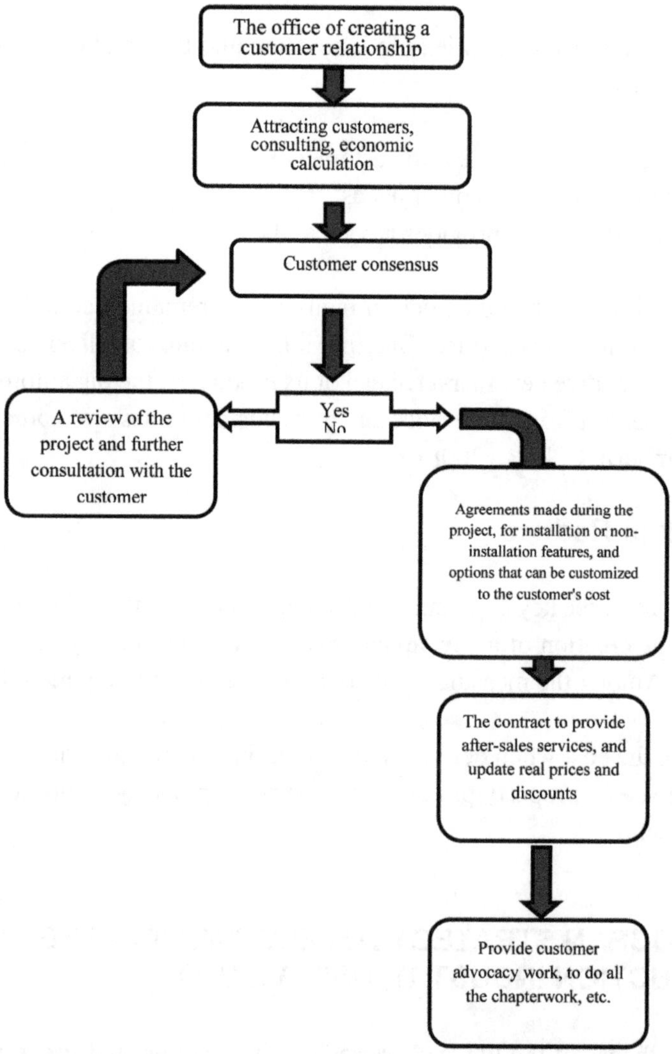

The objective of this study is to measure and determine the amount of Blue Ocean Strategy training in construction companies, and offer some ways to improve it. This study, in terms of purpose, is an applied research, and in terms of data collection, is a descriptive research, and is a part of field studies. The research method is survey. In order to collect research data, the questionnaire is used. To determine the main components of Blue Ocean Strategy in the components in the scientific literature, those with frequency usage had been selected for use in this study, which are: innovation, value, pattern making four attempts, review the structure of market boundaries, focus on the big picture, reach beyond the status quo to request the establishment of strategic steps correct (idea of Blue Ocean) overcome on the key barriers, and providing process of implementation of the strategy in the strategy formulation process..

Based on Kano model and the pillars of the Blue Ocean Strategy, a questionnaire based on the Likert scale questionnaire was adjusted to 5 points, and was sent to 50 people, and received responses were ranked from 1 "extremely important" to 5 "very important" and then, out of every item in the column was relevant and its significance was determined based on the classification of Kano, and based on four attempts, it was determined that which one of the features is in need to be created, invented, eliminated or reduced.

Table 3. Characteristics of the priorities of the customer, which has been arranged in order of preference

Row	Characteristics of Attracting Customers	Average Importance	Average Satisfaction	Kano Model Category	Classification on the Divided Sub-Cathegories of Kano
1	Granting buy low-interest, long-term loans	5	2.05	One-dimensional	High value-added
2	The electronic administrative bureaucracy	5	2.95	One-dimensional	High value-added
3	Building Investment Insurance	4.53	2.95	Must-be	Critical
4	Home insurance completely when buying	3.82	3.08	One-dimensional	High value-added
5	Easy access to public transportation	4.59	3.45	Must-be	Critical
6	Recreational facilities	3.65	3.63	Must-be	Care-free
7	Smart Fire Fighting System	5	2.95	Attractive	Necessary attribute
8	Houses with small size	4.59	2.08	One-dimensional	High value-added
9	Heat regulation system	3.12	3.09	Attractive	Care-free
10	Limited sales of residential units	5	2.71	One-dimensional	Critical
11	Internal power consumption optimization system	2.12	2.95	Attractive	potential
12	Air settlement system	2.09	2.02	Attractive	Care-free

Figure 3. Average of characteristics of Attracting customers, the Kano Model

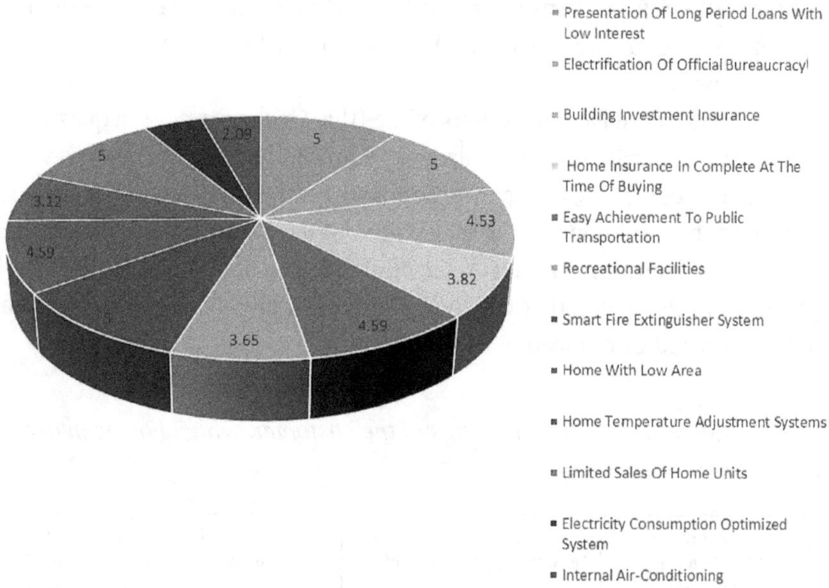

**For a more accurate representation of this figure, please see the electronic version.*

Figure 4 . Average satisfaction level in Kano model

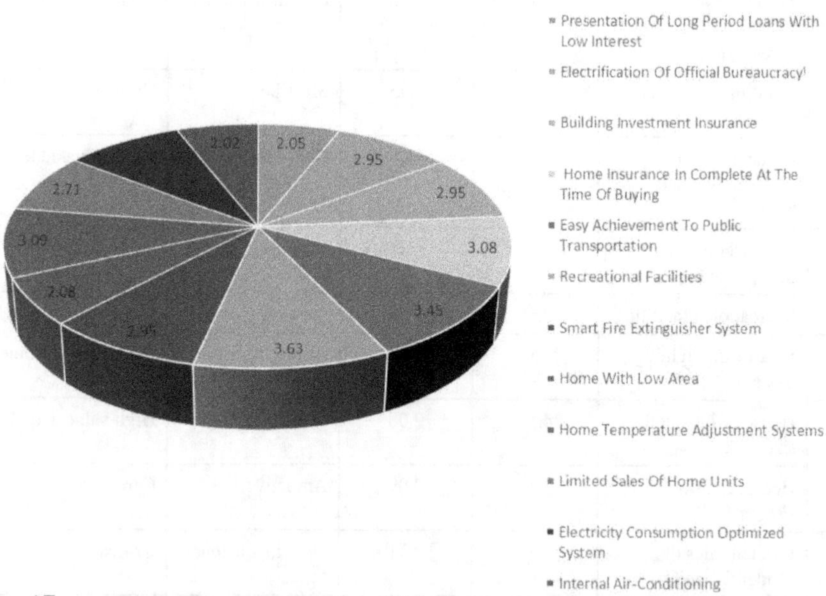

**For a more accurate representation of this figure, please see the electronic version.*

Table 4. integration of Improved models of Kano and Four- step approaches Blue Ocean Strategy

Column	Features	Classification in Kano Divided Subgroups	Recommended Actions
1	Presentation for long period loans with low interest	High value-added	Raise
2	Electrification of official bureaucracy	High value-added	Raise
3	Building investment insurance	Critical	Raise
4	Home insurance in complete at shopping time	High value-added	Raise
5	Easy achievement to public transportation	Critical	Raise
6	Recreational facilities	Care-free	Eliminate
7	Smart fire extinguisher system	Necessary attribute	Maintain or Reduce
8	Home with low area	High value-added	Raise
9	Home temperature adjustment systems	Care-free	Eliminate
10	Limited sales of home units	Critical	Raise
11	Electricity consumption optimized system	potential	Maintain or Reduce
12	Internal air-conditioning	Care-free	Maintain or Reduce

6. CONCLUSION

In this chapter, the Blue Ocean Strategy in the construction industry, so as to be reviewed to identify and evaluate adhered to, the spaces that have not been recognized in the industry, and due to the new ideas, the construction industry has changed and according to the theory of kano and Tisuji who believed, two features should be evaluated to assess the quality of anything placed, intuitive features and mental characteristics, according to the model and the qualitative characteristics fit into five groups and based on the Features the questionnaire was set, and each of these features were divided into two groups: absorbing characteristics and dimensional features.

In this article it is tried that, according to prioritizing the importance of the customer, and according to a series of charts and questionnaires, to clear blue ocean path, in order to optimize the construction industry; but in other articles about Blue Ocean, a multi-stage process of implementation, and in modern strategic management, it does not provide choice and distinctive building on competitive strategy or blue ocean, but instead, there will be a more complex problem, which is the identification of a Optimal and efficient integration process. These two strategies are the short and long term, and that, in other chapters presented in the ocean blue, not used, the questionnaire and field research to fully and transparently. And that, in this chapter, the problem is strategic management of business survival, and winning the competition within the enterprise, but the other articles in this issue, by long run imitating, causes that companies do not follow the competition completely, and thus they lag behind competitors and innovation, initiative and creativity, could be a short-term solution for these companies.

Kim and Renée Mauborgne drew a lot of attention among academics and experts. This approach is formed from two strategies at the same time, the strategy of differentiation and cost reduction strategies. At the same time, the organization offers a series of methodologies and management tools to create an unrivaled, new market space. The authors of Blue Ocean Strategy believe that the only way to win the competition, is stop trying to win the competition and instead of entering the red ocean of bloody competition, to enter the infinite market space of ocean water, and to create demand.

Blue Ocean Strategy has a motivating message: success is not dependent on serious and tough competition marketing costs and research and development budget.

Nowadays the Blue Ocean Strategy in the world is rapidly penetrated all industries and markets, and its cause is more willingness of manufacturers to innovate which is the basis of this strategy. Todays consumers unlike the consumers of decades ago do not seek for meeting the needs of, and are looking for something new for the price they pay. Basic and strategic industries, such as construction, are not removed from this basic, and should be in line with this development. Therefore, a combination of several methods to creat value, and estimate the degree of importance of features that customers are looking for, and other competitors are not able to hire, creates new ways of making and selling the product, which is inevitable. What is now seriously threatening the industry, is the high volume of non-professional producers that market without the need, merely produce and it causes market disruption Shvndf balance and are a waste of resources. Innovative production and development of new fields, the product allows not only to provide more customer satisfaction, but also the producers themselves get free of severe competition with other competitors, to win more market share. The practice causes to itself, non-specialist producers and the industry like other industries become removed from the market and this process get more toward specialization and development. In this chapter as mentioned, with inovating some methods which verbally attract customer needs, and then turn it into quantitative data, to make the best decision, take the necessary measures to carry out continuous improvement. Kano mix method with blue ocean strategy can create value, which is the foundation of Blue Ocean Strategy and make diversification and improvement of the construction market and sell, in all areas from shopping centers to home.

REFERENCES

Ballesteros Perez, M. C. G. C., & Pastor-Ferrando, J. P. (2010). Analysis of construction projects by means of value curves. *International Journal of Project Management, 28*(7), 719–731. doi:10.1016/j.ijproman.2009.11.003

Burke & Thurik. (2009). *Blue Ocean versus Competitive Strategy: Theory and Evidence*. Erasmus Research Institute of Management.

Ching-Chow Yang, K.-J. Y. (2011). An integrated model of value creation based on the refined Kanos model and the blue ocean strategy. *Total Quality Management & Business Excellence, 22*(9), 925–940. doi:10.1080/14783363.2011.611358

Jaka Lindiˇca, M. B. (2012). Higher growth through the Blue Ocean Strategy: Implications for economic policy. *Research Policy, 41*(5), 928–938. doi:10.1016/j.respol.2012.02.010

Kavyani, A. A. (2013). Blue Ocean Strategy and its role in marketing banking services. *Market Engineering Development. Bi-monthly, 13*(2), 9.

Majid Golpayagani, S. P. (2000). Blue Ocean Strategy uncontested market Competition. *Monthly Tadbir, 20*(2), 202.

Mina, A. K. (2010). *Strategic management is based on the blue ocean and the role of creativity and innovation in its implementation*. Paper presented at the First International Conference on Innovation and Management, Tehran, Iran.

Noorian, H. (1999). Strategic management method based on Blue Ocean. *The Quality Assurance Journal, 3*(2), 11.

Pitta, D., & Pitta, E. (2012). Transforming the nature and scope of new product development. *Journal of Product and Brand Management, 21*(1), 35–46. doi:10.1108/10610421211203097

Slocum & Papa. (2014). Envisioning a global role for osteopathic medicine in the 21st century: Using Blue Ocean Strategy to promote osteopathic health care as the World's leader in healthcare education and do it more efficiently, effectively and at the lowest cost. *International Journal of Osteopathic Medicine, 17*, 38-42.

Toulayi, R. (2008). Blue Ocean Strategy as revolution in the field of strategic anagement. *Police Human Development, 24*.

Yang, J. (2012). Effects of ownership change on organizational settings and strategies in a Taiwanese hotel chain. *Hospitality Managment, 31*(2), 428–441. doi:10.1016/j.ijhm.2011.07.001

Chapter 11 Entrepreneurship and Innovation in Lebanese Healthcare: Road to Employee Job Satisfaction

Johnny Chalita Chaanine
Lebanese University, Lebanon & Notre Dame University, Lebanon

ABSTRACT

In a world that is swiftly evolving, working life conditions are continuously changing too; this chapter will deal with changing environment and its impact on our lives; it will cover the historical background of healthcare in Lebanon, the entrepreneurial factors affecting the Lebanese hospitals stressing on the working life needs especially the skills needed to learn new things which will provide a better ability to adapt to changing working environments. This chapter also stresses on the role of core competences among entrepreneurs in special fields of social and health care. The healthcare industry has experienced a worldwide growth and proliferation of innovation aimed at improving our lives, its quality and providing better treatment in addition to creating a good working environment enhancing employee performance and self-satisfaction.

DOI: 10.4018/978-1-5225-2066-5.ch011

INTRODUCTION

It was in those dark days of those dark ages that humans had to give up on finding ways to help patients heal leaving them either in the hands of their gods or in the hand of fate, unable neither to assist them nor to provide support beyond the basic and primitive health and medical knowledge that was transferred to them from earlier generations.

The world kept advancing, the era of ignorance slowly vanished, and with the introduction of computer and technology, the 20th century came to be known as the time of innovation.

It has been said that innovation is to look at things and see what everybody has seen yet think of things that nobody has thought. Innovation is the key driver that affects our economic growth, provides standards for safety in our daily lives and most of all delivers better healthcare, better products and better quality leading for a better environment. With innovation, our productivity increased to the extent of creating what is known nowadays as the knowledge community and knowledge economy.

Never forget this mantra "Innovate or Die"; this applies to one of the top Lebanese organization: "Healthcare."

BACKGROUND

Innovation in the healthcare domain mainly in Lebanon passed through several phases; the introduction of healthcare to the country was not easy; it passed through many difficulties. Historically, the existence of healthcare organization can be tracked back to the crusaders era.

Historical Background

The healthcare system in Lebanon can be tracked back to the nation's existence where Phoenicians used to practice primitive healthcare indicators; this primitive knowledge was taken from the Egyptians through the trade they used to do together. Lebanon used to be an intermediate ground between the Crusaders' and Salah el din's armies where both armies introduced what was called the field hospitals. These hospitals were designated to deliver treatment and rest for the wounded soldiers (Punoose, 2004).

World War I and II played a role in the progress of the medical sector; however, it was only in the first fifteen years of independence (1943 – 1958) that we witnessed the birth of the primitive infrastructure of district and rural hospitals with a governmental policies aiming to create orders and rules to provide healthcare for the society (Regional Health Systems Observatory, 2006). The Lebanese government encouraged social development and community participation.

In 1964, the social security fund was established and the private sector became more and more involved in the healthcare sector by building many private hospitals.

One year after (1965), the Syndicate of Private Hospitals was established; it was the gathering of all private hospitals whose aim was to represent private hospitals and to play the role of a task force enforcer for laws and regulations. One of its main purposes is to organize and set a unified strategy on how to cooperate with the government drawing together a road map for the healthcare sector. Moreover, the establishment of "The Order of Nurses" played an important role in shaping the healthcare system through organizing the nursing work in Lebanon.

Lebanese Hospitals Nowadays

Recently, Lebanon has been facing a demographic change and an epidemiological transition with millions of Syrian, Iraqi and Palestinian refugees living in the small country of 10452Km Square. This crowded population in a small geography creates concerns of a double burden of diseases. Nowadays, there is a noticeable rise in the incidences of communicable diseases, which increases the risk level among the population (Ammar, 2003) in a country with an increasing rate of public debt, increasing poverty among the population, and a minimal growth since 1999 (Sfeir, 2007).

The growth in the number of private hospitals and the tough competition among them have given the Lebanese healthcare system a competitive advantage over the hospitals in the region noting that Lebanon has 2.88 beds per 1000 population making this country one of the highest ratios in the Middle East (Sfeir, 2007).

Healthcare Innovation

Defining healthcare innovation is not an easy task; first we must define innovation: West (1990) defined innovation as the intentional introduction and application of ideas, products, processes or procedures that are designed to significantly benefit the individual, the group, the organizations or the wider society. This definition has been largely accepted among scholars in the field of management (Anderson, et al., 2004).

According to Lanisalmi et al, (2006) innovation focuses on three main factors that are considered as the three characteristics of innovation:

1. Novelty.
2. Application component.

3. Intended benefit.

Several Stakeholders were identified as being directly influenced by innovation; these stakeholders are mainly the entrepreneurs in the organization who are in charge of the performance and the overall success of the enterprise. However, those entrepreneurs have unique needs with specific expectations. In many cases, those entrepreneurs delegate some of their control to the different types of stakeholders. In the Lebanese healthcare context, we can identify four main types of stakeholders:

1. Board of directors in the hospital.
2. Patients.
3. Physicians.
4. Regulatory Agencies.

Each of the above has his/her expectations toward innovation usage in order to create ease of use at work, concerning:

- The board of directors', their aim through innovation usage is to create smooth processes, systematized flow of work and high degree of job satisfaction among their employees and subordinate, especially that the healthcare sector deals with delicate issues and put the patients at the center of the organization universe;
- Patients expect improvement in the physiological well-being, a reduced waiting time and a reduced delay in the medication treatments;
- Physicians expect an improved diagnosis and assistance in the treatment process;
- Regulatory agencies expect risk reduction and more patient safety while they reside in hospitals.

However, in many cases, some of the innovation introduced can be considered as a disruptive innovations or radical innovations (Harvard Business Essentials, 2003), other scholars called it revolutionary nonlinear innovation (Govindarajan, 2007; Hamel, 2000). The Disruption refers to an innovation that disorders an old system, and replaces it by new one thus creating new players in completely new markets while neglecting and marginalizing old ones. It has also the ability to deliver dramatic value to stakeholders who successfully implement and adapt to the new innovation (Varkey, et al., 2008). Innovations in healthcare are related to the product being delivered by the hospitals i.e. the service, the processes and the structures being followed by the entrepreneur of these facilities and the employees working in (Varkey,et al., 2008). The aim of the innovation, whether it is a disruptive or not, is to deliver a good product; this product is what the customer pays for and typically consists of goods or services (for example, clinical procedure innovations). The reduction of paper work is one of the aims of introducing innovation into hospitals. Paperwork is prone to costly errors; huge savings can be realized by more and better use of electronic record keeping and error reduction and money saving is achieved through employing software that can issue prompts and detect mistakes (Grose, 2008).

In the old days, Lebanese healthcare providers had to rely on paper records only; the sharing of information and the delivery of care was not only a challenge but sometimes even impossible. Nowadays sharing information and patient medical records between the ministry of public health and the hospitals and among the hospitals themselves became less time consuming and straightforward (Sfeir, 2007).

UNESCO makes distinction among four different types of innovations; these distinctions are as follows:

1. Product Innovations.
2. Marketing Innovations.
3. Process Innovations.
4. Organizational Innovations.

In product innovation, healthcare organizations must introduce significant improvements to the technical specifications phase (for instance better machinery and more user friendly systems). Such enhancement will improve the hospitalization experience which in turn will improve the services provided ranging from patient admission till patient check-out.

As for marketing innovations, these involve creating the product image, the name and the reputation for the hospital in addition to providing a patient-friendly design; The process innovation includes changes in techniques in order to faster and better services; and finally the organizational innovation, it includes new method in the business practices that shape the overall policies and procedures that in turn will impact the overall strategy of the company.

Lebanese Healthcare Informatics

With the increasing number of population and the advances in technology, the need to automate the processes in the medical field became a necessity. Many attempts have been made to introduce informatics, automation and robotics into Lebanese hospitals. Some have succeeded while others failed, but in general the healthcare information system in Lebanon is considered to be a weak system due to several factors, mainly due to the lack of timely information and a transparent dissemination of data (EMRO, 2007).

The data to be collected by the Ministry of Public Health ranges from first the geographic and demographic information and the distribution of patient; second, the pharmaceutical use of drugs and confidential information of patients and third the quality management information (Ammar, et al., 1999).

Even though the serious attempts toward full automation of patient data in the hospitals seem far from being achieved, there exists a link between all the districts and the central administration from one part, and the ministry and the other public funding agencies from the other (EMRO, 2007). A direct connection between the Ministry of Public Health (MOPH) and the other third party payers like the military forces, social security service, and insurance companies was created, where critical information is registered in the MOPH database. Expenses of both private and public hospitals are to be reported monthly to the MOPH in order to control the overall yearly expenses. This phase of national patient registration is a success as it became fully automated reducing the cost and effort of patient data management. The beneficiary-connecting databases project is the first step toward a national information system (EMRO, 2007).

ENTREPRENEUR: THE DEFINITION AND THE BIGGER PICTURE

We all heard about entrepreneurship importance in a way or another, but how do we define an entrepreneur? And what distinguishes an entrepreneur from other organizational actors and what impact does it have on our lives?

The term entrepreneur appeared in 1253 for the first time, then it was used through time by many scholars; however, this definition differs according to the authors' paradigms. "Entrepreneur" is derived from a French word; it comes from the verb "entreprendre", meaning to do, to take and act or to undertake. This word is divided into two parts; the first is "entre", meaning "between", and the second is "preneur" that means "taker". (Filion, 2008). In order to define the term entrepreneur in this chapter we will refer to the definition of Schumpeter (1928) stating that "the essence of entrepreneurship lies in the perception and exploitation of new opportunities".

In his study that aims showing the importance of innovation in the entrepreneurial world, Filion (2008) referred to Schumpeter study stating that innovation is associated with entrepreneur based on five main factors:

1. Introducing new method of production;
2. Introducing new goods;

Table 1. Role, value, and main key terms

Elements Defining the Entrepreneur	Authors
Innovation and Risk Management	Julien (1998, 1989); Drucker (1985); Reuters (1982); Rosenberg (1983)
Coordination of resources for Production; Value Creation	Fayolle (2008); Bruyat and Julien (2001); Casson (1982); Pearce (1981)
Visionary thinking and Projective decision maker	Filion (2004)
Opportunity recognition; Good Leadership Skills	Shane and Venkataraman (2000); Dana (1995); Hornaday and Aboud (1971)
Catalist of Creativity, Control and Change	Pinchot (1985); Zaleznik and Kets de Vries (1976); Shapiro (1975); McClelland (1961)

3. Carrying out of the new industry and organization;
4. The conquest of a new source of supply of raw material;
5. The ability to open new markets.

Moreover, entrepreneurship is often classified and discussed under the title of the entrepreneurial function, initiative, factor, and entrepreneurial behavior; it is also referred to as the entrepreneurial "spirit"; in this context, entrepreneurial functions implies the assessment, exploitation and discovery of opportunities, i.e. the discovery of new products and services in addition to different production processes, strategies and organizational forms that did not exist previously (Shane and Venkataraman, 2000). This is referred to as the entrepreneurial opportunity (unexpected and unvalued economic opportunity).

Table 1 summarizes the role, value and main key terms used in the definition of an entrepreneur.

Hence through reviewing the literature, the study of entrepreneurship facilitates the attempt to answer the questions of what, why and how; what happens when entrepreneur acts in an organization and mainly in healthcare organization, why do they act and how do they act? The answers to those questions can be found among employees themselves… they simply act like that because they are good leaders.

Entrepreneurship Success is Being a Good Leader for Your Employee

In any successful firm, an entrepreneur should focus on human factors, "employee", by enhancing their skills, providing good working environment, motivating them hence boosting their creativity. If this is achieved, employees' satisfaction will become a reality.

Many scholars studied and proposed motivational theories in order to define variables that affect organizational behavior and employee's performance. The management science recognizes Herzberg, Maslow, Vroom and McGregor to be cornerstone of this science. While Herzberg in his two-factor theory stresses on what he called hygiene and motivating factors working conditions, job security, company policies, and quality of supervision, salary, and relations with others (Herzberg, 2003; Gordon, 2002; Herzberg, 1987) Maslow emphasized on a sequential chain from the bottom to the top of a pyramid as follows: satisfying the physiological needs, safety, belonging, esteem and finally the self-actualization need (Maslow, 1943, 1970).

We stress in this chapter on Victor Vroom theory called the "Expectancy Theory". It was first developed by Edwards Tolman and Kurt Lewin then finalized in the 1964 by Vroom (Moorehead and Griffin, 1989). This theory stresses that employees' behavior depends on expectations based on outcome generated due to this behavior (Vroom, 1982, 1964).

Moreover, Vroom stressed that a "momentary belief concerning the likelihood that particular act will be followed by a particular outcome" (Vroom, 1964, p. 17) which is the case of employees working in Lebanese healthcare organizations, expecting specific outcomes based on specific behavior, this behavior is shaped through technology.

Moreover, the expectancy theory is affected by three inter-related factors: the belief that effort will result in a desired performance level (valence); the value of performing and accomplishing a task and the associated believed reward for that performance and finally the attained performance will eventually lead to rewards at work (expectancy). See Table 2 for a visualization of motivational force.

But how could this theory shape employees satisfaction in Lebanese healthcare? This needs to be linked to two main theories that complement what Vroom developed.

The first theory is the theory of reasoned action which was complemented by another theory the technology acceptance model.

Table 2. Motivational force

Motivational Force = Expectancy X Instrumentality X Valence ***Expectancy: Effort → Performance (E→P);*** ***Instrumentality: Performance → Outcome (P→O);*** ***Valence: Individual places on the rewards based on his needs, and goals.***

Source: Vroom, 1964

Theory of Reasoned Action (TRA)

The theory of reasoned action was first developed by Martin Fishbein and IcekAjzen (1980); this theory is deduced from previous studies targeting employees attitudes at work and "born largely out of frustration with traditional attitude–behavior research, much of which found weak correlations between attitude measures and performance of volitional behaviors" (Hale, Householder and Greene, 2003, p. 259).

The researchers built a model that was based on social and psychological attitudes focusing mainly on intended behaviors (Ajzen and Fishbein, 1980), it stressed also on distinguishing between the beliefs and attitudes among individuals and their impact on the overall motivation at work.

The theory of reasoned action emphasizes that a person's exhibition of a specific behavior depends on his behavioral intention (BI) to perform this behavior; however, this BI is determined by the person's attitude (A) and subjective norms (SN).

Thus, social influence plays a major role in this theory and its impact on satisfaction and performance.

As shown in Figure 1, the theory focuses on the beliefs and motivation that affect the attitude and the subjective norm where those two variables will eventually affect the behavioral intention and the actual behavior among employees.

From these theories, another theory saw the light: a more specialized theory dedicated to test the impact of technology directly on employees motivation and thus their overall satisfaction at work; it's the technology acceptance model.

Technology Acceptance Model (TAM)

Ajzen and Fishbein (1980) conclude that TAM is proven successful in predicting about 40% of a system's use. Three main factors determine the intention to use a given technology (Davis, 1993); those factors are a) usefulness; b) ease of use, and c) the attitudes toward technology usage.

The objective of TAM is "to provide an explanation of the determinants of computer acceptance that is general, capable of explaining user behavior across a broad

Figure 1. Beliefs and motivation

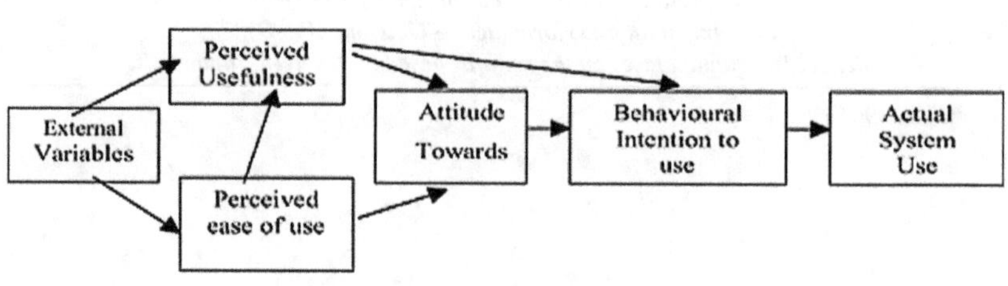

range of end-user computing technologies and user populations" (Davis, Bagozzi and Warshaw, 1989, p. 985).

The perceived ease of use refers to one's belief that using the technology will be free from effort while the usefulness refers to one's belief that using the technology will lead to desirable outcomes, higher productivity, more safety, better quality, and thus more satisfaction.

The third predictor is the attitudes or the subjective norms and this is important when technology is mandatory (Gagnon, Godin, Gagne, Fortin, Lamothe, Reinharz and Cloutier, 2003; Venkatesh & Morris, 2000).

Hence, the technology acceptance model TAM has a direct impact and influence on employees' job satisfaction due to the fact that it studies users' behavior based on their perception toward information system implementation.

In addition, TAM is concerned in tracing the impact of external variables on internal beliefs, attitudes, and intentions, where perceived usefulness (PU) and perceived ease of use (PEOU) are important factors in explaining system use which will affect the user perception toward using information system and the degree of satisfaction of employees toward this information system (see Figure 2).

The Theories in the Lebanese Healthcare Domain

But how can we link these theories together, how can Vroom's expectancy theory be related to the theory of reasoned action and mainly how can expectancy correlates with Ajzen and Fishbein (1980) technology acceptance model especially in Lebanese healthcare. The first relationship targets the Expectancy that deals with the effort of employees at work hence having a direct impact on employee's attitude toward their job and how they perceive the information system as useful in their daily tasks. Moreover, Instrumentality and Valence in the Vroom theory can be linked to the ease of use and perception toward a specific information system hence we conclude that both theories are strongly inter related to each other, complementing each other in order to shed light on the strong influence of innovation on entrepreneurs and decision makers.

Figure 2. Effect of external variables

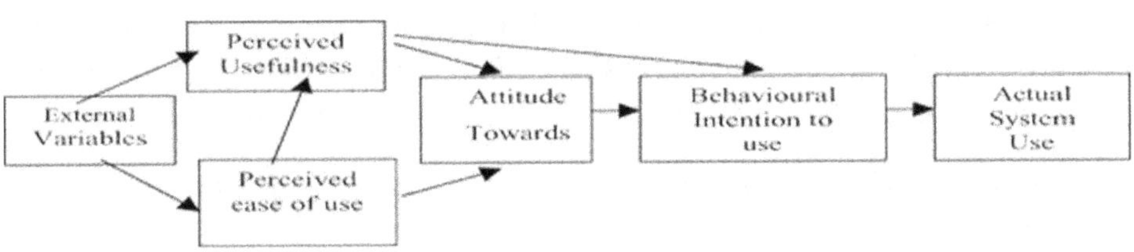

LESSON LEARNED AND CONCLUSION

Only a few years ago, the main lesson of life about the survival of the fittest would have been that Big eats Small; nowadays, with the changes that the world has undergone, we can safely say that Fast beats Slow. If you are too slow to improve and change then you will be beaten by the fastest. Innovation has been said to distinguish the leader from the follower: an idea is born, you plan and you lead your team towards advance.

To innovate you need an entrepreneurial spirit: you assess and then discover opportunities whether products, services, processes or strategies. You use your visionary thinking for opportunity recognition.

REFERENCES

Ajzen, I., & Fishbein, M. (1980). *Understanding Attitudes and Predicting Small Behavior*. Englewood Cliffs, NJ: Prentice-Hall.

Ammar, W. (2003). *Health System and Reform in Lebanon*. Beirut: World Health Organization Eastern Mediterranean Regional Office.

Ammar, W., & Wakim, R. (2005). *Lebanon's Hospital Accreditation Program: A case study*. Beirut: Ministry of Public Health.

Anderson, N., De Dreu, C. K. W., & Nijstad, D. A. (2004). The routinization of innovation research: A constructively critical review of the state-of-the-science. *Journal of Organizational Behavior*, *25*(2), 147–172. doi:10.1002/job.236

Davis, F. (1993). User acceptance of information technology: System characteristics, user perceptions and behavioral impacts. *International Journal of Man-Machine Studies*, *38*(3), 475–487. doi:10.1006/imms.1993.1022

Davis, F. D., Bagozzi, R. P., & Warshaw, P. R. (1989). User Acceptance of Computer Technology: A Comparison of Two Theoretical Models. *Management Science*, *35*(8), 982–1003. doi:10.1287/mnsc.35.8.982

Gagnon, M. P., Godin, G., Gagne, C., Fortin, J. P., Lamothe, L., Reinharz, D., & Cloutier, A. (2003). An adaptation of the theory of interpersonal behavior to the study of telemedicine adoption by physicians. *International Journal of Medical Informatics*, *71*(2-3), 103–115. doi:10.1016/S1386-5056(03)00094-7 PMID:14519403

Gordon, J. R. (2002). *Organizational Behavior: A diagnostic approach* (7th ed.). Upper Saddle River, NJ: Pearson Prentice Hall.

Hale, J. L., Householder, B. J., & Greene, K. L. (2003). The theory of reasoned action. In J. P. Dillard & M. Pfau (Eds.), *The persuasion handbook: Developments in theory and practice* (pp. 259–286). Thousand Oaks, CA: Sage.

Hamel, G. (2000). *Leading the Revolution*. Boston, MA: Harvard Business School Press.

Herzberg, F. (1987). One more time: How do you motivate employees? *Harvard Business Review*, *65*(5), 109–120. PMID:12545925

Herzberg, F. (2003). One more time: How do you motivate employees? *Harvard Business Review*, *81*(1), 86–86. PMID:12545925

Legris, P., Ingham, J., & Collerette, P. (2001). Why do people use information technology? Critical review of the technology acceptance model. *Information and Management, 40*(2003), 191–204.

Maslow, A. (1943). A theory of human motivation. *Psychological Review*, *50*(4), 370–396. doi:10.1037/h0054346

Maslow, A. (1970). *Motivation and Personality*. New York: Harper.

McClelland, D. C. (1985). *Human Motivation*. New York: Scott, Foresman.

Moorhead, G., & Griffin, R. (1989). *Organizational Behavior* (2nd ed.). Boston: Houghton Mifflin Company.

Punnose, J. (2004). *History of Hospitals.* Oyster Healthcare. Retrieved December 17, 2012, from http://johnpunnoose.com/

Regional Health Systems Observatory. (2006). *EMRO, Health Systems Profile-Lebanon*. World Health Organization.

Regional Health Systems Observatory. (2006). *EMRO, Health Systems Profile-Lebanon*. World Health Organization.

Sfeir, R. (2007). Strategy for National Health Care Reform in Lebanon. *Ministry of Public Health Magazine, 3*(3), 10-13.

Venkatesh, V., & Davis, F. (2000). A theoretical extension of the technology acceptance model: Four longitudinal field studies. *Management Science*, *46*(2), 186–204. doi:10.1287/mnsc.46.2.186.11926

Venkatesh, V., Davis, F., & Morris, M. G. (2007). Dead or alive? The development, trajectory and future of technology adoption research. *Journal of the Association for Information Systems*, *8*(4), 267–286.

Vroom, V. H. (1964). *Work and Motivation*. New York: John Wiley and Sons.

Vroom, V. H. (1982). *Work and motivation* (Rev. ed.). Malabar, FL: Robert E. Krieger Publishing Company.

Chapter 12
The Lebanese Way: A Cultural Propensity Toward Entrepreneurship

John Stephen Hess
AUB, Lebanon

ABSTRACT

Within this diverse and often unstable environment, the social phenomenon of entrepreneurship has emerged. Although this concept is found in many segments of society and individuals, it is often linked to the small business venture, and this environment is where our research will take place. Defining the term presents some challenges because it is more of an activity encompassing a wide range of character traits and skills than just a static concept. Additionally, the Lebanese context may share in the collective nature of a definition, but will also offer unique displays of entrepreneurship that may differ from other societies.

LEBANON IN CONTEXT

Just a short walk along any city street, a drive out to a sub-urban neighborhood or a further trip into Lebanon's many villages, and one finds the ever present family owned business. These small to medium sized enterprises (SME) not only mark the landscape of the country, but they account for 98% of the business environment and employ 72.4% of the population (ESCWA report 2001). At the heart of each business venture is an entrepreneurial spirit that thrives on freedom, opportunity, and at times, desperation.

DOI: 10.4018/978-1-5225-2066-5.ch012

The vast majority of these family enterprises are set within a society that has known recent war, civil unrest, and political and economic disparity. The latter conflicts are also set in the backdrop of the country's civil war from 1975-1990 which claimed 150,000 lives and displaced nearly one million citizens through emigration (Hourani, 2006).

The country's ancient history does not appear as bleak as the past few decades of strife. Modern day Lebanon traces its origins back to the ancient Phoenicians who were known for their maritime trade. In addition to being traders, the Phoenicians were cultural intermediaries, explaining to the West the heritage of the East, and introducing the East to the modern material and spiritual civilization of the West (Salibi, 1965). Even today, the Lebanese are still just as adventurous and dynamic and awed neither by strange lands nor by foreign tongues as their Phoenician patriarchs (Sayigh, 1962). This trade legacy was also evident in the seventeenth century as Lebanon emerged as a major exporter of silk to Europe, namely France and Italy. As demand for this product grew, Lebanon also developed its expediency in manufacturing and shipping. In so doing, the country established itself as a center for European trade along the Mediterranean for the next 200 years (Gates, 1997). This event also solidified their outward orientation for economic opportunity.

Also unique in the Middle East is Lebanon's blend of religious, political and educational diversity. Although no formal statistics are kept, it is estimated that 59.7% of the current population adhere to the faith of Islam and 39% practice Christianity. These two faiths and their many sects have coexisted since the inception of the country in 1943. Homes, shops, and touristic sites all bear the marks of religious symbolism and colloquial sayings. The country's parliamentary system of governance reflects this diversity as each major office of the government is chosen along religious identity. Through war, a history of trade, and the recent effects of globalization, Lebanon has adopted a multi lingual, namely French and English, system of education and has privatized schooling for nearly 65% of its student population (Freyha, 2003). It is not uncommon to find a vast majority of Lebanon's population to be at least conversant in French or English. The same can be said of advertisement, mass media, and conventional road signs in the county. In short, these events and experiences have brought not only exposure, but savviness to the latest trends, products, and opportunities from foreign lands.

Entrepreneurship

Within this diverse and often unstable environment, the social phenomenon of entrepreneurship has emerged. Although this concept is found in many segments of society and individuals, it is often linked to the small business venture, and this environment is where our research will take place. Defining the term presents some challenges because it is more of an activity encompassing a wide range of character traits and skills than just a static concept. Additionally, the Lebanese context may share in the collective nature of a definition, but will also offer unique displays of entrepreneurship that may differ from other societies. Initial research into this topic finds Robert Hisrich and Michael Peters' definition to include generally shared terms from the field and the Lebanese business environment. They define entrepreneurship as a process of creating something new with value by devoting the necessary time and effort, assuming accompanying financial, psychic, and social risks, and receiving the resulting rewards of monetary and personal satisfaction and independence (Hisrich & Peters, 1998).

Entrepreneurship is also a key component to the economic cycle from two perspectives. First, ideas and innovation lead to products and services that enhance our daily lives. Secondly, whether it is from an individual's self employment or to a SME's staff team, entrepreneurship contributes to the economy in the form of job creation. In the case of Lebanon, with such s high percentage of SMEs, they are indirectly acting as gatekeepers of the economy.

Entrepreneurship and Innovation

Ideas, products, and methods all have a variable life cycle based on either need or time. From this, innovation either disrupts or begins this cycle with something new or improved. Renowned economist Joseph Schumpeter first introduced the concept of innovation into understanding entrepreneurship through an approach called creative destruction. He describes *creative destruction* as a process in which the old ways of doing things are endogenously destroyed and replaced by new ways (Schumpeter, 1942). To Schumpeter, innovation consists of new ideas whose impacts are so great that they eliminate obsolete products in the marketplace and replaces them with higher quality and equitable cheaper prices (Parhizgar, 2007) In Schumpeter's account, it is the entrepreneur who creates innovation. For Schumpeter, risk was not essential in the concept of entrepreneurship unless the entrepreneur was identified as the resource-owner. The entrepreneur was not the risk bearer, but the driving force in economic development (Ripsas, 1998). The entrepreneur disturbs this equilibrium and is the prime cause of economic development, which proceeds in cyclic fashion along several time scales. According to Schumpeter, the hero of economic development is the entrepreneur.

Entrepreneurship and Opportunity Recognition

As a follow up to Schumpeter's emphasis on innovation, new products and services enter the market only if there is a need or desire for them. According to Scott Shane and Sankaran Venkataraman, the process by which entrepreneurs study the consumer and bring profitable concepts to the market is called opportunity recognition and exploitation (2000). The added value to this approach would be that no matter how good the product or service, it could fail if the opportunity is not the right fit or simply does not exist. By defining the field in terms of the individual alone, entrepreneurship researchers have generated incomplete definitions that do not withstand the scrutiny of other scholars (Gartner, 1988). The authors further state that to have entrepreneurship, you must first have entrepreneurial opportunities. Entrepreneurial opportunities are those situations in which new goods, services, raw materials, and organizing methods can be introduced and sold at greater than their cost of production (Casson, 1982).

Recognizing an opportunity appears to be a joint function of the characteristics of the opportunity and the nature of the individual. Simply enough, the decision to exploit is based largely upon if the amount of profit will compensate for the amount of time and effort that went into the opportunity. An entrepreneur has to have prior information that is complementary with the new information, which triggers an entrepreneurial conjecture (Kaish & Gilad, 1987). Finally, opportunity recognition is a setting in which people can achieve, providing a valuable cue for those who possess a high need for achievement (McClelland, 1961).

Entrepreneurship and Risk

The term *entrepreneur* appears to have been introduced into economic theory by Richard Cantillon (1755), an Irish economist of French descent. According to Cantillon, the entrepreneur is a specialist in taking on risk. He/she 'insures' workers by buying their output for resale before consumers have indicated how much they are willing to pay for it. The workers receive an assured income (in the short run, at least), while the entrepreneur bears the risk caused by price fluctuations in consumer markets. (Casson, 2010) The profit resulted from the entrepreneur accepting uncertainty, and the function of the entrepreneur was to carry out these risky ventures.

THE ENTREPRENEUR

Central to entrepreneurship is the entrepreneur. And probably the most recent and well known successful entrepreneur, by definition, would be Mark Zuckerberg, co-founder and CEO of the social network, *Facebook*. As a Harvard University student in 2004, Zuckerberg created a website that first enabled college students to post their personal information, such as pictures and interests, on his company's website. Shortly after its inception with university students, Facebook opened its site to the general public and today has attracted over 500 million members worldwide. What is interesting about the phenomenon of Facebook is that Zuckerberg did not invent the computer, software, or the concept of social networking. He did however, recognize an opportunity; improve upon the work of others, assume financial risk, and finally, he started an organization. Along this entrepreneurial process, Zuckerberg displayed both behavior and character traits that define the entrepreneur. Understanding entrepreneurs like Zuckerberg will require a look at both their personalities, and their behavior, in this case, the creation of Facebook. Although the relationship between both of these paradigms can be somewhat contentious in the literature, they reveal both character traits and behavior (activity) that help to define the entrepreneur. Moreover, the differences in these two approaches are important as they reveal cultural influences and analyze the entrepreneur outside of the economic context.

Probably the most referenced and quoted approach to codifying some sort of character trait or profile of the entrepreneur was accomplished by Psychologist, David C McClelland in his 1961 seminal work, *Achieving Societies* (Gilleard, 1989). Briefly, McClelland argued that a society's economic growth depends on a psychological motive called *need for achievement* McClelland refers to achievement as the desire to do something better, faster, and more efficiently, and with less effort. It is peculiarly associated with moderate risk taking because any task that allows for a level of difficulty also permits one to become more efficient to maximize the benefit for the least cost. His research begins with codifying character traits for levels of achievement in adolescent boys from 41 countries in comparing years1925 and 1950. With the 1925 sample of national schoolbooks, McClelland demonstrated a positive correlation between achievement imagery and subsequent rates of economic development over a twenty five year time span. For the 1950 sample, however, he used a six to seven year time span and, again demonstrating a positive correlation, he then argued that the books' achievement imagery reflected the motivational level of the adults at the time they are published (Gilleard, 1989). McClelland found that when children with high levels of achievement mature, they are inclined to engage in entrepreneurial activity which is reflected in economic progress for the society (1961).

Although some words have changed since McClelland's work in 1961, several concepts have appeared to remain constant through the research. Anisya Thomas and Stephen Mueller, in their cross cultural comparative study of entrepreneurs from 9 different countries, revealed similar findings (2000). For example, *innovation, risk-propensity, internal locus of control, and energy level* not only marked their study, but were prevalent in entrepreneurial literature. Further, Thomas and Mueller stated that these traits were not a comprehensive list, but they were the ones that appeared repeatedly in economics, psychology, sociology, and entrepreneurial research (Thomas &Mueller, 2000). The most apparent new comer to the list is the phrase, *internal locus of control*. Internals are individuals who believe they have considerable influence over outcomes in their lives, while externals feel dominated by outside forces such as luck, fate, or powerful others (Rotter, 1966). Shapero (1975), for example, found that entrepreneurs tend to have a higher internal locus of control orientation than non-entrepreneurs.

Further observation of the trait's model reveals another quandary between when entrepreneurship begins and when it ends. For example, is a small business considered and an entrepreneurial venture even after 15 years from its inception? A limiting factor to the traits approach is that when entrepreneurs cease to act as entrepreneurs they can still display a personality that conforms to a definition. Moreover, this same business owner mentioned above ceases to be an entrepreneur once they stop introducing innovative behavior into their enterprise (Carland, et al., 1984).

The concept of Entrepreneurship is a basic response to economic survival which has co-existed with man since the creation of time. In principle, it can appear simple, yet once placed under the microscope; its complexities are revealed. For starters, both the system and the individual operate in dynamic environments. Therefore, the entrepreneur will always prove to be an elusive target for universal definitions and fixed paradigms. Comparing past and present literature also reveals a difficult scenario because there is still no persuasive approach to integrate human behavior into economic theory (Ripsas, 1998). Further, critics acknowledge the heritage of Western classical theories, but face difficulty applying them to developing economies and global business trends (Thomas & Mueller, 2000). These hurdles also reveal that entrepreneurship cannot be explained by economic models alone. Entrepreneurship is a subsystem of other societal factors where culture, psychology and sociology must be integrated into an interdisciplinary approach to research (Cauthorn, 1989). The numbers alone remind us that entrepreneurship has proven itself a worthy contributor to societal value and economic growth. Therefore, in applying good business etiquette, answering the questions: "what is entrepreneurship," and, "who is the entrepreneur", should yield a good return on investment.

ENTREPRENEURIALSHIP IN THE LEBANESE CONTEXT

Lebanese have one foot in the Mediterranean and the other in the desert. This statement reveals quite a telling commentary on the nation's entrepreneurs. According to numerous scholars on Lebanon, their story begins with the ancient Phoenicians, a maritime people, who capitalized on the region's strategic location and became intermediaries for both culture and commerce (Sayigh 1962; Salibi 1971). The degree of continuity between today's Lebanese and ancient Phoenicia has been a contested proposition. Yet, consensus remains as to their mercantile influence in the region. Along with trade, the Lebanese entrepreneur is marked by a long association with foreigners. Through Europe's desire for Levant silk, Beirut's port experienced tremendous import and export growth throughout much of the 19th century (Fawaz, 1983). As their interest continued, foreign relations resulted in regional companies, schools and political influence. Lastly, the Lebanese entrepreneur has had to master the art of surviving the chaos. Since its independence in 1943, the country has known a devastating civil war, feudal politics, and an elusive economic system begun by its bourgeoisies. The results have led to a weakened state leaving many to fend for themselves (Abraham, 2010). Taken as a whole, the research will further explore the historical narrative of trade, an outward orientation, and a fragmented society and their influences on Lebanese Entrepreneurship.

Merchants of the Mediterranean

As a newly recognized country by 1920, Lebanon sought to formulate its own identity. Just a couple of years prior to this date, Lebanon was merely a region of greater Syria during the Ottoman Empire. Now, under the French Mandate, Lebanon attempted to distance itself from an Arabian influence and search for its own heritage. The "New Phoenicians" emerged under the influence of Michael Chiha, banker and co-author of the Lebanese constitution, and prominent Christian writer, Charles Crom (Gates, 1989). Their appeal was largely inclusive of portraying the Christian community of Lebanon as traders like their ancestors, the Phoenicians. The problem with this view is that it left out the Muslim community as fellow heirs to a Phoenician heritage. This coupled with the fact that a closer look at the Phoenician people revealed their Canaanite roots from the Arabian Peninsula (Salibi, 1971). All things considered, this movement, although popular among a then Christian majority, has done little to promote itself as a unifying identity for today's Lebanese.

A more agreeable approach to understanding is found in their origins, as it relates to the region, and their influence on trade. Based upon historical and archaeological sources, there is some agreement that the Phoenicians and their society emerged from the local Canaanite people of the Levant around the year 3200 B.C. One documented characteristic of this people group was their successful maritime trade within the Mediterranean. Specifically, the modern day Lebanese cities of Tyre, Sidon, and Jbal were central to Phoenician trade which extended to Egypt, Italy, Carthage and Cyprus. Along with profits from trade, the Phoenicians also brought back customs and languages form their travels and thus became cultural intermediaries between the East and West (Salibi, 1965). Some archeologists even contend that one of our oldest alphabets and inhabited cities dates back to the Phoenician city of Jbal (Sacks, 2003). Although time and numerous empires have removed Phoenicia as a place and people, their legacy lives on in many of today's entrepreneurs who are neither awed nor intimidated by foreign tongue or travel (Sayigh, 1962).

The literature also reveals the Ottoman occupation as a significant era of trade in the Levant. From 1516 to 1918, The Ottoman Empire controlled much of Arabia through Central Asia and over to North Africa. At the time, modern day Lebanon existed only as Mount Lebanon and Beirut while the remainder of the country was part of greater Syria. While under the Ottomans, capitulations were given to Europe's co-religionist in the Levant. These concessions soon afforded the Greek Orthodox, Maronite Catholics, and other minority Christian faiths and opportunity to leverage their status, which in turn became a privileged position for trade and other cultural exchanges (Abraham, 2010). Probably the most lucrative commodity during this era was brought about by Mount Lebanon's sericulture. Raw silk, cocoon harvesting, and production soon became Mount Lebanon's leading industry and employer (Fawaz, 1983).

As the silk industry began to flourish in the 19th century, Beirut's port witnessed 40% of its silk exports head to France and later that number would increase to 90% by 1873 (Fawaz, 1983). Soon France would send their own entrepreneurs to establish silk reeling companies. By 1863, 67 French silk factories were established in Mount Lebanon and soon grew to over 100 by 1900. Along with exports, Lebanon's imports from Europe grew from 50,000 tons a year in 1830 to over 600,000 tons by 1886. It is of interest to note that during this time, Beirut's trade was the least tied to Egypt and Turkey and the most active with Europe (Fawaz, 1983). Even so, the Ottomans did not allow for total foreign domination as they monitored the market to make things equal for the Lebanese merchant. This allowed for locals, who knew the language, culture, and business landscape, to compete as middle men and soon as silk manufactures as well. Consequently, from the emergence of competitive trade routes in the region after World War One, the invention of artificial silk substitutes like rayon, and a world economic depression of the 1930s, Lebanon's sericulture industry was greatly debilitated (Owen, 1984). Nonetheless, the 19th century was a pivotal era for Beirut establishing itself as a modern and competitive port (Gates, 1998).

By the first quarter of the 20th century, Lebanon would experience not only its independence from the Ottomans, but the formation of a new economy which would take its trade practices in a new direction. Although Lebanon's silk industry was in disarray by the 1930s, a redeeming element of its former success would surface, Western access. At this point Lebanon and Syria were under the French Mandate and their prior relationship would give further access to the Beirut's port for its own products. Several writers from this period contend that western penetration of capital and goods greatly diminished exports and increased dependence on cheaper import products (Gates 1998, Owen 1984, Nasr 1978). The formation of Lebanon's open market economy in the 1950s furthered this activity and set the Lebanese entrepreneur on an intermediary course. From this point through 1975, Lebanese foreign trade would reflect its function as a recipient and a regional channel for Western products. Over 70% of the country's imports came from the West. And, the 60% of its exports were predominantly industrial finished products again from Western manufacturers, thus ensuring a transit trade role (Nasr, 1978). Although this era was marked by profitable years of banking and foreign trade, two adverse effects also emerged. First, the apparent success of imports greatly diminished local agriculture and industry. And second, a few politically influential merchants used their position to disarm the competition and soon monopolized profitable trade sectors. It was estimated by 1974, four big trade houses (Fattal, Kettaneh, Pharaud and Chiha, and Abou-Adal) accounted for nearly two-thirds of all Lebanese imports from Western countries (Dunbar & Nasr, 1976).

Outward Orientation

Remnants of Rome, Ottoman Turkey, and France are still quite visible in the culture and language. Today's global products such as electronics, automobiles, and medical equipment have also found a market in Lebanon and predominantly in the business language of English (Braine, 2005). By little in the way of industry, agriculture, and natural resources, Lebanon has continued to look beyond its borders for both survival and to remain contemporary (Gordon, 1983). This next section will explore the factors which have contributed to the Lebanese Entrepreneur's outward orientation.

Whether through trade, occupation, or development, Lebanon has grown acustom to a foreign presence for much of its existence. Early on, the country's relationship to Europe came largely from the silk industry. As this relationship solidified, foreign national companies soon set up their headquarters and regional offices in Lebanon. From the latter part of the 19th century on up to the civil war in 1975, Lebanon was home to 250 foreign companies (Gordon, 1983). Throughout this time, Lebanese entrepreneurs emerged as middle men, intermediaries who could take finished and semi-finished products into the country and also transit them to the rest of the Middle East. As natives of the land, they were hindered neither by language or bureaucratic red-tape that awaited their foreign employers. During this process, these intermediaries soon mastered not only an understanding of foreign products, but also the languages that accompanied them, namely French (Fawaz, 1983). As various forms of instability threatened the Lebanese market, foreign national companies soon found it more advantageous to rely on these middlemen rather than the costs of large infrastructure. Soon agreements and sole proprietary rights were given to locals who established distribution channels and created a customer base for European and American products.

Emigration

Through economic opportunities, civil unrest, and war, Lebanon has known the painful trials of emigration. Conservative estimates place the Lebanese Diaspora at 8 million people, reaching all four corners of the globe (Lebanese Emigration Research Center, 2006). For Lebanon, the past 120 years of emigration has also meant gradual, but sometimes immediate, submersion into their host countries. For many, this has meant a second nationality and exposure to a new way of life. With salaries and employment standards often better in their host countries, Lebanese Expatriates have continued to send money back home to support less fortunate family members. Some estimate these remittance monies into Lebanon amount to 6 billion dollars a year, almost 20 percent of the nations GDP. In regards to emigration and remittances impact on entrepreneurship, the research is almost non-existence. Additionally, there is no empirical data on the number of emigrants who have returned for entrepreneurial ventures. Nonetheless, two observations have surfaced. First, via personal or business travel, the Lebanese have been exposed to foreign markets. They are aware what their host countries have and what Lebanon does not. So, from the percentages of family SMEs in the country, new enterprises will reflect foreign exposure and globalization. Secondly, if Lebanese ex-patriots did not provide the business idea, they often contribute financially as silent family partners. Once again, I draw these conclusions from anecdotal evidence as observed in the literature and during my interviews (Gordon 1983).

Education and Exposure

A salient feature of the Lebanese culture is the value that they place on education. According to World Bank reports, Lebanon spends an unusually high share of its gross domestic product (GDP) – 9.3% – on education, with private expenditure alone representing 5.6% of GDP. Furthermore, the Lebanese, like many of its neighbors, and gulf countries today share rather high literacy rates. 99 percent of Lebanon, Jordan and Qatar's youth are literate. These statistics further reveal Lebanon's exposure to foreign curriculum and languages from both private and public schools. Trying to draw a correlation from these statistics, education level and entrepreneurial career choice through the literature has yielded minimal findings. In 2010, Fahed-Sreih et al., found their sample of entrepreneurs to be highly educated, but did not analyze education as a contributing factor. Besides, the same could be said of others who chose different careers who also could be labelled "highly educated." However, the literature does shed light on two entrepreneurial characteristics brought about by the countries emphasis on education.

First, in a mercantile economy like Lebanon, so many of the foreign products shipped in utilize an intermediary to act as a liaison from manufacture to end user (Nasr, 1978). Along with having to be familiar with import laws, this person would also have to know how to conduct business in another language. For the Lebanese, their long standing relationship with the French culture has also ushered in the language to its schools and business networks. Furthermore with the emergence of other European and Western products into Lebanon, middle men have continued to learn the language of their manufactures (Braine, 2005). Entrepreneurs from both private and public education would have been exposed to the Minister of Education's directive for each student to master at least one language for the purpose of interacting with other cultures.

Secondly, with the ability to travel and communicate in a foreign language, education brought about exposure. From this, travel in itself can act as an almost informal means of education. In his book, *Entrepreneurs of Lebanon*, Sayigh (1962) found that over 70% of his respondents traveled outside the country for business and nine tenths of them bought technical literature for themselves and their staff both in Arabic and in foreign languages. A closer look at Sayigh's research reveals a more established and affluent entrepreneur compared to my recent survey of Beirut's SMEs. Initial demographics reveal that although the travel was not as extensive as higher profile entrepreneurs, owners of SMEs educate themselves via the internet. Both observations are reminiscent of Dib's findings from the late nineteenth century where a merchant from the Levant was known to be conversant in at least three languages (Dib, 2004). Thus, in this sense, the knowledge of language and advanced education equipped entrepreneurs with an ability to recognize opportunities.

Creation of an Open Market Economy

Another outcome of Lebanon's outward orientation was the creation of an open market economy. Shortly after the country's independence, there was political consensus that the national economy should basically be market oriented (Gates, 1998). This was fostered by the existence of a traditionally affluent business class operating close to government leadership that supported liberal economic policies and the opening of the national economy to the outside world (Makdisi, 2007). As early as the 1950s, these same leadership principles led to the flow of foreign goods and capital into a banking system that adopted secrecy and profitable return on investment. While the foundations of a *lassies faires* economy were being established, Lebanon was soon branded as the "Switzerland of the Middle East" for its attractive banking opportunities. Consequently, this era also observed the formation of a powerful entrepreneurial class who began to use their political positions to recognize and exploit profitable trade opportunities (Dib, 2004). Two trends seem to have emerged from this event. First, a socio-economic hierarchy of entrepreneurs began to take shape. Secondly, as previously stated, those at the top of the entrepreneurial tier effectively moved the country toward a mercantile economy with less emphasis on industry and agriculture (Gates, 1998). Although this event furthered the work of the merchant and the private sector, it neglected an indigenous agriculture industry whose return has been a decade's long battle.

Fragmented Society

In Lebanon if one's family name does not give away your religious identity, then your place of residency often will. These two pieces of information are usually discovered within the first few minutes of a greeting or conversation. And, what makes this information so useful is that it reveals one's political allegiance and affiliation. This brief scenario reveals not only the diversity of the country but also the competition that the state and its institutions must contend with. Once again, the seeds of this problem were sown long before the notions of a state existed. While under the Millet system of Ottoman rule, from 1516-1918, the Levant region was given enough autonomy to govern themselves according to their own religious laws and customs (Abraham, 2008). Christians, Jews, and Muslims of all denominations were afforded equal protection and representation in their judicial systems as well. Shortly after the fall of the Ottoman Empire, modern Lebanon fell under the jurisdiction of the League of Nations in 1920. In turn, the French were given authority over both Syria and Lebanon for protection and development; this period was also known as the French Mandate. In similar fashion while under the Ottomans, this era also continued to recognize governing bodies according to religious affinities, or confessions of faith. Today, from an agreement know as the *National Pact,* a Maronite Christian holds the office of the President, a Sunni Muslim is the Prime minister, and a Shiite Muslim acts as the Speaker of the Parliament (Salibi, 1971). The rest of the 128 seats of parliament are also shared along in-country religious representations as well.

As the Millet and Confessional systems evolved, it gave birth to the country's officially recognized 18 political sects, which also have an affinity to their various religious beliefs and values. Even within these political parties, consensus leaders emerge and attract a following to promote their own ideology and version of what the country should be (Abraham, 2008). Kamel Dib, in his book, *Warlords and Merchants* further identifies these individual as a *za'im.* As a transliteration of this Arabic word, a za'im was thought to be an all inclusive type of leader, particularly with political and economic capital contributing to their influence. A za'im from each tribe or sect creates their own economic landscape often apart from any notions of national development (Dib, 2004). Although this narrative has weakened the state and furthered social fragmentation, resilient individualism and the family unit have emerged. These two factors have not only been a consistent theme for the Lebanese throughout their history, but they have also contributed to the country's entrepreneurial spirit (Sayigh, 1962).

Emergence of the Private Sector

As the state kept itself busy keeping its political powers balanced, the private sector emerged. Being mostly non-interventionist and supportive of the private sector, government policy has been business friendly (Makdisi, 2007). This scenario has worked quite well in Lebanon where the individual was free to pursue business interests in an unrestrictive and open market. So the old adage, *necessity is the mother of invention* could be re-stated as *opportunity is the mother of invention* in the case of Lebanese entrepreneurship. With a minimalist state, a spirit of individualism ensued along with the struggle to survive and the personal pride to thrive. This opportunity was also met with fierce competitiveness which was brought about further by the country's social and political fragmentation (Sayigh, 1962). The need to prove oneself had not only economic incentives, but also an appeal to promote one's broader family name or sect.

The private sector has also operated in a *laissez faires* economy which, in theory, allows for an unrestricted flow of capital, goods, and service into the market under minimal supervision from government entities. By the mid 1950s, Lebanon's economy was thriving and was soon branded as "Switzerland of the Middle East" due to its successful secrecy in banking and lucrative interest rates (Kliot, 1987). Also behind much of this success, were the country's elite families who shaped much of the country's mercantile economy that Lebanon has today (Gates, 1989). Other Lebanese scholars and historians, such as Dib, Gates, and Abraham recognize this era where roughly 100 families emerged as the country's power block. As this dominant class began to shape the political and economic landscape two outcomes emerged.

First, the notion of capitalism and an open market economy were no longer accessible to all. Through position and status, Lebanon's mercantile bourgeoisie emerged and created a political economy. At this point, capitalism had been transplanted into a feudal system where Lebanon's elite shaped the economic direction of the country often through their close proximity to political positions (Gates, 1989). Although this era, namely between 1950 –1965, experienced tremendous growth specifically in the banking sector, it began to reveal the dividing effects of sectarianism. So, for the Lebanese entrepreneur, the private sector, although open, now too had its restrictions. These scenarios created a secondary or alternative network where political favors and *wasta* (connections) were needed from *za'ims* to get things done (Abraham, 2008).

Secondly, as Lebanon's mercantile elite shaped their open economy, their outward orientation drastically affected the country's agriculture and industry sectors (Nasr, 1978). By inflating the costs of production, shippers of pesticides, fertilizer, and seeds soon made the cost of production too high to compete. The farmer that did survive did so under the umbrella of several monopolies that controlled agriculture (Nasr, 1978). The industrial sector faced a similar fate due to the high imports of finished and semi-finished products. Eventual loss of land and emigration into the cities for employment soon followed. As for the entrepreneur, their role as intermediaries was kept alive but narrowed through monopolies and trade agreements that were beyond their influence. As this paradigm has continued, the notion of "privately owned" has revealed Lebanon's feudal networks emerging over the State. Nonetheless, the private sector has continues to contribute to economic growth and job creation far better that the public sector (Makdisi, 2007).

The Family Enterprise

Through the ongoing saga of political instability, the Lebanese entrepreneur has continued to look to their family as one of the only viable institutions for moral and financial encouragement. The family business constitutes 85% of the private sector, accounting for 1.05 million of 1.24 million jobs, offering a clear indication of the strength of this relationship (Fahed-Sreih, 2006). With such a pivotal role in the lives of the entrepreneur and the economy, the research will focus on the family unit from two perspectives. First, I will identify characteristics of the Lebanese family owned business as revealed in the literature. And secondly, I will explore key factors within the family that have influenced entrepreneurship.

Current literature on the family firm in Lebanon reveals two qualities. Generally speaking, start-up ventures are risky for conventional financial institutions and Lebanon shares in the statistics with most start-ups failing within the first 5 years . From this, Lebanon has looked to the family for support. In Lebanon, 80% of the family firms have one or more family members investing in the business. Furthermore, 70% of these companies employ at least one member of the family (Fahed-Sreih et al., 2010). These financial bonds also lead the business to be passed down to other family members and thus ensuring generational identity and security.

Secondly, there is a presupposition in the Lebanese family that outsiders are antagonistic and may take advantage of you at anytime (Khalaf, 1966). Therefore the family has emerged as one of the only places where trust can be found. Furthermore, the home is also where work ethics and values are taught and modelled. As Lebanon's political history has shown, feudal allegiances have always come at an expense of the state. So, it leaves little reason to speculate why the family has emerged as a social institution influence to self-employment. Lebanon also has a generational impetus behind it when it comes to working for your family, 28% of new startups are actually a continuation of a previous family business (Fahed-Sreih et al., 2010). Lastly, being a successful entrepreneur also brings about social status which further strengthens a family name in the community (Sayigh, 1962).

PROFILE OF THE LEBANESE ENTREPRENEUR

The Force behind Creative Destruction

Although most entrepreneurs are not aware of their impact on an economy, their influence as individuals has a much broader influence. Joseph Schumpeter's Theory of Economic Development continues to serve as a foundation to understanding the phenomenon of entrepreneurship. Within this theory, the concepts of creative destruction and innovation are central to Shumpeterian theory. In creative destruction, a continuous flow of new entrants into the market causes a disequilibrium effect in the economy and thus stimulates growth. Secondly, through innovation, creating new ways of doing things, the entrepreneur acts as the catalyst of the economic cycle. These two concepts are also evident feature of the Lebanese entrepreneur.

First, since Lebanon operates as a mercantile economy with openness and minimal restrictions, its entrepreneurs are engaging a healthy cycle of creative destruction. Lebanon's openness to the Western world is evident by its considerable supply of the latest trends in electronics, fashion, and entertainment. Globalization and exposure through personal travel and emigration has also brought ideas and products into the country to stimulate this cycle. As the study revealed, trade and commerce establishments account for nearly 50% of the enterprises surveyed from the greater Beirut business district. From this, Lebanon's economic structures are stimulating the business cycles and promoting entrepreneurship.

Secondly, Lebanese entrepreneurs bring innovation to the forefront of the business environment. It should be mentioned that innovation is different than invention. For Schumpeter, the entrepreneur is constantly bringing something new to the market, whether a product, service, or new way of doing something. The Lebanese society has made this easy for the entrepreneur is some ways. For starters, through exposure and globalization, consumer's interests span the market from niche products to everyday consumables. Additionally, the country's inconsistent legal system almost forces its entrepreneurs to be on the lookout for new ways of doing things.

Relying on Schumpeterian theory for a full explanation of Lebanese entrepreneurship would reveal its cultural shortcomings. First of all, capital and funding for firms comes from large impart, the family (Sreih et al, 2010) Secondly, notions of innovation in the west are closely connected to efficiency and invention. Since

Lebanon is largely a mercantile economy, research and development, are often not utilized in the traditional sense by local entrepreneurial process. However, merchants could greatly assist the manufacturing process by sharing feedback from end users, the customers.

Opportunist

If I were to attempt to follow the evolution of the word entrepreneur in Lebanon, it might look something like this: from merchant, to family business owner, and finally the opportunist. The opportunity recognition framework posed by Shane and Venkataraman (2000) adds context to Schumpeterian theory. Without heavy reliance on manufacturing or invention, the Lebanese entrepreneur has emerged as an intermediary. In the simplest of terms, intermediaries and merchants find the right market for products and services. From their time, effort, and risk, they can draw a salary or commission as a pecuniary reward. The process of recognizing opportunities appears to be a joint function of the characteristics of the opportunity and the nature of the individual (Zgheib, 2011).

As Kirzner (1973) also observed, only a certain segment to the population will discover a given opportunity. For the Lebanese entrepreneur, this ability has been created by a number of factors. First, with average monthly salaries far below the lifestyle that they have been exposed to, young entrepreneurs would rather work for themselves than give their time and effort to an employer with little recognition or recompense. Moreover, with little help from governing institutions or employment agencies, the entrepreneurs are left to create their own job, self employment, or to carry on the heritage of their family owned business. Lastly, as reflective in such high remittance monies, emigration, and foreign exposure, the Lebanese have developed a keen sense of products and services that would bode well in the country. From mere survival to having a chance to make more than an average monthly salary, the Lebanese entrepreneurs have developed an affinity toward recognizing profitable opportunities.

For the Lebanese entrepreneur, the ability to capitalize on opportunities centers on the current cycle of instability. Accurately identifying cycles of instability greatly affect not only how and when to buy, but it also what type of business to establish. Whether it was electronics, luggage, clothes, or beauty products, most items could be stored away for a later, more peaceful time. In summary, the nation's entrepreneurs monitor "stability" in the country as if it were the weather. During times of peace, they buy the right products and open their doors for business. If instability should ensue, products that are immune to civil unrest have to be given preference.

In addition to foreseeing instability, Lebanese entrepreneur have developed a keen sense of knowing which profitable opportunities exist beyond its borders.

This ability is influenced by a number of factors. First, through various types of emigration, there is more Lebanese living outside of Lebanon than in the country itself (Hourani, 2006). From this, travel and exposure to outside market has become almost second nature for most. Participants from the surveys were known to have family connections literally at all four corners of the globe. Some of these connections turned into profitable trade routes keeping Lebanon both competitive and up to date from a global perspective. Even without travel, the surveys revealed that 89% of entrepreneurs kept themselves up to date on potentially profitable opportunities within and outside their current field of business. Much of their personal research came from the internet. I was amazed at how quickly information and tutorials could be accessed online in relation to a host of products. Everything from price comparisons to advertising and marketing tips was available. For the Lebanese Entrepreneur, this type of knowledge whether through travel or media is just another capability that one must possess to recognize and exploit opportunities.

Within the process of opportunity recognition and exploitation, the entrepreneurs experiences varying degrees of risk. Many factors affect risk. By not studying the market or simply overbuying, entrepreneurs risk profit loss and not yielding a good return for their investors. For the Lebanese, the country's ongoing saga of instability has become more than just a historical narrative; it has become an antecedent to risk management. For the Lebanese context, this approach would mean that cycles of instability usually end and business resumes. Through what means they end may not be pertinent to the entrepreneur, just that eventually, a cycle of growth will emerge. Once again, this type of risk assessment affects the type of products and services an entrepreneur would pursue. Participants in the interviews were quick to point out this type of risk assessment as they experienced a quick rise in sales once the parliament agreed on PM designate Najib Miqati toward the end of January 2011. For the Lebanese entrepreneur, time may be the only thing against them, because their history and resiliency has shown, business will eventually resume.

Emergence of the Individual

Stepping away from some of the entrepreneurial systems and function, the research also revealed some characteristics unique to the entrepreneur. Although it was not an objective of this research to test these character traits, they do however confirm somewhat of a universal nature of the entrepreneur. Specifically, McClelland's work with adolescent boys from 41 countries shares some similar outcomes compared to the Lebanese entrepreneurs. His finding revealed six traits, all of which find some common ground for the local entrepreneur. However, with attention to the trait on individual responsibility, respondents from the survey share a rather close affinity. Results from the local context have revealed that 94% of Beirut entrepreneurs preferred to work for themselves than someone else. Later in this chapter I will revisit this finding, but at face value, retaining responsibility and personal freedom were high values for the local entrepreneur. On the ground, this trait has manifests itself as self-employment through the SME or a family owned business. McClelland also found that when children with high levels of achievement matured they were inclined to engage in entrepreneurial activity (McClelland, 1961). In turn, this would result in economic progress of the society. Given Lebanon's high rate of SMEs and family owned business, entrepreneurs have become a considerable influence on the economy.

The literature has also shown that entrepreneurs tend to have a high internal locus of control compared to non-entrepreneurs (Shapero, 1975). Individuals with a high locus of control tend to internally motivate themselves, regardless of external factors that may appear to be against them. This trait also appeared to to find acceptance across cultures and nationality (McGrath, et al. 1992). In agreement with the literature, results from the surveys and interviews also find the Lebanese entrepreneur to hold a high locus of control. With little support from the government and cycles of political and regional instability, there are certainly enough external factors that could keep one pessimistic about pursuing a business venture. Yet, these factors reveal the entrepreneurs will to survive, thus making him fiercely independent and competitive.

Influences from the Lebanese Culture

Although classical approaches to understanding entrepreneurship find some universal appeal, their concepts don't always apply the same way in another culture (Thomas and Mueller, 2000). For example, western concepts of innovation from Schumpeter may convey notions of large scale investment capital, production, and finally a new product. This is reflective of a highly developed industrial economy. Developing economies like Lebanon, with less natural resources and infrastructure, view the end product as a means to innovation, bringing something new to the market, opposed to having to create the whole business cycle. Furthermore, the entrepreneurial field of research has yet to agree upon a unified dentition or produce its own theory dedicated to entrepreneurship (Ripsas, 1998). Lastly, with the introduction of interdisciplinary approaches, this has further fragmented an understanding of entrepreneurship in unifying terms. Although some terms and concepts find application in the culture, gaps still exist that the local context could only resolve. In this next section, I will revisit some of the findings from the literature on Lebanese entrepreneurship and then compare them to the findings from the surveys to finalize the profile of the local entrepreneur.

The Lebanese Way

One consistent theme through Lebanon's past has been its narrative of trade. From the ancient Phoenicians, through the silk industry of the 19th century, and now with an open market economy, the country's outward orientation has become part of its identity. The shaping of this trade based culture is built upon a number of factors. First, with limited natural resources and infrastructure, large scale manufacturing and industry are just not cost competitive opportunities. So, finished and pre-finished goods from abroad come into the country cheaper and yield a better return than manufacturing locally. Secondly, even before the emergence of globalization, decisions were made in the early 1950s to solidify Lebanon's mercantile economy (Gates, 1998). Principles of *liaises faires* afforded the countries elite families a stake in Beirut's lucrative shipping industry. Consequently, the capitalistic nature of the economy soon brought about an economically competitive environment which further stratified the society and its entrepreneurs.

For starters, the elite merchants mentioned above were not the central figures included in my Beirut sample. They were the SME on the corner with relatively few employees, some being inclusive of just family members. Yet, every business surveyed from the Beirut sample, appeared to be somehow affected by this over arching trade based economy. Even service oriented companies and restaurants had to retain an expediter or intermediary to obtain their equipment. It appeared to be well established concept in the economy and job market. The surveys also affirm this with 91% of respondents acknowledging the nation's historical link to trade. There were some vague notions of the Phoenician past, but most of the influence was accredited to the countries location and that trade through the years had become a cultural tradition.

In close association to trade, Lebanon's open market economy provides enough opportunities to keep an interest in entrepreneurship higher than other employment options. As mentioned earlier, earning potential and working for oneself was a favorable response to over 92% of Beirut's entrepreneurs. With comparably lower salaries and minimal labor laws, the work environment has not proved to be an inviting alternative. Given these findings and a historical emphasis on trade, entrepreneurship appears to be a socially embedded choice of employment.

Through its political, religious and economic diversity, Lebanon and all of its institutions have become fragmented. This situation has also has revealed an extremely competitive and territorial environment that existed long before the formation a state in the 1920 (Dib, 2004). Although space and focus prohibit a deeper look at how feudal systems react to statehood, the effects on the ground are evident in a decade's long demonstration of a weak Lebanese state. Because of a weak state, allegiance is given to personal institutions over public entities created by the government. Out of this breakdown, the private sector continues to provide what the entrepreneur needs to exist, opportunities. Although political and economic restriction may stand in the way of these opportunities, they are still tantamount to financial success and survival. Along with opportunities, the business environment mentioned above has produced several character traits unique in application to the local entrepreneur.

As discussed earlier, The Lebanese entrepreneur has demonstrated traditionally abilities common to most entrepreneurs, namely innovation, risk management, and opportunity recognition. However, the local context has produced a specific character trait; being *shauter* رطاش. And the Lebanese entrepreneur epitomizes this Arabic word. Its closest English equivalents would be, clever or resourcefulness, but an explanation from the culture would more accurately define this trait.

First of all, knowing the laws, more specifically, the business laws and the legal system in most societies requires the assistance of a lawyer and Lebanon is no different. However, the perception of whose interest the laws serves comes into question in Lebanon. Just as trust is rarely given outside the family network, the government and its bureaucracy are no exception, so they also are viewed with suspicion. Also, given the confessional nature of Lebanon, violating the law does little to effect the conscience of those who do not believe in a unified state. In fact, breaking the law is looked more upon as "beating the system" or "out-smarting" your opponent. Furthermore, according to some interviews, allegation of corruption within public institutions greatly diminishes the notion what is legal and illegal. Incidentally, adherence to the law still emerges in a general sense of the term. For example, starting a new business under a pre-existing business license bypasses registration fees and prohibits an increase in rent. The legal requirements were met; one business still exists, but the letter of the law was not upheld. The new business was never legally registered. Yet, under the umbrella of the old name, taxes and other charges are still being collected. So, in this sense, the spirit of the law was followed. In this scenario, local officials were even aware of this and may have even "helped" with making the transition.

Secondly, *Shauter* entrepreneurs find solutions to obstacles more often than labeling them right or wrong. In response to the amount of "tips" that business owners had to pay to get things done, I found myself responding in rather judgmental value statements, like, "That is unfair." One interviewee even corrected me by saying; "it is not a matter of right or wrong, it is just a system that we have to operate in." Later on, another individual informed me that complaining, for example, about the electricity problem, is not going to change it. Renting ten amps of electricity is just a means to staying operational in business. To operate at any level of success, one has to have a thorough knowledge of this system and this is what usually frustrates the outsider. To the foreigner, it can be viewed as corrupt, but some locals hesitantly admiedt that attempting to change it may make things worse. Several entrepreneurs who once worked outside the country commented that being *shauter* is what makes the Lebanese stand out in the region. In fact, this commentary may explain why 94 percent of the survey respondents answered positively in regard to being unique business people in the region.

Secondly, the Lebanese entrepreneur possesses a unique style of individualism. Before qualifying this statement, I will refer to individualism as being motivated by self-interest and achievement of personal goals over those of the group. Also implicit in the literature is the assumption that the entrepreneurial process is a highly individualistic pursuit (Gartner, 1985). However, what makes individualism unique to the local entrepreneur, generally speaking, is that Lebanon has been considered a collective society similar to many of their eastern neighbors (Hofstede, 2005). However, due to the country's fragmentation, individualism has been brought to the forefront of the culture.

A root cause of much of the individualism stems from the country's ongoing struggle between power sharing among the confessional parties. This often tense relationship has caused each group to promote and protect their own interests often times at the expense of allegiance to the state (Abraham, 2008). Even private education, which accounts for nearly 60% of schools in the country, has a questionable record when it comes to promoting social cohesion (Frayha, 2003). Yet, throughout the saga of political and civil unrest, the family unit has remained one of the only consistent social institutions where the entrepreneur has found support (Fahed-Sreih Et, al., 2010). However, by grouping the three questions related to the family unit, 53% answered agreeably and 47% disagreed to the family influence on entrepreneurship. Several findings from the literature and the most recent interviews, reveal the several factors that may be mitigating the family's impact. One, deeply rooted in eastern culture is the subordination of the individual to his family (Khalaf, 1966). . So for business owner, there is little escape from the consuming presence of the family. This may account for statements such as, "I started this business on my own". In fact, 60% of the Beirut sample did not have parents who were entrepreneurs. Given the responses and research, the strength of the family appears to be both a blessing and a curse. The family is looked to for support and protection, but there are times when that overarching power becomes too much.

Lastly, the Lebanese entrepreneur is shown to be extremely resilient. In the truest sense of the word, history has shown that he bounces back and returns to his entrepreneurial tendencies no matter what the circumstance. Of course, every society faces challenges and has known economic and political struggle. It is also a rare individual who makes it through life without some personal tragedy or setback to work through. Yet, what makes the Lebanese narrative of struggle unique is its frequency and variety.

For Lebanon, the last decade has witnessed numerous high profile assassinations, intermittent conflict with Israel, and its most recent political coup of former Prime Minister, Saad Al Hariri. Moreover, each episode of unrest has brought considerable losses to the economy and more directly to the local SME. However, between each episode of instability, the Lebanese economy reflects considerable growth due large impart by the work of the entrepreneur. After the 2006 war with Israel and a further 18 month boycott of the capital's business district, the economy bounced back with a 9 percent growth rate from 2008-2009. 2009 also witnessed a 40% surge in tourism yielding the country 7 billion dollars in revenue of which was responsible for 30 percent of the country's GDP.

Even within the country, keeping the balance of power between 18 political parties does not always lead to an equitable resolve. As political leaders further show favoritism to their families and sect, a patron-client relationship has developed. These relationships are marked by powerful patrons (leaders) giving jobs, financial rewards, and other privileges to their clients (followers) in exchange for allegiance and support. Unfortunately with little accountability, these relationships are often corrupt and unfair, thereby obstructing the processes of implementing true sustainability. The result of this system has further divided the country into mini-states providing their own political, social, and economic structures (Hamzeh, 2001). For the entrepreneur, this arrangement forces him to meander in and out of relationships with power brokers who may hold the keys to opening a market of restricting his access. Although this reflects poorly on the notion of a truly open market economy, it keeps the entrepreneur busy building his social capital.

Finally, the volatile nature of the Lebanese environment has lead to one constant, its inconsistency. As previously mentioned, this societal dysfunction is evident in the government, national identity, and daily life. And at times, the entrepreneur needs a respite from his overbearing, yet supportive family. Yet, each shortcoming and setback has introduced another angle or possible solution. Waiting for things to change or become stable could mean a missed opportunity. And for the entrepreneur, like the rest of the general public, this deviation from the norm has meant living for the moment. Looking back through each era of struggle, it has been the resilient entrepreneurs who have consistently returned the country back to productivity.

REFERENCES

Armstrong, P. (2005). *Crtique of Entrepreneurship*. New York: Palgrave Macmillan. doi:10.1057/9780230554955

Audretsch, D. B. (Ed.). (2003). *Handbook of Entrepreneurship Research: An Interdiciplinary Survey and Introduction*. Dordrecht, The Netherlands: Kluwer Academic Publishers.

Bhargava, S. (Ed.). (2007). *Developmental Aspects of Entrepreneurship*. New Delhi: Academic Press.

Cantillon, R. (1755). *Essay on the nature of general commerce*. London: Macmillan.

Carland, J. W., Hoy, F., Boulton, W. R., & Carland, J. A. C. (1984). Differentiating entrepreneurs from small business owners: A conceptualization. *Academy of Management Review*, *9*(2), 354–359.

Casson, M., & Buckley, P. J. (2010). *A theory of cooperation in international business*. Palgrave Macmillan.

Casson, M., & Buckley, P. J. (2010). Models of the multinational enterprise. In *The Multinational Enterprise Revisited* (pp. 147–176). Palgrave Macmillan.

Casson, M. Y. (Ed.). (2006). *The Oxford Handbook of Entrepreneurship*. New York: Oxford University Press.

Cauthorn, R. C. (1989). *Contributions to a Theory of Entrepreneurship*. Garland Publishing.

Dana, L.-P. (Ed.). (2007). Handbook of Research on Ethnic Minority Entrepreneurship. Norhthampton, UK: Edward Elgar Publishing Inc. doi:10.4337/9781847209962

Davisson, P. (2008). *The Entrepreneur Research Challenge*. Edwrard Elgar Publishing, Inc. doi:10.4337/9781848442764

De Bruin, A. A. (Ed.). (2003). *Entrepreneurship: New Perspectives in a Global Age*. Hampshire, UK: Ashgate Publishing Limited.

Dib, K. (2004). *Warlords and Merchants: The Lebanese Busiess and Political Establishment*. Reading: Garnet Publishing Limited.

Dunbar, C., & Nasr, S. (1976). *Les Classes Sociales au Liban*. Paris: Presses De La Fondation Nationale Des Sciences Politiques.

ESCWA. (2001). *ESCWA Report 2001. "The Role of SMEs in National Economies in East Asia*. ESCWA.

Falcone, T. A. (2005). Entrepreneurship: A Diverse Concept in a Diverse World.*2005 USASBE/SBI National Conference*, (pp. 1-8). Academic Press.

Fawaz, L. T. (1983). *Merchants and migrants in nineteenth-century Beirut* (Vol. 18). Harvard Univ Pr. doi:10.4159/harvard.9780674333550

Gartner, W. B. (1988). Who is an entrepreneur? Is the wrong question. *Entrepreneurship, Theory and Practice*, *12*(2), 47.

Gates, C. L. (1998). *The Merchant Republic of Lebanon: Rise of on an Open Economy*. London: I.B Tauris and Co Lrd.

Gilleard, C. J. (1989). The achieving society revisited: A further analysis of the relation between national economic growth and need achievement. *Journal of Economic Psychology*, *10*(1), 21–34. doi:10.1016/0167-4870(89)90055-X

Herbert, R. F. (1982). *The Entrepreneur*. New York: Preager.

Hisrich, R. D., & Peters, M. P. (1998). *Entrepreneurship*. Boston, MA: Irwin/McGraw-Hill.

Hofstede, G. a. (2005). *Cultures and Organizations: Software of the Mind*. New York: McGraw-Hill.

Hourani, A. a. (1992). *The Lebanese in the World: A Century of Emigration*. London: I.B Tauris and Co. Ltd.

Hourani, A. (2002). *A history of the Arab Peoples*. Cambridge, MA: The Belknap Press of Harvard University Press.

Hourani, G. G. (2006). The impact of the summer 2006 war on migration in Lebanon: Emigration, remigration, evacuation and return – A preliminary study. Louaize, Lebanon: Lebanese Emigration Research Center; Notre Dame University Press.

Jacobs, J. J. (1991). *The Anatomy of an Entrepreneur: Family,Culture, and Ethic*. San Francisco: ICS Press.

Jarillo, C. J. (1990). A Paradigm of Entrepreneurship: Entrepreneurial management. *Strategic Management Journal, 11*, 17-27.

Kaisch, S., & Gilad, B. (1991). Characteristics of opportunities search of entrepreneurs versus executives: Sources, interests, general, alertness. *Journal of Business Venturing*, *6*(1), 45–61. doi:10.1016/0883-9026(91)90005-X

Kirby, D. A. (2003). *Entrepreneurship*. London: McGraw-Hill Education.

Makdisi, S. (2007). *Rebuilding Devastated Economies in the Middle East* (L. Binder, Ed.). Ney York: Palgrave Macmillan.

McClelland, D. C. (1961). *The Achieiving Society*. Princeton, NJ: D. Van Nostrand Company, Inc. doi:10.1037/14359-000

Mezher, T. S. (2008). Entrepreneurship in Lebanon: A Model for Success and Failures. *International Journal of Arab Culture. Management and Sustainable Devlopment*, *1*(1), 34–52.

Nasr, S. (1978). Backdrop to civil war: The crisis of Lebanese Capitalism. *Merip Reports*, (73), 3-13.

Parhizgar, K. D. (2007). *Global Business Environments: Understanding Multicultural Behavior*. Jaico Publishing House.

Parhizgar, K. D., & Parhizgar, S. S. (2007). Comparative strategic positioning of four academic administrative models: bureaucracy, technocracy, meritocracy, and kakistocracy. *Competition Forum, 5*(1).

Phan, P. H. (Ed.). (2008). *Entrepreneurship in Emerging Regions around the World: Theory, Evidence, and Implications*. Edward Elgar Publishing, Inc. doi:10.4337/9781848441446

Rotter, J. B. (1966). Generalized Expectancies for Internal Versus External Control of Reinforcement. *Psychological Monographs*, *80*(1), 1–28. doi:10.1037/h0092976 PMID:5340840

Sacks, R., & Myers, J. (2003). Tools, Techniques and Tightropes: The Art of Walking and Talking Private Sector Management in Non–profit Organisations, is it Just a Question of Balance? *Financial Accountability & Management*, *19*(3), 287–306. doi:10.1111/1468-0408.00175

Salibi, K. S. (1965). *The modem history of Lebanon*. New York: Academic Press.

Salibi, K. S. (1971). The Lebanese Identity. *Journal of Contemporary History*, *6*(1), 76–86. doi:10.1177/002200947100600104

Sayigh, Y. A. (1962). *Entrepreneurs of Lebanon: The role of the business leader in a developing economy*. Cambridge, MA: Harvard University Press. doi:10.4159/harvard.9780674422247

Schumpeter, J. (1942). Creative destruction. *Capitalism, socialism and democracy*, 82-5.

Schumpeter, J. A. (1942). *Capitalism, Socialism, and Democracy*. New York, NY: Harper.

Shane, S. A. (2000). The Promise of Entrepreneurship as a Field of Research. *The Academy of Management Review*, 217-226.

Shapero, A. (1975). The displaced, uncomfortable entrepreneur. *Psychology Today*, *9*(6), 83–88.

Thomas, P., & Mueller, S. (2000). Culture and Entrepreneurial Potential: A Nine Country Study of Locus of Control and Innovativeness. *Journal of Business Venturing*, *16*, 51–75.

Vinig, G. a. (Ed.). (2005). The Emergence of Entrepreneurial Economics. Oxford, UK: Elsevier.

Zgheib, P. W. & Kowatly, A. K. (2011). Autonomy and Locus of Control for Overseas Lebanese Entrepreneurs Operating Worldwide. *Journal of Small Business and Entrepreneurship, 24*(3), 345-360.

Chapter 13
Expatriate Lebanese Entrepreneurship

Philippe W. Zgheib
American University of Beirut, Lebanon

ABSTRACT

The Lebanese have always been great travelers and emigration played an important role in their history. It became inevitable then that entrepreneurship played a major role in shaping the life of those Lebanese residing outside their motherland, as they had to rely on new and creative ways to sustain their living. Although Lebanese entrepreneurs know how to pinpoint opportunities, they still have limited knowledge of the administrative aspects of managing a business. In other words, Lebanese entrepreneurs have the talent but lack organizational skills. Lebanon is a country where management styles are still traditional. Thus, trying to apply modern management practices can be rather difficult. New technology and product diversification are introduced informally through individual efforts of entrepreneurs.

HISTORY OF ENTREPRENEURSHIP IN LEBANON

The revitalization of the industrial sector in Lebanon happened in the 1920s. Lebanon and the Syrian Arab Republic possessed some resources in the industrial sector before the outcomes of World War Two. This was a fact for Lebanon, where entrepreneurship was a factor which was prominent in the country. (Sayigh, 1962). The typical business structure in Lebanon is small family-owned companies. A major load that small entrepreneurial firms have to face is a limited resource base

DOI: 10.4018/978-1-5225-2066-5.ch013

in relation to what is obtainable to larger firms (Jarillo, 1989). Therefore, Lebanese entrepreneurs get capital chiefly through autofinancing, which builds a heavy load on enterprises.

Debt financing is considered as a barrier to entrepreneurship in Lebanon. Debt financing problems grows from a lack of understanding of the needs of the entrepreneurial segment. (Chakour, 2001). Lebanese people do not think that there are enough opportunities and these people consider it difficult to acquire the information necessary to assess business opportunities. "Successful entrepreneurs not only are accepted but also are often considered 'champions of industry' and presented as role models for others" (Chakour, 2001).

INNOVATION

"Schumpeter posits a single constitutive entrepreneurial function: innovation" (Kilby, 2001). "The entrepreneur is looked upon as the innovator or the introducer of new products to new markets" (Haddad, 1992). According to Sayigh, "Perhaps, more important than a creative or primary form of innovation introduced only infrequently and in a few isolated cases, is a much more frequent and more widely diffused introduction of derivative innovations—indeed, of mere adaptation to local conditions and imitation of innovations generated outside the underdeveloped locale". Lebanese enterprises need to apposite more funds for the innovation of products and services and the improvement of internal processes to attain improved quality.

INDIVIDUALISM/ COLLECTIVISM

Societies differ from each other in terms of their focus on individual goals as contrasting to collective goals (Steensma, 2000). Hofstede (1991) defines individualism as a characteristic of "societies in which the ties between individuals are loose: everyone is expected to look after himself or herself and his or her immediate family". The nature of the Arab family restricts entrepreneurship because Arab families are in general patriarchal and extended. Furthermore, the Arab family is characterized by a pyramid relative to age and gender (Barakat,1992).

Collectivism is seen in societies where citizens are united (Hofstede, 1991). According to the National Human Development Report (Lebanon 2001-2001) "exports cannot thrive on individual initiative alone. Efforts made through institutions pursuing collective interests could lead to sustainable and more efficient results. The Lebanese citizens perceive Lebanon as a country where individualism dominates, without depending on the government for help (Chakour, 2001).

PUBLIC ROLE

To be effective, government programs to encourage entrepreneurship ought to be designed. In Lebanon, Financial agencies ought to be involved more in the development of new firms. Moreover, "increasing the level of entrepreneurship needs considerable government dedication to support research and development and to encourage the transfer of technology from research institutions to the business world. Also, tax reform regarding profit realization could ease some of the financial pressures that Lebanese entrepreneurs face" (Zein, 2001).

According to Eugene Staley and Richard Morse, "Government must provide a framework of stability and progress which encourages foresighted private planning. It must also take lead in developing the human and material foundations for economic modernization and growth" (Kilby, 1971).

THE ROLE OF THE ASSOCIATION OF LEBANESE INDUSTRIALISTS IN THE CREATION OF INDIGENOUS ENTREPRENEURSHIP

The Association of Lebanese Industrialists is a private organization that promotes and grows industries Lebanon. It was founded in 1943. It is the representative body for Lebanese industry and plays a "macro" role at the national and international levels. (Ladki, 2001). Small firms being dominant in Lebanon is ingrained by the lawful standing of enterprises. Around 85 percent of firms are still of the private, individual-ownership type, and less than 1.3 percent are joint stock companies (Ministry of Industry, Industrial survey, 1999). Furthermore, it is worth mentioning that half of the enterprises were produced after 1990.

THE IMPORTANCE OF SMES IN LEBANON: EDUCATION AND TRAINING

Entrepreneurial education activities are starting to be a part of the school curriculum (Gibb, 1993). Effective initiatives in entrepreneurship education are required to produce entrepreneurs through educational systems. "Developing the skills and capabilities required to start a business should be integrated into educational training programs at all levels." (Zein, 2001). Training programs to improve productivity are important for developing management skills. In Lebanon, there is a huge need to improve the technical and vocational training programs. (UNDP, 2002).

REPUTATION OF ENTREPRENEURIAL SPIRIT OF LEBANESE IMMIGRANTS

The Lebanese have always been great travelers and emigration played a vital role in their history. It became inevitable then that entrepreneurship played a major role in shaping the life of those Lebanese residing outside their motherland, as they had to rely on new and creative ways to sustain their living. The focus is on the Lebanese entrepreneurial emigrant spirit from both: an individualistic approach, and a community approach. Major geographical areas of Lebanese emigration include mainly: Canada, Australia, West Africa, the United States, Brazil and South America, France and the Arab Gulf.

WEST AFRICA

The first Lebanese immigrants arrived in West Africa in the late 1800's and mostly settled in the following countries: Senegal, the Ivory Coast, Mali, Liberia, Sierra Leone, Ghana, Gambia, Guinea, Portuguese Guinea, and Nigeria. Lebanese people first started working as peddlers: their job consisted in traveling from one area to another, advertising then selling their merchandise. These activities further developed as Lebanese started buying some items -like rubber- directly from the Africans on better terms than French or other colonial businessmen could. (Bartels, 1973)

As business increases, they bring in friends and relatives, and throw out a line of little shops along the traveled roads and thickly settled native districts. In five years or so, they became the middlemen between the factories and the natives, taking the place of the old European sub-factories.

Success Factors

The success of the Lebanese in outdoing the Europeans in Africa is based on two features:

1. The Lebanese people had somehow lower personal consumption levels than the Europeans; and
2. The Lebanese skill was in some regards greater to that of the Europeans.

CHANGING TIMES: REFLECTION OF LEBANESE ADAPTATION IN AFRICA

However, the beginning of the end for small Lebanese retail merchants started after the Second World War. One of the reactions was to enter fields where the Africans were still unable to compete. Ghana is an example, where at one time, all identifiable motor vehicle spare parts dealers were Lebanese. There was also a high percentage of Lebanese in motor vehicle distribution, and in categories such as General Merchandising, Provision Merchandising, and Textile Merchandising.

Lebanese enterprise reached higher levels, such as in Nigeria with piggeries, shoe factories, soap factories, and other truck businesses. Things got to such an extent, that a responsible British official in Kano (one of the biggest cities in Nigeria) made the statement that if Mr. Khalil Marun (the largest Lebanese entrepreneur in that area) were leave the city, more unemployment would result.

So we can clearly see that the Lebanese brilliantly responded to the challenge faced by increasing African competition and diversified their business activities in multiple fields. (Winder, 1962) Other sectors such as Real Estate and Entertainment were considerably developed under Lebanese enterprise. In terms of entertainment, most of the dance halls and cinemas in West Africa belonged to Lebanese people.

THE UNITED STATES: 1880-1940

Former US President Ronald Reagan is quoted as saying that if he didn't know better, he would say that 'entrepreneur' is another word for America. If that view is adopted, the Lebanese were American before they discovered that entrepreneurial Eden in the late 1870s." (Naff, 1992). This tribute to the Lebanese entrepreneurial spirit speaks well about their achievements in the New World. Since the late 1880s, waves of immigrants started heading for areas such as New York, Boston, and the like.

As was the case in West Africa, Lebanese immigrants in America found success in peddling. In fact most Lebanese were repulsed by the idea of working in factories, or by being isolated in American farm life.In addition, it took them into the homes of Americans, raised their aspirations and forced them to learn English it spared them the uncertainty of finding factory work, of long job lines and layoffs; and finally, because they were itinerant most of the time, it spared them a ghetto mentality:

- **The Supplier's Role and Networking:** Most pioneers were attracted or recruited by a supplier (a veteran peddler who had chosen a suitable site in a small town or city to open a business as a supplier of peddlers). He then sent for relatives or friends. Soon villager drew villager until a peddling settlement developed around the supplier's leadership. By 1900, a network of supplier's settlements filled the nation, providing opportunities for thousands of newcomers and distributing the Lebanese all over the United States. By 1910, Syrian-Lebanese were reporting destinations in all the states and territories (Naff, 1992);
- **The Peddler's Way:** In the settlement, newcomers were given a notions case that was the peddler's prime and constant companion. They were taught the value of American currency; a few tricks of the trade and in a day or two joined the road. Peddlers experienced unexpected hardships on the road: Loneliness, fatigue, and fear were permanent companions. The Lebanese were neither depressed nor discouraged, and feat in touting not only raised their perspectives but persuaded them to settle in America (Naff, 1992);
- **From Peddling to Settling Down:** By about 1910, pioneers had outgrown the trade, the Americans had outgrown the services of peddlers, and new arrivals no longer needed it. Also, the peddlers help America's economy prosper.When Lebanese peddlers settled down, most of them engaged in family businesses in small cities. Grocery goods were among the most peddled. The average business usually began as a small family concern. Operating on minimum capital and opening 16 to 18 hours daily, it required the assistance of the whole family. Children stocked shelves and made deliveries and women relieved or managed the store along with their traditional family obligations;
- **Individual Success Story:** In 1905, Mansour Farah made his way from Lebanon to New Mexico. He began working in the dry- goods business and later moved to New York to study shirt design and manufacturing. He then moved to to El Paso, Texas and started a small factory which produced blue chambray shirts. Farah was designer, cutter, salesperson, and porter: a clear image of an entrepreneur (Naff, 1992);
- **The Lebanese Community of Worcester (Massachusetts):** The study the case of a precise Lebanese community in the US leads to Worcester which illustrates it well.

Lebanese immigrants in Worcester brought with them little education and virtually no professional skills. However they had a lot of energy, the spirit of individualism and the determination to succeed financially.They were willing to take practically any unskilled job, whereas one is struck by the diverse ways they tried to make a living.

There was considerable job mobility among the Lebanese. Lacking in professional skills, they changed jobs based on the demands of the moment. One immigrant, for example, moved from a peddler to a shoe-shop job, and then became a factory worker, a job that he later quit to become a tailor, a driver, and finally an automobile mechanic and real estate investor.

THE LEBANESE IN THE UNITED STATES AFTER 1945

In this part I will focus more on the political and social sides of things, and how new immigrants were different in many respects from members of the earlier community (1880s and on). In general, the more recent arrivals were university students or professionals. While they were not necessarily wealthy, they were benefiting from a wealthy, technologically advanced age. They were politically sophisticated and democratically oriented. Finally, they thought of themselves as nationalists, particularly Arab nationalists. Major sectors from the two communities, the earlier and the later immigrants, were then brought together almost immediately after the 1967 Arab-Israeli war which was the spark that galvanized and solidified the community. (Suleiman, 1992)

It was in 1967 that the first national, non-sectarian organization was formed, which included elements from both communities: The Association of Arab-American University Graduates (AAUG) was established to educate Americans about the Arab world, to improve Arab-American understanding, and to combat prejudice and slander directed at Arabs and Arab countries. (Suleiman, 1992)

Other organizations followed, such as the Lebanese American Association (LAA), the American Lebanese Medical Association (ALMA), the Lebanese American Business Association, plus many others, and helped improve the general conditions of Lebanese people in the United States.

FAMOUS MODERN LEBANESE PEOPLE IN THE UNITED STATES

The list of successful Lebanese-American goes on… However, in the provided list aims to represent individuals from different fields that truly portray the vibrant Lebanese entrepreneurial spirit.

- **Philip Habib:** Responsible for some of the United States' major acts of foreign diplomacy from the 1960s to the 1980s. He was not a high-profile diplomat but rather worked behind-the-scenes to bring diplomats together and prepare them for necessary compromises;

- **Joseph J. Jacobs:** A chemical engineer who developed processes for mass-producing penicillin, B and C vitamins, and fertilizers. As an entrepreneur, he developed a one-man business into a $ 1.7 billion-a-year company with more than 15,000 employees. As a patriot with two heritages, he gives his time, energy, and knowledge to organizations dedicated to strengthening the political and economic bases of both Lebanon and the United States;
- **Ralph Nader:** One of the most brilliant Lebanese to have succeeded abroad. He leads the consumer movement in the States, calling for citizen and consumer rights. Through his activism, he's responsible for at least eight major federal consumer protection laws. Nader ran for the US presidential elections in 2000 and got 3% of the total votes (or 2,781,109 votes). This alone speaks by itself on the dimension this man attained;
- **Michael Ellis DeBakey:** A Lebanese-American surgeon and inventor. He developed several new types of lifesaving surgery on the heart and blood vessels. He also invented revolutionary medical devices such as artificial arteries and the blood pump used in heart-lung machines. He built Texas's Baylor College of Medicine into one of the US's most respected medical research and teaching institutions, and he led the effort to establish the National Library of Medicine (Hall, 1999).

THE ENTREPRENEURIAL SPIRIT OF GREAT LEBANESE WRITERS IN USA

- **Ameen Rihani:** At age 12, Ameen Rihani migrated with his family to New York. Two years later, he left school to handle the bookkeeping in the family business. He later on joined, without the knowledge of his father, a touring theater group. After the group went bankrupt, he re-entered school preparing for law. In the following years, Rihani started writing for Arabic papers in New York, he published his first books at age 27, and what followed is a long list of works that made his fame. Rihani was also renowned for his trip to Arabia with the declared purpose of creating a United States of Arabia. During his visit, he acted as a mediator between different parties, especially in oil related issues between the ruling British authorities and the locals;
- **Khalil Gibran:** Gibran was born in 1883 in Bsharri and emigrated to Boston at the age of 11 with his older brother and two sisters. Early on Gibran showed strong drawing and painting skills, and at age 22 he published his first pamphlet, called "Music". The following years witnessed a series of mas-

terpieces such as "Spirit Rebellious", "Broken Wings" and much others. He moved to the city of New York where he got closer to the artistic scene, and joined along with Ameen Rihani and Mikhaïl Naïmi the young Arabic literary movement in New York. The greatest of all-times Lebanese writers died on April 10, 1931 at St. Vincent Hospital, in New York;

- **Mikhaïl Naïmi:** Mikhaïl Naïmi was 22 years old when he migrated to the west coast of the United States, more precisely to the state of Washington. Later on, he joined Al-Funun group in New York where he met Khalil Gibran. Naïmy had a lot of publications during his lifespan and founded with 12 others of his colleagues "The Pen Society" (Al Rabita al Qalamiyya). He went back to Lebanon where he continued publishing great pieces of work and ended his life here.

LEBANESE ENTREPRENEURS IN CANADA

It is true that the first Lebanese immigrants came to Canada in the early 1880s, however they were very few and until the mid 1940s, the Lebanese population in this country was negligible. It is only since 1946 that the number of Lebanese people increased on a steady rate, due to multiple factors such as the liberalization of Canada's immigration policy for Third World countries and more especially for Lebanese. Some numbers about the Lebanese population of Canada in 1986 indicate that they were rather youthful (modal age: 25-34), family oriented (42% were married), linguistically competent, highly literate, and occupationally well placed. They also were quite secure financially (Abu-Laban, 1992).

LEBANESE INSTITUTIONS IN CANADA

The Lebanese-Canadian community has undergone a respectable degree of institutional development, which focused mainly on three axes:

- **Religious Organizations:** After reaching a sufficiently large population size, the Lebanese community started establishing churches in Montreal, Ottawa, and Toronto (the most influential localities). An important development has been the establishment of the Maronite Diocese of Canada in 1982. The same happened with Lebanese Muslim immigrants, whereby Canada's first mosque was built in Edmonton, Alberta in 1938;
- **Secular Organizations:** Many organizations of this sort were formed, and they performed social, cultural, charitable, and political functions. One par-

ticular example would be the World Lebanese Cultural Union (WLCU) that was committed to building bridges between Lebanon and its descendants abroad;

- **Newspapers:** Only four newspapers and periodicals were started by the Lebanese Canadians in the first half of the 20th century. After the 1960s and the 1970s, scores of newsletters, newspapers, and periodicals, published in Arabic and one or both of the official languages, circulated widely in the Lebanese-Canadian community.

MONTREAL AS THE MAJOR LEBANESE CENTER

Historically, the Lebanese immigrants' first major destination in Canada was Montreal. Upon arrival in Montreal, many started as peddlers or unskilled workers in a variety of service jobs. At first peddlers confined their activities to Montreal and its environs. They were supported in their endeavors by yet a more enterprising group of Lebanese immigrants (those who opened wholesale stores to replenish the peddlers' merchandise). The Montreal experience was very encouraging and the energetic Lebanese entrepreneurs, driven by a dream of success, began to move to other cities and provinces as early as one hundred years ago. The fact remains that the strongest organized structures within the Lebanese community in Montreal are the religious institutions and their leaders. Networks are based on family, business, and ideological ties; and remain strong in Montreal's Lebanese community. Finally, there is a new gap developing within the Lebanese community and that is, between the parental or immigrant generation and their children who are in their young adult years.

- **The Communitarian Support:** A major characteristic of the Lebanese institutions and organizations in Montreal was the strong support they showed to new Lebanese immigrants, as virtually each church, mosque, and other voluntary associations established committees to provide humanitarian aid when needed. The religious institutions also provided shelter. The coexistence between Lebanese from different religions was also exemplary and further asserted the ties of the Lebanese community.

In 1985-1986, and with strong support from Montreal's old Lebanese community, an Ottawa-based national network was organized: the National Council on Canada-Arab Relations (NCCAR). The NCCAR arranged meetings with top Canadian officials to find a peaceful ending to the Lebanese Civil War that was still going on at that time. The Council also stressed on more Canadian humanitarian assistance to Lebanon, co-ordination and co-operation between Canada and the United States; and the facilitation of Lebanese immigration to Canada.

LEBANESE ENTREPRENEURS IN BRAZIL AND SOUTH AMERICA

As the Lebanese flourished in the Northern part of the Americas, however the South was also a major destination, especially countries like Brazil, Argentina, Colombia, Mexico, Jamaica, Cuba, and others. The focus on Brazil and Argentina illustrattes most of the prosperity of Lebanese immigrants.

The Lebanese in Brazil

The first Lebanese immigrants in Brazil were recorded in 1871. Also several life stories of Brazilian-born Lebanese residents in the city of Sao Paulo claim that their fathers had entered Brazil by the early 1880s. Lebanese immigrants first appeared in certain cities of the country and then slowly penetrated the interior other cities as peddlers. Major concentrations developed early in the Amazonas because of the rubber boom around the turn of the century, and in the neighboring states of Minas Gerais and Sao Paulo.

Lebanese peddlers covering the state opened stores in promising urban communities. They prospered, and many became wealthy. Profits were invested in ranches and farms, cotton gins, warehouses, as well as in retail and wholesale stores selling clothing, textiles and haberdashery. Textile manufacturing was one of the most lucrative activity, one could hire or buy sewing machines cheaply, find space in a low-rent building, employ relatives or friends, and go into business at little cost. Many failed but many succeeded:

- **Peddling: Again a Success Story:** No ethnic group could compete with the Lebanese peddlers in Brazil. They usually sold at low prices while having the support of their relatives and other immigrants. In an uncertain dangerous world, Syrian and Lebanese peddlers traveled in groups of two or three. At first, they carried heavy packs on their backs. Later, with a little money, they bought mules and wagons, until they could afford pick-up trucks and boats. Lebanese peddlers were willing to travel long distances to reach isolated populations.

As they moved through the countryside, they looked for promising sites at crossroads or for urban centers with growth potential to start a shop. Once that was done, they sent home fore relatives to work on the premises or to peddle on a commission-basis. In time, they often set up their own outlets in the same urban community if there was room, so that several Lebanese interior towns eventually had clusters of merchants who were related:

- **The Shift from Commerce to Industry:** During the 1930s there has been an accelerated shift from commerce to industry, and by 1940, the Lebanese in the city of Sao Paulo were in second place among ethnic groups in total invested capital. The largest Lebanese investments in 1940 were in textiles, paper and wood products, furs and leather, and in soft drinks. In all these areas, except in wood products, they achieved a commanding position. They were second only to the Italians in the manufacture of ready-made clothing and shoes, and in wood products they were preceded only by the Italians and Portuguese.

It was not until the 1930s and the 1940s that the Lebanese have become important players in the political game. By 1938, eight urban municipalities had Lebanese mayors, rising to 28 in 1947. The first Lebanese were also elected to the state legislature in 1947. Since then, their number has increase and many have been appointed to high office in state and federal governments.

The Lebanese in Argentina

The Lebanese arrived in Argentina in the late 19th and early 20th centuries as part of the wave of Syro-Lebanese emigration during the Ottoman rule. Since 1945 Lebanese emigration to Argentina has virtually ceased because it is no longer an attractive destination for emigrants. Most of the Lebanese that live in Argentina have been there for at least two, three or four generations. (Valverde, 1992)

Back in the first waves, the newly arrived Lebanese immigrants faced many difficulties, so they soon organized themselves to support each other. The more established ones would lend the new arrivals money or create partnerships with them while they taught them their own trade. The ones who would have already bought a shop would act as bankers for the newcomers, not only lending them money but also providing deposit boxes where they could keep their earnings while traveling. In this Argentine society, the Lebanese emigrants had to choose commerce because all the usual jobs were taken. However, they were maligned because they could undercut prices as they had no rent, salaries or intermediaries to pay.

Upper mobility was very much linked to geographical mobility. The Lebanese moved from being peddlers in the remotest areas of the country where only the Indians and the most marginalized people lived, to become small shopkeepers in rural towns. From there they could move to a secondary city and become a "Minoristas". The most successful would then become "Mayoristas" and if they were wealthy enough they would move to Buenos Aires as a mark of success and upper mobility achievement. From the most peripheral position they would move inwards trying to reach the center, where power and control resided.

An example of the Lebanese entrepreneurial spirit in Argentina would be the Asociacion Libanesa which opened in 1937. Funded by donations from the most successful members of the community, the names of all its donors and the amount donated was published, with the result that everybody wanted to outshine the other, as generosity is the source of community respect for the Lebanese in general. This association worked for the general welfare of Lebanese immigrants in the area of Tucuman, a major city in the north of Argentina. Other associations included the World Lebanese Cultural Union, and a youth branch: the Organizacion del Intercambio Cultural Argentino Libanes that organizes cultural activities and attracts young Lebanese to keep links with the culture of their ancestors.

- **Adversity Faced by the Lebanese in Argentina:** Once in Argentina, the Lebanese lack of enthusiasm for agriculture initially played a large part in their prejudicial characterization. In a country where the shortage of farm laborers was a very powerful motivation for its immigration policies, most Middle Easterners devoted their energies to tertiary activities, namely trade. At one point, representatives for the Lebanese community in Argentina started motivating new immigrants into opting for farming: They took care of their travel and accommodation, and helped them settle in agricultural estates. This was considered as a major achievement in order to enhance the Lebanese public image in Argentina.

LEBANESE ENTREPRENEURS IN AUSTRALIA

A few individuals or small groups of Lebanese arrived in Australia in the 1870s. However, it was not until the late 1880s and early 1890s that Lebanese began arriving in numbers large enough to attract the attention of colonial census officials. Most of the early Lebanese settled in New South Wales and were followed there by later immigrants. They found a niche in hawking, an occupation that Lebanese immigrants in all parts of the world heavily practiced.

The early Lebanese typically purchased their goods from Jewish or Lebanese merchants and began peddling their wares in the country areas of New South Wales and Victoria. Those who had amassed enough capital settled in businesses such as shop-keeping, warehousing, or manufacturing. In Victoria, shop-keeping included grocery, hairdressing and drapery shops; in New South Wales and Queensland, drapery stores predominated (Batrouney, 1985).

During that period, half of the Lebanese in Australia resided outside metropolitan areas. In order to minimize economic competition they seldom congregated in substantial numbers in any one place, so it was rare to find more than one Lebanese family in each provincial urban area. In Sydney the Lebanese quickly established churches, voluntary associations and businesses in and around the inner-city suburbs. (Batrouney, 1985). By the 1920s second-generation Lebanese began making inroads into more prestigious occupations. During this decade the first lawyers and medical practitioners of Lebanese descent graduated from Sydney University. They are well represented in professional, technical and managerial positions, and some have received national and international acclaim for their achievements in Australian politics, literature, music, academia, medicine, commerce and sport.

THE NEW LEBANESE (POST WORLD WAR II) IN AUSTRALIA

With the development of more efficient farming methods and greater employment opportunities in manufacturing industry, people began to move to the cities. During this period most Lebanese found their first jobs in the manufacturing industries which had prospered in the immediate post-war years. Many Lebanese women would take jobs as machinists and pressers in clothing factories owned by either Lebanese or non-Lebanese. Those women who stayed at home to care for their children, would take in work from clothing factories (outwork) to contribute to the family income. Others played an important role in establishing Lebanese businesses. Often they would work in the family milk bar or delicatessen while their husbands retained their factory jobs during the day. When the potential of the small business was realized, the husband would quit his factory work and become a full-time shopkeeper with his wife and other members of the family (Batrouney, 1985).

NOTORIOUS LEBANESE IN AUSTRALIA

- **Jack Nasser:** Was born in Lebanon and migrated to Australia when he was four years old. While he was enrolled at the Royal Melbourne Institute of Technology he purchased used old cars, fixed them up, and then sold them, making a profit. Nasser's love of cars and desire to have a career in global industry drove him into the automotive industry. Nasser was hired at Ford Australia as a junior trainee in 1968. He earned the title "Jack the Knife" for his cost-cutting moves that resulted in plant closures and job cuts in the early 1990s. At a certain point, Nasser shared leadership of Ford Motor Company;

- **Louis Fleyfel:** Migrated to Australia in 1949 at the age of 21 and his first job was with Ford Motor Company in Melbourne for a weekly wage of 5 pounds. Two years later he bought his first corner store in the Victorian suburb of Geelong. In 1962, he moved to Melbourne and opened the famous Walnut Tree restaurant. Another three classy restaurants soon followed, which catered to the city's elite. During his career, he was elected president of the Victorian Lebanese Association and appointed Lebanese Honorary Counsel;
- **Steve Bracks:** Is famous for his political career as he was ministerial adviser to Premiers John Cain and Joan Kirner. Moreover, he was principal adviser to Neil O'Keefe, the federal parliamentary secretary for transport and communications. His parliamentary and portfolio positions commenced with his election as the Member for Williamstown in the Victorian Parliament. The posts he has held include the deputy chair public accounts and estimates committee (1996-99) and premier of Victoria.

LEBANESE ENTREPRENEURS IN FRANCE

Because of the historical relation between France and Lebanon, France has always been a special destination for Lebanese immigrants. This was mostly true during the Lebanese wars of the end of the 20th century whereby the rate of migration increased drastically. What sharply differentiates Lebanese immigration from other foreign implantations in France is the disparity between the size of its population and the strength of its economic presence.

One of the strongest ideas which contribute to shape French perception of the Lebanese community in France is Lebanese individualism. The Lebanese community in France may be divided into 3 social groups:

1. Traders, merchants, and liberal professionals;
2. Lebanese employees working for companies; and
3. Students.

The majority of different Lebanese businesses in France were started within five years of their founders' arrival in the country, nearly half of them within the first year. Most of them had built up their capital in Lebanon or in other countries of emigration. Lebanese businessmen also launched into buy-outs of French firms which were experiencing difficulties either with their management or among their shareholders. The Lebanese bought in the hotel and fashion sectors in particular.

Many bankrupt businesses were also acquired at a low price, and the Lebanese methodically worked on making them winning companies once again.

THE LEBANESE BANKING SECTOR IN FRANCE

Following the success of its national immigrants, many Lebanese banks opened subsidiaries in France and started playing an increasingly important role in the foreign banking system. Lebanese banks play a direct role as purveyors of a variety of financial services to their clientele in the management and investment of their capital. They also expand their operations beyond the internal French market in the financing of commercial ventures abroad, especially in Arab and African countries which want to take advantage of the facilities offered by the Lebanese banking and community network.The great flexibility of the Lebanese banking system is above all due to family ties between bankers and their clients, who on occasions give them discretionary powers to act on their behalf: this very unusual type of service has attracted a select clientele which by comparison tends to find the service offered by French banks less competitive.

THE CATERING SECTOR: A SUCCESS STORY

Lebanese restaurants proliferated in France as a result of the massive arrival of Lebanese immigrants since the beginning of the civil war. Those restaurants have paid careful attention to their choice of location, both as regards the cities as well as particular areas within these cities.Thus in Paris, the highest concentration is to be found in the tourist and business sectors, or in up-market areas with a high concentration of Lebanese and other Arabs. In the south of France restaurants have also concentrated in tourist and leisure areas, especially in busy town centers by the seaside.

Capitalization for such businesses is of mainly foreign origin, sometimes supplemented by a bank loan, while the rest is either borrowed or drawn from family savings. The success of most of these restaurants has resulted in an important accumulation of profit which has encouraged managers to reinvest either through expansion or by opening new restaurants, or by investing in a new area altogether. This success is due to good management, often by a family group, and the ability to adapt to the French market by creating a niche of their own in what was previously a gap in the catering industry. The ability to adapt is also apparent in the diversification into new styles of catering, such as the business lunch restaurant, the night-club restaurant, supply-to-order, and the combination of fast-food and traditional gastronomy within the same unit.

LEBANESE ENTREPRENEURS IN THE ARAB GULF

Over the past 30 years, the growth in the trend of Lebanese emigration to the Gulf has to be understood against the background of two factors: the oil price increase after 1973, and the effects of the Lebanese civil war:

- **Profile of Lebanese Emigrants in the Gulf Region:** The Lebanese emigrant tends to be an educated worker in the high salary bracket. The long-standing traditions of education within Lebanon as well as abroad have contributed not only to the prosperity of the home country, but also to a substantial brain drain. From the highly skilled or staff worker to the semi-skilled or unskilled, the typical Lebanese emigrant to the Gulf is not an illiterate migrant seeking his chance in a far-off land, but a cultured and skilled worker (Maaouia, 2001).

Most Lebanese in the Gulf tend to emigrate with their families, which is obviously a more expensive proposition, especially when one takes the children's education into account. Single emigrants send their surpluses back home; the purpose of emigration for them is not so much the ability to make savings as to supplement their family income. Here another factor has to be borne in mind: by what may be termed "wage-scale segregation" in well-paid professions, the salaries commanded will vary according to the worker's origins, a mixture of status and education: thus in the higher salaried positions, a Lebanese can expect to earn one and a half times more than an Indian or a Pakistani, while the French or the English in turn will have a still higher wage (Maaouia, 2001):

- **The Host Countries - How to Get There:** In order to immigrate to the Gulf, it is necessary to go through a local sponsor. This is as true for immigrants who wish to invest as those who seek to work. There are no defined official formalities to obtain a sponsor, rather the procedure is arbitrary. The sponsor acts as a guarantor who eventually expectsto be remunerated for his services.

The demand for foreign labor in the Gulf has declined in recent years. Firstly, countries such as Saudi Arabia have been training their own managerial and executive class, sending students abroad. Secondly, few Gulf countries had any sort of economic development program, as in the early years of the oil boom strong growth was possible without any planning. With the subsequent decrease in the price of crude, they have begun adopting more coherent policies and giving up certain developmental projects. Thirdly, Gulf countries are willing to employ workers without rights or guarantees of protection, namely Asian workers: Indians, Pakistanis, South Koreans and Filipinos have fewer rights in terms of wages or conditions of stay. Contracts are increasingly becoming shorter term, whereas some Arab workers try to settle or are at any rate likely to stay longer. An in-built competition between Arab and Asian workers is developing, and one which the Arabs stand to lose as countries like Korea and the Philippines already export goods, or manufacturing goods to the Gulf and are thus at an economic advantage (Maaouia, 1992).

Obviously, Lebanese emigrants played a major role in Lebanon's economic life, even when they're abroad. The sums of money sent back to their families, or invested in various projects were enough to support a fragile Lebanese economy over the years.

Today however Lebanon is facing a potential disaster with the excessive amounts of debt that our government has contracted. Part of the solution could start by suggesting the creation of a company for economic, financial, and technical studies. This company would include representatives from various Lebanese communities abroad and should help them implement projects that they had in mind, but that no one was listening to. Such a company will also include experts from the Lebanese private and public sectors and will be funded both by emigrants and the Lebanese government. Continuing in the spirit of getting emigrants more involved, one could recommend an "Emigrants' Club" which will act as a social center for emigrants on their return to Lebanon.

REFERENCES

Barakat, K. L. (1993). *Proceedings of the Expert Group Meeting on Creation of Indigenous Entrepreneurship and Opportunities from Small- and Medium-Scale Industrial Investment.* Damascus, Syria: Academic Press.

Bartels, K. G. (1973). *Stranger groups in developing societies: the Lebanese in Liberia and Ghana.* Harvard College.

Batrouney, T. R. (1985). *The Lebanese in Australia.* Melbourne: AE Press.

Chakour, D. Z. (2001). *Entrepreneurship in Lebanon- Situation and Informational Framework.* American University of Beirut.

Erkkila, K. (2000). *Entrepreneurial Education: Mapping the Debates in the United States, the United Kingdom and Finland.* New York: Garland Publishing.

Gibb, A. (1990). Entrepreneurship and Intrapreneurship – Exploring the differences. In *New findings and perspectives in entrepreneurship*. Hant: Gower.

Gibb, A. (1993). The Enterprise Culture and Education. *International Small Business Journal, 11*(3), 11–34. doi:10.1177/026624269301100301

Hall, L. T., & Hall, B. K. (1999). *Arab American Biography*. U.X.L.

Hofstede, G. (1991). *Cultures and organizations. Software of the mind*. Berkshire, UK: McGraw Hill.

Hourani, A. L., & Shehadi, N. D. (1992). *The Lebanese in the world: a century of emigration*. Centre for Lebanese Studies.

Jacobs, J. J. (1991). *The anatomy of an entrepreneur: family, culture, and ethics*. ICS Press.

Jarillo, J. C. (1989). Entrepreneurship and Growth: The strategic use of external resources. *Journal of Business Venturing*, *4*(1), 133–147. doi:10.1016/0883-9026(89)90027-X

Kilby, P. T. (1971). *Entrepreneurship and Economic Development*. Hunting the Heffalump.

Klich, I. G., & Lesser, J. F. (1998). *Arab and Jewish immigrants in Latin America: images and realities*. Frank Cass.

Ladki, N. L. (1993). *The Role of the Association of Lebanese Industrialists in the Creation of Indigenous Entrepreneurship. In Proceedings of Indigenous Entrepreneurship*. Damascus: ESCWA.

Maamari, R., & Ghaleb, J. R. (2002). Microfinance in Lebanon and the Case of Al Majmoua. Making Markets Work for The Poor. WBI MENA Debates, Beirut, Lebanon.

Maaouia, M. L. (2001, January 26). Children of the Cedars who made a mark down under. *The Daily Star*, p. 2.

Manassa, G. B. (1950). *For a Lebanese economic renovation with the collaboration of Lebanon overseas*. Lebanese Political Economy Society.

Naff, A. L. (1985) Becoming American: The Early Arab Immigrant Experience. South Illinois University Press.

Naimy, N. A. (1985). *The Lebanese prophets of New York*. American University of Beirut.

Saliba, N. E. (1992). *Emigration from Syria and the Syrian-Lebanese Community of Worcester*. Association Press.

Sayigh, Y. A. (1962). *Entrepreneurs of Lebanon: the role of the business leader in a developing economy*. Cambridge, MA: Harvard Business Press. doi:10.4159/harvard.9780674422247

Sayigh, Y. A. (1978). *The Determinants of Arab Economic Development*. London: Croom Helm Ltd.

Staley, E., & Morse, R. (1965). *Developing Entrepreneurship: Elements for a Program*. McGraw Hill.

Steensma, K. E., Marino, L. S., & Weaver, M. A. (2000). Attitudes Toward Cooperative Strategies: A Cross-Cultural Analysis of Entrepreneurs. Journal of International Business Studies, 31(4), 591-608.

Suleiman, M. W. (1999). *The Arab Immigrant Experience, From Arabs in America*. Temple University Press.

Triandis, H. Y. (1993). Collectivism and individualism as cultural syndromes. *Cross-Cultural Research*, *27*(1), 155–180. doi:10.1177/106939719302700301

UNDP. (2002). United Nations Development Programme, Globalization: Towards a Lebanese Agenda, Lebanon 2001-2002. National Human Development Report, Beirut, Lebanon.

Winder, R. B. (1962). *The Lebanese in West Africa*. Mouton.

Zein, F. M. (2001). *Strategies in the Development of Venture Businesses: A Study on the Lebanese Entrepreneurial Status*. American University of Beirut.

Chapter 14
Social and Civic Entrepreneurship in Lebanon and the Middle East

Salaheddine M. Chukri
Lebanese American University, Lebanon

ABSTRACT

The Middle East has acknowledged the importance and need of entrepreneurial activities which would flourish the economy and open new opportunities for employment. Providing employment to a young and growing population is the major challenge faced by countries in the MENA (Middle East and North America) region. Everywhere in the world, it is small firms that contribute most to job creation. Their ability to thrive and generate jobs is a function of the environment in which they operate and their capacity to deal with continuous change and build assets for the future. Hence firm competitiveness is high on the development agenda. In today's global environment, firms rather than nations have become the engine of growth, and competitiveness is the key for firms to survive.

DOI: 10.4018/978-1-5225-2066-5.ch014

SOCIAL ENTREPRENEURSHIP IN LEBANON AND THE MIDDLE EAST

People are attracted to entrepreneurs like Muhammad Yunus, the Nobel Peace Prize laureate, the same way they are attracted to Steve Jobs, they believe that these people are extraordinary with the ability to do extraordinary things. Muhammad Yunus and Steve Jobs are both examples of social entrepreneurs that have worked long and hard in order to change and improve people's lives (Martin, Osberg 2007). The exact definition of social entrepreneurs can vary depending on the situation and on the person. Entrepreneurship is the ability to create a viable and prospective business that would have promising abilities to expand and regenerate to form several other successful businesses. Social entrepreneurship, is a sub group that focuses on the social impact of business. (Alvord, et al., 2002). Social entrepreneurship is summarized as a person, who has acquired a social idea, pursued a goal in mind that is set to develop and expand that idea, regardless of the limitations and obstacles, in order to help and improve society and its population. (Peredo, McLean 2005). Firstly, it can focus on the commercial aspect of entrepreneurship. Secondly, it can focus on the innovation of social entrepreneurship and its impact toward other businesses. Thirdly, social entrepreneurship can be viewed as solving a potential social problem before acquiring it (Alvord, et al., 2002). In Lebanon, findings have suggested that the Lebanese population are motivated to work depending on the availability of independence and flexibility, this could be due to the long war history that affected the Lebanese population physically and psychologically. Most Lebanese have acquired the skill of working from a relatively young age with an average of 17 years of experience (Sreih, 2010). However, Lebanon is not considered as part of the top innovating countries in the world, despite the long years of experience, due to the fact that at some point and time, Lebanon lacked a sense of stability and creativity. This instability has led to the Lebanese population shift from local corporate businesses, to private businesses in order to gain direct advantage over the long run. More than 90 percent of the businesses in Lebanon are family-owned, whereas the state-owned businesses dominate the economy today. (Charbaji, 2009).

Social and Civic Entrepreneurship revolve around the central question of who should and can take responsibility for the needs of civil society (Haugh, 2005). Two main social democracy models have been applied following the Second World War until today: The Keynesian model and the free market neo-liberalism or Laissez faire. But there also exists a third model, a compromise between the two models, which looks for the rebuilding of a strong civil society through community effort in partnership with the government (Thompson *et al.,* 2000).

Social entrepreneurship and civic entrepreneurship follow the same definition and comprise the same actions (Sud *et al.,* 2009); a converging consensus to the meaning of it states: "it is an independent organization with social and economic objectives that aim to fulfill a social or environmental purpose as well as achieving financial sustainability". It plays the role of change agents in the social/civic sectors by adopting a mission to create and sustain social and civic value (Murphy and Coombes, 2009).

Furthermore, social enterprises often come with a "triple bottom line" (TBL) mandate. The triple bottom line refers to people, profits, and the planet, and implies that businesses should be run in a financially, socially, and environmentally responsible manner; whence derive environmental enterprises which are "for-profit businesses that pursue business strategies designed to capture a growing market for environmentally sustainable products and services while simultaneously "greening" their operations" (Gliedt and Parker, 2007).

Looking at the sectors by ownership, we see the following models of social entrepreneurship: a) Social entrepreneurship in the private sector: This model has the advantage of latitude in terms of the orienting to planning, profit, and innovation, and CEOs have more freedom to pursue values they cherish. b) Social entrepreneurship in the public sector: This model of social entrepreneurship does not easily innovate or adapt to change due to the political and administrative constraints attached to it (Roper and Cheney 2005).

Consequently, there are two kinds of entrepreneurs: a) CEO as social entrepreneur: CEOs who style themselves and their organizations as innovative and socially responsible. The relative autonomy of the company allows for the consistent pursuit of social values. *[Ex: Dame Anita Roddick- founder of The Body Shop]* b) Social entrepreneurs in the public and third sectors: Despite financial constraints being greater in these sectors, new organizations still arise and governmental agencies often engage in public-private partnerships that involve creative combinations of organizational interests in a project-focused way. *[Ex: Grameen Bank of Bangladesh* – the concept of microfinance] (Roper and Cheney, 2005).

Social entrepreneurship is an active field in Lebanon, more and more seminars, workshops and awareness campaigns are being done and people are highly interested. Sarah's bag, Souk el Tayeb, and YASA are few examples.

Although social entrepreneurship is a "noble" field, should everyone aspire to be a social entrepreneur? The answer is no, society is built on diversity. The need for entrepreneurs is important in both the business and social part alike; society has a need for different leadership types and styles.

Psychological View

A psychological view of the social patterns that influences the creation and development of national entrepreneurs' character in different societies provides a clear description of personality factors empowering competitive or cooperative behavior among entrepreneurs. The following traits were identified by different studies summarized by the researcher Yang, with universal application:

1. Collective orientation.
2. Other-Orientation.
3. Relationship Orientation.
4. Authoritarian Orientation.
5. Submissive disposition.
6. Inhibited disposition.
7. Effeminate disposition.

These factors raises social-oriented entrepreneurs character as the Yang (1986) study reveals. The collective form of behavior is shaped by the principles of Confucian Ideals. This ideology bases its foundation on the assumption that man only exist in relationship to others. How the new generation will be raised within the family and the society later, plays a critical role in shaping the in favor for "cooperative strategies" individuals. Relational dimensions help explain the personality of entrepreneurs. The relationship between sovereign and subject, father and son, husband and wife, friend and friend structures the personality of the individual and his perception of his role as a relational being. It defines as well, subjects' rights and obligations, which mainly revolve around interpersonal harmony leading to social welfare and stability among social-oriented groups. Other societies cherish a different kind of value such as:

1. High achievement.
2. Competition.
3. Equalitarian values.
4. Enjoyment.
5. Autonomy.
6. Expression of Oneself (Sum Lam, 1999, pp. 138-139).

Norms and Values

This individualistic relational factor could best be explained by Hofstede's definition of competition driven societies: "individualism stands for a preference for a loosely knit social framework in society wherein individuals are supposed to take care of themselves and their immediate families only." (Sum Lam, 1999, pp. 186). Norms and values that societies adopt greatly influence the individuals' orientation. A matrix table is presented in the Appendix to show how different societies view cooperation and competition.

To summarize the previous findings on influential norms and values of societies, it is significant to point out another research conducted on the correlation between national cultural values and the attitude of entrepreneurs toward cooperative strategies, and which revealed the following: entrepreneurs emerging from masculine and individualistic driven societies were less favorable of cooperative strategies. In all cases, contractual safeguards seemed as a proper tool to protect oneself against other parties' individual goals and aspirations. The authors, Steensman, Marino and Weaver concluded that societies with uncertainty avoidances tendencies had their entrepreneurs appreciate cooperation; both safeguards and partner commonality were considered, in this case. The results of this study as were advanced, stressing the differences among entrepreneurs, bring about some notable implications on the competitive advantage level. Where as feminine and collective societies can see its entrepreneurs rely on cooperative strategies to position their businesses on the global level or to improve innovations developed by other societies. Masculine and individualistic societies would rather focus and be competitive on the technological level. (Steensman, Marino, Weaver, "Attitudes Toward Cooperative Strategies", 2000). This point was advanced and further discussed by Wilken who explained this divergence as "with the transition to collective forms of entrepreneurship expansion and innovation are likely to decrease, either because of the greater caution of collective actors or the unwieldiness of attempting to act in concert" (Wilken, 1979, p. 66).

Also on the socio-cultural norms level, the trust factor seems critical in developing cooperative strategies among market players. As entrepreneurial behavior is often defined as "the pursuit of opportunity without regard to resources currently controlled", a conflict arises naturally as both parties have similar attitudes towards opportunistic behavior (Burt, 1992). An environment or a society that is supportive of a high level of trust will basically promote: effective communication, lower cost of coordination, high level of exchange, low monitoring efforts and costs and a more performance or goal oriented venture. These factors would eventually lead to lucrative cooperative strategies supporting expansion and efficiency. (Steensman, Marino, Weaver, "Attitudes Toward Cooperative Strategies", 2000).

Economic Perspective

On the economic level, the emergence of cooperative strategies came as the result of the rise in capital requirement of new ventures on one hand, and the limitation that faced individual entrepreneurs on the other. As the result, a group of individuals responded better to the new market conditions and were through the "one for all and all for one" team game, more able to take advantage of the present opportunities (Wilkin, 1979, p. 66). Individual entrepreneurs contribute to the growth of the economy. Their contribution takes many faces: from the introduction of a high level of competitiveness, to the introduction of all sorts of innovative products and services.... The authors of The Entrepreneurship dynamic, allege that it is time to put the myth of the power of "the Entrepreneur" as a lonely individual to rest and consider more closely the teams of entrepreneurs who work formally or informally together to build new organizations and "create new legitimate market spaces" as specified by the authors.

Direct Application

The following section is a historical overview of the entrepreneurial predisposal towards cooperative strategy since the emergence of the entrepreneurial concept. This overview is interesting as it considers different countries with different social norms and values.

Historical Snapshots of Entrepreneurs Around the Globe

The British Entrepreneur

Entrepreneurship in Britain was first seen as individual rather than collective. "During the English industrial revolution, more than in any subsequent industrialization, ... one man often combined two or more of the roles of capitalist, inventor, innovator, and manager, so that high success demanded wide ability" (Harwell, 1971, p.301). Nevertheless, small partnerships of six players –mostly friends or family- were the prevalent form of entrepreneurship as it was permissible by law during the mid-nineteenth century (Wilken, 1979, p.90).

The French Entrepreneur

A more collective-cooperative form on entrepreneurship prevailed in France. However, the last half of the nineteenth century witnessed some cases of individual entrepreneurs especially in textiles and metallurgy. French people were criticized for their individualism and indisposition to cooperate with each other by some researchers such as Dunham and Kindleberger. Others like Palmade, highlighted that French were on the contrary highly cooperative with each other and that they were not really in favor of market competition. It is noteworthy to mention that partnerships (commenda) prevailed in the country by 1850 which indicates that French entrepreneurs were more inclined towards cooperation among themselves. (Wilken, 1979, p.119).

The German Entrepreneur

Germans were most probably among the first in Europe to grasp the benefits from cooperation or team play structure as explains Bowen. This cooperation emerged as activities mainly involved several players from different organizations. Bank financing, the rise of cartels and other factors required a high level of cooperation and shaped the entrepreneurship form in the country. (Wilken, 1979, pp. 147-148).

The Japanese Entrepreneur

Until 1880, entrepreneurship in Japan had one face: Government. Whether is started or not in the form of competition, entrepreneurship was tailored back to fit the "cooperation" oriented society. "Zaibatsu" a popular business form, is a multi-organizational entrepreneurship that provides a clear picture on the nature of most of the ventures taking place during the period. (Wilken, 1979, pp. 180-182).

The US Entrepreneur

Rockefeller, Carnegie, and Ford to name a few, reveal the individual-competitive form of entrepreneurship that has been prevailing in the US since the commencement of any entrepreneurial activity in that country. Yet, one would be surprised that this was not always the case, as during the period extending from 1810 and 1830, entrepreneurial activities in the United States were also cooperative in many instances. Corporations emerged as a resulting from the needs of raising funds and the popularity of the limited liability form of establishments. Individual entrepreneurs, however, had a significance presence. Their definition of individualism or competition slightly deviated from that of other society studied in this paper, as these individual never hesitated to surround themselves with an experienced team and therefore never had the "one man show" status (Wilken, 1079, p. 209).

The Russian Entrepreneur

Surprisingly, Russia had individual entrepreneurship form in the late 1800s. Blakwell asserted as he was quoted by Wilken:" if New York had twenty millionaires by 1855, Moscow at the same time had at least a dozen, St. Petersburg an equal number (although many of these were of foreign birth), and Ivanovo, three". Many industries were lucrative as for example the textile industry.

Corporation and share associations soon found its place in the Russian economy which led to a transition from competitive to cooperative entrepreneurship (Wilken, 1979, p. 245).

The Chinese Entrepreneur

Chinese entrepreneurship has been following a change pattern from a solely social-oriented or collective form to a more individualistic approach. These changing patterns are mainly due to exposures to western values and inspiration by Chinese who worked oversees in Taiwan and the United States. (Sum Lam, 1999, p.139). Motivation of entrepreneurs in China falls under the social-oriented achievement as dictated by the country's traditions. Nevertheless, modern views are stressing the personal achievement traits to be primordial, to be followed by moral character and sociability of the individual. Perhaps, this new modern view of the person in China was mainly brought about by the requirement of capitalist economy. (Sum Lam, 1999, p.189).

ENTREPRENEURSHIP

Entrepreneurship is a crucial component of a decentralized, market-based approach to the efficient organization of economic activity. Virtually all-successful private enterprises of all sizes in all sectors of an economy, in the developed and developing worlds, originate from the efforts of individual or small groups of entrepreneurs. The prospect for entrepreneurship in most developing countries has improved remarkably as distortions created in the past are diminishing substantially. The elimination of such distortions will foster sound entrepreneurship for the benefit to societies. A corollary to this situation is that the receding nature of the State in the economies in developing countries also propels greater entrepreneurship as State dominance diminishes and as new opportunities occur with privatization. *(Is Privatization Necessary?, May 1994).*

The private sector's contributions towards economic growth and sustainable development are numerous and multifaceted. An active and growing private sectors - whether small-, medium- or large-sized operations - is the principal means by which a society generates employment, creates wealth and promotes material well-being of its population. Its contribution towards the alleviation of poverty can be substantial.

Furthermore, a free and vibrant private sector contributes to human development by opening up opportunities and options for people to choose occupation, consumption and investments. An equally important factor is that a flourishing private sector will become the main generator of resources in society and contribute to a stable and growing revenue base from which Governments can draw resources to develop and operate other mechanisms, systems and activities supporting economic growth and sustainable development. As a result, the role of the market has been put to the fore in national and international policy discussions, as it has been increasingly recognized that market-based approaches may often present a more effective means of performing activities that were originally undertaken by the State or in quasi-public organizations. *(The Global Report, 1992).*

Entrepreneurship in the Middle East

The Middle East has acknowledged the importance and need of entrepreneurial activities which would flourish the economy and open new opportunities for employment. Providing employment to a young and growing population is the major challenge faced by countries in the MENA (Middle East and North America) region. Everywhere in the world, it is small firms that contribute most to job creation. Their ability to thrive and generate jobs is a function of the environment in which they operate and their capacity to deal with continuous change and build assets for the future. Hence firm competitiveness is high on the development agenda. In today's global environment, firms rather than nations have become the engine of growth, and competitiveness is the key for firms to survive. (*Globalization and Firm Competitiveness in the Middle East and North Africa Region, Samiha Fawzy).*

To this end, the Middle East, in different regions, has opened facilities which enhance entrepreneurial skills. Organizations like the "Mediterranean Development Forum (MDF), the "World Bank", and the United Nations Development Programme, have been established to address and answer questions like: It addresses key issues for the future of the region, including: What are the real challenges facing firms' operations and efficiency? Can MENA firms compete in global markets? Which are the key institutional constraints that they face? What are the standards of good corporate behavior that they should follow? How can small- and medium-size enterprises (SMEs) play a more effective role as an engine of growth in the region? What are the reasons behind the observed gap between the actual and potential performance of the tourism sector in MENA? How can MENA's potential in this sector be achieved? Finally, how can governments, firms, business associations, the media, think tanks, and universities participate in building firm competitiveness in the MENA region?

Major actions are being taken to promote statistics databases and "Business Incubators", starting with university campuses and going to privately and publicly owned places.

Lebanon's Background

Since independence, whenever the economic situation deteriorated, the private sector always found good reasons to blame the public sector. This backbiting has only worsened since the end of civil strife in 1990 and does very little to further the cooperative public-private effort that is necessary to revive the country. The business community simply cannot wait for the public sector to reform itself. It must forge ahead with reforms of its own house and contribute to government effort to improve administrative efficiency. If one goes back in time, the track record of the Lebanese economic "miracle" in the 1950s and 1960s, which lasted until the outbreak of the civil war in 1975, was the doing of the private sector while the role of the public sector remained marginal. The steps taken to modernize state administration, which were initiated by former President Fouad Chehab, remain the only real reforms that Lebanon has known in 59 years of independence. It is ironic that the Lebanon of the 1950s and 1960s, which lacked any real structural economy, benefited from all the upheavals that the region witnessed after the 1948 catastrophe or nakba in Palestine, not to mention the rise to eminence of the oil-rich Arab countries. The flow of capital and entrepreneurs into Lebanon from those countries and the new opportunities that were opened to entrepreneurs benefited Lebanon in a miraculous way and were responsible for what were the country's golden years.

"The Switzerland of the Middle East," as many Lebanese liked to call their country, became an oasis in the midst of considerable regional turmoil. But it was the de facto arena where most of the Arab world's internal wars were fought through the media. Nobody realized at the time that these wars were a prelude to the bloody strife that the Lebanese had to endure for more than 15 years, and the aftermath of which we are still enduring. During those days, no one complained about an inefficient state administration, corruption or tax evasion, because most of the country's powerful and intelligent elite were benefiting from the chaotic state of things and were reaping huge benefits from the economy. Everybody lived as if each was his last day and no one cared about the future. But the prosperity of the laissez-faire era bore the seeds of calamities to come.

When one considers the entrepreneurship that led to a prosperous Lebanon in the 1950s and 1960s and the resolve of the people of this country to survive the war years, it seems incredible now to see so little enthusiasm or private initiative to revive the country's economic health. All sorts of excuses are brought out to explain the lack of proper conditions and measures to save the country as if they did not exist before of course in different weights and calibers. The Syrian presence, the Palestinian threat of upsetting the delicate sectarian balance, sectarianism, the interference of security bodies in public life, the lack of an independent judiciary,

Israel and globalization are but a few of the culprits blamed by different segments of Lebanese society and especially the business community.

Today things have changed. Most of the political and economic elite, who are convinced that Lebanon cannot survive in the world's free market economy, are calling for state intervention and a centrally planned economy to salvage privileges that will not be salvageable in the coming decades. For this elite, all means are acceptable to reach the ultimate goal. Quite unrealistically, they want tailor-made reforms to enable the Lebanese to live like the Scandinavians in a tax-free haven as if Lebanon were an oil-rich country. It is true that the state lacks the basic ingredients for real reform but the private sector suffers from many of the same shortcomings. It is disheartening to know that the private sector lacks a multitude of essentials such as reliable data, transparency and a serious plan to reform its structure. This lack of strategic vision in the business community is most evident in the constant bickering between traders and industrialists. Any effort to raise customs duties raises the ire of merchants, but the failure to protect local producers only leads to the industrialists accusing the government of taking sides. Support for the tourism and banking sector only antagonizes those in agriculture and industry. Stuck in the middle is the citizen, who suffers the most. Since 1990, no private institution has prepared any serious plan of reform for the different sectors of the economy. The various chambers of commerce or associations could have given the government an economic vision, but instead have been plagued by egos and feuds. The statistical data occasionally presented by these institutions is not accurate and serves neither a serious plan for the restructuring the economy nor an effort to build a sound database that could be of use to the government. As former Prime Minister Salim Hoss rightly said: "Statistical data in Lebanon is nothing more than a point of view."

Growth Factors

Economic growth occurs mainly because of high rates of capital accumulation, some in the form of education (human capital) but most in machines, equipment and factories. But the accumulation of capital and educated labor must be backed by improvements in technology. Historically, long-term economic growth has been sustained by significant increases in productivity due to technological and organizational advances. This increase in productivity is then translated into higher real wages, increasing the workers' standards of living and giving impetus to further entrepreneurial investments.

Government Regulations

The major obstacles to forming new businesses or attracting foreign investments are government regulations, red tape and bribery - all proliferating in the Lebanese economy. As a result, many foreign investors and entrepreneurs have pulled out of Lebanon, even though overseas Lebanese individuals have been successful in business in the U.S., Canada, Australia, Brazil, Africa, Saudi Arabia, etc.

Only sympathetic business environments prompt talented entrepreneurs to invest in the local economy. This lesson can be learned by looking at different nations in Europe, South America or North America. A good example in Europe is Sweden, famous today for the competitive efficiency of companies such as L.M. Ericsson, Volvo, ABB (Asea Brown Bovery); with few exceptions, they all came into being from 1875 to 1915, the heyday of Swedish free markets and growth. But they are frustrated nowadays; some of the most successful Swedish companies, such as ABB, have moved their headquarters and factories abroad. Even in European nations, like Italy, with many small companies, executives complain about obtrusive regulations that discourage and hinder entrepreneurial activities.

Statistics from the Organization for Economic Cooperation and Development confirm that venture capital is more abundant in the U.S. than in Europe, and that America invests much more of this capital in startups. Moreover, much startup money is devoted to risky high-tech companies in centers of entrepreneurial energy like Silicon Valley.

The Lebanese government needs to create a Lebanese "Silicon Valley" where entrepreneurial talent and energy would be nourished and promoted, not only by the usual pro-market talk service, but by abolishing taxes on the profits of newly created firms, abolishing red tape on investments, lowering capital gains and estate taxes, promoting and encouraging investments in technology, and by promoting capital accumulation and productivity. In short, the government should be pro-business and work for high rates of economic growth. The Lebanese government invests a lot of its resources in barren political maneuvers. It is time to shift all our resources into high-yield economic investments, thereby promoting and sustaining economic growth. *(Fadi Asrawi, The Daily Star Online).*

Through my research, I realized that most of the information generated about Lebanon indicates that Lebanon is characterized by the presence of SME or in other words "Individual Enterprises", where the father owns, then the son, then the grand son. Moreover, *Banks are too busy lending to the government to worry about the private sector.* Without the right connections, raising finance for small businesses isn't always easy in Lebanon.

As I present the simple case of an entrepreneur named Badr Hassoun, a soap maker in Tripoli who wanted to advertise his football-shaped bars to visiting fans and players during the recent Asian Cup tournament.

Because he makes soap in a traditional way with little capital investment and no credit history, he was unable to quickly raise the few thousand dollars he needed to publicize his product and take advantage of the influx of tourists to Tripoli.

Banks and capital markets, the traditional external sources of financing for companies, are largely closed off to entrepreneurs such as Hassoun who want to expand their businesses.

Conventional bank loans come with double-digit interest rates and are hard to obtain without a bank account, signatories, and collateral. And even if small businesses are ready to take on this debt, banks are generally unwilling to lend because of the increased likelihood that these borrowers will be unable to make the repayments in the current recession.

This fact of "family owned" businesses, could be considered the main cause of not having adequate cooperative entrepreneurship in Lebanon. Lebanon, in its current position, as the center of the Middle East should be promoting cooperative entrepreneurs, however, this is not yet the case.

Places like AUB, where cooperative entrepreneurship is enhanced are starting to establish their identities as places of reference in the entrepreneurial world. Yet, a lot more effort should be done on both, the private and the public sector.

Special action, I also discovered, is being taken for this aspect, and there are individuals as well as organizations who are working for the promotion of cooperative entrepreneurship in Lebanon. An example would be the (ARCEIT).

The Arab Regional Center for Entrepreneurship and Investment Training (ARCEIT), which is attached to the UNIDO Investment and Technology Promotion Office (ITPO) in Bahrain, has just made an agreement with the Beirut Association for Social Development (BASD), to be its focal point in Lebanon. With focal points already in Jordan, Sudan and Syria, BASD is the fourth focal point established by ARCEIT since its inauguration in February this year.

The programme in Lebanon has the full support of the Prime Minister of Lebanon, a protocol formalizing the arrangements is currently being concluded with the Prime Minister's office. Capacity building activities (training of trainers) will be initiated soon at the BASD. (*Lebanese small businesses are starved for financing, The Daily Star Online*).

The ARCEIT is itself a focal point of the Inter-Regional Centre for Entrepreneurship and Investment Training (IRC) of Ahmedabad, India. IRC is the international arm of the Entrepreneurship Development Institute of India and is responsible for building the capacity of institutions in Africa, Asia, Central Asia and Arab countries.

SOCIAL ENTREPRENEURSHIP: A CURRENT CASE SCENARIO IN BEIRUT

Social entrepreneurship is looking at what is happing around you and coming up with an idea or business plan to take help solve the situation. Social Entrepreneurship pushes a person to become more aware of what i happing around them from all aspects of life, it also allows the person to see a problem or situation and come up with a solution.

Value Proposition

"Connect to Collect"

I unpacked the problem and explored it, it is time to be creative and innovative like an entrepreneur. The best solution is to recycle all the garbage. This way we can reduce and reuse. My value proposition is that I will provide a recycling service that is the simplest, easy to use and quick to learn. I will also make it easy to have access to recycling cans for all interested persons. The business will benefit both the environment and consumer because of the return they both will get. Efficiency is also a key attribute because we do not want the trash lying around, this service comes with a software application that would allow the consumer to contact us, so we come empty the can when it is full. This way we do not have to come around every couple of days.

Stakeholder Map

The stake holder map looks at everyone who is involved in this issue, which is the trash in Lebanon. There are two ways people can get effected, directly and indirectly. Almost most people who walk in the streets every day or who need a clean environment to work like farmers and directly affected. But there on the other hand even if you are not in contact with the trash I can also be effective. For example, city hall has to find a solution:

- **Direct:**
    - Students
    - Patents
    - Tourists
    - Farmers
    - Fisherman
- **Indirect:**

- City hall
- Police department
- Shops
- Restaurants
- Hospitals
- Ecosystem

User Persona

I finally looked at who would be interested in this idea, who my partners will be, what resources I will need, and the channels of distribution. That achievement I would like to reach from my business.

SWOT

Recycling is the best solution but it was done inefficiently, and majority of the population was not aware of it. The best two ideas I came up with was recycling in return for something and recycling at your door step, this idea came up because people wanted to recycle but didn't know how and where. This idea makes it easy to access recycling cans:

- **Strength:**
  - Helping the environment;
  - Reducing the potential of viruses and diseases that could be born out of it;
  - Helping the community;
- **Weakness:**
  - Hard to change or motivate people to recycle;
  - Expansive because there are very little facilities;
- **Opportunities:**
  - Lots of garbage;
  - Reach out to the public who want a change;
  - Build more jobs and opportunities for people in need;
- **Threats:**
  - Close minded people;
  - Completion from other firms;
  - Government isn't helping.

Business Model Canvas

- **Key Resources:**
    - Garbage
    - Bags
    - Recycling cans
    - Pickup Trucks
    - Warehouse
    - Labor
    - Tools
- **Key Partners:**
    - Other recycling companies
    - Transportation companies
- **Type of Intervention:**
    - Service that collects garbage to recycle
- **Key Activities:**
    - Collection
    - Distribution and collection
    - Transportation
    - Creating awareness
- **Channels:**
    - Provide cans to consumers
    - Logistics to collet garbage in the most efficient way
- **Segments:**
    - Middle and upper class educated part of the population

Current Condition: Promoting Awareness about Recycling

In Lebanon there is a garbage crisis, social Entrepreneurship creates a motive to first look at this crisis and then find ways to solve the problem. There are disagreements within the government and confusion on where the trash should be disposed of and who should do it.

First I looked at unpacking the problem of why there is a crisis and why is has not been solved. The public can't really help with government disagreements, but they can find solutions that could help reduce and eliminate this problem. Schools and universities teach about not littering and recycling but only apply in their own communities. I then looked at exploring the problem more deeply to see why people are not taking action about the issue, but I found out they are. Small communities such as schools and universities only care about cleaning what's inside and forget the outside but as soon as you leave the problem is apparent again. This shows how these communities are not teaching about the cause but only showing it can be done. What these communities are trying to teach is not being implanted. Another problem is households do not take initiative towards that garage at home there is a low level of commitment towards the Ecosystem. There is a lack of facilities is a major issue, there are very little places to disposed of garbage which should motivate the idea of recycling but sadly there is lack of facilities for that too.

REFERENCES

Alvord, H. S., Brown, D., & Letts, W. C. (2002). *Social Entrepreneurship and Social Transformation: An Exploratory Study.* Harvard University: Hauser Center for Nonprofit Organizations Working Paper No. 15, 1-26.

Axelrod, R. M. (1997). *The complexity of cooperation: Agent-based models of competition and collaboration*. Princeton, NJ: Princeton University Press.

Burt, R. S. (1992). *Structural holes: The social structure of competition*. Cambridge, MA: Harvard University Press.

Charbaji, A. (2009). The effect of globalization on commitment to ethical corporate governance and corporate social responsibility in Lebanon. *Social Responsibility Journal.*, *5*(3), 376–387. doi:10.1108/17471110910977294

Collins, O. F., & Moore, D. G. (1964). The enterprising man. East Lansing, MI: Bureau of Business and Economic Research, Graduate School of Business Administration, Michigan State University.

Dearlove, D. (1999). *Business the Bill Gates way: 10 secrets of the world's richest business leader*. Oxford, UK: Capstone.

Gliedt, T., & Parker, P. (2007). Green community entrepreneurship: Creative destruction in the social economy. *International Journal of Social Economics*, *34*(8), 538–553. doi:10.1108/03068290710763053

Hakim, Y. (2002, March 16). Time for private sector to pull its weight, stop 'unending lament'. *The Daily Star*.

Haugh, H. (2005). A research agenda for social entrepreneurship. *Social Enterprise Journal*, *1*(1), 1–12. doi:10.1108/17508610580000703

Ismoisili, C. (2000). *Cooperative Entrepreneurship: The Challenge for Unions in the New Millennuim*. International Labor Organization.

Lam, S. K. (1999). *Portraits of successful entrepreneurs and high-flyers: A psychological perspective*. Aldershot, UK: Ashgate.

Littunen, H. (2000). Entrepreneurship and the characteristics of the entrepreneurial personality. *International Journal of Entrepreneurial Behaviour & Research*, *6*(6), 295–310. doi:10.1108/13552550010362741

Martin, L, R., Osberg, S. (2007). Social Entrepreneurship: The Case for Definition. *Stanford Social Innovation Review,* 1-3.

Mead, M. (1937). *Cooperation and competition among primitive peoples*. New York: McGraw-Hill Book Company, Inc. doi:10.1037/13891-000

Murphy, P. J., & Coombes, S. M. (2009). A Model of Social Entrepreneurial Discovery. *Journal of Business Ethics*, *87*(3), 325–336. doi:10.1007/s10551-008-9921-y

Peredo, A. M., & McLean, M. (2006). Social Entrepreneurship: A Critical Review of the Concept. *Journal of World Business*, *41*(1), 56–65. doi:10.1016/j.jwb.2005.10.007

Roper, J., & Cheney, G. (2005). The meanings of social entrepreneurship today. *Corporate Governance: The International Journal of Business in Society*, *5*(3), 95–104. doi:10.1108/14720700510604733

Schoonhoven, C. B., & Romanelli, E. (2001). *The entrepreneurship dynamic: Origins of entrepreneurship and the evolution of industries*. Stanford, CA: Stanford University Press.

Sreih, F. J., Pistrui, D., Huang, V. W., & Welsch, P. (2010). Family and cultural factors impacting entrepreneurship in war time Lebanon. *International Journal of Entrepreneurship and Innovation Management*, *12*(1), 35–51. doi:10.1504/IJEIM.2010.033166

Steensma, H. K., Marino, L., & Weaver, K. M. (2000). Attitudes Toward Cooperative Strategies: A Cross-Cultural Analysis of Entrepreneurs. *Journal of International Business Studies J Int Bus Stud*, *31*(4), 591–609. doi:10.1057/palgrave.jibs.8490924

Sud, M., Vansandt, C. V., & Baugous, A. M. (2009). Social Entrepreneurship: The Role of Institutions. *Journal of Business Ethics*, *85*(S1), 201–216. doi:10.1007/s10551-008-9939-1

Swedberg, R. (2000). *Entrepreneurship: The social science view*. Oxford, UK: Oxford University Press.

Thompson, J., Alvy, G., & Lees, A. (2000). Social entrepreneurship – a new look at the people and the potential. *Management Decision*, *38*(5), 328–338. doi:10.1108/00251740010340517

Wilken, P. H. (1979). *Entrepreneurship: A Comparative and Historical Study*. Ablex Publishing Corporation.

Chapter 15
Entrepreneurial Innovation in Islamic Banking

Philippe W. Zgheib
Lebanese American University, Lebanon

Lama I. Massalkhy
Lebanese American University, Lebanon

ABSTRACT

Instruments of Islamic finance have recently reemerged as an innovative tool for entrepreneurial transactions. Purpose of this chapter is to: a) define Islamic banking Product; b) compare with nearest western banking equivalent; c) highlight advantages and disadvantages of product; d) state future progression of banking towards convergence or divergence between Islamic and Western banking; and e) finally evaluate the role of client focus and customer driven performance in the future trends of entrepreneurial Islamic funding. This chapter highlights the concept of Islamic Banking. Business is slowly adopting Islamic banking as a rival market to western fractional reserve banking from the perspective of delivering customer value. This synopsis covers 19 instruments of Islamic banking by comparing the advantages and disadvantages of each one to that of conventional banking. Interestingly, the comparative methods result in several findings including the fact that banks must be completely devoted to providing customers with excellent service standards, and must also cater for customers' needs and demands. In addition, if Islamic services are desired, then the ones who cater for those needs will survive. Whereas western

DOI: 10.4018/978-1-5225-2066-5.ch015

banks have a higher chance to penetrate the Islamic banking sector, Islamic banks can't provide any conventional banking services due to Sharia'a rules that prohibit fixed or floating payment or acceptance of specific interest or fees for any service. This chapter also concludes with a contrast between Islamic and western banking from a customer perspective.

ISLAMIC FUNDS AND GLOBAL MARKET

The events of global financial meltdown of 2008 have had drastic impact on business globally; particularly serious implications on financial institutions – banks and investment houses. So, like any other commercial and financial organizations, banking institutions face a stiffer challenge than ever before. Banking is a service oriented business where customers are at the core of the bank's missions. As such, business's success to become the premier Arab bank depends on its ability to provide superior service and products to its customers to cater their growing needs. Islamic banking is growing over the coming years but the gap still big between Islamic and Western banking due to the global market and most population around the world still operates in conversion banking (non-Islamic). The global market and economy is connected to western n banks rather than Islamic banks. Also, the central banks in these Islamic operating banking still connected and works fully with western banking system. Business had chosen to be part of a new Islamic bank "Rival" as a step to be closer to Islamic market, business Continuously improving customer service levels to meet escalating expectations and the competitive Marketplace by offering Islamic products that doesn't include interests rates to avoid "Riba", And as supported by the article: "Future proofing your bank through an effective core banking strategy", the bank should be covering customer's needs and channels, knowing the market preferences and work to be there for their customers.

Client Focus and Customer Driven Performance

The role of customer focused performance on business future is crucial for maintaining future competitiveness given the intensifying multinational competition. Business should engage in systems/process re-engineering that will aid in delivering customized, high quality timely solutions while benefiting from cross-country operational synergies. Listening is a very import attribute in a future proof organization. Being customer driven will immensely help business in efficient adapting. Customer focus helps in anticipating future potential development potential. Business's proactive strategy of regional expansion, makes it ready for opportunity whenever/wherever it arises. Customer focus and customer driven performance are critical to future proofing multinational banking strategy. There are many factors that are involved in implementing such a strategy. One important factor is "evolving customer needs". This involves the bank being up to date with the latest innovations and technological advancements as a tool for customer interaction. Another factor is the "availability of skilled professionals". The bank needs to hire the best human capital available in the market. The use of appropriate and up-to-date technology is critical for the organization's success in the digital age. In a highly competitive environment, this will give business an edge over its overseas competition. Focusing on a customer driven performance both locally and internationally and meeting customers' needs wherever they are abroad will definitively strengthen customers' loyalty and encourage our existing customers to spread the word about our high service delivery standards. Customer orientation is pivotal to strengthening business foothold regionally, aiding penetration into untapped markets and customer acquisition.

Regional Business Expansion

As business expands its regional and international operations it should ensure that it caters to all segments of its customer base. A backbone of any banking operation is excellence of service. As their popularity and efficiency are increasing, Islamic banking services are appealing to many customers and id flexible to work with different cultures and expanding in different countries. It has succeeded to fulfill the customer requirements in different aspects. In order to future proof the expanding market of Islamic Banking, the bank needs to enter in alliance with a top tier fully fledged sharia complaint bank by white labeling their products and presenting them to their customers to safe guard their position and steer clear of any doubts that might arise by issuing a declaration prior to circulation. By entering in an alliance the bank will actually increase its product base, meet its customer requirements and follow the future market requirements and trend. The future business strategy emphasizes on customer's relationship in each country it is operating in. Ultimately, synergy & alignment is created between these countries, in an effort to reach its shared objectives driven by customers' needs.

Delivering Customer Value

Future proofing will always strive to offer customer satisfaction whether in retail, corporate or private banking and across all departments through quality products and services locally, regionally and internationally. In retail banking new future campaign is created to offer the best service for customers and making sure that we help achieve customer satisfaction. Customer is at the core of business strategy.. Additionally a regional service network aims to serve the customers at any regional branch irrespective of where the account is initially opened. Business strategically focuses on enhancing customer relationship management to improve profitability, which can provide a sustainable competitive advantage. Business is future-proofing itself from an IT perspective using it for targeted customer segmentation, but is yet to build on internal resources to ensure commitment and service quality, and marketing processes to actively capture market openings.

Listing of Islamic Finance Tools

- **RIBA:** Interest.
- **MUBADALA:** Swap.
- **GHARAR:** Risk.
- **QARD AL HASSAN:** Interest free.
- **HIBAH:** Voluntary payment.
- **WADIIA:** Guarantor.
- **WAKALAH:** Power of attorney.
- **KAFALAH:** Guarantee.
- **MUSHARAKA:** Sharing.
- **MURABAHA:** Cost-plus financing.
- **TAKAFUL:** Insurance.
- **MUSAWAMAH:** Bargaining on a price.
- **SUKUK:** Securities.
- **BAII MUAJJAL:** Deferred Sale.
- **BAII DAYN:** Sale of debt.
- **IQTINA:** Leasing.
- **SAALAAM:** Advance payment.
- **IJARA:** Rent.
- **HARAM:** Illegitimate.

RIBA: INTEREST

Riba, an Islamic Banking tool that means Interest, is forbidden in Islamic Banking. Simply put, it stands for unjust gains in trade or business, generally through exploitation. Taking advantage of one's need for money borrowed by requesting returns above and beyond the lended amount; making gain without "working for your money (Sharjah Islamic Bank, 2010). This is the essential difference between Islamic Banking and Western Banking.

Advantages

- The profits to the lender from loaning money; this encourages the flow of credit;
- The return rewarded to those who invest money into savings since they're relatively risk free compared to other investments;
- During high inflation, riba is applied to curb price of goods and services.

Disadvantages

- Riba is favored significantly unfairly towards the profit of banks and lenders and grossly disadvantage the borrower;
- Riba contributed to the current recession due to banks irresponsibly distributing high-risk loans on under the premise of returns from interest.

With regards to these two forms of banking, Islamic and Western, as different as they may seem, they are methods of doing business. With Islamic banking, those details are put to better protect the society we live in. With the future outlook, western banking might realize that this form/method of banking can be applied for two main reasons:

1. To protect themselves as a business where returns/risks are evenly shared with depositor based on the performance of the bank and convergence is a valid option;
2. Banks have to become absolutely customer oriented, as competition has become fierce over time and with the current economic situation, it's becoming increasingly difficult to find customers who are "good" to do business with and will not default, causing them problems.

MUBADALA: SWAP

Islamic banking differs from conventional banking mainly in the types of products offered to consumers. Islamic banks provide Shariah compliant products, i.e. products that adhere to the principles of Islamic law but still serve the benefits of traditional banking products. An example of a Shariah compliant product is *aqd mubadala*, which literally means swap contract. One of the common swap contracts, provided by many Islamic banks in the Middle East, is the Islamic Profit Rate Swap (IPRS)[1]. The Saudi Hollandi Bank, the first bank in the Kingdom of Saudi Arabia, defines the product as a "profit rate hedging product that allows customers to manage their

Islamic floating or fixed rate liability by exchanging their floating rate for the fixed rate or by exchanging their fixed rate for the floating rate respectively" (Saudi Hollandi Bank, 2012).

Derivative instruments are the Western banking equivalent to the IPRS. A derivative is a sophisticated type of security; the price of the security depends mainly on one or more underlying commodity, financial asset or interest and foreign currency rates. It involves the transfer of risk, that arise from a variable factor such as a currency's exchange rate, from one person to another who is willing to accept the uncertainty risk (Malkawi, 2011). Derivatives come in different forms, such as swaps, options, future and forward contracts. The uncertainty associated with the future delivery of the underlying assets is the key reason behind forbidding such activity in Islamic banking; however, the alternative Islamic profit rate swap product presents some advantages and disadvantages. On the positive side, unlike conventional derivatives, the IPRS offers customers the ability to limit funding costs by hedging their cash flows against profit rate movements (Mashreq Al Islami, 2010). Hence, it provides a risk control mechanism to protect the parties involved, this includes financial institutions, from fluctuations in interest rates (Hussain & Mehboob, 2008). It gives borrowers and investors the option to turn their floating rate liabilities and assets into fixed rates by entering into "payer" or "receiver" swaps (Mashreq Al Islami, 2010). In terms of limitations, unlike traditional derivatives, the Islamic derivatives are mainly used for hedging reasons and cannot be traded (Garbois et al., 2012). Another disadvantage is the lack of Islamic derivatives' benchmarks; this is mainly due to the varied market practices in the absence of a consolidated Shariah approval process, which leads to higher legal risks (Jobst & Sole, 2012).

Islamic banking is witnessing significant growth in the Middle East and South-East Asia. According to a study conducted by Garbois et al. (2012), the world's most active Islamic markets are located in the Gulf Cooperation Council (GCC) countries and Malaysia. Islamic banking is growing at yearly rates that range between 15 to 20 percent (Jose, 2011). Bahari (2009) argues that Western banks, such as HSBC, are seeking to establish Islamic footprints in many countries due to the rapid growth in the Islamic finance industry. Although regulations restrict conventional banks in the GCC countries to launch Islamic windows, the presence of Islamic banking services remains a future-proofing imperative to sustain profitability and increase market share. In addition to the tight regulations, "suspicion would be less when dealing with a full-fledged Islamic bank than dealing with conventional banks having Islamic windows" (Jose, 2011). As a result, the future progression of banking towards convergence between Islamic and traditional banking cannot be achieved. Large conventional banks, therefore, need to consider acquiring smaller Islamic banks to launch a gateway into the growing Islamic market. BANK's acquisition of Rival bank few years ago is an example of a strategic acquisition. According to BANK's Vice

Chairman, Nasser Al-Sayer, "the management and operations of BANK and Rival Bank would be kept separate and fully independent of each other in accordance with Islamic Banking law and regulation" (AME Info., 2009). Garbois et al. (2012) state that such strategic moves "allow banks to compete more effectively by expanding branch networks, taking advantage of operational synergies, and expanding their financial clout" (Garbois et al., 2012:8). BANK Group has now positioned itself in the local market to meet the needs of religious conservatives seeking Shariah compliant banking products and services as well as Western financing activities. In addition, BANK's regional expansion strategy could potentially cover established as well as emerging Islamic markets, such as India and Indonesia.

The intense market competition and the regulatory restrictions are two major obstacles BANK faces towards pursuing higher revenue and continuous growth. Attracting new customers and retaining existing ones require BANK to shift from an account-focused operation to a customer-centric approach (CSC, 2011). BANK must continuously identify the customers' needs and ensure the delivery of innovative services to maximize their satisfaction and maintain stronger relationships. Hence, for the future-proofing of BANK, progressive modernization approach is required. As defined by CSC (2011), a progressive modernization approach "provides a bank with the modern technology and framework for transformation of all applications, processes and delivery channels while lessening the operational impact."(CSC, 2011: 5). It gives BANK the ability to cope with the speed of industry developments by aligning new technologies with business imperatives to pursue multinational exposure. Investment in technology will help BANK tailor its services based on the targeted segments' desires, such as:

- Harmonize different banking channels, traditional and electronic, to enable customers use their preferred point of contact;
- Real-time delivery of information;
- Automate operational processes for integrated global banking;
- Comprehensive understanding of customer's behaviour that leads to efficient cross-sell actions across all channels.

In parallel, the Human Resources Department's role towards acquiring and preparing the right skill-sets amongst employees is vital to ensure maximum utilization of technology. Management learning is a key aspect for effective future-proofing, which in turn, will enable us to deal with the unknown (Najjar, 2012). The organization's culture, a body of core values and beliefs, must encourage the share of ideas to accelerate the development of innovative products (Najjar, 2012). As we are dealing with future-proofing, we don't know what the outcome is; we should be focusing on the process (Rao, 2009).

GHARAR: RISK

1. Business contracts and financial transactions in Islamic banking have to follow the guidelines of Holy Quran and Sunna. Gharar is any elements of risk, uncertainty and hazard involved in financial transactions, trade and contracts. Islamic products and services need to be risk free to make sure that it does not lead to distraction and loss (Said, n.d.);
2. **Loan contracts in western banking (no Islamic) were interest rate is variable and can be changed over time which leads to future loss of money due to change of interest, increase of monthly payments and increase of length of repayment period;
3. **Housing loans suppose to be for buying or refinancing a house but people use the cash from the loan to buy a car a holiday and other things which loss the credibility use of the loan which create uncertainty and future hazard compare to Murabaha in Islamic Banking which created for specific purpose of buying goods, car or furniture;
4. **Advantage and Disadvantage of Gharar:**
    a. **Advantages:** Identify the uncertainty and risk from any product and services and make sure transactions and contracts are risk free with compliance of (Quran and Sunna);
    b. **Disadvantages:** There usually low profit and return as the risk is usually low in Islamic Banking transactions. The transaction can be also affected the environments and the country where the Islamic products and services are operating (it differ from one country or another).

QARD AL HASSAN: INTEREST FREE

1. Qard Al Hassan is an interest free loan and is the only loan acceptable in Islamic finance. The loans is profit free and is mostly given to a customer on charitable basis and usually sourced by the bank's own funds. The bank might require supporting documents for the purpose of the loan and/or collateral guarantees;
2. This product is primarily offered to support the Islamic bank in positioning itself as Shariah-compliant and to highlight the fact that its values are deeply rooted and coincident with Islamic beliefs and values (charity). Accordingly, this Islamic banking product has no real equivalent in conventional banking. What can be considered as similar is the 1 month or so interest free period conventional banks offer on their credit cards. Both products, though of dif-

ferent structure and features, serve a common purpose of marketing the bank and attracting potential customers;

3. Qard Al Hassan is obviously a riskless and free facility from the perspective of the borrower. The lender on the other hand can capitalize on this product to enhance its image as a fully fledged Islamic bank while hooking in new customers (once a relationship is established with a Qard Al Hassan customer, eventually the bank can start selling him/her other products). On the downside, however; this product is a risky investment without any direct financial return. There is also a moral hazard issue because the borrower is not baring any of the risk involved;
4. Governing and regulatory authorities are becoming all the more aware of the need to separate between conventional and Islamic banking. The most recent example being the Qatari central bank which last year issued a directive requiring conventional banks to shut down their Islamic banking windows. From a pure regulatory perspective, the separation allows for much more effective oversight of the banks under supervision. First, Islamic banks include additional risks related to asset ownership inherent in some Islamic products and operations. Second, Islamic banking is a growing industry still undergoing major changes and development in addition to being very innovative which makes it essential for supervising bodies to continually develop their policies and proactively respond to market dynamics and developments. Finally, from a customer perspective, while Islamic banking may appeal to a wide range of clientele, those with religious interests remain the major player in this industry. It is therefore ethically crucial for governing authorities to ensure that no commingling of funds or operations is possible and that the "purity" of Islamic banking is not compromised. Clearly there have been reasons to believe that this is not the case when banks operate as dual intermediaries.

QARD HASSAN

1. An interest free loan is a loan that is given for reasons other than monetary gain. It is quite popular in charitable circles as well as governmental social support programs. The way it works is simple; you borrow a dollar and pay it back without interest after a defined period;
2. The nearest thing to this in western banks is a credit card limit in some instances. Some banks allow for a grace period in which you get a number of days or months of interest-free financing, after which a normal interest rate is applied;

3. An advantage of this product is that it allows for the use of credit cards without charging interest. What Islamic banks do is provide an interest-free credit line in return for an annual fee. A disadvantage to this is the time value of money for outstanding amounts and the opportunity costs that could exceed the fees charged—especially for longer periods;
4. Modern financing tools that use buy and sell agreements as substitutes for conventional lending are not inventions of modern day Islamic theologians. In fact, back in the 1400's in Italy, the Catholic Church banned the lending of money with interest. A bank by the name of Medici Bank pioneered creative ways to profit from lending without directly charging interest. It did this by manipulating the value of mediums such as currencies and commodities in the lending scheme (Tim Parks, 2006). Just as Italian banks evolved into modern banks in 600 years, modern sharia compliance banking is bound to converge with conventional banking. With time, the customer will note see the distinction between Islamic and conventional banking.

HIBAH: VOLUNTARY PAYMENT

Definition of Hibah (Gift) Product

Hibah is a voluntary payment of a nominal amount for customers holding deposits or saving accounts. It may not be announced in advanced, nor can it be announced in a binding contract. The bank may or may not pay a Hibah at the maturity of the deposit. Hibah is a form of incentive for encouraging customers to depositing into Shariah compliant products.

Another form of Hibah would be a reward for an early settlement of a debt, whereas the borrower would pay the customer an amount, upon a prepayment of his loan.

Nearest Western Banking Equivalent

The equivalent of Hibah in conventional banking would be interest. Either paid on deposits, or paid back upon settlement of a pre-matured loan.

Advantages and Disadvantages of Hibah

The concept of Hibah was introduced to give Islamic Banking the ability to compete with non shariah compliant banks', in terms of interest payment and interest re-imbursement.

What gives Hibah the competitive edge is that even though it is not guaranteed, it may be very rewarding if the bank excels in performance. That being said, its main disadvantage is that it is not guaranteed and the customer may not receive any interest.

Future Progression of Banking towards Convergence or Divergence between Islamic and Western Banking

In my opinion, the recent economic crisis and the US credit crunch's were driven by highly leveraged mortgages. In the definition of Islamic banking, you would find a lot of reassuring words. Such as "fair, reasonable, just" which at these times can be very attractive to concerned customers. Furthermore, the fact that Islamic Banking's main profit generators are fees rather than interest and are less controlled by the Central Bank, makes it very attractive for investors and shareholders. As a form of future proofing and given the current trend in Kuwait, having an Islamic Banking arm, as well as the ability to convert entirely as an Islamic Bank should be available.

WADIIA: GUARANTOR

In a Wadiia, the depository or bank acts like a trust; it becomes the guarantor, the keeper and trustee of funds. The bank guarantees repayment of the full amount deposited, or any component of the outstanding amount, upon the depositor's request.

This product most closely resembles a fixed deposit in a western conventional bank. The main difference between a conventional deposit and an Islamic safekeeping Wadiia is the interest component that is paid at the end of a fixed deposit (Friends, 2009).

The main advantages of this product are that it's guaranteed and can be withdrawn whenever demanded by a customer. Additionally, the usage of the Wadiia by the institution is subject to the permission of the depositor and the depository may provide returns in the form of a Hibah (gift) as a token of appreciation, although it is not obligated to do so. The main disadvantage of this product is that the customer is not entitled to participate in any share of the Bank's profits which will not allow the funds to grow.

Islamic Banking requires human interpretation of the Sharea, which certainly provides a variety of opinions. Islamic banks should work more on standardization and synchronization of interpretations and opinions as it is very difficult to achieve full convergence. Thus, convergence with Western banking will be an even bigger obstacle and divergence will most likely be the outcome.

WAKALAH: POWER OF ATTORNEY

According to the US Legal Dictionary, the term "Power of Attorney" called as "Wakalah" in Arabic refers to "an instrument containing an authorization for one to act as the agent of the principal that terminates at some point in the future either by its terms or by operation of law such as death of the principal or agent. They are also called letters of attorney. The person appointed is usually called an Attorney-in-Fact. The person making the power of attorney appointment is called the principal. A power of attorney can be either general, durable or limited. (U.S. Legal Dictionary, 2012) In the Islamic banking context, the term implies the same meaning - Wakalah "occurs when a person appoints a representative to undertake transactions on his/her behalf, similar to a power of attorney" (Wikipedia, 2012). A close review of the terms in both traditional banking as well as in Islamic banking clearly highlights its vital role and scope – particularly in the context of future proofing. For example, there is a strong need both in the traditional as well as in the Islamic banking to ensure the future well-being and successful sustainability of opportunities. So, from a future proofing perspective the need for 'power of attorney' or wakalah as in the case of Islamic banking is very vital to formulate 'tactical process so as to anticipate and take remedial measures to minimize possible negative effective.

There are both pros and cons in executing a power of attorney. Some of the major advantages are: establishing a power of attorney is inexpensive, a loved one can decide who should make decisions on his or her behalf, and thirdly the power of attorney as a document can require the agent to become bonded or to give an account of his or her transactions. On the other hand, some major disadvantages are: a person's competence at the time of writing the power of attorney might be questioned later. Some financial institutions such as a banking institution require that the "power of attorney" be written on special forms. Some institutions may refuse to recognize a power of attorney after a lapse of a long period - say 6 months or so. Lastly giving a general power of attorney could lead to, the agent misusing it. For example, the agent could turn out to be untrustworthy. (National Library, 2012) An evaluation of the pros and cons of 'power of attorney' or 'Wakalah' clearly highlights its scope in banking, particularly for banking customers in diverse areas ranging from personal banking to corporate banking operations.

Support for future progression of the banking towards an integration or convergence between Islamic and Western banking operations is obvious in all areas of products and services. For example, the best example of such a convergence is evident in the case of one of the most reliable and oldest financial institutions that provide uniquely a wide range of traditional banking products and services, while at the same time also catering exclusively to Sharia compliant customers – by providing them Sharia compliant products and services. In the convergence process, the element of "power of attorney" or "Wakalah" would serve as an effective tool for both the banks as well as to customers.

KAFALAH: GUARANTEE

Kafalah is an agreement in which one party assumes responsibility for the debt of another if the debtor fails to pay. In Western banking Kafalah is also known as guarantee. Guarantee is defined as a promise by one party (the guarantor) to assume responsibility for the debt obligation of a borrower if that borrower defaults. There are many different types of guarantee in the western banking while in Islamic banking Kafalah has only 3 types. In Kafalah fees and charges (mainly paper work fees) to provide this service are taken from the customer in advance and without any interests on any amounts taken while in western banking there is a percentage to be taken on any type of guarantee provided to the customer.

Kafalah Advantages

- It bails out customers when they face difficulties and can't pay the seller, acts as a safety measure for the opposing party in the transaction;
- Support Group and community by providing trust and support to establish businesses and make profit.

Disadvantages

- For banks acting as guarantor will have to pay back what their customers owed;
- Issues with lawsuits against fallouts;
- Banks cannot track down fraud/bad intentions in customers who are looking to miss use the Kafalah product.

Banks will go towards Islamic products as a result of the Arabic revolutions in the region to attract more customers, their trust and to explore the market of Islamic banking and depending on their location abiding laws they will either convert completely or add Islamic products. It helps the bank to have a clear view on the market trend for each region/location, to reflect its values, to apply the appropriate customer driving principals for action and gives a comprehensible view on where the bank is and what's its weakness and strength.

MUSHARAKA: SHARING

1. Musharaka is the Islamic contract for establishing a joint venture partnership. In Musharaka, two or more parties contribute capital and expertise to a business and participate with the related profits (in agreed percentages) and losses (pro rata to initial capital);
2. The equivalent for Musharaka in the conventional banking is the joint venture. Those two concepts are very similar as both parties in a specific venture share capital, profits and risks. However, the main difference lies when one party is the financer/creditor. In Musharaka, the creditor will still have to share the losses unlike in conventional banking where the creditor charges interest;
3. Musharaka is regarded as the purest form of Islamic financing because it is based on the principles of sharing risks and profits and it is considered to be convenient for long term ventures. However, while profits are distributed on the basis of agreed ratios, risks are proportionate to the initial capital: That is risks and profits are not equally shared among related parties. This might glooms the risk/return assessment. Another disadvantage is that different parties can take part in managing the venture which could turn into threat when points of view diverge;
4. With Islamic banking growing in size and complexity, I believe it should be separate from conventional banking. While both conventional and Islamic banking share the same core role and offer equivalent products to cater customers' needs, their models differ in function and structure and, thus, in risk assessment. In addition, each has a different set of regulations at the operational levels (i.e investments) and internally (auditing and financials). Separating Islamic and conventional banking would allow regulators to better regulate and monitor the market.

MURABAHA: COST-PLUS FINANCING

There has been rapid growth of Islamic banking the past couple decades in the Gulf Cooperation Council (GCC) region and other Muslim nations like Malaysia and Indonesia. Some Western or conventional banks offer Islamic-based products or changed their philosophies on some products in an attempt to attract a segment of diverse customer-base. Due to the recent global economic crisis many conventional and western financial institutions have been hit with declining growth rates and eroding profitability. In an effort to recover from the crisis a majority of these institutions have revisited their strategies and operational efficiency. Despite unexpected hurdles and change in its banking approach, the attraction of customers and maintaining their loyalty remains essential for a bank's survival. In order to compete with Islamic banks, many conventional banks are now offering Islamic products in an effort to maintain a part of the market share. One of the most popular of these products is *Murabaha.*

Murabaha is a Shariah compliant contract type of form similar to the Western banking equivalent of a corporate or trade-financing solution. Murabaha "is often referred to as 'cost-plus financing' and frequently appears as a form of trade finance based upon letters of credit. In its simplest form, this contract involves the sale of an item on a deferred basis. The item is delivered immediately and the price to be paid for the item includes a mutually agreed margin of profit payable to the seller. In this contract, the market cost price (true cost) of the item is shared with the buyer at the time of concluding the sale (2007). In a Western banking structure the equivalent is a consumer loan to acquire assets, usually for automobiles and real estate, or short-term financing for small to medium enterprises without specifying the product.

An advantage of Murabaha is that the customer, at the time of finalizing and signing the "murabaha contract" with the bank, is aware of the profit mark-up at the time of finalizing and signing the "murabaha contract" with the bank, and the required repayments which do not change during the financing term. An additional advantage is the opportunity for the customer to have the option for a long repayment period.

"The advantage is that [the customer] knows [the bank's] profit mark-up and [the] installments at the time of signing the deal, and it never changes throughout the financing term. This arrangement allows [the customer/client] to take immediate possession and ownership of your vehicle and spread your capital expenditure over a period of time."

The disadvantages of Murabaha are that products or assets purchased though Murabaha have a mark-up in the price compared to conventional banks. Another disadvantage with Murabaha is that the assets purchased must be compliant with Shariah law, and for any unforeseen circumstance the financial institution may end up owning or managing this product. "The second main disadvantage is the issue of cost. Put simply, developing and providing Shari'a compliant banking products costs more than the typical banking product. Costs are incurred in developing the knowledge base to put the products in place, to retain Shari'a scholars to ensure constant compliance (having regard to the fluid nature of Islamic law), and in owning and managing the properties themselves. In Murabaha transactions, for example, additional land transfer taxes will be incurred on resale." ("Shari'a Compliant Financing" Silvana M. D'Alimonte and Lauren Temple of Blake, Cassels & Graydon LLP) A major disadvantage with Murabaha is that there is minimum flexibility by the purchaser when the product is purchased in the sense that the product cannot be traded.

"The disadvantage of the Commodity Murabaha is that it is not tradable under Shariah principles and may carry some market, commodity price, counterparty, credit and even Shariah risk. Some observers emphasize that it is also not flexible enough to be used for monetary policy operations. ("*Major Milestone*" Cash & Trade Magazine, July 30, 2011)

Islamic banking with its Shariah laws and restrictions do not comply with the western capitalistic banking systems in any way. Islamic banking seems to place many restrictions on the customer based on the Shariah laws, which is perceived negatively by Western societies generally. "On the other hand, it could be harmful where compromises are made on the Islamic prohibitions of riba and gharar." (*Reappraising the Islamic Financial Sector: A Short Report*, Harvard-LSE Workshop, London School of Economics, London, UK. February 24, 2011) Islamic banking has been subject to some disagreements on its functionality that is based on either professed beliefs or practice even within Muslim countries.

"It was further contended that the convergence of the Islamic financial sector with the conventional financial sector is caused by a dichotomy between professed beliefs and practice, a problem which is also faced by Muslims in other spheres of life. "Islamization" of finance, like the "Islamization" of some Muslim-majority countries, has not brought a change in substance." (*Reappraising the Islamic Financial Sector: A Short Report*, Harvard-LSE Workshop, London School of Economics, London, UK. February 24, 2011).

Recently during the real estate crisis which contributed to the economic downturn of most of the global economies, Islamic banks actually financed some these properties, especially in the GCC region.

"A similarly critical view was that if Islamic financial services have the same economic substance as conventional financial services, they will likely contribute to the same economic ills. The real estate speculative bubble experienced in Dubai was financed by both the conventional and Islamic financial sector." (*Reappraising the Islamic Financial Sector: A Short Report*, Harvard-LSE Workshop, London School of Economics, London, UK. February 24, 2011)

Even though I personally do not believe in the convergence between Islamic and Western banks, I must admit I find it intriguing that some Western banks are including Islamic products as part of their services, with guidance from Islamic legal experts. "Some, such as HSBC, have done this by creating a dedicated Sharia advisory board, attached to a specific Islamic banking unit.

TAKAFUL: INSURANCE

Takaful is Islamic insurance fund geared towards providing financial aid to the participants (who are also the owners) in a case of a tragedy or crisis. The money is drawn from a mutual pool, which is created by the fund owners to help recover the loss (Abdul Wahab et el, 2007). Takaful is equivalent to life and family insurance in the conventional banking system but with the exception of charging participants a premium fee.

The Takaful insurance concept has both advantages and disadvantages in its business model. One of the main advantages is that participants have a low risk of financial loss. In the case of surplus or no usage of the money invested, participants will receive their money back. The drawback of Takaful however does not take participants credit score into consideration, some participants may be of a higher risk to insure than others. (Nikolas, 2011)

In my perspective, Islamic and Western banking systems should diverge to ensure the progression of the banking sector mainly due to image reasons. The trust factor becomes an issue to those consumers who base their banking decisions based on their religious beliefs. Combining both Islamic and western banking frameworks will raise consumer's suspension to how finances are operated since they are not verified in financial statements and strictly depend on the monitoring of the Sharia board (Jose, 2011). Consumers trust and confidence is the main contributor to banks sustainability, especially during tough economic times.

MUSAWAMAH: (BARGAINING ON A PRICE)

- **Definition:** The most common type of Islamic trade where the selling price of a commodity is negotiated between the seller and the buyer, with the cost price being unknown to the latter. Following Shari'ah law, there are restrictions for this kind of trade to exist:
    - The product or services being traded need to be wholly owned by the seller;
    - The sale must take place at the time the product or service is being traded, not at any future time;
    - The product or service must be valuable and usable.

The Nearest Concept in Western Banking: Cost-Plus Pricing

Definition: A pricing method, in which the selling price is established by adding a markup to total variable costs. The expectation is that the markup will contribute to meeting all or a part of fixed costs, and generate some level of profit.

Variable cost-plus pricing is especially useful in competitive scenarios such as contract bidding, but is *not* suitable in situations where fixed costs are a major component of total costs.

Advantages and Disadvantages of Musawamah

Disadvantages

- May lead to corruption and mismanagement at a micro level;
- The seller may or may not know the actual price of the sold goods.

Advantages

- An appealing service to the customers, as it targets the feeling of win/win situation.

Banking Progression

YES, western banks will progress towards implementing Islamic banking principles.

WHY? Western banks are based on the principle that the more you have, the more you can get, their aim is to increase their market share and maximize profits. Especially international banks that have branches in Muslim countries will respect and follow the tendencies and cultures will open dedicated branches for Islamic products and services, as the Western banks have a higher chance to penetrate the Islamic banking sector, the Islamic banks can't operate any conventional banking services because its controlled by Sharia'a rules that prohibits the fixed or floating payment or acceptance of specific interest or fees for any service.

SUKUK: SECURITIES

Derived from the Arabic word Suk meaning certificate, Sukok are securities that comply with the sharia and its investment principles. Sukuk represent the ownership of real assets; whereas conventional bond are holders of debt. As per the Islamic regulations (money now for money later) will always fall under the scope of Riba (receiving interest); therefore, between the purchase and return should stand a purchased asset that is why Sukok should never be referred to as an Islamic Bond. Like bonds, sukuk have a maturity date and holders are entitled to a regular stream of income over the life of the sukuk along with a final payment at maturity. Advantages of the foresaid product are that they are monetized real assets that are liquid, easily transferred and traded in the market. On the other hand the major disadvantage is presenting an appropriate sharia compliant structure to achieve the set objectives given the fact that there are no global sharia standards to employ. Islamic Banks should be fully segregated from conventional banks in order to safeguard their position in terms of purification of the assets; by doing so the bank will have no room for any customer doubt. Of all the faiths Islam is the most pragmatic when it comes to finance. Islamic Banks are distinguished from other financial institutions in their avoidance of interest (Riba); sharia compliant banks enter with their customers in joint investments sharing the reward and risk. Even though regional banks had the first access to the Islamic market, international banks are offering alternative facilities with their Islamic arms and windows bringing with them level of experience, technology and market share which will result in a conflict of interest within the institution and external doubt of the assets used and structuring of the facilities involved.

BAII MUAJJAL: (DEFERRED SALE)

Literally, *baii muajjal* means a credit sale. Technically it is a financing technique adopted by Islamic banks that takes the form of *Murabaha Muajjal*. It is a contract in which the seller earns a profit margin on his purchase price and allows the buyer to pay the price of the commodity at a future date in a lump sum or in installments. The bank has to expressly mention the cost of the commodity and the margin of profit is mutually agreed. The price fixed for the commodity in such a transaction can be the same as the spot price or higher or lower than the spot price. *Baii muajjal* is also called a deferred-payment sale.

Baii bithaman muajjal: Deferred price sale: it refers to the sale of goods at a higher price than its actual cost against periodic deferred payments. It is compared with the consumer loan at conventional bank. Interest is replaced by the extra amount added (profit margin) on the actual cost of goods.

Comparison with Nearest Western Banking Equivalent

An equivalent to *baii muajjal* in western banking is any credit sale (loans or credit cards for instance) on an installment plan with payments delayed or postponed until a future date. However *bai muajjal* is a contract whereby the seller charges fixed profit on sale of goods. Unlike Islamic banking, in case of western banking, the assets are fictional in nature and there is no physical sale or purchase of assets. Yet, if we are to consider the contract between the buyer and the seller of the goods, then we can compare the *baii muajjal* to a lease financing contract in western banking where the bank grants the individual leasing the product (such as an automobile or machinery) the ability to use/own the commodity while making specific monthly payments.

Advantages and Disadvantages of Baii Muajjal (Deferred Payment Sale)

Advantages of the product for the borrower include that he/she can structure his payments over time, by paying the total balance at an agreed future date or make installments over a pre-agreed period. Hence, the use of a deferred payment strategy allows the debtor to receive the benefit of the goods now rather than having to pay for the commodities in full at the present time. Advantages of the product for the bank could be to defer income into the next years. Moreover the product *baii muajjal* is asset backed and adequately collateralized. Therefore the default risk is mitigated by the fact that the Islamic banks can foreclose the asset in case of default. On the other hand, the most obvious disadvantage of the product for the bank is that the risk of asset is transferred to the bank. From a legal perspective, the most striking is that the bank, for the interval between the sale of the goods, bears the risk that the goods will be harmed or destroyed.

Convergence/Divergence between Islamic and Western Banking

The financial crisis of 2008 has increased the need for instruments that really cater to risk-sharing, and this has spread the trend of convergence between Islamic and Western banking. The crisis has highlighted the flaws of fractional reserve banking and debt leveraging. It may thus be a major force for change in western banking, toward greater reliance on equity financing and risk sharing schemes, innovations in financial instruments and thus increase the likelihood for convergence of Islamic and Western banking. Moreover, there is an obvious emergence and expansion of Islamic finance in Kuwait which came about through a favorable convergence of government support, popular sympathy and innovative marketing. Also, due to the nature of competition, conventional banks are keen on opening Islamic windows to enter into the Islamic banking business which is leading to a future progression of banking towards convergence between Islamic and western banking.

BAII DAYN: (SALE OF DEBT)

1. Dayn is debt acquired as the result of any agreement or contract of exchange. Bai' Dayn in the context of Islamic banking, or Sale of Debt, is the selling of debt instruments between different parties, either with the debtor himself, or with any other independent third party;
2. It can be compared to securitization in conventional banking, which is the practice of pooling different kinds of debts into securities that are later sold to investors;
3. First, this instrument helps companies reduce cash flow problems since it provides immediate cash to businesses. Second, it will somewhat reduce administrative costs because it reduces the time spent on credit control and some other costs like record keeping.

However, it has the disadvantage of reducing profit margins as the business has to share part of the profits with the company which buys the debt. Also, this sale can be costly as the company could pay more if the buyer of debt demands more to cover the liability for the bad debt.

4. The trend nowadays is towards customization. Customers are becoming more educated and sophisticated, and so is the banking industry as a whole. Additionally, the past decade has witnessed the proliferation of myriad innovative products in the Islamic banking which created a divergence between conventional and Islamic banking. Even large international banks have understood this reality a while back and started offering Islamic products. I believe this trend is bound to continue in the future, considering also the Islamic wave hitting the Gulf region.

IQTINA: LEASING

Iqtina is a mode of financing adopted by Islamic banks. It is a contract under which the Islamic bank finances equipment, building or other facilities for the customer against an agreed rental together with a unilateral undertaking by the bank or the customer that at the end of the lease period, the ownership in the asset would be transferred to the lessee. The promise does not become an integral part of the lease contract to make it conditional. The purchase price is fixed; the bank gets back its cost price along with some profit, which is usually determined in advance.

This concept is very close to the Western idea of *leasing*. Iqtina process is asset-based rather than credit-based Islamic financing method that has been used in the U.S. for more than 20 years. Similar to conventional auto leases.

Iqtina contract allows small, medium, and large-scale business owners to enjoy the benefits of using an asset or a piece of property without having to buy it. The option of being able to transfer the ownership of an asset is also beneficial for the lessor, because it means that it is not saddled with the responsibility of owning an asset at the end of the leasing period. On the other hand, if the customer decided to cancel the rental contract, the bank profit, which they agreed on previously, will not be waived and the customer is obligated to pay it.

The future progression of banking towards convergence between Islamic and western banking, There has been significant growth in Islamic financial services in recent years and there is every reason to expect that this growth will continue at a rapid pace. Clearly, there is expanding demand for these products, and a closely associated desire on the part of banks, including non-Islamic banks, to provide Islamic financial services. in the case of "Sharjah Islamic bank-2010", and from the statement of the year of the bank, the net profit is increased by 12.33%, which is an indicator that he market is expanding in that region and that chances are high to achieve more in the coming years.

ISTISNA'A: (ORDER TO MANUFACTURE)

Definition

Istisna'a is a sales agreement between the Bank as Al-sani (the seller) and the customer as Al-mustasni (the ultimate purchaser) whereby the Bank based on the order from the customer undertakes to have manufactured or otherwise acquire the subject matter (Al-masnoo) of the contract according to the specifications stipulated by the customer and sell it to the customer for an agreed upon price and method of settlement whether that may be in advance, by installments or deferred to a specific future date.

The nearest western banking equivalent is Project Financing.

Advantages

- Huge infrastructure and development projects can be financed through this type of contracts;
- Both parties bare the risks;
- The aspects of the contract is finalized and agreed upon by both parties beforehand. So the there is no speculation or hidden cost involved;
- The Bank as Al-sani receives a markup on the manufacturing activity and no interest is charged.

Disadvantages

- There is much debate among scholars whether Istisna is sharia compliant;
- There are no approved Standards prescribed for these contracts;
- These contracts can be terminated by either parties any time before the actual work starts;
- This type of contracts is more or less the same as in the case of conventional banking and at time more expensive for the customer.

In my opinion there is equal scope for both Islamic and western banking. With the amount of growth recorded in the past few years and the back to basics type of banking done by Islamic banks, would in my opinion compel conventional banks to come up with products similar to the Islamic products. Lack of International standards, difference in the interpretation of Sharia, lack of adequate knowledgeable staff and the notion that Islamic financing is only for Muslims are the major stumbling blocks in the growth of Islamic Banking.

SAALAAM: ADVANCE PAYMENT

Salam is an Islamic financing tool consisting of a contractual sale in which the buyer makes full advance payment to the seller for the deferred supply of specified goods of specific quantity, quality and workmanship at a specific date as contractually agreed.[2],3

Advantages

- **Intention:** betterment of small farmers and traders;
- **Higher Profits:** Salam at a lesser price and parallel Salam at a higher price.

Disadvantages

- Trade allowed only in specific definable goods;
- Desire for higher profits can override the intention of farmer/trader assistance;
- The nearest conventional banking equivalent is an agricultural [or trading] loan.

Islamic banking, convergent as it is on the fundamentals of basic banking, will stay divergent from Western banking in that it will perform as an alternative system, operating basis different mechanisms, with differently packaged banking products serving mainly a niche community.

Islamic banking evolved in opposition to the modern banking economics of an interest-based financial structure and functions based on a trading/PLS structure. Its fundamental difference would cause it to stay distinctive from the Western banking culture.

IJARA: RENT

Definition

Ijara: An agreement under which an Islamic bank (lessor) leases assets to a customer (lessee) against an agreed fixed rent and for an agreed period after which the bank

Table 1. Contrasting Islamic Salam and agricultural loan in western banking

	SALAM	Agricultural Loan
Produce supported	Halal produce	Any produce
Bank's involvement	Output oriented-deals with downward chain. Importance: Use of proceeds.	Input oriented-no further involvement. Importance: Collateral
Bank's primary concern	Societal growth	Interest Income
Relationship style	Buyer-seller	Lender-borrower
Borrower default probability	Lesser (bank's interest in project viability)	Higher (no further association with project)

recovers its investment plus a profit. Asset is then disposed based on Shari'ah rules. Example: option to own the asset.

Comparison

Ijara mainly replaces conventional interest-based financing (loans) with Islamic-lease financing as the concept of usury (interest) is prohibited in Shari'ah. Hence instead of lending money on interest, profit is earned on rentals of an asset. Unlike loans, with Ijara ownership of the asset is not transferred to the customer until the end of the lease period.

Beyond financing, Ijara investment funds can be compared to any conventional investment funds with the difference of being backed by secured leased assets, with pre-determined tenure and fixed monthly returns.

Advantages and Disadvantages

Advantages

- Entails financing tangible marketable assets, hence less risk associated with defaults;
- Entails commitment to avoid (Haram), thus assets are used in a more socially responsible way.

Disadvantages

- Intangibles cannot be leased (edibles, money…etc.);
- In case of total asset loss, contract is void and bank cannot charge rental;
- Interest rate increases cannot be passed on to the customer as bank profit has to be fixed.

Convergence vs. Divergence

Convergence is not feasible because Islamic banking system limits flexibility of bank dealings as many products/services are lawful but not necessarily ethical in Islamic banking terms plus "Shari'ah compliance" can be interpreted differently by different Islamic scholars increasing incongruities and thus difficulty to converge. Also, divergence will better serve the needs of hard core Islamic customers not willing to deal with banks offering non-Shari'ah based solutions.

HARAM BANKING: ILLEGITIMATE

1. Haram is everything that is prohibited by Sharia'a- such as businesses that sell alcohol or pork, or businesses that produce media such as gossip columns or pornography, which are contrary to Islamic values;
2. All Islamic banking products e.g. Eljara, Murabaha…etc. must define the profit and the destination of money spending in advance to make sure that it is acceptable by Islamic fundamentals and Sharia'a. On the other hand; the conventional banks do not consider that as a must to do;
3. The aim of this is to engage in only ethical investing, and moral purchasing. All that is Haram was prohibited for a good reason and for a better life on individuals or economics or societies and that's why I don't see any disadvantage;
4. I support the converting to Islamic Banking because Islamic banking is an example of full-reserve banking. Islamic banking is a complete system of social and economic justice. It deals with property rights, the incentive system, and

Table 2. Overall comparison between Islamic and western banking

	Islamic-Banking	Western-Banking
Sharia compatible	Yes	No
profits	added value on goods sold	Interest
Goods	Mandatory	Not mandatory
Cash loans	No	Yes
Profit-on-investments	Shared risk (Bank & customer)	Predetermined
Core-business	Emphasis on viability of projects/ goods	Emphasis on credit worthiness of customer
Customer-relationship	Partnership, buyer, seller, etc…	Creditor/Debtor

Table 3. Difference between customer and bank perspective in Islamic Banking

	Customer-Perspective	Bank-Perspective
Advantages	Compatible with Sharia Known & fixed cost Shared risk with the bank	Profit margin is known Customer's satisfaction Availability of tangible assets (Goods)
Disadvantages	Higher profit margin Cannot benefit from Discounted Interest rate (if decreased) Cannot be in Cash (goods must be available)	Cannot benefit from Discounted Interest rate (if increased) More difficult (availability of goods) Constraints of Sharia

the allocation of resources, economic freedom and decision-making and the proper role of government.

Customer Focus

- **Understand and Respond to Customer Needs:**
  - Using appropriate questioning techniques;
  - Implementing customer feedback systems and acting on findings;
  - Building and maintaining excellent relationships with customers;
  - Ensuring diversity policies and practices are followed when dealing with customers;
- **Deliver Excellent Customer Service:**
  - Using skills and resources to deliver the best possible service;
  - Dealing with customer requests, queries and problems;
  - Meeting customer service standards and requirements;
  - Monitoring customer service performance and taking action to resolve poor quality service;
  - Sharing good practice and identifying opportunities for customer service improvements cross the organizational boundaries.

REFERENCES

Al Nasser, L. (2010). *The Differences between Sukuk and Bonds. Gulf Business Intelligence.*

Al-Tamimi, H. (2010). *Sharjah Islamic Bank. University of Sharjah.*

AME Info. (2009). *National Bank of Kuwait acquires 13.2% stake of KIA's holding in Rival Bank.* Available at: http://www.ameinfo.com/204572.html

Anonymous, . (2011). *Reappraising the Islamic financial sector. Harvard Law School.*

Anonymous. (2011). Islamic microfinance and socially responsible investments. Microfinance at the University, University of Torino.

Bahari, Z. (2009). The Changes Of Product Structure In Islamic Banking: Case Study Of Malaysia.*International Conference On Islamic Perspective On Management And Finance.*

CSC. (2011). *Future-Proof Banking Strategies with Agile Technology.* Computer Science Corporation.

Garbois, C., Gourp, C., von Pock, A., & Bhatnagar, M. (2012). *The Future Of Islamic Banking*. A. T. Kearny.

Hussain, K., & Mehboob, F. (2008). Hedging Market Risk in Islamic Finance. *World Commerce Review*, *2*(3), 22–27.

Jobst, A., & Sole, J. (2012). *Operative Principles of Islamic Derivatives – Towards a Coherent Theory*. International Monetary Fund.

Malkawi, B. (2011, January). Financial Derivatives In The West And In Islamic Finance: A Comparative Approach. *Banking Law Journal*, *128*(1), 50.

Mateeha, F. (2006). *Differences and similarities between operating lease contracts*. College of Management Since, PAF-Karachi Institute of Economics and Technology.

Najjar, G. (2012). *High Fliers Program Cohort III: Future Proofing*. Executive Education BANK Program.

Power of Attorney. (n.d.). In *U.S. Legal Dictionary*. Academic Press.

Rao, S. (2009). Islamic Finance WIKI. Plug into your hard-wired happiness. *Islamic Finance Encyclopedia*.

Said, P., & Javaid, F. (2012). Handbook of Islamic Banking Products & Services. Academic Press.

Saudi Hollandi Bank. (2012). *Shariah Compliant Profit Rate Hedging*. Author.

Usman, H. (2013). Islamic Finance and Socially Responsible Investment. *CFA Institute Magazine*, *24*(2), 2–8.

Compilation of References

AACSB. (2014). *Business School Data Guide.* Retrieved January 03, 2015 from: http://www.aacsb.edu/~/media/AACSB/Publications/data-trends-booklet/2014-business-school-data-guide.ashx

Abbasi, M. Z. (2009). Legal analysis of agency theory: An inquiry into the nature of corporation. *International Journal of Law and Management, 51*(6), 401–420. doi:10.1108/17542430911005936

Abdnor, J. (1988). The Spirit of Entrepreneurship. *Journal of Small Business Management, 1*(3), 1–6.

Adams, R. H. Jr, & Page, J. (2003). Poverty, inequality and growth in selected Middle East and North Africa countries, 1980–2000. *World Development, 31*(12), 2027–2048. doi:10.1016/j.worlddev.2003.04.004

Adendorff, C., Venter, E., & Boshoff, C. (2008). The impact of family harmony on governance practices in South African Greek family businesses. *Management Dynamics: Journal of the Southern African Institute for Management Scientists, 17*(3), 28–44.

Admin. (2011). *The three circle model - Family business framework.* Retrieved Sept.9, 2015 from http:/www.symcoandco.com/resources/article/family-business-framework

Afifi, M. (2002). Compatibility between the characteristics of family businesses and the requirements of successful change management. Family Business Forum in the Arab World, Jeddah, Saudi Arabia.

Agrawal, A., & Mandelker, G. (1987). Managerial Incentives and Corporate Investment and Financing Decisions. *The Journal of Finance, 42*(4), 823–837. doi:10.1111/j.1540-6261.1987.tb03914.x

Ajzen, I., & Fishbein, M. (1980). *Understanding Attitudes and Predicting Small Behavior.* Englewood Cliffs, NJ: Prentice-Hall.

Al Ardhi, M. M. (2016, June 4). Arabs Unseen: Golden age of innovation looms for Arab world's entrepreneurs. *The National.* Retrieved July 30, 2016, from http://www.thenational.ae/business/economy/arabs-unseen-golden-age-of-innovation-looms-for-arab-worlds-entrepreneurs

Al Nasser, L. (2010). *The Differences between Sukuk and Bonds. Gulf Business Intelligence.*

Albawaba. (2015, November 22). *MENA must create 100 million jobs by 2020 to meet unemployment numbers.* Retrieved July 28, 2016, from http://www.albawaba.com/business/mena-must-create-100-million-jobs-2020-meet-unemployment-numbers-771664

Al-Dajani, H., & Marlow, S. (2010). Impact of women's home-based enterprise on family dynamics: Evidence from Jordan. *International Small Business Journal,28*(5), 470-486.

Alfaro, L., Chanda, A., Kalemli-Ozcan, S., & Sayek, S. (2004). FDI and economic growth: The role of local financial markets. *Journal of International Economics, 64*(1), 89–112. doi:10.1016/S0022-1996(03)00081-3

Al-Ghazali, B. M., Yusoff, R. M., & Sadi, M. A. (2013). Women Entrepreneurs in Bahrain: Motivations and Barriers. *Jurnal Teknologi, 64*(2), 139–143. doi:10.11113/jt.v64.2251

Allen, S. (2006). *Entrepreneurship is an attitude.* Retrieved from http://entrepreneurs.about.com/b/2006/10/07/

Al-Masri, S. (2016, February 24). *Numbers Don't Lie: Self-Employment Is Thriving In The Middle East.* Retrieved July 28, 2016, from https://www.entrepreneur.com/article/271238

Al-Tamimi, H. (2010). *Sharjah Islamic Bank. University of Sharjah.*

Alvord, H. S., Brown, D., & Letts, W. C. (2002). *Social Entrepreneurship and Social Transformation: An Exploratory Study.* Harvard University: Hauser Center for Nonprofit Organizations Working Paper No. 15, 1-26.

AME Info. (2009). *National Bank of Kuwait acquires 13.2% stake of KIA's holding in Rival Bank.* Available at: http://www.ameinfo.com/204572.html

Ammar, W. (2003). *Health System and Reform in Lebanon.* Beirut: World Health Organization Eastern Mediterranean Regional Office.

Ammar, W., & Wakim, R. (2005). *Lebanon's Hospital Accreditation Program: A case study.* Beirut: Ministry of Public Health.

Anderson, N., De Dreu, C. K. W., & Nijstad, D. A. (2004). The routinization of innovation research: A constructively critical review of the state-of-the-science. *Journal of Organizational Behavior, 25*(2), 147–172. doi:10.1002/job.236

Angeles, M. S., & Soriano, D. R. (2011). Human Resource Management and Corporate Entrepreneurship. *International Journal of Manpower, 32*(1), 6–13. doi:10.1108/01437721111121198

Anonymous. (2011). Islamic microfinance and socially responsible investments. Microfinance at the University, University of Torino.

Anonymous, . (2011). *Reappraising the Islamic financial sector. Harvard Law School.*

Antoncic, B., & Hisrich, R. D. (2000). Intrapreneurship modeling in transition economies: A comparison of Slovenia and the United States. *Journal of Developmental Entrepreneurship*, *5*(1), 21–40.

Antoncic, B., & Hisrich, R. D. (2003). Clarifying the intrapreneurship concept. *Journal of Small Business and Enterprise Development*, *10*(1), 7–25. doi:10.1108/14626000310461187

Aramco. (2016, May 30). *Aramco Entrepreneurship Center*. Retrieved July 29, 2016, from http://www.saudiaramco.com/en/home/citizenship/economy/aramco-entrepreneurship-center.html

Armstrong, P. (2005). *Crtique of Entrepreneurship*. New York: Palgrave Macmillan. doi:10.1057/9780230554955

Aronoff, C. E., & Ward, J. L. (2000). *La prueba suprema de la grandeza familiar: La elección del nuevo líder*. McGraw-Hill.

Arzeni, S. (1992). Encouraging the Entrepreneur. Organization for Economic Cooperation and Development. *The OECD Observer*, (174), 19.

Asad Sadi, M., & Henderson, J. C. (2007). In search of greener pastures: Al-Marai and dairy food business in Saudi Arabia. *British Food Journal*, *109*(8), 637–647. doi:10.1108/00070700710772426

Astrachan, J. H., & McMillan, K. S. (2003). *Conflict and communication in the family business (No. 16)*. Marietta, GA: Family Enterprise Publisher.

Ataya, L. (2016, May 10). *An Open Call To Innovators: The Middle East Needs More Women Entrepreneurs*. Retrieved July 29, 2016, from https://www.entrepreneur.com/article/275417

Audretsch, D. B. (Ed.). (2003). *Handbook of Entrepreneurship Research: An Interdiciplinary Survey and Introduction*. Dordrecht, The Netherlands: Kluwer Academic Publishers.

Audretsch, D. Z., & Acs, Z. J. (1991). Innovation and Size at the Firm Level. *Southern Economic Journal*, *57*(3), 739–744. doi:10.2307/1059787

Axelrod, R. (1997). *The complexity of Cooperation*. Princeton, NJ: Princeton University Press.

Axelrod, R. M. (1997). *The complexity of cooperation: Agent-based models of competition and collaboration*. Princeton, NJ: Princeton University Press.

Ayranci, A. E., & Ayranci, E. (2015). A Research on Job Satisfaction Factors of Private Entrepreneurs: The Case of Beylikduzu Organized Industrial Zone. *Procedia: Social and Behavioral Sciences*, *195*(1), 268–277. doi:10.1016/j.sbspro.2015.06.156

Badulescu, A., & Dodescu, A. (2010). Entrepreneurial training and attitude toward entrepreneurship: Assessing the impact of Antr ES programme.*Proceedings of the 5th WSEAS International Conference on Economy and Management Transformation, 2.*

Bahari, Z. (2009). The Changes Of Product Structure In Islamic Banking: Case Study Of Malaysia. *International Conference On Islamic Perspective On Management And Finance.*

Bakir, H. A. (2001). Sustainable wastewater management for small communities in the Middle East and North Africa. *Journal of Environmental Management*, *61*(4), 319–328. doi:10.1006/jema.2000.0414 PMID:11383104

Ballesteros Perez, M. C. G. C., & Pastor-Ferrando, J. P. (2010). Analysis of construction projects by means of value curves. *International Journal of Project Management*, *28*(7), 719–731. doi:10.1016/j.ijproman.2009.11.003

Baporikar, N. (2002). *Entrepreneurship and Small Industry (Theory and Practice)*. Mumbai, India: Himalaya Publishing House.

Baporikar, N. (2007). *Entrepreneurship Development and Project Management*. Mumbai, India: Himalaya Publishing House.

Baporikar, N. (2011). *Entrepreneurship. In Emergent Trends* (1st ed., p. 14). VDM Verlag.

Baporikar, N. (2014). Strategic Management Overview and SME in Globalized World. In K. Todorov & D. Smallbone (Eds.), *Handbook of Research on Strategic Management in Small and Medium Enterprises* (pp. 22–39). Hershey, PA: Business Science Reference. doi:10.4018/978-1-4666-5962-9.ch002

Baporikar, N. (2014). Youth Entrepreneurship in Indian Scenario. *International Journal of Asian Business and Information Management*, *5*(2), 74–84. doi:10.4018/ijabim.2014040106

Baporikar, N. (2014b). Information Strategy as Enabler of Competitive Advantage. *International Journal of Strategic Information Technology and Applications*, *5*(1), 30–41. doi:10.4018/ijsita.2014010103

Baporikar, N. (2015a). Entrepreneurship in Sultanate of Oman: A Case Approach. *International Journal of Asian Business and Information Management*, *6*(4), 14–26. doi:10.4018/IJABIM.2015100102

Baporikar, N. (2015b). Role of Entrepreneurship in Networked Indian Economy. In P. Ordóñez de Pablos (Ed.), *Technological Solutions for Sustainable Business Practice in Asia* (pp. 36–59). Hershey, PA: Business Science Reference. doi:10.4018/978-1-4666-8462-1.ch003

Baporikar, N. (2015c). Effect of National Culture on Development of International Business in the Sultanate of Oman. In B. Christiansen (Ed.), *Handbook of Research on Global Business Opportunities* (pp. 268–288). Hershey, PA: Business Science Reference. doi:10.4018/978-1-4666-6551-4.ch013

Baporikar, N. (2015d). Societal Influence on the Cognitive Aspects of Entrepreneurship. [IJCESC]. *International Journal of Civic Engagement and Social Change*, *2*(4), 1–15. doi:10.4018/ijcesc.2015100101

Barakat, K. L. (1993). *Proceedings of the Expert Group Meeting on Creation of Indigenous Entrepreneurship and Opportunities from Small- and Medium-Scale Industrial Investment*. Damascus, Syria: Academic Press.

Barnes, L., & Hershon, S. (1976). Transferring power in the family business. *Harvard Business Review*, (July-August), 105–114.

Barnett, C. G. (1993). *Defining Entrepreneurship.* Paper delivered at the 7th annual conference of small business, Southern Africa.

Barringer, B. A., & Bluedorn, A. C. (1999). The Relationship Between Corporate Entrepreneurship and Strategic Management. *Strategic Management Journal*, *20*(5), 421–444. doi:10.1002/(SICI)1097-0266(199905)20:5<421::AID-SMJ30>3.0.CO;2-O

Barro, R. J. (1990). Government spending in a simple model of endogenous growth. *Journal of Political Economy*, *98*(5), 103–125. doi:10.1086/261726

Barro, R. J. (1991). Economic growth in a cross section of countries. *The Quarterly Journal of Economics*, *106*(2), 407–443. doi:10.2307/2937943

Barro, R. J., Mankiw, N. G., & Sala-i-Martin, X. (1995). *Capital mobility in neoclassical models of growth (No. w4206).*National Bureau of Economic Research.

Bartels, K. G. (1973). *Stranger groups in developing societies: the Lebanese in Liberia and Ghana*. Harvard College.

Bastian, B., & Zali, S. (in press). Entrepreneurial motives and their antecedents of men and women in North Africa and the Middle East. *Gender in Management*, *31*(7).

Bates, T., & Nucci, A. R. (1990). *An analysis of small business size and rate of discontinuance.* US Department of Commerce, Bureau of the Census.

Batrouney, T. R. (1985). *The Lebanese in Australia.* Melbourne: AE Press.

Baumol, W. J. (2006). *Entrepreneurship and Invention: Toward Their Microeconomic Value Theory.* Special Session on Entrepreneurship, Innovation and Growth I: Theoretical Approach, American Economic Association Meetings.

Baumol, W. J. (1968). Entrepreneurship in Economic Theory. *The American Economic Review*, *58*, 64–71.

Baumol, W. J. (1993). *Entrepreneurship, Management, and the Structure of Payoffs*. Cambridge, MA: MIT Press.

Baumol, W. J. (2002). *The Free-Market Innovation Machine: Analyzing the Growth Miracle of Capitalism.* Princeton, NJ: Princeton University Press. doi:10.1515/9781400851638

Baumol, W. J., Litan, R. E., & Schramm, C. J. (2007). *Good Capitalism, Bad Capitalism, and the Economics of Growth and Prosperity*. New Haven, CT: Yale University Press.

Baysinger, B., & Butler, H. (1985). Corporate governance and the board of directors: Performance effects of changes in board composition. *Journal of Law Economics and Organization*, *1*(1), 101–124.

Becker, T. E. (2013). Nepotism and the Commitment of Relevant Parties. *Nepotism in Organizations*, 129.

Beckhard, R., & Dyer, W. G. (1983). Managing continuity in the family-owned business. *Organizational Dynamics*, *12*(1), 5–12. doi:10.1016/0090-2616(83)90022-0

Beck, T., & Honohan, P. (2008). *Finance for all? Policies and pitfalls in expanding access* (Vol. 41792). World Bank Publications.

Beetham, D. (Ed.). (1994). *Defining and measuring democracy* (Vol. 36). Sage.

Begley, T. M., Wee-Liang, T., Larasati, A. B., Rab, A., & Zamora, E. (1997). *The Relationship Between Social-Cultural Dimensions and Interest in Starting A Business- A Multi-Country Study, Frontiers of Entrepreneurship Research.* Wellesley, MA: Babson College.

Bellone, G., & Goerl, G. F. (1992). Reconciling public entrepreneurship and democracy. *Public Administration Review*, *52*(2), 130. doi:10.2307/976466

Benhabib, J., & Spiegel, M. M. (1994). The role of human capital in economic development evidence from aggregate cross-country data. *Journal of Monetary Economics*, *34*(2), 143–173. doi:10.1016/0304-3932(94)90047-7

Bergh, A., & Magnus, H. (2011). Government size and growth: A survey and interpretation of the evidence. *Journal of Economic Surveys*, *25*(5), 872–897. doi:10.1111/j.1467-6419.2011.00697.x

Berle, A., & Means, G. (1932). *The Modern Corporation and Private Property*. New York: Macmillan Co.

Berl, R., Powell, T., & Williamson, N. (1984). Industrial Sales force Satisfaction and Performance with Herzbergs Theory. *Industrial Marketing Management*, *13*(1), 11–19. doi:10.1016/0019-8501(84)90003-8

Berns, M., Townend, A., Khayat, Z., Balagopal, B., Reeves, M., Hopkins, M. S., & Kruschwitz, N. (2009). The business of sustainability: What it means to managers now. *MIT Sloan Management Review*, *51*(1), 20–26.

Berrone, P., Cruz, C., & Gomez-Mejia, L. R. (2012). Socio-emotional wealth in family firms theoretical dimensions, assessment approaches, and agenda for future research. *Family Business Review*, *25*(3), 258–279. doi:10.1177/0894486511435355

Bhargava, S. (Ed.). (2007). *Developmental Aspects of Entrepreneurship*. New Delhi: Academic Press.

Bhide, A. (2000). *The origin and evolution of new businesses*. New York: Oxford University Press.

Binder. (1994). *The quest for growth: A survey of UK private companies*. London: Author.

Bird, C. H., & Romanelli, E. E. (2001). *The entrepreneurship Dynamic: Origins of entrepreneurship and the evolution of industries*. Stanford, CA: Stanford University Press.

Birdsall, N., Ross, D., & Sabot, R. (1995). Inequality and growth reconsidered: Lessons from East Asia. *The World Bank Economic Review*, *9*(3), 477–508. doi:10.1093/wber/9.3.477

Birley, S. (1985). The role of networks in the entrepreneurial process. *Journal of Business Venturing*, *1*(1), 107–117. doi:10.1016/0883-9026(85)90010-2

Blair, M. (1995). *Ownership and Control*. Rethinking Corporate Governance for the Twentieth Century.

Block, J. H. (2012). R&D investments in family and founder firms: An agency perspective. *Journal of Business Venturing*, *27*(2), 248–265. doi:10.1016/j.jbusvent.2010.09.003

Blodgett, M. S., Dumas, C., & Zanzi, A. (2011). Emerging trends in global ethics: A comparative study of US and international family business values. *Journal of Business Ethics*, *99*(1), 29–38. doi:10.1007/s10551-011-1164-7

Bocatto, E., Gispert, C., & Rialp, J. (2010). Family-Owned Business Succession: The Influence of Pre-performance in the Nomination of Family and Nonfamily Members: Evidence from Spanish Firms. *Journal of Small Business Management*, *48*(4), 497–523. doi:10.1111/j.1540-627X.2010.00306.x

Bonazzi, L., & Islam, S.M.N. (2007). Agency theory and corporate governance: A study of the effectiveness of board in their monitoring of the CEO. *Journal of Modelling in Management, 2*(1).

Bonnett, C., & Furnham, A. (1991). Who Wants to be An Entrepreneur? A Study of Adolescents Interested in a Young Enterprise Scheme. *Journal of Economic Psychology*, *12*(3), 465–478. doi:10.1016/0167-4870(91)90027-Q

Bostjan, A. N., & Hisrich, R. D. (2000). Intrapreneurship modeling in transition economies: A comparison of Slovenia and the United State. *Journal of Developmental Entrepreneurship*, *5*(1), 21.

Boyd, N. G., & Vozikis, G. S. (1994). The influence of self-efficacy on the development of entrepreneurial intentions and actions. *Entrepreneurship Theory and Practice*, *18*, 63–63.

Braun, M., & Sharma, A. (2007). Should the CEO also be the Chair of the Board? An Empirical Examination of Family-Controlled Public Firms. *Family Business Review*, *20*(2), 111–126. doi:10.1111/j.1741-6248.2007.00090.x

Brenes, E. R., Madrigal, K., & Requena, B. (2011). Corporate governance and family business performance. *Journal of Business Research*, *64*(3), 280–285. doi:10.1016/j.jbusres.2009.11.013

Brennan, M. J. (1994). Incentives, Rationality, and Society. *Journal of Applied Corporate Finance*, *7*(2), 31–39. doi:10.1111/j.1745-6622.1994.tb00403.x

Bruno, G., De Bonis, R., & Silvestrini, A. (2012). Do financial systems converge? New evidence from financial assets in OECD countries. *Journal of Comparative Economics*, *40*(1), 141–155. doi:10.1016/j.jce.2011.09.003

Bruyat, C. A., & Julien, P. A. (2001). Defining the field of research in entrepreneurship. *Journal of Business Venturing*, *16*(2), 165–180. doi:10.1016/S0883-9026(99)00043-9

BudisJ. (2014). Retrieved fromhttp://www.newrepublic.com/article/112278/paul-krugman-vs-joseph-stiglitz-inequality-slowing-recovery

Burke & Thurik. (2009). *Blue Ocean versus Competitive Strategy: Theory and Evidence*. Erasmus Research Institute of Management.

Burns, P. (2008). *Corporate Entrepreneurship*. Palgrave Macmillan.

Burt, R. O. (1992). *Structural Holes: The social structure of competition*. Cambridge, MA: Harvard University Press.

Burt, R. S. (1992). *Structural holes: The social structure of competition*. Cambridge, MA: Harvard University Press.

Burt, R. S. (2000). The network structure of social capital. *Research in Organizational Behavior*, *22*, 345–423. doi:10.1016/S0191-3085(00)22009-1

Cantillon, R. (1755). *Essay On The Nature Du Commerce in General*. London: Fletcher.

Cantillon, R. (1755). *Essay on the nature of general commerce*. London: Macmillan.

Carayannis, E. G., & Papadopoulos, C. B. (2011). The innovation diplomacy concept and the Hellenic-American innovation bridge as a special case-in-point. *J Knowl Econ*, *2*(3), 257–326. doi:10.1007/s13132-011-0056-5

Carland, J. W., Hoy, F., Boulton, W. R., & Carland, J. A. C. (1984). Differentiating entrepreneurs from small business owners: A conceptualization. *Academy of Management Review*, *9*(2), 354–359.

Casson, M. (1982). *The Entrepreneur: An Economic Theory*. Totowa, NJ: Barnes & Noble Books.

Casson, M. Y. (Ed.). (2006). *The Oxford Handbook of Entrepreneurship*. New York: Oxford University Press.

Casson, M., & Buckley, P. J. (2010). *A theory of cooperation in international business*. Palgrave Macmillan.

Casson, M., & Buckley, P. J. (2010). Models of the multinational enterprise. In *The Multinational Enterprise Revisited* (pp. 147–176). Palgrave Macmillan.

Cater, J. J., III. (2006). *Stepping out of the shadow: The leadership qualities of successors in family business* (Doctoral dissertation). Wake Forest University.

Cates, N. (1987). S.A.M. *Advanced Management Journal*, *52*(3), 41.

Cauthorn, R. C. (1989). *Contributions to a Theory of Entrepreneurship*. Garland Publishing.

Chakour, D. Z. (2001). *Entrepreneurship in Lebanon- Situation and Informational Framework*. American University of Beirut.

Chamlou, N., Klapper, L., & Muzi, S. (2008). *The environment for women's entrepreneurship in the Middle East and North Africa*. World Bank Publications. doi:10.1596/978-0-8213-7495-5

Chang, J. (2000). Model of Corporate Entrepreneurship. *Intrapreneurship and Exopreneurship, 12*(4), 69–104.

Charbaji, A. (2009). The effect of globalization on commitment to ethical corporate governance and corporate social responsibility in Lebanon. *Social Responsibility Journal., 5*(3), 376–387. doi:10.1108/17471110910977294

Chau, F., Deesomsak, R., & Wang, J. (2014). Political uncertainty and stock market volatility in the Middle East and North African (MENA) countries. *Journal of International Financial Markets, Institutions and Money, 28*, 1–19. doi:10.1016/j.intfin.2013.10.008

Chen, C., Green, R., & Crick, A. (1998). The self-efficacy expectations and occupational preferences of females and males. *Journal of Business Venturing, 13*(4), 295–316. doi:10.1016/S0883-9026(97)00029-3

Chen, J., Zhu, Z., & Anquan, W. (2005). A system model for corporate entrepreneurship. *International Journal of Manpower, 26*(9), 529–543. doi:10.1108/01437720510625449

Chen, Y. F., & Lai, M. C. (2010). Factors influencing the entrepreneurial attitude of Taiwanese tertiary-level business students. *Journal of Social Behavior and Personality, 38*(1), 1–12. doi:10.2224/sbp.2010.38.1.1

Chesson, P. (2012). Scale transition theory: Its aims, motivations and predictions. *Ecological Complexity, 10*, 52–68. doi:10.1016/j.ecocom.2011.11.002

Ching-Chow Yang, K.-J. Y. (2011). An integrated model of value creation based on the refined Kanos model and the blue ocean strategy. *Total Quality Management & Business Excellence, 22*(9), 925–940. doi:10.1080/14783363.2011.611358

Chris, I. M. (2000). *Cooperative Entrepreneurship: The Challenge for Unions in the New Millennuim*. International Labor Organization.

Chung, C. N., & Luo, X. R. (2013). Leadership succession and firm performance in an emerging economy: Successor origin, relational embeddedness, and legitimacy. *Strategic Management Journal, 34*(3), 338–357. doi:10.1002/smj.2011

Chung, L., & Gibbons, P. (1997). Corporate entrepreneurship: The roles of ideology and social capital. *Group & Organization Management, 22*(1), 10–30. doi:10.1177/1059601197221004

Churchill, N. C., & Hatten, K. J. (1997). Non-market-based transfers of wealth and power: A research framework for family business. *Family Business Review, 10*(1), 53–67. doi:10.1111/j.1741-6248.1997.00053.x

Clawson, M., Landsberg, H. H., & Alexander, L. T. (1971). *The agricultural potential of the Middle East*. Academic Press.

Cohen, D., & Soto, M. (2007). Growth and human capital: Good data, good results. *Journal of Economic Growth, 12*(1), 51–76. doi:10.1007/s10887-007-9011-5

Collins, O. F., & Moore, D. G. (1964). The enterprising man. East Lansing, MI: Bureau of Business and Economic Research, Graduate School of Business Administration, Michigan State University.

Collins, O., & Moore, D. S. (1964). *The enterprisingman.* MSU Business Studies, Michigan State University.

Contessi, S., De Nicola, F., & Li, L. (2012). *International trade, female labor, and entrepreneurship in MENA countries.* FRB of St. Louis Working Paper.

Core, J., Holthausen, R., & Larcker, D. (1999). Corporate governance, chief executive officer compensation, and firm performance. *Journal of Applied Corporate Finance.*

Covin, J. G., & Slevin, D. P. (1986), The development and testing of an organizational-level entrepreneurship scale. Frontiers of Entrepreneurship Research, 1(3), 628-639.

Covin, J. G., & Slevin, D. P. (1991). A conceptual model of entrepreneurship as firm behavior. *Entrepreneurship Theory and Practice, 16*(1), 7–25.

Creane, S., Goyal, R., Mobarak, A. M., & Sab, R. (2006). Measuring financial development in the Middle East and North Africa: A new database. *IMF Staff Papers*, 479–511.

Creţu, R. F. (2012). Corporate governance and corporate diversification strategies. *Review Of International Comparative Management/Revista De Management Comparat International, 13*(4), 621-633.

CSC. (2011). *Future-Proof Banking Strategies with Agile Technology.* Computer Science Corporation.

Dahl, R. A. (1973). *Polyarchy: participation and opposition.* Yale University Press.

Daily, C. M., & Dollinger, M. J. (1993). An empirical examination of ownership structure and family and professionally managed firms. *Family Business Review*, (5): 117–136.

Dana, L.-P. (Ed.). (2007). Handbook of Research on Ethnic Minority Entrepreneurship. Norhthampton, UK: Edward Elgar Publishing Inc. doi:10.4337/9781847209962

Dana, L. (1997). A contrast of Argentina and Uruguay: The effects of government policy on entrepreneurship. *Journal of Small Business Management, 35*(2), 99.

Danco, K. (1981). *From the other side of the bed: A woman looks at life in the family business.* Cleveland, OH: University Press.

Dash, S. (2016, April 17). *Family First: Securing Continued Growth For Family Businesses In The MENA Region.* Retrieved July 30, 2016, from https://www.entrepreneur.com/article/274231

Davies, J., Hides, M., & Powell, J. (2002). Defining the development needs of entrepreneurs in SME's. *Emerald Insight, 44*(8/9), 24.

Davis, P. S., & Harveston, P. D. (1998). The influence of family on the family business succession process: A multi-generational perspective. *Entrepreneurship Theory and Practice, 22*, 31-54.

Davis, F. (1993). User acceptance of information technology: System characteristics, user perceptions and behavioral impacts. *International Journal of Man-Machine Studies*, *38*(3), 475–487. doi:10.1006/imms.1993.1022

Davis, F. D., Bagozzi, R. P., & Warshaw, P. R. (1989). User Acceptance of Computer Technology: A Comparison of Two Theoretical Models. *Management Science*, *35*(8), 982–1003. doi:10.1287/mnsc.35.8.982

Davisson, P. (2008). *The Entrepreneur Research Challenge.* Edwrard Elgar Publishing, Inc. doi:10.4337/9781848442764

Dawson, M. (2005). *The Consumer Trap: Big Business Marketing in American Life*. Urbana, IL: University of Illinois Press.

De Bruin, A. A. (Ed.). (2003). *Entrepreneurship: New Perspectives in a Global Age*. Hampshire, UK: Ashgate Publishing Limited.

De Jordy, H. (1988). Ottawa introduces national policy for entrepreneurs. *Toronto Star*, p. B3.

de Vries, M. F. K. (1994). The dynamics of family controlled firms: The good and the bad news. *Organizational Dynamics*, *21*(3), 59–71. doi:10.1016/0090-2616(93)90071-8

Dearlove, D. (1999). *Business the Bill Gates way: 10 secrets of the world's richest business leader*. Oxford, UK: Capstone.

Dearlove, D. S. (1999). *Business the Bill Gates way*. San Francisco, CA: Capstone Publishing Limited.

Dechow, P. M., & Sloan, R. G. (1991). Executive Incentives and the Horizon Problem: An Empirical Investigation. *Journal of Accounting and Economics*, *14*(1), 51–89. doi:10.1016/0167-7187(91)90058-S

Delmar, F., & Davidsson, P. (2000). Where do they come from? Prevalence and characteristics of nascent entrepreneurs. *Entrepreneurship & Regional Development*, *12*(1), 1–23. doi:10.1080/089856200283063

Demirgüç-Kunt, A., & Levine, R. (Eds.). (2004). *Financial structure and economic growth: A cross-country comparison of banks, markets, and development*. MIT Press.

Denis, D. J., & Denis, D. K. (1995). Performance Changes Following Top Management Dismissals. *The Journal of Finance*, *50*(4), 1029–1057. doi:10.1111/j.1540-6261.1995.tb04049.x

Denis, D. J., Denis, D. K., & Sarin, A. (1997). Agency Problems, Equity Ownership, and Corporate Diversification. *The Journal of Finance*, *52*(1), 135–160. doi:10.1111/j.1540-6261.1997.tb03811.x

Denscombe, M. (1998). *The Good Research Guide*. Buckingham, UK: Open University Press.

Devlin, J. (2010). *Challenges of Economic Development in the Middle East and North Africa Region* (Vol. 8). World Scientific. doi:10.1142/6762

Dib, K. (2004). *Warlords and Merchants: The Lebanese Busiess and Political Establishment.* Reading: Garnet Publishing Limited.

Djeflat, A. (2002). *National systems of innovation in the MENA region.* World Bank Working paper/ Maghtech. http://lnweb18.worldbank.org/mna/mena.nsf/attachments/innovation/$file/rapfin.pdf

Duh, M. (2012). *Family businesses: the extensiveness of succession problems and possible solutions.* INTECH Open Access Publisher.

Dunbar, C., & Nasr, S. (1976). *Les Classes Sociales au Liban.* Paris: Presses De La Fondation Nationale Des Sciences Politiques.

Dyer, W. G. (2003). The Family: The Missing Variable in Organizational Research. *Entrepreneurship Theory and Practice, 27*(4), 401-416.

Easterbrook, F. H. (1984). Two Agency Cost Explanations of Dividends. *The American Economic Review*, *74*(4), 650–659.

Easterly, W., & Levine, R. (2001). What have we learned from a decade of empirical research on growth? Its Not Factor Accumulation: Stylized Facts and Growth Models. *The World Bank Economic Review*, *15*(2), 177–219. doi:10.1093/wber/15.2.177

Eisenhardt, M. K. (1989).. . *Agency Theory: An Assessment and Review, The Academy of Management Review, Vol*, *14*(1), 57–74.

Ekanem, I. (2007). Insider Accounts: A qualitative research method for small firms. *Journal of Small Business and Enterprise Development*, *14*(1), 105–117. doi:10.1108/14626000710727926

Erdem, F. (2010). *Family Business Reputation: A Literature Review and Some Research Questions. Electronic Journal of Family Business Studies*, 4(2).

Erkkila, K. (2000). *Entrepreneurial Education: Mapping the Debates in the United States, the United Kingdom and Finland.* New York: Garland Publishing.

Ernst & Young. (2012). *Built to last Family businesses lead the way to sustainable growth.* Available: http://www.ey.com/Publication/vwLUAssets/Built_to_Last/$FILE/ Built_to_Last.pdf

Erogul, M. S., & McCrohan, D. (2008). Preliminary investigation of Emirati women entrepreneurs in the UAE. *African Journal of Business Management*, *2*(10), 177–185.

ESCWA. (2001). *ESCWA Report 2001. "The Role of SMEs in National Economies in East Asia.* ESCWA.

Etzo, S., & Collender, G. (2010). Briefing: The mobile phone revolution in Africa: rhetoric or reality? *African Affairs*, *109/437*(437), 659–668. doi:10.1093/afraf/adq045

Ezell, H. (1993). Economic Fears Turn Younger Americans to Entrepreneurship. Journal of Bus[ness. *Record*, *1*(3), 23–32.

Falcone, T. A. (2005). Entrepreneurship: A Diverse Concept in a Diverse World.*2005 USASBE/SBI National Conference*, (pp. 1-8). Academic Press.

Fama, E. F. (1980). Agency Problems and the Theory of the Firm. *The Journal of Political Economy, Vol*, *88*(2), 288–307. doi:10.1086/260866

Fama, E. F., & Jensen, M. C. (1983). Separation of Ownership and Control. *The Journal of Law & Economics*, *88*(2), 301–325. doi:10.1086/467037

Farazmand, A. (2014). *Crisis and emergency management: Theory and practice*. Boca Raton, FL: CRC Press-Taylor & Francis. doi:10.1201/b16715

Fasano-Filho, M. U., & Goyal, R. (2004). Emerging strains in GCC labor markets (No. 4-71). International Monetary Fund.

Fawaz, L. T. (1983). *Merchants and migrants in nineteenth-century Beirut* (Vol. 18). Harvard Univ Pr. doi:10.4159/harvard.9780674333550

Fawzy, S. (Ed.). (2002). *Globalization and firm competitiveness in the Middle East and North Africa region* (Vol. 3). World Bank Publications. doi:10.1596/0-8213-4989-9

File, K. M., & Prince, R. A. (1996). Attributions for family business failure: The heirs perspective. *Family Business Review*, *9*(2), 171–184. doi:10.1111/j.1741-6248.1996.00171.x

Floyd, S. P. (2000). Strategizing throughout the Organization: Managing Role Conflict in Strategic Renewal. *Academy of Management Review*, *25*(1), 154–177.

Forbes, K. J. (2000). A Reassessment of the Relationship between Inequality and Growth. *The American Economic Review*, *90*(4), 869–887. doi:10.1257/aer.90.4.869

Frankel, J. A., & Romer, D. (1999). Does Trade Cause Growth? *The American Economic Review*, *89*(3), 379–399. doi:10.1257/aer.89.3.379

Frynas, G., & Mellahi, K. (2011). *Global Strategic Management*. New York: Oxford University Press.

Gagnon, M. P., Godin, G., Gagne, C., Fortin, J. P., Lamothe, L., Reinharz, D., & Cloutier, A. (2003). An adaptation of the theory of interpersonal behavior to the study of telemedicine adoption by physicians. *International Journal of Medical Informatics*, *71*(2-3), 103–115. doi:10.1016/S1386-5056(03)00094-7 PMID:14519403

Galloway, L., & Brown, W. (2002). Entrepreneurship Education at University, A Driver in the Creation of High Growth Firms? *Education + Training*, *44*(8/9), 398–405. doi:10.1108/00400910210449231

Galor, O. (2011). *Inequality, human capital formation and the process of development (No. w17058)*. National Bureau of Economic Research. doi:10.3386/w17058

Galor, O., & Moav, O. (2004). From physical to human capital accumulation: Inequality and the process of development. *The Review of Economic Studies*, *71*(4), 1001–1026. doi:10.1111/0034-6527.00312

Garbois, C., Gourp, C., von Pock, A., & Bhatnagar, M. (2012). *The Future Of Islamic Banking*. A. T. Kearny.

Gartner, W. B. (1988). Who is an entrepreneur? Is the wrong question. *Entrepreneurship, Theory and Practice*, *12*(2), 47.

Gates, C. L. (1998). *The Merchant Republic of Lebanon: Rise of on an Open Economy*. London: I.B Tauris and Co Lrd.

GEM (Global Entrepreneurship Monitor). (2012). *Global Entrepreneurship Monitor 2012 Women's Report*. Retrieved March 20, 2016, from: http://www.babson.edu/Academics/centers/blank-center/global-research/gem/Documents/GEM 2012 Women's Report.pdf

Gerard, M., & Al-Riyami, R. (2003). Women entrepreneurs in Oman: Some barriers to success. *Career Development International*, *8*(7), 339–346. doi:10.1108/13620430310505296

Gersick, K. E., McCollom-Hampton, M., Davis, J. A., & Lansberg, I. (1997). *Generation to generation: Life cycles in the family business*. Cambridge, MA: Harvard Business School Press.

Gibb, A. (1990). Entrepreneurship and Intrapreneurship – Exploring the differences. In *New findings and perspectives in entrepreneurship*. Hant: Gower.

Gibb, A. (1993). The Enterprise Culture and Education. *International Small Business Journal*, *11*(3), 11–34. doi:10.1177/026624269301100301

Gilleard, C. J. (1989). The achieving society revisited: A further analysis of the relation between national economic growth and need achievement. *Journal of Economic Psychology*, *10*(1), 21–34. doi:10.1016/0167-4870(89)90055-X

Gliedt, T. R., & Parker, P. (2007). Green community entrepreneurship: Creative destruction in the social economy. *International Journal of Social Economics*, *34*(8), 538–553. doi:10.1108/03068290710763053

Global entrepreneurship Monitor. (2000). London: GEM Research Association, London Business School.

Goel, A., Vohra, N., Zhang, L., & Arola, B. (2007). Entrepreneurs and entrepreneurship: A cross cultural comparison of India and China. Indian Institute of Management Ahmedabad Journal, 1-33.

Goodbody Economic Consultants. (2002). *Entrepreneurship in lreland*. Dublin, Ireland: Goodbody.

Gordon, J. R. (2002). *Organizational Behavior: A diagnostic approach* (7th ed.). Upper Saddle River, NJ: Pearson Prentice Hall.

Greig, C. (2002). So just what is an entrepreneur? And why it actually matters. *Profit Review*, *21*(2), 14.

Gromb, D., & Scharfstein, D. (2005). *Entrepreneurship in Equilibrium*. Working Paper. London Business School.

Gupta, S. K. (1989). Entrepreneurship development: The Indian case. *Journal of Small Business Management*, *27*(1), 67.

Guth, W. D., & Ginsberg, A. (1990). Guest editors' introduction: Corporate entrepreneurship. *Strategic Management Journal*, *11*(3), 5–15.

Hakim, Y. (2002, March 16). Time for private sector to pull its weight, stop 'unending lament'. *The Daily Star*.

Hakim, Y. H. (2002, March 16). Time for Private Sector to Pull its Weight, Stop "Unending Lament". *The Daily Star*.

Hale, J. L., Householder, B. J., & Greene, K. L. (2003). The theory of reasoned action. In J. P. Dillard & M. Pfau (Eds.), *The persuasion handbook: Developments in theory and practice* (pp. 259–286). Thousand Oaks, CA: Sage.

Hall, L. T., & Hall, B. K. (1999). *Arab American Biography*. U.X.L.

Hamel, G. (2000). *Leading the Revolution*. Boston, MA: Harvard Business School Press.

Hančlová, J., & Tvrdý, L. (2004). *Classification of the Regions. In Multiregional and Regional Models*. Ostrava: Faculty of Economics, Technical University of Ostrava.

Handler, W. C. (1994). Succession in family business: A review of the research. *Family Business Review*, *7*(2), 133–157. doi:10.1111/j.1741-6248.1994.00133.x

Hattab, H. (2012). Towards understanding female entrepreneurship in Middle Eastern and North African countries: A cross-country comparison of female entrepreneurship. *Education. Business and Society: Contemporary Middle Eastern Issues*, *5*(3), 171–186. doi:10.1108/17537981211265561

Haugen, R. A., & Senbet, L. W. (1981). Resolving the Agency Problems of External Capital through Options. *The Journal of Finance, Vol*, *36*(3), 629–647. doi:10.1111/j.1540-6261.1981.tb00649.x

Haugh, H. L. (2005). A research agenda for social entrepreneurship. *Social Enterprise Journal*, *1*(1), 1–12. doi:10.1108/17508610580000703

Healy, P. (1985). The Effect of Bonus Schemes on Accounting Decisions. *Journal of Accounting and Economics*, *7*(1-3), 85–108. doi:10.1016/0165-4101(85)90029-1

Hellmann, T. (2007). Entrepreneurs and the Process of Obtaining Resources. *Journal of Economics & Management Strategy*, 16.

Henderson, R., & Robertson, M. (2000). Who Wants to be An Entrepreneur? Young Adult Attitudes to Entrepreneurship as a Career. *Career Development International*, *5*(6), 279–287.

Herbert, R. F. (1982). *The Entrepreneur*. New York: Preager.

Herzberg, F. (1987). One more time: How do you motivate employees? *Harvard Business Review*, *65*(5), 109–120. PMID:12545925

Herzer, D. (2013). Cross-Country Heterogeneity and the Trade-Income Relationship. *World Development*, *44*, 194–211. doi:10.1016/j.worlddev.2012.09.014

Hills, G. (1988). Variations in university entrepreneurship education, An empirical study of an evolving field. *Journal of Business Venturing*, *3*(2), 109–122. doi:10.1016/0883-9026(88)90021-3

Hisrich, R. D., & Peters, M. P. (1998). *Entrepreneurship*. Boston, MA: Irwin/McGraw-Hill.

Hofstede, G. (1991). *Cultures and organizations. Software of the mind*. Berkshire, UK: McGraw Hill.

Hofstede, G. (1992). *Cultural Dimensions in People Management-The Socialization Perspective. In Globalizing Management–Creating and Leading the Competitive Organization*. New York, NY: Wiley & Sons.

Hofstede, G. a. (2005). *Cultures and Organizations: Software of the Mind*. New York: McGraw-Hill.

Hofstede, G. H. (2001). Culture's consequences: Comparing values, behaviors, institutions and organizations across nations. *Sage (Atlanta, Ga.)*.

Hornsby, J., Kuratko, D., & Zahra, S. (2002). Middle managers perception of the internal environment for corporate entrepreneurship: Assessing a measurement scale. *Journal of Business Venturing*, *17*(1), 253–273. doi:10.1016/S0883-9026(00)00059-8

Hourani, A. (2002). *A history of the Arab Peoples*. Cambridge, MA: The Belknap Press of Harvard University Press.

Hourani, G. G. (2006). The impact of the summer 2006 war on migration in Lebanon: Emigration, remigration, evacuation and return – A preliminary study. Louaize, Lebanon: Lebanese Emigration Research Center; Notre Dame University Press.

Hourani, A. a. (1992). *The Lebanese in the World: A Century of Emigration*. London: I.B Tauris and Co. Ltd.

Hourani, A. L., & Shehadi, N. D. (1992). *The Lebanese in the world: a century of emigration*. Centre for Lebanese Studies.

Hussain, K., & Mehboob, F. (2008). Hedging Market Risk in Islamic Finance. *World Commerce Review*, *2*(3), 22–27.

IFC. (2008). *Guidebook on corporate governance of family-owned enterprises*. Beirut: The Lebanese Transparency Association.

IFC. (2014). *Women, Business and the Law 2014*. Retrieved January 16, 2015 from: http://wbl.worldbank.org/~/media/FPDKM/WBL/Documents/Reports/2014/Women-Business-and-the-Law-2014-Key-Findings.pdf

IFERA (The International Family Enterprise Academy). (2003, December). Family businesses dominate. *Family Business Review*, *16*(4), 235–250.

ILO. (2013). *Global Employment Trends for Youth 2013: A generation at risk.* Retrieved 27.4.2015 from: http://www.ilo.org/global/research/global-reports/global-employment-trends/youth/2013/lang--en/index.htm

Inter American Development Bank. (2014a). *WEGrow: Unlocking the Growth Potential of Women Entrepreneurs in Latin America and the Caribbean.* Retrieved on January 16, 2015, from: http://services.iadb.org/mifdoc/website/publications/98704705-c7cc-416c-b103-7797dac0844a.pdf

International Finance Corporation (IFC). (2014b). *Women owned SMEs: A business opportunity for financial institutions. A market and credit gap assessment and IFC's portfolio gender baseline.* Retrieved 3 Jan. 2015 from: http://www.ifc.org/wps/wcm/connect/b229bb004322efde9814f-c384c61d9f7/WomenOwnedSMes+Report-Final.pdf?MOD=AJPERES

International Labor Organization. (2015, October 8). *MENA region retains highest youth unemployment rate in the world.* Retrieved July 28, 2016, from http://www.ilo.org/beirut/media-centre/news/WCMS_412797/lang--en/index.htm

International Monetary Fund. (2015). *Islamic finance and the role of the IMF.* Retrieved from: http://www.imf.org/external/themes/islamicfinance/

Investopedia. (2008). Retrieved from: www.investopedia.com

Isenberg, D. J. (2010). How to start an entrepreneurial revolution. *Harvard Business Review*, *88*(6), 40–50.

Jacobs, J. J. (1991). *The anatomy of an entrepreneur: family, culture, and ethics.* ICS Press.

Jacobs, J. J. (1991). *The Anatomy of an Entrepreneur: Family, Culture, and Ethic.* San Francisco: ICS Press.

Jaka Lindiˇca, M. B. (2012). Higher growth through the Blue Ocean Strategy: Implications for economic policy. *Research Policy*, *41*(5), 928–938. doi:10.1016/j.respol.2012.02.010

Jamali, D. (2008). A stakeholder approach to corporate social responsibility: A fresh perspective into theory and practice. *Journal of Business Ethics*, *82*(1), 213–231. doi:10.1007/s10551-007-9572-4

Jamali, D. (2009). Constraints and opportunities facing women entrepreneurs in developing countries: A relational perspective. *Gender in Management: An International Journal*, *24*(4), 232–251. doi:10.1108/17542410910961532

Jarillo, C. J. (1990). A Paradigm of Entrepreneurship: Entrepreneurial management. *Strategic Management Journal, 11*, 17-27.

Jarillo, J. C. (1989). Entrepreneurship and Growth: The strategic use of external resources. *Journal of Business Venturing*, *4*(1), 133–147. doi:10.1016/0883-9026(89)90027-X

Jassim, A., & Dexter, C. R. (1988). Agency theory: Implications for financial management. *Managerial Finance Year Journal, 14*(4).

Javadian, G., & Singh, R. P. (2012). Examining successful Iranian women entrepreneurs: An exploratory study. *Gender in Management: An International Journal*, *27*(3), 148–164. doi:10.1108/17542411211221259

Jensen, M. C. (1986). Agency Costs of Free Cash Flow, Corporate Finance and Takeovers. *The American Economic Review*, *76*(2), 323–329.

Jensen, M. C. (1993). The Modern Industrial Revolution, Exit and the Failure of Internal Control Systems. *The Journal of Finance*, *48*(3), 831–880. doi:10.1111/j.1540-6261.1993.tb04022.x

Jensen, M. C., & Meckling, W. H. (1976). Theory of the Firm: Managerial Behavior, Agency Costs and Ownership Structure. *Journal of Financial Economics*, *3*(4), 305–360. doi:10.1016/0304-405X(76)90026-X

Jensen, M. C., & Murphy, K. J. (1990). Performance Pay and Top-Management Incentives. *Journal of Political Economy*, *98*(2), 225–264. doi:10.1086/261677

Jensen, M. C., & Ruback, R. S. (1983). The Market for Corporate Control: The Scientific Evidence. *Journal of Financial Economics*, *11*(1-4), 5–50. doi:10.1016/0304-405X(83)90004-1

Jenssen, H. S. (2002). Public intervention in the entrepreneurial process. *International Journal of Entrepreneurial Behavior and Research, 8*(3), 173-187.

Jobst, A., & Sole, J. (2012). *Operative Principles of Islamic Derivatives – Towards a Coherent Theory*. International Monetary Fund.

Johnson, D. (2001). What is innovation and entrepreneurship? Lessons for larger organizations. *Industrial and Commercial Training*, *33*(4), 135–140. doi:10.1108/00197850110395245

Jones, S. (2013). *Gendered Discourses of Entrepreneurship in HE: The Fictive Entrepreneur and the Fictive Student*. Retrieved January 03, 2015 from: http://www.google.com/url?sa=t&rct=j&q=&esrc=s&frm=1&source=web&cd=6&ved=0CD0QFjAF&url=http%3A%2F%2Fwww.isbe.org.uk%2Fcontent%2Fassets%2FBest_Conference_Paper-_Sally_Jones.pdf&ei=0QmvVIjEA4rtatPVgLAE&usg=AFQjCNE45n0jg8ECHs8RlGaaxg2v3hs2ig&bvm=bv.83339334,d.d2s

Kabbani, N., & Kothari, E. (2005). Youth employment in the MENA Region: A situational assessment. *World Bank, Social Protection Discussion Paper, 534.*

Kaisch, S., & Gilad, B. (1991). Characteristics of opportunities search of entrepreneurs versus executives: Sources, interests, general, alertness. *Journal of Business Venturing*, *6*(1), 45–61. doi:10.1016/0883-9026(91)90005-X

Kanbur, R., & Michael, S. (2008). *Globalization, Growth, and Distribution: Framing the Questions*. World Bank.

Kanoo, K. H. (1995). Family Businesses and the Road to Survival. *Eastern Region Chamber of Commerce Economic Symposium.* Kingdom of Saudi Arabia.

Kanter, R. M. (1984). *The Change Masters*. New York: Touchstone, Simon & Schuster.

Kanter, R. M. (1989). *When Giants Learn to Dance*. New York: Touchstone,Simon & Schuster.

Kaplan & Reishus. (1990). Outside Directors and Corporate Performance. *Journal of Financial Economics, 27*(2), 389-410.

Kaplan, J. A. (2010). *Patterns of Entrepreneurship Management* (3rd ed.). John Wiley and Sons, Inc.

Kaplan, S. N. (1989). The Effects of Management Buyouts on Operating Performance and Value. *Journal of Financial Economics*, *24*(2), 217–254. doi:10.1016/0304-405X(89)90047-0

Kauffman Foundation. (2014). *Sources of economic hope: Women's entrepreneurship*. Retrieved 3 Jan. 2014 from: http://www.kauffman.org/~/media/kauffman_org/research%20reports%20and%20covers/2014/11/sources_of_economic_hope_womens_entrepreneurship.pdf

Kaufmann, D., Kraay, A., & Zoido-Lobatón, P. (1999). *Aggregating governance indicators* (Vol. 2195). World Bank Publications.

Kavyani, A. A. (2013). Blue Ocean Strategy and its role in marketing banking services. *Market Engineering Development. Bi-monthly*, *13*(2), 9.

Kazemi, F. (2000). Gender, Islam and politics. *Social Research*, *67*(2), 453–474.

Kemp, L. J. (2013). Modern to postmodern management: Developments in scientific management. *Journal of Management History*, *19*(3), 345–361. doi:10.1108/JMH-02-2011-0005

Kenney, M., & Mujtaba, B. (2007). A Practitioner View of Organizational Intrapreneurship. *The Journal of Applied Management and Entrepreneurship*, *12*(3), 73–81.

Kenwood, A. G., Graff, M., & Lougheed, A. L. (2013). *Growth of the International Economy, 1820-2015*. Routledge.

Kets de Vries, M. F. (2012). Star Performers: Paradoxes wrapped up in enigmas. *Organizational Dynamics*, *41*(3), 173–182. doi:10.1016/j.orgdyn.2012.03.010

Kets de Vries, M. F. R. (2013). *Organizational paradoxes: Clinical approaches to management*. New York: Routledge.

Khandwalla, P. N. (1977). *The Design of Organizations*. New York: Harcourt Brace Jovanovich.

Khandwalla, P. N. (1987). Generators of Pioneering-innovative Management: Some Indian Evidence. *Organization Studies*, *8*(1), 39–59. doi:10.1177/017084068700800104

Kilby, P. T. (1971). *Entrepreneurship and Economic Development*. Hunting the Heffalump.

Kirkwood, J. (2009). Is a lack of self-confidence hindering women entrepreneurs? *International Journal of Gender and Entrepreneurship*, *1*(2), 118–133. doi:10.1108/17566260910969670

Kirzner, I. (1999). Creativity and/or Alertness: A Reconsideration of the Schumpeterian Entrepreneur. *The Review of Austrian Economics, 11*(1), 5–17. doi:10.1023/A:1007719905868

Klein, K. (2014). Rise of female Angel investors fuels women-run companies. *Business Week.* Retrieved on January 03, 2015 from: http://www.businessweek.com/articles/2014-09-10/angel-investing-rise-of-women-investors-fuels-women-run-companies

Klich, I. G., & Lesser, J. F. (1998). *Arab and Jewish immigrants in Latin America: images and realities.* Frank Cass.

Kliot, N. (2005). *Water resources and conflict in the Middle East.* Routledge.

Knight, F. H. (1921). *Risk, Uncertanity and Profit.* Chicago: University of Chicago Press.

Knight, F. H. (1971). *Risk, Uncertainty and Profit.* Chicago: University of Chicago Press.

Kogut, B., & Zander, U. (1992). Knowledge of the Firm, Combinative Capabilities, and the Replication of Technology. *Organization Science, 3*(3), 383–397. doi:10.1287/orsc.3.3.383

Koh, H. (1996). Testing hypotheses for entrepreneurial characteristics. *Journal of Managerial Psychology, 11*(3), 12–35. doi:10.1108/02683949610113566

Koiranen, M. (2003). Understanding the contesting ideologies of family business: Challenge for leadership and professional services. *Family Business Review, 16*(4), 241–250.

Kootstra, G. L. (2009). *The incorporation of design management in today's business practises: An analysis of design management practises in Europe.* Design Management Europe: ADMIRE programme.

Krugman & Obstfeld. (2000). *International economics: theory and policy.* Addison-Wesley.

Kuran, T. (1997). Islam and Underdevelopment: An Old Puzzle Revisited. *Journal of Institutional and Theoretical Economics, 153*(1), 41–71.

Kuran, T. (2004). Why the Middle East is Economically Underdeveloped: Historical Mechanisms of Institutional Stagnation. *The Journal of Economic Perspectives, 18*(3), 71–90. doi:10.1257/0895330042162421

Kuratko, D. (2009). *Entrepreneurship: Theory, Process, & Practice* (8th ed.). Mason, OH: Cengage/South Western Publishing.

Kuratko, D., Morris, M., & Covin, J. (2011). *Corporate Innovation and Entrepreneurship: Entrepreneurial within Organizations* (3rd ed.). South-Western.

Kuznets, S. (1955). Economic growth and income inequality. *The American Economic Review*, 1–28.

Ladki, N. L. (1993). *The Role of the Association of Lebanese Industrialists in the Creation of Indigenous Entrepreneurship. In Proceedings of Indigenous Entrepreneurship.* Damascus: ESCWA.

Lam, S. K. (1999). *Portraits of successful entrepreneurs and high-flyers: A psychological perspective.* Aldershot, UK: Ashgate.

Lander, G. P. (2002). The Sarbanes-Oxley Act of 2002. *Journal of Investment Compliance, 3*(1), 44–53.

Lansberg, I., Perrow, E. L., & Rogolsky, S. (1988). Family business as an emerging field. *Family Business Review, 1*(1), 1–8. doi:10.1111/j.1741-6248.1988.00001.x

Leftwich, A. (1993). Governance, democracy and development in the Third World. *Third World Quarterly, 14*(3), 605–624. doi:10.1080/01436599308420345

Legris, P., Ingham, J., & Collerette, P. (2001). Why do people use information technology? Critical review of the technology acceptance model. *Information and Management, 40*(2003), 191–204.

Lichtenstein, G. A., & Lyons, T. S. (2010). *Investing in Entrepreneurs: An Approach for Strengthening your Regional and Community Economy*. Santa Barbara, CA: Praeger/ABC-CLIO.

Ling, Y., Simsek, Z., Lubatkin, M., & Veiga, J. (2008). Transformational Leaderships Role in Promoting Corporate Entrepreneurship: Examining the CEO –TMT Interface. *Academy of Management Journal, 51*(3), 557–576. doi:10.5465/AMJ.2008.32626023

Lin, W. T. (2014). Founder-key leaders, group-level decision teams, and the international expansion of business groups: Evidence from Taiwan. *International Marketing Review, 31*(2), 129–154. doi:10.1108/IMR-07-2012-0120

Littunen, H. (2000). Entrepreneurship and the characteristics of the entrepreneurial personality. *International Journal of Entrepreneurial Behavior and Research, 6*(6), 295–310. doi:10.1108/13552550010362741

Litz, R. (2012). Double roles, double binds? Double bind theory and family business research. In Understanding Family Business: Unique Perspectives. Springer New York.

Litz, R. A. (2008). Two Sides of a One-Sided Phenomenon: Conceptualizing the Family Business and Business Family as a Möbius Strip. *Family Business Review, 21*(3), 217–236.

Litz, R. A., Pearson, A. W., & Litchfield, S. (2012). Charting the future of family business research perspectives from the field. *Family Business Review, 25*(1), 16–32. doi:10.1177/0894486511418489

Lobato, R. (2010). Creative industries and informal economies: Lessons from Nollywood. *International Journal of Cultural Studies, 13*(4), 337–354. doi:10.1177/1367877910369971

Longenecker, J., & Schoen, J. (1975). The essence of entrepreneurship. *Journal of Small Business Management, 13*(3), 26.

Lumpkin, G. T., & Dess, G. G. (1996). Clarifying the entrepreneurial orientation construct and linking it to performance. *Academy of Management Review, 12*(1), 135–172.

Lumpkin, G. T., & Dess, G. G. (1996). Clarifying the entrepreneurial orientation construct and linking it to performance. *Academy of Management Review, 21*(1), 135–172.

Lüthje, C., & Franke, N. (2003). The Making of an Entrepreneur: Testing A Model of Entrepreneurial Intent among Engineering Students at MIT. *R & D Management*, *33*(2), 135–147. doi:10.1111/1467-9310.00288

Lyman, A. R. (1991). Customer service: Does p make a difference. *Family Business Review*, *4*(3), 303–324. doi:10.1111/j.1741-6248.1991.00303.x

Lyons, J. S. (2009). *Communimetrics*. New York: Springer. doi:10.1007/978-0-387-92822-7

Maamari, R., & Ghaleb, J. R. (2002). Microfinance in Lebanon and the Case of Al Majmoua. Making Markets Work for The Poor. WBI MENA Debates, Beirut, Lebanon.

Maaouia, M. L. (2001, January 26). Children of the Cedars who made a mark down under. *The Daily Star*, p. 2.

MacMillan, I. C. (1986). Progress in Research on Corporate Venturing. In D. L. Sexton & R.W. Smilor (Eds.), The Art and Science of Entrepreneurship, (pp. 241-263). Cambridge, MA: Ballinger Publishing Company.

Madichie, N. O., & Gallant, M. (2012). Broken silence: A commentary on womens entrepreneurship in the United Arab Emirates. *The International Journal of Entrepreneurship and Innovation*, *13*(2), 81–92. doi:10.5367/ijei.2012.0071

Mahroum, S. (2016, May 4). *The Triumphs and Struggles of Arab Startups*. Retrieved July 28, 2016, from https://www.project-syndicate.org/commentary/startups-entrepreneurship-middle-east-by-sami-mahroum-2016-05

Majid Golpayagani, S. P. (2000). Blue Ocean Strategy uncontested market Competition. *Monthly Tadbir*, *20*(2), 202.

Makdisi, S. (2007). *Rebuilding Devastated Economies in the Middle East* (L. Binder, Ed.). Ney York: Palgrave Macmillan.

Malkawi, B. (2011, January). Financial Derivatives In The West And In Islamic Finance: A Comparative Approach. *Banking Law Journal*, *128*(1), 50.

Manassa, G. B. (1950). *For a Lebanese economic renovation with the collaboration of Lebanon overseas*. Lebanese Political Economy Society.

Marom, D., Robb, A., & Sade, O. (2015). Gender Dynamics in Crowdfunding (Kickstarter): Evidence on Entrepreneurs, Investors, Deals and Taste-Based Discrimination. *Investors, Deals and Taste-Based Discrimination.* Retrieved 26.10.2016, from: file:///C:/Users/bb21/Downloads/sade_presentation.pdf

Martin, L, R., Osberg, S. (2007). Social Entrepreneurship: The Case for Definition. *Stanford Social Innovation Review,* 1-3.

Maslow, A. (1943). A theory of human motivation. *Psychological Review*, *50*(4), 370–396. doi:10.1037/h0054346

Maslow, A. (1970). *Motivation and Personality*. New York: Harper.

Mateeha, F. (2006). *Differences and similarities between operating lease contracts*. College of Management Since, PAF-Karachi Institute of Economics and Technology.

Matriano, M. T., & Suguku, D. (2015). Entrepreneurship Growth in Oman: Position, Prospects and Growth of Entrepreneural Education. *IJAEDU-International E-Journal of Advances in Education*, *1*(2), 127–131. doi:10.18768/ijaedu.58791

Mazzarol, V. G., & Doss, T. N. (1999). Factors influencing small business start-ups. *International Journal of Entrepreneurial Behavior and Research*, *5*(2), 48–63. doi:10.1108/13552559910274499

McCarthy, B. (2003). Strategy is personality-driven, strategy is crisis-driven: Insights for entrepreneurial firms. *Management Decision*, *41*(4), 327–339. doi:10.1108/00251740310468081

McClelland, D. C. (1961). *The Achieiving Society*. Princeton, NJ: D. Van Nostrand Company, Inc. doi:10.1037/14359-000

McClelland, D. C. (1985). *Human Motivation*. New York: Scott, Foresman.

McClelland, D., & Pilon, D. (1983). Sources of adult motives in patterns of parent behavior in early childhood. *Journal of Personality and Social Psychology*, *44*(3), 564–574. doi:10.1037/0022-3514.44.3.564

McGivem, C. (1989). The dynamics of management succession: A model of chief executive succession in the small family firm. *Family Business Review*, *2*(4), 401–411. doi:10.1111/j.1741-6248.1989.tb00007.x

Mead, M. J. (1937). *Cooperation and competition among primitive peoples*. New York: McGraw-Hill Book Company, Inc. doi:10.1037/13891-000

MEE. (2015, February 12). *Rail network project to link GCC states begins*. Retrieved July 30, 2016, from http://www.middleeasteye.net/news/rail-network-project-link-gcc-states-begins-1070205078

Merrifield, D. B. (1993). Intrapreneurial Corporate Renewal. *Journal of Business Venturing*, *8*(5), 383–389. doi:10.1016/0883-9026(93)90020-6

Mervyn, D. K. (2015, August 10). *Are Entrepreneurs Born Or Made?* Retrieved July 28, 2016, from https://www.entrepreneur.com/article/249375

Mezher, T. S. (2008). Entrepreneurship in Lebanon: A Model for Success and Failures. *International Journal of Arab Culture. Management and Sustainable Devlopment*, *1*(1), 34–52.

Millan, J. M., Hessels, J., Thurik, R., & Aguado, R. (2013). Determinants of job satisfaction: A European comparison of self-employed and paid employees. *Small Business Economics*, *40*(1), 651–670. doi:10.1007/s11187-011-9380-1

Miller, D., & Friesen, P. H. (1983). Strategy-making and environment. *Strategic Management Journal*, *4*(3), 221–235. doi:10.1002/smj.4250040304

Miller, W. D. (1998). Siblings and succession in the family business. *Harvard Business Review, 76*, 22–40.

Mina, A. K. (2010). *Strategic management is based on the blue ocean and the role of creativity and innovation in its implementation.* Paper presented at the First International Conference on Innovation and Management, Tehran, Iran.

Ministry of Economy and Planning. (2009). *Statistical Yearbook.* Riyadh: Author.

MOM. (2005). *Third symposium on employing national manpower.* Shinas, Oman: Ministry of Manpower.

Moorhead, G., & Griffin, R. (1989). *Organizational Behavior* (2nd ed.). Boston: Houghton Mifflin Company.

Morck, R., Strangeland, D., & Yeung, B. (2000). *Inherited wealth, corporate control and economic growth: the Canadian disease.* Working Paper. National Bureau of Economic Research: 6814.

Morelli, N., & Sangiorgi, D. (2006). Managing globalization and local issues in service design: on the convergence between opposing demands of industrialisation and personalisation of service performance. *Proceedings: D2B – The first international design management symposium.*

Morrison, A. (2000). Entrepreneurship: What triggers it? *International Journal of Entrepreneurial Behavior and Research, 6*(2), 59–71. doi:10.1108/13552550010335976

Morrison, A. (2001). Entrepreneurs transcend time: A biographical analysis. *Management Decision, 39*(9), 784–790. doi:10.1108/EUM0000000006222

Mouritsen, J. N. (2003). Intellectual capital and the capital market: The circulability of intellectual capital. *Accounting, Auditing & Accountability Journal, 16*(1), 223–234. doi:10.1108/09513570310464246

Munck, G. L. (2009). *Measuring democracy: A bridge between scholarship and politics.* JHU Press.

Murphy, P. J., & Coombes, S. M. (2009). A model of social entrepreneurial discovery. *Journal of Business Ethics, 87*(1), 325–336. doi:10.1007/s10551-008-9921-y

Naff, A. L. (1985) Becoming American: The Early Arab Immigrant Experience. South Illinois University Press.

Naguib, R., & Jamali, D. (2015). Female entrepreneurship in the UAE: A multi-level integrative lens. *Gender in Management: An International Journal, 30*(2), 135–161. doi:10.1108/GM-12-2013-0142

Naimy, N. A. (1985). *The Lebanese prophets of New York.* American University of Beirut.

Najjar, G. (2012). *High Fliers Program Cohort III: Future Proofing.* Executive Education BANK Program.

Nakauchi, M., & Wiersema, M. F. (2014). Executive succession and strategic change in Japan. *Strategic Management Journal*.

Nasr, S. (1978). Backdrop to civil war: The crisis of Lebanese Capitalism. *Merip Reports*, (73), 3-13.

Nielsen, L. (2011). *Classifications of countries based on their level of development: how it is done and how it could be done*. International Monetary Fund.

Noorian, H. (1999). Strategic management method based on Blue Ocean. *The Quality Assurance Journal, 3*(2), 11.

Nordqvist, M., Wennberg, K., & Hellerstedt, K. (2013). An entrepreneurial process perspective on succession in family firms. *Small Business Economics, 40*(4), 1087–1122. doi:10.1007/s11187-012-9466-4

O'Sullivan, A., Rey, M.-E., & Mendez, J. G. (2011). Opportunities and Challenges in the MENA Region. *Arab World Competitiveness Report, 2012*, 42–67.

OECD. (2014). *Women in Business 2014. Accelerating Entrepreneurship in the Middle East and North Africa Region*. Retrieved January 15, 2014 from: http://www.keepeek.com/Digital-Asset-Management/oecd/development/women-in-business-2014_9789264213944-en#page1

Olson, P. D., Zuiker, V. S., Danes, S. M., Stafford, K., Heck, R. K., & Duncan, K. A. (2003). The impact of the family and the business on family business sustainability. *Journal of Business Venturing, 18*(5), 639–666. doi:10.1016/S0883-9026(03)00014-4

Omair, K. (2008). Women in Management in the Arab Context. Education, Business and Society. *Contemporary Middle Eastern Issues, 1*(2), 107–123. doi:10.1108/17537980810890293

Panizza, U. (2002). Income inequality and economic growth: Evidence from American data. *Journal of Economic Growth, 7*(1), 25–41. doi:10.1023/A:1013414509803

Parhizgar, K. D., & Parhizgar, S. S. (2007). Comparative strategic positioning of four academic administrative models: bureaucracy, technocracy, meritocracy, and kakistocracy. *Competition Forum, 5*(1).

Parhizgar, K. D. (2007). *Global Business Environments: Understanding Multicultural Behavior*. Jaico Publishing House.

Pearce, D. (2011). *Financial Inclusion in the Middle East and North Africa: Analysis and Roadmap Recommendations*. World Bank Policy Research Working Paper Series.

Pedersen, P. O., & McCormick, D. (1999). African Business Systems in a Globalising World. *The Journal of Modern African Studies, 37*(1), 109–135. doi:10.1017/S0022278X99002955

Peredo, A. M., & McLean, M. (2006). Social Entrepreneurship: A Critical Review of the Concept. *Journal of World Business, 41*(1), 56–65. doi:10.1016/j.jwb.2005.10.007

Perotti, R. (1996). Growth, income distribution, and democracy: What the data say. *Journal of Economic Growth, 1*(2), 149–187. doi:10.1007/BF00138861

Phan, P. H. (Ed.). (2008). *Entrepreneurship in Emerging Regions around the World: Theory, Evidence, and Implications.* Edward Elgar Publishing, Inc. doi:10.4337/9781848441446

Pistrui, D., Welsch, H. P., & Roberts, J. S. (1997). The [Re]-Emergence of Family Businesses in the Transforming Soviet Bloc: Family Contributions to Entrepreneurship Development in Romania. *Family Business Review, 10*(3), 221–238. doi:10.1111/j.1741-6248.1997.00221.x

Pitta, D., & Pitta, E. (2012). Transforming the nature and scope of new product development. *Journal of Product and Brand Management, 21*(1), 35–46. doi:10.1108/10610421211203097

Porter, H. (2003). A Culture of Enterprise. *Business Today,* 51-52.

Power of Attorney. (n.d.). In *U.S. Legal Dictionary.* Academic Press.

Praag, M. (1999). Some classic views on entrepreneurship. *The Economist, 147*(3), 311.

Pradhan, S., & Ranajee, J. (2012, December). Value Creation by Family-Owned Businesses: A Literature Review. *The IUP Journal of Business Strategy, IX*(4), 35–45.

Prendergast, C. (2001). *Consumers and Agency Problems.* NBER Working Paper No. 8445. National Bureau of Economic Research.

Prosser, D. (2015, November 16). *Silicon Roundabout is getting congested, but it isn't the only hub for tech start-ups.* Retrieved July 29, 2016, from http://www.independent.co.uk/news/business/comment/silicon-roundabout-is-getting-congested-but-it-isnt-the-only-hub-for-tech-start-ups-a6735736.html

Pryor, A. K., & Shays, E. M. (1993, Spring). Growing the business with intrapreneurs. *Business Quarterly, 57*(3), 42.

Punnose, J. (2004). *History of Hospitals.* Oyster Healthcare. Retrieved December 17, 2012, from http://johnpunnoose.com/

Ramady, M. A. (2010). *The Saudi Arabian economy: policies, achievements and challenges.* Spingler.

Rao, S. (2009). Islamic Finance WIKI. Plug into your hard-wired happiness. *Islamic Finance Encyclopedia.*

Ravallion, M. (2001). Growth, inequality and poverty: Looking beyond averages. *World Development, 29*(11), 1803–1815. doi:10.1016/S0305-750X(01)00072-9

Rebernik, M., Tomnic, P., & Duh, M. (2007). Pitanja sukcesije unutar obiteljskih poduzeća u tranzicijskim privredama. *Društvena istraživanja-Časopis za opća društvena pitanja,* (4-5), 751-779.

Regional Health Systems Observatory. (2006). *EMRO, Health Systems Profile- Lebanon.* World Health Organization.

Rein, P. (1988). Understanding and Encouraging Entrepreneurship Internationally. *Journal of Small Business Management, 3*(1), 111–114.

Reynolds, P. D., Bygrave, W. D., Autio, E., & Arenius, P. (2004). *GEM 2003 global report.* Babson College.

Robbins, S. M. (2007). *Management* (9th ed.). Pearson Prentice Hall.

Robinson, M. (2001, December). The Ten Commandments of Intrapreneurs. *New Zealand Management. Auckland, 48*(11), 95.

Rodrik, D. (2005). Growth strategies.Handbook of Economic Growth, 1, 967-1014.

Rogal, K. H. (1989). Obligation or Opportunity: How Can Could-Be Heirs Assess Their Position? *Family Business Review, 2*(3), 237–255. doi:10.1111/j.1741-6248.1989.00237.x

Romer, P. M. (1989). *What determines the rate of growth and technological change?* (Vol. 279). World Bank Publications.

Roper, J. T., & Cheney, G. (2005). The meanings of social entrepreneurship today. *Corporate Governance, 5*(3), 95–104. doi:10.1108/14720700510604733

Rotter, J. B. (1966). Generalized expectancies for internal versus external control of reinforcement. *Psychological Monographs, 80*(1), 609. doi:10.1037/h0092976 PMID:5340840

Sachs, G. (2014). *Giving credit where it is due. How closing the credit gap for women owned SMEs can drive global growth.* Retrieved January 03, 2015 from: http://www.goldmansachs.com/our-thinking/investing-in-women/gmi-report-pdf.pdf

Sacks, R., & Myers, J. (2003). Tools, Techniques and Tightropes: The Art of Walking and Talking Private Sector Management in Non–profit Organisations, is it Just a Question of Balance? *Financial Accountability & Management, 19*(3), 287–306. doi:10.1111/1468-0408.00175

Saddi, J., & Soueid, R. (2011). Accelerating entrepreneurship in the Arab world. In *The Forum of Young Global Leaders, World Economic Forum, and Booz & Company.* Retrieved from http:// www3. weforum. org/docs/WEF_YGL_AcceleratingEntrepreneurshipArabWorld_Report_

Sadeq, T., & Setti, Z. (2013). Effects of entrepreneurs networking with national values on job growth expectations: A two-level analysis for the MENA region and Denmark. *International Journal of Business and Globalisation, 11*(4), 443–459. doi:10.1504/IJBG.2013.056879

Sadi, M. A., & Al-Ghazali, B. M. (2010). Doing business with impudence: A focus on women entrepreneurship in Saudi Arabia. *African Journal of Business Management, 4*(1), 1–11.

Said, P., & Javaid, F. (2012). Handbook of Islamic Banking Products & Services. Academic Press.

Saliba, N. E. (1992). *Emigration from Syria and the Syrian-Lebanese Community of Worcester.* Association Press.

Salibi, K. S. (1965). *The modem history of Lebanon.* New York: Academic Press.

Salibi, K. S. (1971). The Lebanese Identity. *Journal of Contemporary History, 6*(1), 76–86. doi:10.1177/002200947100600104

Santiso, C. (2001). International Co-operation for Democracy and Good Governance: Moving Towards a Second Generation? *European Journal of Development Research*, *13*(1), 154–180. doi:10.1080/09578810108426785

Sarbanes, P. (2002, July). Sarbanes-oxley act of 2002. In *The Public Company Accounting Reform and Investor Protection Act*. Washington, DC: US Congress.

Saudi Hollandi Bank. (2012). *Shariah Compliant Profit Rate Hedging*. Author.

Sayigh, Y. A. (1962). *Entrepreneurs of Lebanon: The role of the business leader in a developing economy*. Cambridge, MA: Harvard University Press. doi:10.4159/harvard.9780674422247

Sayigh, Y. A. (1978). *The Determinants of Arab Economic Development*. London: Croom Helm Ltd.

Schoonhoven, C. B., & Romanelli, E. (2001). *The entrepreneurship dynamic: Origins of entrepreneurship and the evolution of industries*. Stanford, CA: Stanford University Press.

Schramm, C. J. (2006b). *Entrepreneurial Capitalism and the End of Bureaucracy: Reforming the Mutual Dialog of Risk Aversion*. Presented at the American Economic Association meetings, Boston, MA.

Schramm, C. J. (2006a). *The Entrepreneurial Imperative: How American's Economic Miracle Will Reshape the World (and change your life)*. New York: Harper Collins.

Schuler, R. (1986). Fostering and facilitating entrepreneurship in organizations: Implications for organization structure and human resources management practices. *Human Resource Management*, *25*(4), 607–629. doi:10.1002/hrm.3930250408

Schumpeter, J. (1942). Creative destruction. *Capitalism, socialism and democracy*, 82-5.

Schumpeter, J. A. (1942). *Capitalism, Socialism, and Democracy*. New York, NY: Harper.

Schwartz, E. L. (1954). Will Your Business Die With You? *Harvard Business Review*, *32*(5), 110–122.

Sdralevich, M. C. A., Sab, M. R., Zouhar, M. Y., & Albertin, G. (2014). *Subsidy Reform in the Middle East and North Africa: Recent Progress and Challenges Ahead*. International Monetary Fund.

Sfakianakis, J. (2009). *Challenges facing family businesses in Saudi Arabia*. Accessible at: www.Arabnews.com

Sfeir, R. (2007). Strategy for National Health Care Reform in Lebanon. *Ministry of Public Health Magazine*, *3*(3), 10-13.

Shahbaz, M. (2012). Does trade openness affect long run growth? Cointegration, causality and forecast error variance decomposition tests for Pakistan. *Economic Modelling*, *29*(6), 2325–2339. doi:10.1016/j.econmod.2012.07.015

Shane, S. A. (2000). The Promise of Entrepreneurship as a Field of Research. *The Academy of Management Review*, 217-226.

Shanker, M. C., & Astrachan, J. H. (1996). Myths and realities: Family businesses contribution to the US economy—A framework for assessing family business statistics. *Family Business Review*, *9*(2), 107–123. doi:10.1111/j.1741-6248.1996.00107.x

Shapero, A. (1975). The displaced, uncomfortable entrepreneur. *Psychology Today*, *9*(6), 83–88.

Shapero, A. (1985). Why entrepreneurship? A worldwide perspective. *Journal of Small Business Management*, *23*(4), 25–42.

Sharma, P., & Hoy, F. (2013). Family business roles. *The Landscape of Family Business*, 113.

Sharma, P. (2004). An overview of the field of family business studies: Current status and directions for the future. *Family Business Review*, *17*(1), 1–36. doi:10.1111/j.1741-6248.2004.00001.x

Shaw, E. (1999). A guide to the qualitative research process: Evidence from a small firm study. *Qualitative Market Research: An International Journal*, *2*(2), 59–70. doi:10.1108/13522759910269973

Shivdasani, A., & Yermack, D. (1999). CEO involvement in the selection of new board members: An empirical analysis. *The Journal of Finance*, *54*(5), 1829–1853. doi:10.1111/0022-1082.00168

SIDF. (2016). *About Us*. Retrieved July 29, 2016, from http://www.sidf.gov.sa/en/AboutSIDF/Pages/AboutUs.aspx

Slocum & Papa. (2014). Envisioning a global role for osteopathic medicine in the 21st century: Using Blue Ocean Strategy to promote osteopathic health care as the World's leader in healthcare education and do it more efficiently, effectively and at the lowest cost. *International Journal of Osteopathic Medicine, 17*, 38-42.

Smallbone, D., & Welter, F. (2001). The distinctiveness of entrepreneurship in transition economies. *Journal of Small Business Economics*, *16*(4), 249–262. doi:10.1023/A:1011159216578

Smith, W. L. (2006). Goals and characteristics of family-owned small businesses: An international replication and comparison between Middle America and Western Australia Hospitality Providers. *International Journal of Management and Enterprise Development*, *3*(3), 212–226. doi:10.1504/IJMED.2006.008821

Sobel, P. (2005). *Auditor's Risk Management Guide: Integrating Auditing and ERM*. CCH Inc.

Solow, R. M. (1956). A contribution to the theory of economic growth. *The Quarterly Journal of Economics*, *70*(1), 65–94. doi:10.2307/1884513

Sonnenfeld, J. (1985). Shedding Light on the Hawthorne Studies, *Journal of occupational. Behaviour*, *6*(2), 111–130.

Sowers, J., Vengosh, A., & Weinthal, E. (2011). Climate change, water resources, and the politics of adaptation in the Middle East and North Africa. *Climatic Change*, *104*(3-4), 599–627. doi:10.1007/s10584-010-9835-4

Springborg, R. (1977). New patterns of agrarian reform in the Middle East and North Africa. *The Middle East Journal*, 127–142.

Spulber, D. F. (2008). *The Theory of the Firm: Microeconomics with Endogenous Entrepreneurs, Firms, Markets, and Organizations*. Cambridge, UK: Cambridge University Press.

Sreih, F. J., Pistrui, D., Huang, V. W., & Welsch, P. (2010). Family and cultural factors impacting entrepreneurship in war time Lebanon. *International Journal of Entrepreneurship and Innovation Management*, *12*(1), 35–51. doi:10.1504/IJEIM.2010.033166

Staley, E., & Morse, R. (1965). *Developing Entrepreneurship: Elements for a Program*. McGraw Hill.

Start-Up Chile. (2016). *About*. Retrieved from http://startupchile.org/about/

Statistics unkind to family business. (2007, June 18). *The Star Magazine*.

Steensma, K. E., Marino, L. S., & Weaver, M. A. (2000). Attitudes Toward Cooperative Strategies: A Cross-Cultural Analysis of Entrepreneurs. Journal of International Business Studies, 31(4), 591-608.

Steensma, M. W. (2000). *Attitudes toward cooperative strategies: A cross cultural analysis of entrepreneurs*. Academic Press.

Steensma, H. K., Marino, L., & Weaver, K. M. (2000). Attitudes Toward Cooperative Strategies: A Cross-Cultural Analysis of Entrepreneurs. *Journal of International Business Studies J Int Bus Stud*, *31*(4), 591–609. doi:10.1057/palgrave.jibs.8490924

Stevenson, H. H., & Jarillo, J. C. (1990). A Paradigm of Entrepreneurship: Entrepreneurial Management. *Strategic Management Journal*, *11*(3), 17–27.

Stiglitz, J. E. (2000). Capital market liberalization, economic growth, and instability. *World Development*, *28*(6), 1075–1086. doi:10.1016/S0305-750X(00)00006-1

Sud, M., VanSandt, C. V., & Baugous, A. M. (2009). Social entrepreneurship: The role of institutions. *Journal of Business Ethics*, *85*(1), 201–216. doi:10.1007/s10551-008-9939-1

Suleiman, M. W. (1999). *The Arab Immigrant Experience, From Arabs in America*. Temple University Press.

Sullivan, K. T., & Perrenoud, A. (2012). *Executive Succession Planning*. ELECTRI International and Arizona State University.

Sum Lam, S. K. (1999). Portraits of successful entrepreneurs and high-flyers: A psychological perspective. Ashgate Publishing Limited.

Sundbo, J. (1999). Empowerment of employees in small and medium-sized service firms. *Employee Relations*, *21*(2), 105–127. doi:10.1108/01425459910266385

Swdberg, R. (2000). *Entrepreneurship: The social science view*. Oxford University Press.

Tagiuri, R., & Davis, J. (1996). Bivalent attributes of the family firm. *Family Business Review*, *9*(2), 199–208. doi:10.1111/j.1741-6248.1996.00199.x

Tagiuri, R., & Davis, J. A. (1992). On the goals of successful family companies. *Family Business Review*, *5*(1), 43–62. doi:10.1111/j.1741-6248.1992.00043.x

TechCrunch. (2016). *The first comprehensive study on women in venture capital and their impact on female founders*. Retrieved on October 17, 2016, from https://techcrunch.com/2016/04/19/the-first-comprehensive-study-on-women-in-venture-capital/

Teh, J., Al-Dhaafri, H., & Isakovic, A. A. (2015). *Entrepreneurial Attitudes and Intentions of Dubai Students*. Academic Press.

Temple, J. (1999). The new growth evidence. *Journal of Economic Literature*, *37*(1), 112–156. doi:10.1257/jel.37.1.112

Thacker, S. (2011). *An exception to the gender gap in education: The Middle East and North Africa*. Retrieved on 30.11.2016, from: http://blogs.worldbank.org/arabvoices/exception-gender-gap-education-middle-east-north-africa

Thomas, P., & Mueller, S. (2000). Culture and Entrepreneurial Potential: A Nine Country Study of Locus of Control and Innovativeness. *Journal of Business Venturing*, *16*, 51–75.

Thompson, J. (1999). The world of the entrepreneur: A new perspective. *Journal of Workplace Learning*, *11*(6), 209–224. doi:10.1108/13665629910284990

Thompson, J. M., Alvy, G., & Lees, A. (2000). Social entrepreneurship- a new look at the people and the potential. *Management Decision*, *38*(5), 328–338. doi:10.1108/00251740010340517

Time. (2009). *Leaders and Revolutionaries* [Online]. Available from http://content.time.com/time/specials/packages/article/0,28804,1894410_1893847_1893841,00.html

Timmons, J. A. (1978). Characteristics and role demands of entrepreneurship. *American Journal of Small Business*, *3*, 5–17.

Tlaiss, H. (2013). Entrepreneurial motivations of women: Evidence from the United Arab Emirates. *International Small Business Journal*.

Tlaiss, H. A. (2015). How Islamic Business Ethics Impact Women Entrepreneurs: Insights from Four Arab Middle Eastern Countries. *Journal of Business Ethics*, *129*(4), 859–877. doi:10.1007/s10551-014-2138-3

Toulayi, R. (2008). Blue Ocean Strategy as revolution in the field of strategic anagement. *Police Human Development, 24*.

Toulin, A. (1988). Policy aims to inspire entrepreneurs. *The Ottawa Citizen*, p. B8.

Triandis, H. Y. (1993). Collectivism and individualism as cultural syndromes. *Cross-Cultural Research*, *27*(1), 155–180. doi:10.1177/106939719302700301

Ugonma, O. E. (2003). Psychological Factors Influencing Perceived entrepreneurial Success Among Nigerian Women in Small-Scale Businesses. *Journal of International Women's Studies*, *5*(1), 234–238.

Uhlaner, L., & Thurik, A. R. (2007). Postmaterialism influencing total entrepreneurial activity across nations. *Journal of Evolutionary Economics*, *17*(2), 161–185. doi:10.1007/s00191-006-0046-0

UK Excellence in Islamic Finance. (n.d.). Retrieved from: https://www.gov.uk/government/uploads/system/uploads/attachment_data/file/367154/UKTI_UK_Excellence_in_Islamic_Finance_Reprint_2014_Spread.pdf

UNDP. (1997). *Governance and Sustainable Human Development*. United Nations Development Programme.

UNDP. (2002). United Nations Development Programme, Globalization: Towards a Lebanese Agenda, Lebanon 2001-2002. National Human Development Report, Beirut, Lebanon.

UNDP. (2004). *Unleashing entrepreneurship: Making business work for the poor: Report to the Secretary-General of the United Nations by the Commission on the Private Sector & Development*. New York: UNDP.

United Nations Department of Economic and Social Affairs (DESA). (1999). *Entrepreneurship and Privatization for Economic Growth and Sustainable Development*. DESA.

Usman, H. (2013). Islamic Finance and Socially Responsible Investment. *CFA Institute Magazine*, *24*(2), 2–8.

Vandenbussche, J., Aghion, P., & Meghir, C. (2006). Growth, distance to frontier and composition of human capital. *Journal of Economic Growth*, *11*(2), 97–127. doi:10.1007/s10887-006-9002-y

Venkatesh, V., & Davis, F. (2000). A theoretical extension of the technology acceptance model: Four longitudinal field studies. *Management Science*, *46*(2), 186–204. doi:10.1287/mnsc.46.2.186.11926

Venkatesh, V., Davis, F., & Morris, M. G. (2007). Dead or alive? The development, trajectory and future of technology adoption research. *Journal of the Association for Information Systems*, *8*(4), 267–286.

Verheul, I., Stel, A. V., &Thurik, R. (2006). Explaining female and male entrepreneurship at the country level. *Entrepreneurship and Regional Development*, *18*(2), 151-183.

Vinig, G. a. (Ed.). (2005). The Emergence of Entrepreneurial Economics. Oxford, UK: Elsevier.

Vroom, V. H. (1964). *Work and Motivation*. New York: John Wiley and Sons.

Vroom, V. H. (1982). *Work and motivation* (Rev. ed.). Malabar, FL: Robert E. Krieger Publishing Company.

Wagner-Tsukamoto, S. (2008). Scientific Management revisited: Did Taylorism fail because of a too positive image of human nature? *Journal of Management History*, *14*(4), 348–372. doi:10.1108/17511340810893108

Wang, C., & Wong, P. (2004). Entrepreneurial interest of university students in Singapore. *Technovation, 24*(2), 161–172. doi:10.1016/S0166-4972(02)00016-0

Ward, J. L. (2011). *Keeping the family business healthy: How to plan for continuing growth, profitability, and family leadership*. Macmillan. doi:10.1057/9780230116122

Warriner, D. (1962). Land reform and development in the Middle East. A study of Egypt, Syria, and Iraq. Land reform and development in the Middle East (2nd ed.). Academic Press.

Weathington, B. L., Cunningham, C. J. L., & Pittenger, D. P. (2010). *Research Methods for the Behavioral and Social Sciences*. Hoboken, NJ: John Wiley & Sons, Inc.

Weeks, J. R. (2009). Women business owners in the Middle East and North Africa: A five-country research study. *International Journal of Gender and Entrepreneurship, 1*(1), 77–85. doi:10.1108/17566260910942354

Welsh, D. H., Memili, E., Kaciak, E., & Al Sadoon, A. (2014). Saudi women entrepreneurs: A growing economic segment. *Journal of Business Research, 67*(5), 758–762. doi:10.1016/j.jbusres.2013.11.040

Wilken, P. H. (1979). *Entrepreneurship: A Comparative and Historical Study*. Ablex Publishing Corporation.

Wilken, P. L. (1979). *Entrepreneurship: comparative and historical study*. Norwood, NJ: Ablex Publishing Corporation.

Wilson, F., Marlino, D., & Kickul, J. (2004). Our entrepreneurial future: Examining the diverse attitudes and motives of teens across gender and ethnic identity. *Journal of Developmental Entrepreneurship, 9*(3), 177–197.

Winder, R. B. (1962). *The Lebanese in West Africa*. Mouton.

Wolcott, R. M. (2007). The Four Models of Corporate Entrepreneurship. *MIT Sloan Management Review, 49*(1), 75–82.

Wolcott, R., & Lippitz, M. (2007). The Four Models of Corporate Entrepreunership. *MIT Sloan Management Review, 49*(1), 75–80.

WOMENA. (2015, October 19). *Exploring Trends and Challenges to Scale for Startups in MENA*. Retrieved from http://womena.co/2015/10/19/challenges-to-scale-in-mena/

World Bank Group. (Ed.). (2012). *World Development Indicators 2012*. World Bank Publications.

World Bank. (2010). *Doing Business 2010*. Washington, DC: The World Bank Group, IFC and Palgrave MacMillan.

World Economic Forum. (2015, May 27). *Solving the problem of youth unemployment in the MENA region*. Retrieved July 28, 2016, from https://www.weforum.org/agenda/2015/05/solving-the-problem-of-youth-unemployment-in-the-mena-region/

Wyk, R. M. (2011). An eight-factor solution for the Corporate Entrepreneurship Assessment Instrument. *African Journal of Business Management*, *5*(8), 3047–3055.

Yahia, M. (2014). *Women's gap from education to research*. Retrieved 30.11.2016, from: http://blogs.nature.com/houseofwisdom/2014/03/womens-gap-from-education-to-research.html

Yang, J. (2012). Effects of ownership change on organizational settings and strategies in a Taiwanese hotel chain. *Hospitality Managment*, *31*(2), 428–441. doi:10.1016/j.ijhm.2011.07.001

Yanikkaya, H. (2003). Trade Openness and Economic Growth: A Cross-Country Empirical Investigation. *Journal of Development Economics*, *72*(1), 57–89. doi:10.1016/S0304-3878(03)00068-3

Yin, R. (2009). *Case Study Research: Design and Methods*. London: Sage.

Yonca, G., & Atsan, N. (2006). Entrepreneurial characteristics amongst university students: Some insights for entrepreneurship education and training in Turkey. *Education + Training,48*(1), 25 – 38.

Yusuf, S. (2014). *Middle East Transitions: A Long*. Hard Road.

Zahra, S. (1996). governance, ownership, and corporate entrepreneurship: The moderating impact of industry technological opportunities. *Academy of Management Journal*, *39*(6), 1713–1735. doi:10.2307/257076

Zahra, S. A. (1991). Predictors and financial outcomes of corporate entrepreneurship: An exploratory study. *Journal of Business Venturing*, *6*(4), 259–285. doi:10.1016/0883-9026(91)90019-A

Zahra, S. A. (1993). Environment, corporate entrepreneurship, and financial performance: A taxonomic approach. *Journal of Business Venturing*, *8*(4), 319–340. doi:10.1016/0883-9026(93)90003-N

Zahra, S. A., & Wright, M. (2011). Entrepreneurships next act. *The Academy of Management Perspectives*, *25*(4), 67–83. doi:10.5465/amp.2010.0149

Zahra, S., Jennings, D., & Kuratko, D. (1999). The Antecedents and Consequences of Firm- Level Entrepreneurship: The State of the Field, *Entrepreneurship. Theory into Practice*, *24*(1), 45–65.

Zakaria, F. (1997). The rise of illiberal democracy. *Foreign Affairs*, *76*(6), 22–43. doi:10.2307/20048274

Zali, M. R., Bastian, B. L., & Qureshi, S. (2013). Promoting innovation in the MENA region: The role of social norms and individual factors in entrepreneurial networks. *International Journal of Business and Globalisation*, *11*(4), 413–426. doi:10.1504/IJBG.2013.056877

Zalivako, A. (2012). *Die Bauten des russischen Konstruktivismus: Moskau 1919-32; Baumaterial, Baukonstruktion, Erhaltung*. Imhof.

Zamberi Ahmad, S. (2011). Evidence of the characteristics of women entrepreneurs in the Kingdom of Saudi Arabia: An empirical investigation. *International Journal of Gender and Entrepreneurship*, *3*(2), 123–143. doi:10.1108/17566261111140206

Zein, F. M. (2001). *Strategies in the Development of Venture Businesses: A Study on the Lebanese Entrepreneurial Status*. American University of Beirut.

Zellweger, T., & Siegcr, P. (2012). Entrepreneurial orientation in long-lived family firms. *Small Business Economics*, *38*(1), 67–84. doi:10.1007/s11187-010-9267-6

Zgheib, P. W. & Kowatly, A. K. (2011). Autonomy and Locus of Control for Overseas Lebanese Entrepreneurs Operating Worldwide. *Journal of Small Business and Entrepreneurship, 24*(3), 345-360.

Zimmerer, T. W., & Scarborough, N. M. (2008). *Essentials of entrepreneurship and small business management: the foundations of entrepreneurship*. Pearson Education.

Zimmerman, J. (2010). Corporate Entrepreneurship at GE and Intel. *Journal of Business Case Studies*, *6*(5), 77–81.

About the Contributors

Philippe W. Zgheib is a senior Fulbright scholar since 2004 in entrepreneurship, strategic management, and business economics. He holds a PhD in economics (1994) and a civil engineering doctorate (1990) from Utah State University in the USA. He has served actively in academia both in Lebanon and in the USA. Also he is a widely established corporate consultant and business moderator of executive workshops with private business as well as in public civic engagement and community service. He has joined LAU in Fall 2012 in Business Management and Entrepreneurship as a director of the Human Resources Institute at LAU, after 12 years at AUB. His publications are specialized in the areas of human resource management, entrepreneurship, business ethics, and business communications. His consulting expertise beyond entrepreneurship includes leadership styles, conflict optimization, advanced negotiations, emotional intelligence, and business communications. He is also a registered professional engineer, and a project development leader. Media exposure includes BBC World, CNN, Voice of America, Executive magazine, and An-nahar daily in economics, and management of integrated systems.

***

Mohammad Abdolshah received his B.Sc. and M.Sc in Industrial Engineering from Amirkabir University of Technology, Tehran, Iran. Later, he obtained his Ph.D. from University of Putra Malaysia, Malaysia in Industrial Engineering. Dr. Mohammad Abdolshah's current research interests are Industrial Engineering, Quality Engineering, Control Project, and Project Management.

Latifah Abdulmohsen Alrossais is a PhD student at Middlesex University. She graduated with MA in International Business Management from Middlesex University in 2014. Latifah is an active member of the board of directors of Abdul Mohsen Alrossais Trading Group - her family business in Saudi Arabia.

Neeta Baporikar is currently Director/Professor (Business Management) at Harold Pupkewitz Graduate School of Business (HP-GSB), Namibia University of Science and Technology, Namibia. Prior to this she was Head-Scientific Research, with Ministry of Higher Education CAS-Salalah, Sultanate of Oman, Professor (Strategic Management and Entrepreneurship) at IIIT Pune and BITS India. With more than a decade of experience in industry, consultancy and training, she made a lateral switch to research and academics in 1995. Dr. Baporikar holds D.Sc. (Management Studies) USA, PhD in Management, University of Pune INDIA with MBA (Distinction) and Law (Hons.) degrees. Apart from this, she is also an External Reviewer, Oman Academic Accreditation Authority, Accredited Management Teacher, Qualified Trainer, Doctoral Guide and Board Member of Academics and Advisory Committee in accredited B-Schools. Reviewer for international journals, she has to her credit 5 conferred doctorates, several refereed research papers, and authored books in the area of Entrepreneurship, Strategy, Management and Higher Education.

Bettina Lynda Bastian is assistant professor of management at the American University of Beirut (AUB). She obtained her PhD in management from the College of Management at the Ecole Polytechnique Fédérale de Lausanne (EPFL), Switzerland. Prior to this, she received a Master degree in political science from the Free University of Berlin. Before going back for her PhD, she obtained a postgraduate Master in Energy from the EPFL and the Institut Français du Pétrole (IFP), Paris. Dr. Bastian's primary area of interest is related to entrepreneurship and innovation under uncertainty conditions, notably, political and institutional instabilities. Dr. Bastian teaches in the areas of entrepreneurship, technology management, and she is currently responsible coordinator for the business ethics section at AUB.

Johnny Chaanine received his BS in Computer Science from Notre Dame University in 2003. He is a software engineer and consultant in the healthcare domain in Lebanon. In 2007, he became an oracle certified. He holds a Doctorate in Business Administration from Grenoble Ecole of Management in 2015. He is currently an assistant professor and lecturer in the Lebanese University and Notre Dame University. He has several publications in the domain of Management, Marketing and Management Information Technology.

Salaheddine M. Chukri is a rising business executive with double focusing in family entrepreneurial management and in marketing. He has a wide cultural background ranging from the Middle East Arabian Gulf, to Asia and to the Eastern Mediterranean. He graduated from the British International School with a wide variety of world different cultures. His social entrepreneurship interests include a major construction project with Habitat for Humanity in Malaysia. He belongs to a family of entrepreneurs with long tradition in autonomous business start-ups.

Ignatius Ekanem holds a PhD in Financial Management of SMEs from Middlesex University, London and MBA from London South Bank University. He is a Senior Lecturer in Business Management at Middlesex University Business School, London. Dr Ekanem specialises in economic regeneration and small business research, with particular focus on the financial management practices of small and medium sized businesses and has published his work in a number of reputable journals, including The British Accounting Review, International Small Business Journal, Journal of Small Business and Enterprise Development, International Journal of Entrepreneurial Behavior and Research and International Journal of Consumer Studies. He has written five book chapters and is a co-author of over 20 official reports. He is a fellow of the Higher Education Academy (FHEA).

Mehtap Isik has BSc degree in Mathematics, MA and PhD degrees in Economics from Bogazici University, Turkey. After she had worked as a Risk analyst at Citibank, İstanbul, she started her academic career as a teaching assistant at Department of Mathematics and Department of Economics, Bogazici University. She joined the Department of International Trade as a full-time faculty member at 2005. Her research interests include microeconomic theory, firm theory, network theory, international trade, development and growth and Middle East political economy. She is also lecturing in these subjects at Department of International Trade, Department of Economics and Institute of Social Sciences, Bogazici University.

Ahmad Jannoun, with an extensive career in SMEs, is pursuing his doctorate degree at the Grenoble School of Management. His work in the field of corporate strategies, corporate trainer and consultant, and member of a number of company board of directors, have allowed him a wide range of insights into today's SMEs of the Middle East in general and of Lebanon more specifically. His research interests include SMEs and family businesses, strategy and corporate performance, succession planning, corporate governance and generation conflicts and gaps in family businesses.

Bassem Maamari, after a long executive career, joined the academic world as a full-time faculty at the Lebanese American University's School of Business. He brings a wealth of practical experience in the areas of sales management, finance, MIS and human resources management. He has a number of studies and his research interests include job satisfaction of employees, emotional intelligence, and the impact of technology on people.

Amir Manzoor is a senior faculty member in MIS/Finance Area at Bahria University, Karachi, Pakistan. He did MBA in General Management from Lahore University of Management Sciences (LUMS), Pakistan and an MBA in Finance from Bangor University, UK. He has about 10 years of corporate experience and more than six years of teaching experience. His research papers and book chapters have been published in reputed journals (such as SAGE Open) and by publishers (such as IGI Global). Amir has authored six books three of them adopted as reference texts in various reputable universities around the world. His research interests are in the areas of technology use for competitive advantage, quantitative analysis, management of academic institutions, and financial modeling.

Lama Issam Massalkhy is a business executive in International Business and Finance from the Lebanese American University with experience in Lebanon's A list of Banks. Her professional background includes assignments in auditing and accounting. Her career goals include executive leadership within corporate and retail operations in commercial banking headquarters in Lebanon, and eventually in London. Her studies include a Baccalaureate in Sociology and Economics with honors. She frequently participates in business events and academic conferences in business. In addition to her work in banking, Lama has received several awards in sales and financial promotion. Lama has been listed among active volunteers aiming for business people to come together.

John Hess is a widely travelled NGO executive officer with extensive experience in the Middle East.

Index

A

B

C

D

E

F

G

H

I

J

K

L

M

N

O

P

Q

R

S

T

U

V

W

www.ingramcontent.com/pod-product-compliance
Lightning Source LLC
LaVergne TN
LVHW080603300926
849162LV00005B/1032